# Attachment, Trauma, and Healing

## Understanding and Treating Attachment Disorder in Children and Families

Terry M. Levy

Michael Orlans

CWLA Press • Washington, DC

CWLA Press is an imprint of the Child Welfare League of America. The Child Welfare League of America is the nation's oldest and largest membership-based child welfare organization. We are committed to engaging people everywhere in promoting the well-being of children, youth, and their families, and protecting every child from harm.

CHILD WELFARE LEAGUE OF AMERICA, INC.
440 First Street, NW, Third Floor, Washington, DC 20001-2085
e-mail: books@cwla.org

CURRENT PRINTING (last digit)
10 9 8 7 6 5 4

Cover design by Veronica J. Morrison

The cover art, "Child in Need," was done by Margaret, 15, Devereux Deerhaven, Chester, New Jersey. The illustrations in Chapter 5 were made by clients at Evergreen Psychotherapy Center in Evergreen, Colorado.

Printed in the United States of America

ISBN # 0–87868-709-2

*Library of Congress Cataloging-in-Publication Data*
Levy, Terry M.
    Attachment, trauma, and healing : understanding and treating
attachment disorder in children and families / Terry M. Levy,
Michael Orlans.
        p.    cm.
    Includes bibliographical references (p.   ).
    ISBN 0-87868-709-2
    1. Attachment disorder in children.    I. Orlans, Michael.
II. Title.
RJ507.A77L49   1998                                     98-25993
    618.92'89--dc21                                         CIP

# Dedication

To my wife, Suzanne, whose love and support provides the "secure base" I need; to my children, Mia, Eliah, and Matthew; and my parents, Donald and Renee, who have taught me much about commitment, attachment, and love.

*T.M.L.*

To my wife, Jeri, and my children, Raina, Ushi, and Jesse, for their unconditional love, support, and wisdom.

*M.O.*

# Contents

## List of Tables

## List of Figures

# Foreword

It is essential to those of us who work with hard-to-reach children that we have a firm understanding of attachment disorder.

Several years ago, I attempted to work with an 11-year-old boy who had been adopted at the age of 5. He was referred for therapy because of his aggressive and uncontrollable behavior. His adoptive mother was exhausted and in despair. Her hair had fallen out due to stress. The adoptive father was angry. He felt betrayed because, in spite of his efforts to establish a relationship, his child continued to treat him like a stranger.

The best I could do was refer the boy to a residential program. In retrospect, he and his parents endured six terrible years together before getting help. Had the mental health community been knowledgeable about attachment disorder at the time of his adoption, the child's quality of life may have been vastly different.

Authors Terry M. Levy and Michael Orlans have written an excellent sourcebook that explains this diagnosis thoroughly. They address the scary stuff that caregivers and professionals felt helpless to treat in the past—erratic, explosive, and often antisocial behaviors within children, including their failure to respond to conventional treatment interventions.

While providing important early childhood development information, the authors carefully discuss how infants connect with or disconnect from caregivers. They describe traits associated with attachment disorder, as well as treatment protocol. They also reinforce the fact that physiological and psychological patterning are equally important when it comes to healing from trauma.

I wish this book had been available years ago. It is a solid clinical guide for professionals who want to know more about attachment disorder in children and families.

*Kathryn Brohl, M.A., L.M.F.T.*
*Licensed Marriage and Family Therapist*
Author: *Working with Traumatized Children: A Handbook for Healing*
*When Your Child Has Been Molested: A Parents' Guide*
*Healing and Recovery*
*Pockets of Craziness: Investigating Suspected Incest*

# Acknowledgments

I express my appreciation to all of my colleagues, friends, and family who have been so supportive during the long process of preparing this book. To my wife, Suzanne, for her limitless patience and understanding. To the many children, parents, and therapeutic foster parents who have inspired me with their courage and determination and helped us to understand and heal the devastating effects of attachment disorder.

*Terry M. Levy, Ph.D.*

I would like to give special thanks to my parents, Rae and Sam Orlans, who taught me about attachment. Most of all, I would like to recognize the parents of the children with attachment disorder whom I have assisted. These individuals have bared their hearts and souls as they toil on the front lines for us all.

*Michael Orlans, M.A.*

From both of us, a special thanks to Anthea Coster, M.A., for her encouragement, dedication, and support.

# Confidentiality

We have used case vignettes throughout this book to illustrate clinical and treatment issues. These vignettes are based on actual children and families who have participated in our treatment program, although names and circumstances have been changed to protect confidentiality.

# 1
# Introduction

There is a time bomb ready to explode. In fact, in many communities the bomb has already exploded. More and more children are failing to develop secure attachments to loving, protective caregivers—the most important foundation for healthy development. They are flooding our child welfare system with an overwhelming array of problems (emotional, behavioral, social, cognitive, developmental, physical, and moral) and growing up to perpetuate the cycle with their own children. Some social service and mental health professionals believe that attachment disorder is rare: the evidence indicates otherwise. Research has shown that up to 80% of high-risk families (poverty, substance abuse, abuse and neglect, domestic violence, history of maltreatment in parents' childhood, depression, and other psychological disorders in parents) create disorganized/disoriented attachment patterns in their children. Since there are 1 million substantiated cases of serious abuse and neglect in the United States each year, the statistics indicate that there are 800,000 children with severe attachment disorder coming to the attention of the child welfare system each year [Lyons-Ruth 1996]. This does not include the thousands of children with attachment disorder who are adopted from other countries.

## Attachment

Attachment is the deep and enduring connection established between a child and caregiver in the first several years of life. It profoundly influences every component of the human condition—mind, body, emotions, relationships, and values. Attachment is not something that parents do *to* their children; rather, it is something that children and parents create *together*, in an ongoing, reciprocal relationship. Attachment to a protective and loving caregiver who provides guidance and support is a basic human need, rooted in millions of years of evolution. We have an instinct to attach: babies instinctively reach out for the safety of the "secure base" with caregivers; parents instinctively protect and nurture their offspring. Attachment is a physiological, emotional, cognitive, and social phenomenon. Instinctual attachment behaviors in the baby are activated by cues or signals from the caregiver (social releasers). Thus, the attachment process is defined as a "mutual regulatory system," in which the baby and the caregiver influence one another over time.

Beyond the basic function of secure attachment—providing safety and protection for the vulnerable young through closeness to a caregiver—there are several other important functions for children:

- To learn basic trust and reciprocity that serve as a template for all future emotional relationships;

1

- To explore the environment with feelings of safety and security ("secure base"), which leads to healthy cognitive and social development;

- To develop the ability to self-regulate, which results in effective management of impulses and emotions;

- To create a foundation for the formation of an identity that includes a sense of competency, self-worth, and a balance between dependence and autonomy;

- To establish a prosocial moral framework that involves empathy, compassion, and conscience;

- To generate a core belief system that comprises cognitive appraisals of self, caregivers, others, and life in general; and

- To provide a defense against stress and trauma, which incorporates resourcefulness and resilience.

Secure attachment can only be established in the context of a relationship that includes nurturing touch, safe holding, eye contact, smile, positive affect, and need fulfillment:

- **Touch.** For millions of years, mothers have held their babies "in arms," providing nurturing touch and safe containment. The communication transmitted through touch is the most powerful way to establish a human relationship [Montague 1986]. Secure attachment involves loving and caring touch, as well as sensitive and appropriate limits and boundaries. Without touch children can die; with abusive touch and/or little loving and nurturing touch, children develop severe biopsychosocial problems and an aversion to the very touch and closeness they desperately need.

- **Eye contact.** A newborn can focus his or her eyes on objects 7 to 12 inches away, the exact distance needed to make eye contact in arms. The caregiver-infant gaze is a primary releaser for the development of secure attachment and is synonymous with closeness and intimacy. Securely attached children are able to communicate and connect through eye contact. Children with attachment disorder are incapable of using eye contact for closeness and positive communication; they use their gaze to manipulate, seduce, control, or threaten.

- **Smile and positive affect**. The baby's smile is an instinctive response that attracts the attention of the caregiver and encourages an ongoing positive caregiver response. The caregiver's smile and positive affect help the baby feel safe and secure. The relationship between caregiver and a securely attached child is characterized by warmth, joy, and love. Caregivers and children with attachment disorder experience rejection, pain, fear, and anger.

- **Need fulfillment**. Successful completion of the first-year-of-life attachment cycle leads to the development of secure attachment. The sensitive caregiver gratifies basic needs, which alleviates the child's arousal and discomfort. Securely attached children learn to trust caregivers and authority and believe that their own needs are valid. Children with attachment disorder mistrust authority and develop negative self-perceptions. ("I am bad, defective, unlovable.")

Children who begin their lives with the essential foundation of secure attachment fare better in all aspects of functioning as they develop. Numerous longitudinal studies have demonstrated that securely attached infants and toddlers do better over time in the following areas:

- Self-esteem;

- Independence and autonomy;

- Resilience in the face of adversity;

- Ability to manage impulses and feelings;

- Long-term friendships;

- Relationships with parents, caregivers, and other authority figures;

- Prosocial coping skills;

- Trust, intimacy, and affection;

- Positive and hopeful belief systems about self, family, and society;

- Empathy, compassion, and conscience;

- Behavioral performance and academic success in school; and

- Promote secure attachment with their own children when they become adults.

## Disrupted Attachment

Children who begin their lives with compromised and disrupted attachment (associated with prenatal drug and alcohol exposure, neglect of physical and emotional needs, abuse, violence, multiple caregivers) are at risk for serious problems as development unfolds:

- Low self-esteem;

- Needy, clingy, or psuedoindependent;

- Decompensate when faced with stress and adversity;

- Lack self-control;

- Unable to develop and maintain friendships;

- Alienated from and oppositional with parents, caregivers, and other authority figures;

- Antisocial attitudes and behaviors;

- Aggression and violence;

- Incapable of genuine trust, intimacy, and affection;

- Negative, hopeless, and pessimistic view of self, family, and society;

- Lack empathy, compassion, and remorse;

- Behavioral and academic problems at school; and

- Perpetuate the cycle of maltreatment and attachment disorder in their own children when they reach adulthood.

Disrupted and anxious attachment not only leads to emotional and social problems, but also results in biochemical consequences in the developing brain. Infants raised without loving touch and security have abnormally high levels of stress hormones, which can impair the growth and development of their brains and bodies [Perry 1994; van der Kolk 1996]. The neurobiological consequences of emotional neglect can leave children behaviorally disordered, depressed, apathetic, slow to learn, and prone to chronic illness. Compared to securely attached children, children with attachment disorder are significantly more likely to be aggressive, disruptive, and antisocial. Teenage boys, for example, who have experienced attachment difficulties early in life, are three times more likely to commit violent crimes [Raine 1993]. Disruption of attachment during the crucial first three years can lead to what has been called "affectionless psychopathy"; the inability to form meaningful emotional relationships, coupled with chronic anger, poor impulse control, and a lack of remorse. These disturbing psychosocial qualities have contributed to a more violent and "heartless" character to the crimes being committed by today's youth. We are experiencing a pace of violence among children that has been steadily rising for more than two decades. The number of youths held in juvenile facilities has increased 41% in the past 10 years. One-third of those arrested for arson in 1994 were under age 15, and nearly 7% were under age 10. More than 110,000 children under age 13 were arrested for felonies in 1994; 12,000 were crimes against people, including murder, rape, robbery, and aggravated assault [Berman et al. 1996]. The vast majority of these children had histories of abuse and neglect, lived in single-parent homes, had young mothers, and/or a parent with a criminal record. These young offenders will become the "superpredators" of tomorrow, likely to go on to commit more numerous and serious offenses.

A recent newspaper article reveals the seriousness of our current problem: "The nation's juvenile courts, long a troubled backwater of the criminal justice system, has been so overwhelmed by the increase in violent teenage crime and the breakdown of the family that judges and politicians are debating a solution that was once unthinkable—abolishing the system and trying most minors as adults" [Butterfield 1997]. The legal and child welfare systems not only find it impossible to keep up with new cases, but have difficulty monitoring and serving the children and families on their current caseloads. As many as 50% of all fatalities that are due to child abuse and neglect occur in cases that have already been brought to the attention of law enforcement and child protection agencies [Lung & Daro 1996].

Attachment disorder is transmitted intergenerationally. Children lacking secure attachments with caregivers commonly grow up to be parents who are incapable of establishing this crucial foundation with their own children. Instead of following the instinct to protect, nurture and love their children, they abuse, neglect, and abandon. There is a "pyramid effect"; with each generation, there is a multifold increase in the number of children with attachment disorder. Consider the following:

- The number of children seriously injured by maltreatment quadrupled from 1986 (140,000) to 1993 (600,000).

- Three million cases of maltreatment were investigated by Child Protective Services in 1995, and more than 1 million were confirmed as serious abuse and/or neglect, with risk for continued maltreatment. *Surveys indicated the actual number of cases are 10 to 16 times higher.*

- Child Protective Services are unable to handle the vast increases; only 28% of seriously maltreated children were evaluated in 1993, compared to 45% in 1986 [NCCAN 1995; Gallup et al. 1995; Children's Defense Fund 1997].

> Awilda Lopez, a 29-year-old mother of three who was addicted to drugs and alcohol, had physically abused her 6-year-old daughter for months. Finally, she smashed little Elisa's head into a cement floor, and for the next 48 hours left her to die alone. What kind of a parent can act that cruel, with total disregard for the instinct to protect, nurture, and love her own child? It is convenient to blame mental illness or substance abuse for such behavior, but that misses the deeper truth: Most parents who abuse and neglect their children are repeating what was done to them; they were not securely attached to their parents, and, therefore, do not securely and lovingly attach with their own offspring.

Compromised attachment early in life not only leads to aggression and antisocial acting out, but also has contributed to the current disorganized and overwhelmed state of our foster care system. Over the past generation, the number of children with severe attachment disorder in out-of-home placements has increased, while the number of foster parents has decreased. Child Protective Services removes many children from violent, substance-abusing, and maltreating birth parents, and places them in foster homes. However, due to the lack of proper diagnosis, effective treatment, and inadequate training and support of foster parents, large numbers of children with attachment disorder are moved aimlessly through the system, their problems increasing in severity with each move.

Many of these children are eventually adopted by well-meaning parents who are intellectually and emotionally ill-prepared to handle the children's severe emotional and behavioral problems. Such children are unable to give and receive love and affection, constantly defy parental rules and authority, are physically and emotionally abusive to caregivers and siblings, and create ongoing stress and turmoil in the family. As a result of insufficient preplacement services (education, training, support, matching) and postplacement services (individual and family therapy, parent education, support), family members and marriages suffer. Traumatized parents may relinquish, shifting the child and his or her problems back to the child welfare system. Others place their children in long-term institutions that drain financial resources and often fail to address the child's attachment difficulties. Many parents choose to maintain the child in their family, which results in years of ongoing stress, neglect of the needs of their other children, and prolonging parenting responsibilities well into their child's adult years.

An adoptive mother describes a typical day in the life of her son:

### Morning

"Kyle it's time to get up." Five minutes later, "Kyle, it's time to get up."

"WHAT! Nobody told me." Now the noises start, low at first, then loud and louder.

"Kyle, please stop."

"Stop what?"

"The noises, you know what."

"I'm just singing."

"Is your bed made and are you ready for school?" More noises. "Kyle, are you ready?"

"If you would get me up earlier, I'd have more time to get ready."

"Kyle, what are you chewing on?"

"Nothing."

"Kyle, what is in your mouth?"

"Oh! The top of my pen."

"Throw it away so you can eat and take your medicine. It's time for the bus."

"Not it's not, she comes at 22 after, not 20 after."

"Good-bye, Kyle, have a nice day."

"Bye, TOOT WOMAN."

Phone is ringing. (Great). I wonder if that's the school?

"Hello, Mom?" (Oh no, what now?) "I lost one of my braces."

"Okay, thanks for calling me." (Thank you, Lord).

### Afternoon

The phone rings: "Hello?"

"This is Mr. Donahue at school. We have a problem. Kyle is farting and belching in class, laughing, and thinking it's funny. I've warned him before, so he has in-school suspension tomorrow, and the next time it happens, a Saturday school. Oh! By the way, Kyle had five milkshakes for lunch today!"

"Hi, Kyle. How was school today?"

"Fine, why? Anything happen?"

"I got a call."

"I DIDN'T DO ANYTHING, IT WAS ANDY, I SWEAR."

"What did you have for lunch?"

"I don't remember."

"Any milkshakes?"

"Maybe one."

"How many?"

"Two or three."

"How many, Kyle?"

"That's all."

"How many, Kyle?"

"I didn't drink all of the last one!!"

"Do you have any homework?"

"No."

"None?"

"I already did it."

"Good, I would like to see it."

"Why? You always have to see everything. I forgot it at school."

"Well, tomorrow bring your homework home whether you have done it or not."

"That's not fair. Jenny never has to do anything. You let her do anything she wants to do. If she had homework, you would not have to see it. You always treat her nice. You love her more than you love me."

"Kyle, that's enough, go sit on the chair in your bedroom."

BANG! He jumps in the air and lands on his bottom.

"That's it! You threw me down, I'm calling Children's Services. I'm telling them you're abusing me."

"Go ahead, here's the phone and the numbers in the front of the book."

"I'm not calling, I'm just leaving. I'll go live with John. His family is nice."

"Bye, Kyle."

Out the door he goes. A few minutes later when I see him peeking in the window, I just ignore him. I hear the door close.

"Oh, I thought you left."

"Didn't you call the sheriff?"

"No, was I supposed to?"

"Can I have another chance?"

"Kyle, please put the drinks on the table for supper. Everyone, supper is ready. Kyle, where are the drinks?"

"No one told me to get them."

"Kyle, please chew with your mouth closed."

"No, you have had three servings of lasagna and two salads. That's enough."

"That's right, just make me starve. I never get what I want to eat. If Jenny wanted it she could have it."

"Kyle, you have had plenty to eat." (noises start) "Now clear the table. Kyle, clear the table."

"My dishes are almost done."

"Kyle, why didn't you finish clearing the table?" (more noises)

"I did!"

"Is that why there are still silverware and napkins on the table?"

"I thought I cleared it!"

**Bedtime**

"Kyle, did you brush your teeth?"

"Nobody told me to."

"What time is bedtime?"

"I don't know."

"Kyle, it's the same time every night. Now brush your teeth and get in bed."

Noises start, the bed creaks and shakes around, there is pecking on the wall.

"Kyle, that's enough."

"What?"

"You heard me."

"I forgot, I didn't go to the bathroom." (back in bed)

"I didn't get a snack."

"Too bad. Get to sleep."

"But Jenny would get one if she wanted one."

"Kyle, tomorrow night bedtime is 8:30. Goodnight. We love you."

"Yeah, make me go to bed early. I didn't do anything. It's your fault. You should have told me!!"

A significant family and societal issue regarding the attachment of young children is substitute child care. Currently, 75% of all women in the United States with young children work full time outside the home. More than half the mothers of infants work [Scarr 1998]. The maternity and nursing benefits given to working mothers in the United States are the least generous in the industrialized world, according to a recent United Nations study [Grimsley 1998]. The same study reported that in 30% of the world's households, women now are the primary source of income. Within 10 years, 80% of all women in industrialized nations will work outside the home during their childbearing years. Although there is ongoing debate regarding the benefits of staying home with your child versus placing the child in day care, the need for substitute child care is a reality. Research has revealed the ingredients of quality substitute child care: proper staff education and training, small staff-child ratios, adequate financial incentives for staff, consistency of one child care provider who remains with a child through developmental stages, staff-parent collaboration, cooperation, and communication. Despite this knowledge, most child care facilities do not meet these requirements. According to a recent study, *every* state in the United States failed to meet the requirements for quality day care [Young et al. 1997].

## Solutions

What are the solutions to the vast problems of attachment disorder in families, the child welfare system, and society? The solutions can be found in four areas: attachment-focused assessment and diagnosis, specialized training and education for caregivers (Corrective Attachment Parenting), treatment for children and caregivers that facilitates secure attachment (Corrective Attachment Therapy), and early intervention and prevention programs for high-risk families.

- **Assessment and diagnosis**. Attachment disorder is one of the most easily diagnosed and yet commonly misunderstood parent-child disorders. Diagnosis rests on four pillars: 1) signs and symptoms, 2) early history, 3) previous diagnoses, and 4) parents' attachment histories. Many social service and mental health professionals who are adept at assessing behavioral and emotional disorders are not trained in the use of an "attachment frame." Chapter 5 provides a comprehensive overview of assessment and diagnosis of attachment disorder in children and families.

- **Training for caregivers**. Parents and other caregivers assume the responsibility of childrearing accompanied by the challenges of children with attachment disorder, often without the information, training, and support they need. These individuals need specialized parenting skills to be successful in their parenting role. Adoptive and foster parents commonly feel frustrated, angry at the child and the "system," demoralized, disillusioned, and burned out. Chapter 9 will cover the basic concepts and skills of Corrective Attachment Parenting.

- **Treatment.** For more than 25 years, Evergreen Consultants in Human Behavior, in Boulder, Colorado, has been developing and refining approaches for the treatment of children with attachment disorder and their families. We have found that effective treatment involves creating secure attachment patterns; systemic, holistic and integrative interventions; and utilizing a developmental structure (Revisit, Revise, Revitalize).

  - *Creating secure attachment patterns.* The primary therapeutic goal is to facilitate secure attachment in the parent-child relationship. To achieve this goal we must recreate the elements of secure attachment that were unavailable in the child's early developmental stages. In the context of the Holding Nurturing Process (HNP), children are provided with structure, attunement, empathy, positive affect, support, reciprocity, and love. The HNP is a therapeutic relationship/milieu that promotes secure attachment through social releasers, safe containment, corrective touch, access to "old brain" functions that control attachment behavior, and the establishment of a secure base in which positive developmental changes can occur.

  - *Systemic interventions.* Attachment develops in the context of overlapping relationship systems, including parent-child, marital, family, extended kin, and community. For example, the quality of the mother-infant relationship is influenced by behaviors and attitudes of the father. Thus, effective treatment must address the various social systems in the life of the child and family.

  - *Holistic and integrative interventions.* Treatment focuses on mind, body, behaviors, emotions, relationships, and morality. Therapeutic interventions and strategies are varied: experiential, psychoeducational, cognitive, and skill based. The holistic approach is based on the concept that many factors interact to create both health and dysfunction.

  - *Revisit, Revise, Revitalize.* Treatment is developmental, requiring the successful completion of each stage, which in turn builds upon the next. Attachment trauma is first revisited to address core issues. Next, the therapist facilitates revisions in belief systems, choices, relationship patterns, and coping skills. Lastly, revitalization includes celebrating achievements, cementing positive changes, and enhancing hope for the future.

- **Early intervention and prevention.** Even with the availability of effective therapeutic interventions, it is impossible to reach all the children and families that need help. A significant amount of evidence accumulated over the past 25 years indicates that early intervention and prevention programs are effective for at-risk children and families [Guralnick 1997; Ramey & Ramey 1998]. For example, high-risk mothers (young, single, poor) who received prenatal and postnatal home visits by a public health nurse had significantly fewer instances (4%) of child abuse and neglect than mothers who did not receive these services (19%)

[Barnett 1997]. Early intervention and prevention programs have been shown to enhance parent-child attachment and children's cognitive and social development. (See Chapter 2).

Traditional psychotherapeutic approaches have not been effective with children with severe attachment disorder, who can not trust or form a working alliance basic to success in therapy. Lack of secure attachment in the early years results in a need to control, a fear of closeness, and a lack of reciprocity. The therapeutic challenge is to take charge in a firm, yet caring way and gradually form a working relationship with the child. Mental health professionals are taught to be empathic, caring, and to allow the child to take the lead. This nondirective client-centered approach is appropriate for many children, but is not effective with children who rarely admit they need help and are not motivated to improve. The same characteristics that make it difficult to help those with antisocial personality (no empathy or remorse, angry, defiant, dishonest, self-centered) are present in these children. The therapeutic challenge is to instill the basics—trust, empathy, cooperation, and conscience—qualities essential for successful living in a family and community.

Attachment during infancy is a physiological, emotional, and social experience. Instinctual attachment behaviors, rooted in biology and evolution, are activated by caregivers' cues (social releasers). The therapeutic challenge is to elicit these primitive, internal attachment feelings, behaviors, and patterns that involve both arousal and redirection. Stimulating the portion of the brain that monitors and controls attachment behavior (the limbic system) is necessary. Physiological and emotional arousal must be redirected for therapeutic and prosocial purposes (see Chapters 6 and 7 for details).

Many parents of children with severe attachment disorder have been "through the mill" of mental health and social service programs. Parents are commonly blamed for their child's problems, denied access to their child's social service records, and thoroughly frustrated in their attempts to get help. They are angry with their child, feel guilty and inadequate, and are often on the verge of relinquishment. The therapeutic challenge is to increase motivation, enhance positive emotion, instill faith and hope, and encourage a more effective framework for conceptualizing their parenting role and understanding their child.

## About This Book

This book addresses the entire scope of attachment from the perspective of the child, family, community, and society. We have three major purposes for writing this book. First, our hope is to increase awareness and understanding of attachment as a critical factor in childhood and family psychosocial functioning and dysfunction. Second, our goal is to provide a specific and effective framework for assessment and treatment of attachment disorder. Lastly, we will offer answers to commonly asked questions regarding attachment-related problems and solutions. The following questions will be considered and answered throughout the text:

• Is attachment instinctual (prewired) or environmental (learned from caregivers)?

- What do an infant and toddler need in order to feel secure, worthwhile, and lovable?

- What are the advantages of secure attachment for the child, family, and society?

- How do attachment experiences during the first three years of life lead to autonomy, confidence, and resilience in the face of adversity?

- Is the need for secure attachment during infancy as important as other basic needs?

- Is attachment a universal phenomenon, or does it vary from culture to culture?

- What role do fathers play in the attachment process?

- Can fathers or other nonmaternal caregivers facilitate secure attachment as effectively as mothers?

- What traits, symptoms, and relationship patterns can be observed at various developmental stages in order to accurately assess attachment disorder?

- What are the similarities and differences between attachment disorder and other childhood psychosocial disorders (e.g., attention deficit/hyperactive disorder, oppositional defiant disorder, conduct disorder, bipolar disorder)?

- In what way does disrupted and disordered attachment contribute to the development of antisocial personality (lack of empathy and conscience, dishonesty, hostility, aggression, exploitation)?

- What high-risk factors in families are most often correlated with the development of severe attachment disorder?

- Why do some children develop major psychosocial problems as a result of early compromised attachment, while other children with similar backgrounds develop normally?

- What are the similarities between the neurobiology of trauma and attachment disorder?

- What are the family system issues in the understanding and treatment of attachment disorder?

- Why do many child welfare caseworkers, mental health professionals, and parents fail to produce positive changes in children with attachment disorder?

- What are the most effective therapeutic interventions for children with attachment disorders and their families?

- How does the Holding Nurturing Process (HNP) contribute to positive therapeutic outcome, and how do you prevent retraumatization?

- What are the effects of day care on attachment patterns in children and families?

- What are the best out-of-home placements for maltreated children with attachment disorders?

- When should sibling groups be placed together in foster homes, and when is it best to separate them?

- How does the foster care system exacerbate the problems of children with attachment disorder, and what are the best solutions for our overwhelmed child welfare system?

- Do all adopted children have attachment-related challenges and problems?

- How do you emotionally and intellectually prepare foster parents and preadoptive parents to address and manage the special needs of children with attachment disorder?

- What are the changes in public policy that must take place in order to foster secure attachment and prevent attachment disorder in the children and families of our society?

# 2
# Historical Perspective

## Early Theory and Research

Not long ago, the standard approach to treating infants and children totally ignored any basic understanding of attachment. This was true in Europe and the United States as recently as the 1950s, and some of these ideas still influence policy today. Hospitals had strict rules against parents visiting their children, or the visits were to be brief and infrequent. Parents were considered a nuisance and were thought to contaminate the children with germs. Similarly, staff were warned against contact with the children. It is not surprising that failure to thrive was the leading cause of death among hospitalized babies. "Experts" in behaviorism who viewed children as "blank slates" to be shaped by the environment provided childrearing advise to parents. They warned parents against picking up a crying baby, as that only resulted in creating a demanding and needy child. "Never hug and kiss them, never let them sit on your lap. If you must, kiss them once on the forehead when they say goodnight. Shake hands with them in the morning," advised John Watson in his book on childrearing [Watson 1928; cited in Karen 1994, p. 3].

The prevailing attitude in the foster care system was to prevent children from becoming attached to caregivers by moving them from home to home—it was wrong, they believed, for a child to attach to someone who would never be her permanent parent. Prospective adoptive parents were discouraged from adopting early, as it was better to allow the child to develop so that defects could be detected [Karen 1994].

Fortunately, there was a new trend developing among social scientists by the middle of the 1900s. John Bowlby, considered to be the founder of attachment theory, was a pioneer in these new "child-friendly" concepts. Bowlby, one of the first British psychiatrists to work at a child guidance clinic, believed that the infant-mother relationship was crucial for healthy psychological and social development. He studied antisocial children and adolescents and found prolonged early mother-child separations to be common. Bowlby concluded that these "affectionless children" developed behavioral disorders and criminal characters as a result of early emotional deprivation, resulting in traumatic loss and depression. Upon assessing the parents, he found that they consistently displayed disturbed attitudes and parenting styles [Bowlby 1944].

Bowlby's report to the World Health Organization in 1951 began a powerful movement toward understanding attachment. He studied homeless children from various cultures and found that significant early deprivation resulted in a variety of severe problems as the children developed: lack of empathy, conduct disorders, inability to give and receive affection, and attentional deficits [Bowlby 1951]. He then went a step further, suggesting that these problems become intergenerational when the children grow to become abusive and neglectful parents. Although these notions seem obvious or even trite today, they created quite a stir in the early 1950s.

Bowlby developed many of his ideas about attachment from studying the research of ethologists, such as Konrad Lorenz and Niko Tinbergen. These ethologists studied imprinting, the bond that develops quickly between adults and offspring in birds and mammals, which is not related to feeding. Lorenz [1971] and Tinbergen [1951] found that bonding behavior is instinctive, but that the young only respond when certain cues or signals from their caregivers are available ("species-specific behavior"). For example, the young herring gull opens its mouth to eat only when it sees a red spot on the beak of the adult gull. Certain birds only develop a song when they hear the song of an adult of their species. Bowlby, and others to follow, applied this idea of the interplay between instinct and environment to the mother-infant relationship. This concept suggests that infants are "prewired" for attachment, but this process only unfolds when activated by certain cues or conditions from primary caregivers. This was the beginning of a long journey involving numerous researchers and clinicians in an effort to explore the mother-child relationship.

Bowlby's work with children and families led him to formulate a number of important conclusions [Bowlby 1988b]:

- Infants possess instinctual behaviors (sucking, clinging, following, crying, smiling, and gazing) that serve to keep the mother close.

- The smile is a "social releaser" for both mother and infant. The baby's smile elicits maternal care, while the mother's smile promotes feelings of security in the baby.

- Anxiety, fear, illness, and fatigue cause increases in attachment behaviors, a need for more closeness and contact.

- Maternal deprivation and separation are traumatic, because they prevent the fulfillment of a biological need.

- The loss of an attachment figure causes pathological mourning, resulting in disturbed development, emotional detachment, inability to love and trust, and depression.

Other researchers and clinicians were coming to similar conclusions regarding the nature of the mother-child bond. David Levy studied children who lacked early maternal care, had several out-of-home placements, and later would not attach to adoptive parents. He found these children to be conduct disordered (lying, stealing, aggression), full of rage, indiscriminately affectionate, demanding, and incapable of genuine affection. They suffered from "primary affect hunger," he suggested, an emotional starvation resulting from maternal deprivation. Loretta Bender studied children who had numerous foster home placements and found them to be delayed in speech and social behavior, indiscriminately affectionate, abusive towards peers, clingy, and displaying attentional deficits and frequent temper tantrums. She diagnosed these children with psychopathic personalities, a result of early emotional deprivation. Harry Bakwin studied babies with failure to thrive syndrome in institutions. He found that they improved when nurses took more of an interest and when they were placed in nurturing homes. Harold Skeels noticed that deprived, institutionalized children had language and cognitive deficits. When he provided these children with older affectionate caregivers, their IQs increased an average of 30 points within one and a half years. Rene Spitz filmed children after they were left in hospitals and institutions by their parents, showing their emotional and physical deterioration. He found that most recovered if the mother returned within three months. After then, they became apathetic and unresponsive [Levy 1937, Bender & Yarnell 1941, Bakwin 1942, Spitz 1947; cited in Karen 1994, pp. 15–24].

James Robertson observed children in British hospitals who were separated from their parents for long periods of time. He made dramatic films depicting their deterioration and described three stages of emotional reaction to separation and loss:

- **Protest.** Child is frightened, confused, screaming, and anxiously looking for mother.

- **Despair.** Child is losing hope of being reunited, becomes depressed and disinterested in surroundings and food.

- **Detachment.** Child is indifferent to maternal care, does not connect with mother during visits nor seem to care when she leaves. Child appears to have adapted to institutionalized life. Feelings for the parents "died" due to repeated disappointment [Robertson & Robertson 1989].

The famous experiments of Harry Harlow validated the importance of a basic attachment need for contact. He found that infant rhesus monkeys preferred a "surrogate mother" covered with cotton terry cloth to a wire mesh "mother" that provided a bottle of milk. These infants spent most of their time clinging to the cloth mother, using her as a secure base from which to explore. These experiments demonstrated the importance of contact comfort and instinctual attachment needs, as separate from the issues of feeding [Harlow 1958]. Subsequent studies showed that monkeys isolated for the first six months of life displayed severe problems over time, including abnormal social and sexual behavior and abusive parenting when they became adults [Suomi & Harlow 1978].

Mary Ainsworth was most influential in moving Bowlby's original ideas and observations to the next level. She began observing mother-infant relationships in Uganda in 1954, in an effort to learn how attachment develops. Through these observations Ainsworth coined the phrase "secure base," using the attachment figure as a base from which to explore the environment without anxiety—a phrase that even today is widely associated with healthy attachment [Ainsworth 1967]. Ainsworth described five phases of attachment:

- **Undiscriminating.** No specific social responses, baby responds to anyone;

- **Differential responsiveness.** Baby knows and prefers mother;

- **Separation anxiety.** Baby cries when mother leaves and is calmed when she returns;

- **Active initiation.** Baby protests when separated from mother and actively pursues her by approaching, following, and greeting upon reunion;

- **Stranger anxiety.** Between 6 and 8 months, baby is uncomfortable with strangers.

In the early 1960s, Ainsworth began a longitudinal study of mother-child relationships in the United States to determine if attachment patterns were universal (cross-cultural) and to compare parenting styles and subsequent attachment. She developed the "Strange Situation," a laboratory assessment procedure designed to study separation and reunion under conditions of low and high stress, which would be utilized by numerous researchers for years to come. In the Strange Situation, the baby is initially in the playroom with the mother only, then a stranger enters; mother next leaves the room, then returns; the stranger next leaves the room, and mother then leaves with the baby now alone; then mother returns. The child's reactions to separation and reunion are observed through a one-way mirror and recorded on film for further analysis.

Similar to the Uganda findings, the babies explored more with mothers present (secure base behavior). Three distinct attachment patterns were discovered, one secure and two insecure/anxious patterns, in 12- to 18-months-olds. *Securely* attached babies actively sought out mother when distressed, maintained contact on reunion, and were easily comforted by mother. *Ambivalently* attached babies were extremely distressed by the separation, but were difficult to soothe on reunion and resisted their mother's comfort. *Avoidantly* attached babies seemed disinterested in their mothers and, in fact, rejected them on reunion [Ainsworth & Wittig 1969].

Why did these babies respond with different attachment patterns? Did it have to do with inborn temperament or environmental factors? Ainsworth was able to answer this question because she had a team of observers who made numerous home visits during the infants' first year of life. Vast differences in parenting style were found on scales of acceptance, cooperation, sensitivity, and availability. Mothers of securely attached babies were rated higher on all four scales; they were more responsive to baby's needs and signals and showed more pleasure in their reactions. Mothers of anxiously attached babies were less likely to respond to baby's needs in sensitive, attuned, and consistent ways. Mothers of ambivalent babies were inconsistent and unpredictable. Mothers of avoidant babies were rejecting.

These studies provided concrete evidence about ways in which parenting style affected individual differences in children. Securely attached babies had mothers who were affectionate, fed them on demand, and picked them up quickly when they cried during the early months. These babies cried less than anxiously attached babies by the end of their first year, indicating that responsive parenting did not create "spoiled," dependent children, but instead, lead to healthy autonomy. Avoidantly attached babies had mothers who were much less affectionate, angry and irritable, displayed gruff physical interactions, and often had an aversion to physical warmth and contact. No wonder these babies rejected their mothers on reunion—they were doing to their mothers (rejection) what had been done to them, and showing indifference to disguise their hurt and anger.

# Developmental Studies

Mary Main and colleagues at the University of California at Berkeley began a longitudinal study of middle class families in the 1970s. Attachment patterns were assessed at 12 and 18 months of age, and aspects of psychosocial development were evaluated. A fourth attachment pattern was discovered—*disorganized/disoriented attachment*—where some children displayed both avoidant and ambivalent styles, and sought closeness to their mothers in strange and bizarre ways [Main & Weston 1982]. Many of these disorganized children were found to have been abused [Crittenden 1988] and to have mothers who had experienced trauma and loss in their own early family life which they never successfully resolved or mourned [Main & Solomon 1990]. Fear and anxiety were somehow communicated to the baby. (See Chapter 4 for more information on disorganized attachment.)

Further studies provided new insights into the emotional, cognitive, and relationship aspects of attachment. The child's early attachment pattern creates an *internal working model*, a mental and emotional reflection of early attachment relationships that determines perception of self, others, and the world [Bowlby 1982]. The internal working model was found to influence not only behavior and emotion, but also attention, memory, and language. When 6-year-olds were asked to react to photographs showing children separated from parents, the differences were profound. Securely attached children talked about their feelings associated with separation, had ideas about coping, and were serious but not distressed. Ambivalent children responded in a contradictory way similar to the responses that they demonstrated at 1 year of age—anger mixed with seeking closeness. Avoidantly attached children became distressed and were not able to suggest ways to cope. Children with disorganized attachment patterns deteriorated; they were extremely frightened, gave aggressive and confusing responses, and expressed fears of annihilation. The researchers were able to accurately guess the children's original attachment classifications by merely observing their reactions to the photos [Main et al. 1985].

Researchers were also able to accurately assess attachment patterns by observing parent-child interactions. Securely attached children had relationships with their parents that were relaxed, friendly, with a warmth and intimacy that was "natural" but not clingy. Children in the ambivalent category had a relationship that mixed closeness with hostility and often seemed artificial or contrived. The avoidantly attached children distanced and rejected their parents, avoiding intimacy and connection in many ways. Disorganized children would either reject their parents or become parental with them, but either way their basic stance was to control or dominate [Main & Cassidy 1988].

The researchers hypothesized that the insecurely/anxiously attached children had developed unconscious strategies to deal with their mothers' neglect, rejection, or inconsistency. Their internal working models (belief systems) and ways of relating showed that these children had learned their lessons well; they were now perpetuating rejection and hostility. Ambivalent children long for a connection, but alienate others by clinging and neediness. They act helpless in order to elicit care, try desperately to get their mother's attention, and are chronically anxious about how mother will respond. Avoidant children are angry about the rejection, but not able to be honest and direct, otherwise this may lead to more rejection. They are "shut-down" and avoid interactions that involve attachment needs, resulting in a detached, "I don't care" attitude. They typically act out their anger towards others in passive-aggressive ways.

Further research, much of it from Alan Sroufe and colleagues at the Institute of Child Development, University of Minnesota, focused on attachment and self-esteem, moral development, social relationships, and school achievement. Attachment patterns were found to be consistent over time, regardless of developmental changes. Babies were assessed at 12 and 18 months, and more than 95% fell into the same attachment category on both occasions [Waters 1978]. In another study, securely attached 18-month-olds were found to share more positive feelings with mother, smile more during play, and share toys, compared to anxiously attached children. By 3 1/2, these secure children were more likely to be sought out by other children, be more empathic, and demonstrate better leadership skills [Waters et al. 1979].

One large-scale research program was initiated that focused on a high-risk population (low-income, young, single mothers, with few resources or support systems). These mothers and their children were followed for 20 years. This study provided a valuable contrast to the results of the Berkeley studies involving middle-class families. The initial finding was both interesting and controversial; mothers who were depressed and had low interest in their babies during pregnancy, were more likely to have anxiously attached children at 1 year [Sroufe 1983]. By ages 4 and 5, the securely attached children scored higher on every measure: social skills, friendships, leadership, empathy, self-esteem, self-reliance, and resilience. Anxiously attached children were much more dependent. Avoidant children made the worst friends; they took pleasure in other's distress, were devious and manipulative, and had trouble sharing. Ambivalent children were socially incompetent and concerned mostly with their own needs [Troy & Sroufe 1987]. These findings were consistent with others who found securely attached children to have better social skills and to be generally more liked by peers [Pastor 1981, Jacobson & Wille 1986].

Similar patterns were found at age 10, but now problems with power and control were more apparent for the anxiously attached children. Avoidant boys were most aggressive and conduct disordered (lie, bully, destructive, angry, defiant). Avoidant girls were also angry, but more likely to internalize and become depressed. Again, secure preadolescents were more competent socially and emotionally [Erikson et al. 1985, Elicker et al. 1992]. These patterns continued throughout adolescence [Sroufe et al. 1993].

In summary, the studies on attachment patterns, development, and psychosocial functioning consistently show that children classified as securely attached in infancy do better in every important area of life as they develop: they make better friends, feel better about themselves, are more competent problem solvers, receive more positive feedback from others, and are more resilient and independent. The anxiously attached children and adolescents are always more dependent, emotionally troubled, and socially incompetent.

# Temperament

The previous section focused on the importance of early parenting influences on the development of attachment patterns. It is also of importance, however, to emphasize the role of genetics, temperament, and other biological factors. The nature-nurture debate has been a controversial issue in the social sciences for many years: to what extent are behavior and personality traits genetic, biological, or a function of inborn temperament? To what extent do early life experiences shape and influence the developing individual? Some theorists and researchers emphasize the biological factor, others point to psychosocial influences, while another group focuses on the interaction between nature and nurture as most relevant.

Jerome Kagan [1962,1984,1989,1994] has been a leading proponent of the importance of inborn temperament. He began a longitudinal study of children in 1957 and followed them into adulthood. Kagan and colleagues found that the children labeled "fearful" during their first three years of life became adults who were introverted, cautious, and psychologically dependent on their spouses [Kagan & Moss 1962]. They concluded that temperament predicted adult behavior more than early family influences. Further studies revealed two temperamental types of children: *inhibited* and *uninhibited.* According to Kagan, inhibited children are more shy with unfamiliar children and adults, smile less with unfamiliar people, take longer to relax in new situations, have more impaired memory recall following stress, take less risks, have more fears and phobias, and have higher muscle tension [Kagan 1994]. Kagan also notes physiological differences: "temperamentally inhibited children have a more reactive circuit from the limbic area to the sympathetic nervous system than do uninhibited children" [Kagan 1994, p. 140].

Karen [1994] reviewed studies that give credence to constitutional and genetic factors. One study of 120 pairs of identical twins reared apart found many traits that were genetic in origin (e.g., imagination, leadership, sociability, stress reactions) [Bouchard et al. 1990]. The Colorado Adoption Project compared adopted children to their biologically unrelated siblings. They found children temperamentally different despite similar family influences [Dunn & Plomin 1990]. Neubauer & Neubauer [1990] reviewed research on the genetic origins of personality traits and listed a variety of traits that appear to have an inherited basis: aggressiveness, alcoholism, depression, empathy, excitability, temper, shyness, and vulnerability to stress.

The New York Longitudinal Study also focused on inborn temperament [Chess et al. 1959; cited in Karen 1994, pp. 274-288]. Researchers followed both middle-class and low socioeconomic status infants into adulthood. They assessed infants' temperamental characteristics using nine variables: activity level, rhythmicity, approach or withdrawal, adaptability, intensity of reaction, threshold of responsiveness, quality of mood, distractibility, and attention span and persistence. The babies were found to fit into four different categories:

- *Difficult* babies (10%) displayed negative mood, were slow to adapt, withdrew in novel situations, and were irregular in biological functioning.

- *Slow-to-warm-up* babies (15%) were similar to the difficult babies, but reacted with less activity and intensity.

- *Easy* babies (40%) showed positive mood, regular body functions, adapted well, and approached rather than withdrew from new situations.

- The last group, *mixed* (35%) displayed combinations of these traits.

Evaluations revealed that children born with difficult temperament developed the most emotional and behavioral problems over time; 70% developed serious symptoms in adulthood. Researchers did not conclude, however, that temperament alone produced these problems. Rather, they pointed to an interaction of nature and nurture (temperament and environment); i.e., children with difficult temperaments were much more likely to experience negative responses from others as they developed. For example, these children were more likely to "trigger" their parents, causing negative parental attitudes and reactions, and provoking old unfinished issues to surface [Thomas et al. 1969]. Only parents who were patient, consistent, firm, and emotionally resolved, could manage these children well. Additional evaluations showed that a "poor fit" between child's and parents' temperaments often accounted for difficulties (e.g., high-activity child and low-activity parent) [Chess & Thomas 1987]. Again, the conclusion was that temperament is influential, but that environmental factors play a critical role. The reaction of parents and others (e.g., teachers) could amplify or diminish any inborn traits and qualities.

There is no doubt that babies with difficult temperaments are more challenging to parents and caregivers than those who are easier and more relaxed. However, family and environmental factors cannot be underestimated, and many studies validate this notion. Mother's personality, assessed prior to the birth of her baby, was found to be a more reliable predictor of later attachment than temperament. Mothers who were more empathic, emotionally mature, and stable, were more likely to have securely attached children [Belsky and Isabella 1988]. Another study of 100 infants irritable after birth found that many more babies (68%) were securely attached at 1 year when their mothers received parenting training to increase sensitivity, compared to babies without parent training (28%) [van den Boom 1988]. Social support does make a difference in families. Mothers of irritable infants who received external support (extended kin, social programs) were found to provide parenting that led to secure attachment significantly more than mothers of irritable infants who lacked such support [Crockenberg 1981].

Thus, it appears that temperament and environment interact in an ongoing manner over the course of development to determine emotional, behavioral, and social traits and outcomes. This is hopeful news for children who are born with difficult temperaments or who receive inadequate or damaging care in the early phases of life. It indicates that outside forces, such as effective parenting programs and therapeutic interventions, can go a long way towards attenuating early difficulties.

# 3

# Roots of Attachment

## Biology and Evolution: The Basis of Attachment

Attachment between the human infant and caregiver is rooted in biology and evolution. During the course of evolution, certain behaviors became incorporated into the biological equipment of our species. These universal adaptations are found in almost all human cultures and include the development of complex language, mating, the care of babies and the very young, and attachment between the young and their parents. These instinctive behaviors have an evolutionary nature with the goal of survival of the offspring and of the species [Bowlby 1969].

Humans are genetically programmed for attachment behavior and family life. The nuclear family evolved over the course of 150 million years as the social environment best suited to provide the necessary ingredients for the survival and development of the young. Mammalian evolution is characterized by helpless and dependent young who require considerable care for survival. Human babies need the longest period of protection and nurturance of any mammal, and the parental burden and responsibility are also the greatest. Prolonged dependency of the young on the mother, father, and family unit, and the concomitant attachment behaviors, are necessary to maximize proximity, adaptability, and survival [MacLean 1982, cited in Donley 1993].

Sociobiologists, ethologists, and others who study naturally occurring behaviors have concluded that infant-mother attachment is primary due to the biological nature of the bond. However, other influences must be considered and understood. For example, the infant attaches to the entire family system, with each family member playing a unique, valuable, and highly specialized role. Temperament, psychological, and cultural influences also affect attachment and are superimposed over the biological and evolutionary forces.

## Development and Function of Family Roles

Patterns in human life emerged over the course of evolution, which led to distinctive gender roles. Humans evolved from isolated gatherers to cooperative hunter-gatherers. Limited food supplies, combined with the demands and dangers of the hunt, created a situation in which females would have difficulty protecting and nurturing their young while traveling far afield to gather food. Additionally, limiting female exposure to the risks of the hunt was based on the greater survival value of females for subsequent generations. For example, assume in a population of an equal number of males and females, all but one of the females died. Only one female would be available for procreation, and the survival of the group would be in jeopardy. If all but one male died, however, the surviving male could impregnate a number of females. Thus, males were the more expendable sex, while females were more valuable for the survival and perpetuation of the species. [Morris 1994; Ornstein 1995].

Evolutionary psychologists believe that men and women differ in those realms in which they confronted different adaptive challenges over the course of evolution [Buss 1995]. Initially, food gathering accounted for most of the diet. As humans developed skills in hunting large animals, they began to develop a level of cooperation, communication, and problem solving not needed previously. An increasingly differentiated set of roles and responsibilities evolved as males became more efficient hunters and females became more effective at gathering food and caring for the young. Males developed more upper body strength, stamina, speed, and other attributes specialized for the chase. Hunting required that they become more courageous, less selfish, and concentrate on long-term goals. The higher protein diet led to increased intelligence in all family members. Females still provided the bulk of the food source in gathering, but also perfected their abilities regarding the care of the young. A monogamous pair, each with specialized roles and functions, provided the best opportunity to perpetuate the species. This led to the "breadwinner" and "homemaker" distinction between men and women, which, of course, is less relevant in our modern society. Although not politically correct in the modern era, these stereotypical gender distinctions appear to be based on adaptation and evolution.

All animals have two basic strategies for procreation, both aimed at passing on genes and ensuring the continuation of the species. The first is to produce and disseminate as many young as possible. The male mates with many successive females, provides little or no protection of and interest in offspring, and relies on quantity for perpetuation of their genes. The second approach is to produce only a few young with one mate, providing quality care and higher levels of protection, involvement, and nurturance. This strategy of increased participation by doubling parental care greatly improved the chances of offspring survival and fostered the establishment of the nuclear family [Morris 1994].

Emotional evolution accompanied the development of gender roles and functions. For example, for the male to leave the family to hunt while the female remained behind unprotected from the advances of other males, required the development of pair-bonds. This social arrangement (rare among primates) required a sense of loyalty, commitment to mutual goals, and affectional attachments. The females remained bonded to their mates, staying faithful while they were away. Because fertilization occurs internally within women, men have faced the uncertainty that their putative children were genetically their own. The development of emotional ties increased the sense of security for both the male and female. The declaration of an exclusive pair-bond inhibited sexual rivalries among males, reducing disharmony and enhancing cooperation among the group. The committed pair-bond greatly benefited the offspring by providing maximum protection and nurturance. The females were assured of their mate's support, allowing devotion to maternal functions. The development of the family unit was instrumental in the crucial task of rearing the slowly developing offspring. [Morris 1967].

## Family as a Natural System

All natural systems operate according to basic principles and processes that are rooted in evolution and occur across cultures and species. The human family is a naturally occurring system and is regulated by the same forces that influence all other living systems.

The concept of an emotional system describes how families operate within this natural-systems framework. The emotional system allows the organism to receive information (from self and environment), to integrate that information, and to respond on the basis of that information. It includes responses that range from instinctual to learned, such as obtaining food, reproducing, fight or flight when threatened, rearing young, and other aspects of social relationships [Kerr & Bowen 1988].

The emotional system is guided by two counterbalancing life forces that govern behavior: *individuality* and *togetherness*. Family members sometimes respond on the basis of self-interest and other times based on the interests of the group. Individuality is a biologically based life force that motivates one to follow inner directives, to be separate and distinct. Togetherness propels an individual to follow the directives of others, to be connected and interdependent. The interplay of individuality and togetherness affects the level of stability, cohesiveness, and cooperation in the family. It is critical for understanding how family members function and how attachment occurs. There is need, for instance, for a child to develop into a separate individual, able to think, feel, and act for himself or herself. Simultaneously, however, there is a need for the child to remain connected to the family; to think, feel, and act as part of the unit. The process of attachment occurs within this dynamic family setting.

Kerr and Bowen [1988] reviewed several other life processes that exist in living systems, including the family system:

- **Reciprocity.** Family members occupy different roles and interact in reciprocal relationship to one another. The mother's familiar smile soothes and calms the infant, while the infant's reciprocal smile brings joy and a sense of warm emotion to the mother. The younger child shapes the behavior of an older sibling as much as the older child shapes the younger. A reciprocal relationship also exists between the individual and the larger system. A child's behavior does not exist in a vacuum, but is part of the larger emotional system of the nuclear and extended family. For example, a symptom (e.g., anxiety, depression) is not viewed as existing inside a child, but rather exists both inside and between the child and the system.

- **Differentiation of self.** There is an instinctively rooted need toward differentiation: to develop emotional separateness and to think, feel, and behave as an individual. A symbiotic, interdependent relationship is a normal state for mother and infant. This profound level of connection and togetherness promotes secure attachment, and allows the child to develop into an autonomous, distinct individual as development unfolds. The higher the level of differentiation, the greater the developing child's ability to direct his or her own functioning. The lower the level of differentiation, the less individuality emerges. A poorly differentiated person (young or old) has virtually no capacity for autonomous functioning. Emotional maturity is associated with the degree of separateness achieved from one's family-of-origin, while still in emotional contact with the group.

- **Anxiety.** All living things experience some form of anxiety, which is a natural response to real or imagined threat. Anxiety is associated with differentiation of self in the family system. The lower an individual's differentiation, the less he or she is able to adapt to stress, and the higher the level of chronic anxiety. For example, a securely attached child has lower levels of anxiety when exploring the environment than a child anxiously attached, knowing the parent serves as a "secure base." Acute anxiety develops into chronic anxiety over time, as the anxiously attached child strives to function independently.

- **Triangles.** The triangle is the basic foundation of an emotional (family) system. Attachment occurs within the context of many interlocking triangles (e.g., mother-father-child; mother-grandparent-child; parent-social service agent-child). Family triangles are influenced by the level of anxiety present. When anxiety increases between two people, a third person becomes involved in the tension, creating a triangle. For example, tension between a mother and child will draw the father into the conflict; conflict between a husband and wife can be avoided by focusing on a "problem child" (scapegoating). The involvement of a third person decreases anxiety in the twosome by spreading it among three.

According to evolution and biology, the mother-infant bond is primary and strongest. However, as will be emphasized throughout this book, many other forces in the family system affect mother-child attachment and the child's process of attachment in general. Attachment occurs in the context of the family network, including the extended family. The larger social context in which mother-child attachment occurs exerts more influence on attachment than the specific characteristics of the mother or child [Donley 1993].

## Triune Brain

Paul MacLean [1978], while director of the Laboratory of Brain Evolution and Behavior, National Institute of Health, developed the triune brain concept. MacLean described the human brain as actually a hierarchy of three brains in one, each significantly different in structure, function, and chemistry. Although the brain has evolved in size and complexity, it still contains the basic components and functions of its reptilian and mammalian past. Thus, all human beings carry in their brains this legacy of millions of years of evolution.

The *brain stem* (reptilian brain), located at the base of the skull, represents the first stage of brain evolution and is shared by all vertebrates, from reptiles to mammals. It controls primitive sexual, territorial, and survival instincts, such as reproduction, circulation, digestion, and muscle contraction in reaction to external stimulation. It regulates automatic behaviors like sleeping, breathing, blood pressure, heart rate, blinking, and swallowing. The brain stem also governs imitative behavior, tendency towards routine and ritual, stress-provoked responses, and tropistic behavior (ability to adapt to environmental changes). Distributed along its length is a network of cells, called the reticular formation, that governs the state of alertness and serves as a gateway to channel information to the higher brain structures.

The *paleomammalian brain* (limbic system), wrapped around the reptilian brain, developed as evolution proceeded to provide mammals with enhanced survival skills and the ability to interact with the environment. This second phase of brain evolution gave humans the capacity to experience and express the emotions and also maintains the immune system, the body's capacity for self-healing. The limbic system governs the general adaptation syndrome, the fight-or-flight response necessary for self-preservation. There are three subdivisions of the limbic system:

- The *amygdala* controls emotion and aggression;

- Procreation, affectionate, and sexual behaviors are incorporated into the *sextal* area; and

- The *mammillary* portion manages maternal functions, such as nursing and other attachment-related behaviors.

The limbic system is the seat of all relationship bonds. The brain stem and the limbic system together are referred to as the "old brain," primarily concerned with automatic reactions and self-preservation.

The *neomammalian brain* (cerebral cortex), the third layer of the brain to evolve, is most highly developed in humans. It is five times larger than its two lower neighbors combined, contains more than 8 billion cells (70% of the nervous system), and is what makes us uniquely human. The prefrontal cortex allows for planning, creative thinking, capacity to observe internal emotional states, and to have choice regarding those internal subjective states. The cerebral cortex, called the "new brain," governs production of symbolic language, decision making and information processing, and is believed to regulate the "higher emotions" of empathy, compassion, and love [Pearce 1992].

There is an ongoing relationship between the three parts of the brain as they continually exchange and interpret information. The reticular activating system (RAS), which begins in the brainstem and is attached to the cerebral cortex, serves as a switching device between the old and new brain. When we become threatened or emotionally aroused, the RAS enables the limbic system to take over and facilitate automatic, instinctual responses (fight or flight). When we are relaxed, not perceiving threat, the cortex is switched back on, allowing logic and reasoning to return. The old brain determines our basic survival reactions, while the new brain allows us to make choices about those reactions and enables us to consider alternative actions.

The work of MacLean and other researchers demonstrates how much of the social behavior of animals is controlled by the old brain. An experiment on rats, for instance, showed they were able to mate, breed, and rear their young with the removal of their neocortex. MacLean also found that, when neocortical development was prevented in hamsters, they were still able to display every behavior pattern found in normal hamsters. Other research showed that monkeys lost the capacity for typical social behavior when their neocortex was left intact, but the reptilian and limbic connections were destroyed [MacLean 1982; cited in Kerr and Bowen 1988, p. 36]. The neocortex is crucial for higher level mental functioning, like speech and language, but the operation of the old brain governs basic instinctual and social functions. Much of attachment behavior is governed by the old brain, and so is rooted in biology and evolution.

Contrary to previous thought, human infants are not born a *tabula rasa* (blank slate), but enter the world equipped with a repertoire of basic survival mechanisms and behaviors. For example, babies are born *without* a fear of water (and instinctively hold their breath when submerged), and *with* an inborn fear of falling and an ability to reach out for support (the Muro reflex); they instinctively orient towards the breast (rooting reflex), and demonstrate a head-turning reflex to prevent smothering. These reflexes disappear after 3 or 4 months, suggesting that we possess biologically rooted capabilities until we are able to learn and adapt to our environment.

The triune brain reflects a pattern of evolutionary progression in which nature builds newer and more complex structures on the foundation of previous structures. Each component of the triune brain has its own specialized capabilities and behaviors that emerge sequentially over the course of development. The successive unfolding and maturation of the triune brain corresponds to the evolution of human behavior and parallels the stages of child development. The old brain (brain stem and limbic system) must be appropriately stimulated and nourished during the early years of life. If this foundational brain system is understimulated, the higher brain (neocortex) does not develop to its full potential [Pearce 1992]. Sensitive and protective caregiving stimulates the natural evolution of the old brain during infancy, the critical phase of prolonged helplessness. When appropriate care is not provided (e.g., abuse, neglect, multiple separations and losses), intellectual, emotional, and social maturation does not occur normally and naturally [MacLean 1978].

## Genesis of Attachment

Fifty years ago "experts" believed that the human fetus was a blank slate, devoid of sensitivity, feeling, and any interactional capability. Over the last 30 years, a wealth of knowledge has been acquired about the fetus, its prenatal environment, and events surrounding the birth experience (perinatal). Pre- and perinatal psychologists, using such modern clinical tools as electronic fetal monitors and ultrasound, have proven that the unborn baby has well-developed senses and reacts to stimuli from mother and the environment. We now have an increased understanding of the physical, emotional, and social influences on the unborn baby. Communication, both physiological and emotional, between parents (particularly the mother) and the fetus can have a significant impact on future health and development.

Prenatal psychologists believe that the core of personality forms in the womb, rather than during the first few years of life. Research and observation have demonstrated the significance of the *in utero* experience [Verny & Kelly 1981]:

- Maternal emotional, as well as physical, messages are transmitted to the fetus.

- Severe maternal stress during pregnancy is associated with prematurity, low birth weight, and infants who are irritable, hyperaroused, and colicky.

- Women who want their babies have easier pregnancies and healthier infants than women who have unwanted pregnancies.

- The 5-month-old fetus can recognize mother's voice and communicate auditorily with the father.

- Synchrony and bonding begin during pregnancy; mother and unborn baby develop reciprocal sleep-activity cycles and styles of reactivity.

- Every sensory system of the baby is capable of functioning prior to birth.

The time of pregnancy offers parents-to-be an opportunity for both physical and psychological preparation. This period of time is truly the dawn of attachment, the time in which mother, father, and baby-to-be begin the process of uniting and connecting. We continue this discussion by examining the physical development of the fetus and the psychological tasks and reactions of the parents that accompany pregnancy.

### First Trimester

The first trimester is divided into three separate stages of *in utero* development: germinal, embryonic, and fetal [Ornstein 1995]. The *germinal* stage begins at the moment of conception, when a sperm fertilizes the egg (only one sperm in a million reaches the egg). It ends two weeks later after the fertilized egg, repeatedly dividing, implants itself on the uterus wall. A few days after fertilization, a small cluster of cells forms that is the beginning of the human heart [Pearce 1992]. This is, in essence, the first "attachment" between mother and offspring.

The *embryonic* stage lasts from implantation of the fertilized egg in the uterine cavity until about the eighth week. Embryologists refer to the baby as an embryo until all of its systems are formed by the end of the second month. This is the time of greatest differentiation, when organs are undergoing their most rapid and extensive changes. New organs and systems are created almost daily. By the end of the third week the embryo is 2 millimeters long and has a working heart and rapidly developing nervous, skeletal, and digestive systems. Between the fourth and eighth weeks, the embryo goes from a primitive shape to one that begins to resemble a human form. By the eighth week, it has a human face with eyes, ears, nose, lips, tongue, and even milk-teeth buds. The brain is sending out impulses that coordinate the functioning of organs; all major organs and structures are beginning to develop. The earliest sense to develop in the human embryo is touch. As early as six weeks, the fetus will bend its head away from the site of stimulation when the face is touched lightly near the mouth [Montagu 1986]. The first smooth, circular movements of the body occur at this time. The life of an embryo is quite tenuous. Due to the rapid growth and development of organs, this is the time when teratogens— agents that cause birth defects—are most likely to harm the embryo [Samuels & Samuels 1986].

The third development period of the first trimester is the *fetal* stage, from the ninth week of pregnancy until birth. The ninth week represents a turning point; only the reproductive system undergoes new formation, while all other organs simply undergo fine differentiation and rapid cell growth. By the end of the third month the fetus can kick legs, turn feet, curl toes, make a fist, move its thumb, turn its head, squint, frown, open mouth, swallow, and breathe. The vocal cords are completed, digestive glands are working, and vital functions of breathing, eating, and motion are rehearsed. The baby shows distinct individuality in behavior, and facial expressions are already similar to those of the parents.

During the first trimester, as the fetus is physically developing, the "work" of pregnancy truly begins for the parents. The mother must prepare herself for the monumental changes that will occur in her anatomy and physiology. Her uterus grows from 500 to 1,000 times its normal size. Her cervix softens, breasts grow, blood volume increases up to 2 1/2 quarts, and she will experience significant weight gain. She will store more protein and water and go through significant hormonal changes. Psychological and emotional issues, both conscious and unconscious, begin to emerge as pregnancy unfolds.

As discussed previously, the "old brain" controls biologically rooted instincts to procreate and attach. The "new brain" (neocortex), however, is responsible for the complex psychological and social factors involved in reproducing and caring for the young. A woman's desire for a baby is prompted by a variety of motives and needs that may include identification, fulfillment of narcissistic needs, and desire to heal old relationships through the baby. Many of these same wishes and desires are true for fathers-to-be, such as narcissistic needs, the desire to heal past relationships, and the drive to provide a link to past generations. Additionally, the wish to reproduce one's own sex is stronger for men than women, which may reflect the need to enhance the masculine identity [Brazelton & Cramer 1990].

The process of attachment begins in this early phase of pregnancy. This is a time of excitement, anxiety, ambivalence, and other emotions. The first task involves accepting and adjusting to the reality of pregnancy. There is often an initial feeling of euphoria, followed by doubts and worries: Can I handle the responsibility? Will I receive the support I need? Will the child be healthy? Am I emotionally prepared to take care of a baby? Family-of-origin issues begin to surface, including memories and unresolved feelings. The woman thinks about her own mother, wondering if she will be better or worse in the nurturing role. Men often consider their early family relationships, with similar concerns and questions regarding their own capabilities. These issues may be conscious, but more often remain out of awareness until later stages of pregnancy (if at all).

The woman may feel ambivalent or anxious about becoming increasingly dependent on her partner, especially if there is marital or relationship conflict. Support from the partner is extremely important at this time and influences maternal adjustment. The nature of the marital relationship during the first trimester—support, trust, security—has a direct bearing on the mother's adjustment before and after birth [Grossman et al. 1980]. Since there is typically less access to, and therefore less support from, extended family in our modern society, the supportive role of the man becomes even more urgent. The distant, unsupportive, or absent father has a strong negative impact on attachment, even in the initial stages of pregnancy. By not supplying the necessary support and emotional engagement, the mother-to-be develops more pressure, responsibility, and anxiety, which may affect her perceptions and feelings about the life growing inside of her. The man's self-identity, self-esteem, and own childhood experiences will affect his ability to provide love and support to his mate and face the prospects of fatherhood [Brazelton & Cramer 1990].

## Second Trimester

The fetus now responds to light, taste, and sound. He or she is capable of learning, intentional behavior, and has a rudimentary memory. By the fourth month the fetus can frown, squint, and grimace. The first embryonic cells are sound sensitive and by 4 1/2 months *in utero*, the auditory system is virtually complete. By 6 to 7 months, the fetus responds with a precise muscular movement to each of the phonemes (smallest unit of sound of which words are formed) of the mother and moves his or her body rhythm to mother's speech. The unborn baby also practices the fine neuromuscular movements of the vocal tract that are used later in crying and vocalizing [Pearce 1992]. The fetus shows preferences for certain kinds of music: she becomes calm and relaxed when listening to gentle music such as Vivaldi and Mozart, or she becomes agitated and kicks violently when exposed to Brahms, Beethoven, or loud rock music [Verny & Kelley 1981].

In the second trimester, the mother experiences "quickening" as she begins to feel the baby's movement. This heightens the mother's awareness of focusing on the baby. The movements soon turn to kicks, and mothers instinctively place their hands gently on their abdomens when this occurs. Mothers calmly talk to their babies. Some believe that this soft, soothing talk makes the fetus feel loved and wanted [Brazelton & Cramer 1990].

Often, as a woman's belly grows, so do her doubts about her sexual attractiveness and anxiety about her husband's attention. As the realities of the impending birth increase, she may wonder if he will ignore her, be totally engrossed in the baby, or ignore her and the baby. The pregnant mother requires a great deal of emotional support and understanding. Couple communication becomes crucial. If the father is feeling resentment, apathy, jealousy, or other conflicts, the mother can easily become anxious, depressed, ambivalent, or angry. Recent studies indicate that the way a man feels about his wife and unborn child is one of the single most important factors in determining the success of the pregnancy [Truman 1991].

Having no partner present can be devastating for a single mother. Lack of financial and emotional support can leave her chronically stressed and worried about her and the baby's future. Maternal depression, ambivalence, or rejection of the fetus can leave a deep scar on the unborn child. The fetus can sense and react to love and hate, as well as ambivalence and ambiguity. Studies demonstrate that accepting mothers, who looked forward to having a family, had children who were healthier emotionally and physically at birth and afterward, than offspring of rejecting mothers. Another study showed that "negative attitude mothers" had the highest rate of premature, low birth weight, and emotionally disturbed infants. Ambivalent mothers bore children with a large number of behavioral and gastrointestinal problems. The situation can be further complicated by a family environment of chronic stress and/or violence. In a study of 1,300 children and families, it was found that women in high-conflict marriages ran a 237% greater risk of bearing psychologically and physically damaged children [Verny & Kelley 1981].

### Third Trimester

There is a great acceleration in growth toward the end of *in utero* gestation. The fetus is showing its greatest weight gain, moving more, and taking on a "personality" of his or her own. He or she is demonstrating preference of activity in day or night, is more receptive to communication from the outside world, and is capable of conditioned learning. All the sensory systems are functioning; i.e., responding to visual, auditory, and kinesthetic stimulation. The unborn baby is affected by touch, noise, and stress and is particularly vulnerable to the ingestion of drugs, alcohol, and tobacco. Babies exposed to drugs *in utero* are often born with low birth weight, extremely agitated, tactilely defensive, and may exhibit developmental, emotional, and intellectual impairments. The effects of Fetal Alcohol Syndrome and Fetal Alcohol Effect have long-term implications for the child's ability to learn and integrate experience [Besharov 1994]. Smoking also has serious effects on the fetus. In addition to injecting the neonate with numerous noxious chemicals (arsenic, cyanide, formaldehyde, carbon monoxide), smoking decreases the oxygen supply to the fetus, carried by maternal blood passing through the placenta. Studies showed that an unborn fetus becomes agitated (measured by significantly increased heart rate) each time mother even thinks about having a cigarette [Sontag 1970].

During the last few months of pregnancy, the increased activity level of the fetus falls into certain cycles and patterns. A receptive mother interacts with her fetus in response to these patterns and knows if he or she is in deep sleep, light sleep, or actively awake and alert. Synchrony is developing; the baby responds to mother's rest activity level, and mother responds to the baby's. The fetus and mother are preconditioned to each other's rhythms, preparing for the mother to respond to the cries, needs, and other signals after birth.

Our brains are like pharmacies, compounding a wide range of chemicals that affect our moods and biological systems. The fetus decodes maternal feelings through a neurohormonal dialogue [Borysenko & Borysenko 1994]. Fear and anxiety, for example, are biochemically induced by a group of chemicals called catecholamines. When a pregnant woman becomes frightened, the hypothalamus orders the autonomic nervous system (ANS) to increase heart rate, pupils dilate, palms sweat, blood pressure rises, and the endocrine system increases neurohormone production. This floods into the blood stream, altering both the mother and fetus' body chemistry. When a mother thinks joyful thoughts, the limbic system releases neuropeptides into her blood stream, which fit into receptor cells throughout her body (and fetus). When she feels joy and acceptance, every cell in her body responds to that emotion. Depression, anxiety, and ambivalence are also broadcast throughout her entire body/mind system and to that of the unborn child. Almost anything that upsets mother also upsets the fetus. (Infrequent or isolated incidents will not cause serious harm; it is the ongoing stressors that produce damaging effects).

## The Birth Experience

Immediately prior to birth, the infant's body releases adrenal hormones that initiate a chain of reciprocal events within the mother. First, the hormones alert the infant's body to mobilize for the challenges of birth. Second, these hormones are transmitted through the umbilical cord to signal the mother's body, which begins its own set of programmed responses. The pregnancy-maintaining hormone progesterone begins to decrease in the mother's blood stream, initiating the birth process. Mother also begins to secrete oxytocin, which induces uterine contractions and signals the start of lactation [Pearce 1992].

There are a variety of factors that influence the degree of difficulty of labor and delivery. The birth experience is affected by mother's medication, diet, level of stress, and general physical and emotional health. Mother's anxiety level before and during birth can be increased by lack of knowledge about or fear of the birth process, apprehension about motherhood, and a lack of emotional support (especially from the child's father). All mammals seek a safe and secure environment to deliver their young, due to their high level of vulnerability. Humans continue to require this ancient need for birth protection. Stress and anxiety send a danger signal to the mother, flooding her body with biochemicals that slow down the birth process. The more anxious the mother, the longer she takes to give birth. Delaying the birth can lead to an increased risk of complications, use of drugs to induce labor, and a higher incidence of cesarean section. Thus, attention to the mother's emotional state and available support are critical factors during the birth experience [Morris 1994].

Our concept of the newborn infant has changed dramatically. The neonate is considerably more sensitive, aware of, and responsive to the environment than previously imagined. The birth experience radically changes the neonate's environment from wet to dry, muffled sounds to loud noises, head down to head up or flat, and these changes have an impact on the sensitive baby. In many instances, the newborn is separated from mother at a time of importance for closeness and connection, designed by nature to reduce the stress of birth. For example, one-third of the infant's blood and oxygen remains in the placenta for 5 to 10 minutes after birth, allowing time for the infant's internal systems to function independently.

The environment in which the birth occurs is also a critical factor. A relaxing, safe, and supportive atmosphere leads to a more positive birth experience for both mother, father, and baby. The birthing environment has come full circle: the place of birth has shifted from the home, to the hospital, and back again to a family focus. Initially, advances in medicine led to a dramatic increase in the survival rate among high-risk infants and mother. What was previously a family-oriented organic event became a medically oriented technical event, and the psychological aspects of the birth experience suffered. The birth experience became more clinical and sterile, consisting of bright lights, loud noises, electronic devices, and cold instruments.

Hospital births required women to lie down as if a "sick patient." Our ancestors knew that squatting was the natural position for childbirth, taking advantage of gravity, and allowing for an easier and more natural birth. Recently, hospital birthing environments have been designed to be more "family friendly" and conducive to a natural experience. For example, family birthing suites offer dim lights, soft music, and a reassuring and comfortable atmosphere. Home births with midwives have also reemerged as a viable alternative in low-risk situations [Brazelton & Cramer 1990].

## Prematurity

Premature birth has been found to affect not only the physiology of the infant, but also early interactions and attachment with caregivers. Preterm infants show a variety of characteristics: less well-defined sleep cycles; less alert and responsive at birth; poor motor coordination; greater percentage of time fussing and crying; and more difficult to feed and soothe, compared to full-term infants [Frodi & Thompson 1985]. Full-term babies have an instinctual protective response, "habituation," that prevents the nervous system from being overstimulated. Premature babies, however, generally lack this protective response, and are easily overstimulated.

Prematurity also affects the biological and psychological reactions of parents. After nine months of pregnancy, parents typically feel a sense of completion and readiness for the birth of their infant. When this process is cut short, parents may feel unprepared and anxious. A mother may blame herself, perceiving the premature birth as her own personal failure. Disrupting the instinctual and biological schedule increases parental anxiety and reduces confidence, which can have detrimental effects on the parent-infant relationship. Some studies have shown that parents of premature babies initiate less body contact, less face-to-face contact, smile and talk less, and play less with their infants [Brazelton & Cramer 1990]. "On the whole, interactions with prematures are more taxing for parents, testing their capacities to attune to a less responsive, less well put together infant. This is also true for 'professional infant handlers' " [Brazelton & Cramer 1990, p. 199]. Other studies of middle class samples, however, have found mothers of premature babies to be more sensitive to cues for contact, more responsive in early face-to-face interactions, and more affectionate and gentle [Field 1987]. Parents who become hypervigilant and overprotective towards their vulnerable infants may inhibit the development of age-appropriate autonomy and independence.

The preemie is physically and emotionally isolated at a time when he or she requires a great deal of contact. The name of the incubator ("isolette") aptly describes this predicament. Corrective touching and caressing of the infant can minimize detrimental effects. Massaging preemies, for example, has enabled these infants to be more alert, active, responsive, sleep better, gain weight faster, and leave the hospitals sooner than untouched babies [Field 1987]. Premature birth alone does not necessarily cause attachment problems. It does place the infant at risk for anxious attachment, however, when combined with other risk factors, such as chronic illness and negative parental responses [Colin 1996].

# Birth to 3 Years

Bonding is the biological, genetic, and emotional connection between mother and baby during pregnancy and at birth. All babies have a bond with their birth mother. Attachment, however, is learned after birth through interactions between caregivers and child during the first three years. "Attachment is an affective bond characterized by a tendency to seek and maintain proximity to a specific figure, particularly while under stress" [Bowlby 1970, p. 12].

Human babies are born earlier in the growth cycle than other mammals. The fetus must be born when its head has reached the maximum size compatible with passage through the birth canal. The female pelvis is relatively small to support an erect posture. The baby must be born after 266 days of gestation in order to pass through the birth canal, due to the rapid growth of the brain during the last trimester. The baby is born well before complete maturation. Extrogestation lasts, on average, the same amount of time as *in utero* gestation (266 days). Thus, significant brain development occurs outside the womb, when the baby is exposed to a variety of social and environmental influences [Montagu 1986; Verny & Kelly 1981].

## *Birth to Eight Months*

The newborn infant's nervous system is not well organized, and it is through the interactions between baby and caregiver during the first year that organization occurs. The attachment relationship is critical for the infant's developing nervous and hormonal systems; lack of healthy attachment can result in deficiencies in cognitive and physical development [Fahlberg 1991]. Studies have demonstrated the importance of early mother-infant interaction. Infants are born with the ability to distinguish their mothers' voice and express a preference for the voice of birth mother [DeCasper & Fifer 1980]. Newborns turn preferentially toward their mother's breast, instead of toward the breast of another lactating woman [MacFarlane 1975]. Brazelton's pioneering study on mother-infant relationships demonstrated that they form a "mutually regulated partnership." The relationship is reciprocal, with the mother and infant moving in synchrony through positive and negative experiences [Brazelton et al. 1974]. The mother's behavior can actually regulate the infant's body and brain: Mother's body warmth affects the infant's endocrine systems, maternal touch stimulates growth hormones, and maternal milk changes the baby's heart rate. Conversely, the infant also affects the mother's mood and behavior. By 3 months of age, more than 50% of the mother's behaviors and almost 40% of the infant's behaviors were found to be influenced by their partner [Tronick & Weinberg 1997]. These ongoing interactive routines between caregiver and infant serve as a meaning system; the infant senses consistency and predictability, which leads to a feeling of security [Bruner 1995].

Mutual regulation is dependent upon three factors: the infant's ability to organize and control physiological states and behavior, the infant's ability to communicate messages to the caregiver, and the caregiver's capacity to read those signals accurately and respond appropriately. Unlike other species, in which the offspring imprints on the mother, the human mother becomes imprinted on the baby. Human infants are born too helpless to follow and too weak to cling to caregivers for protection. The infant's only means of getting its needs met are to signal distress and then hope that assistance is forthcoming. It is critical for survival to have a responsive caregiver who is perceptive of the infant's signals and attentive to his or her needs. This imprinting impulse allows the mother to override her own hunger, fatigue, or self-interest in order to meet the infant's needs and numerous demands [Montagu 1986]. Nature has provided a means to entice the attention and assistance of caregivers. There is a strong instinctual reaction to what is called "kinderschema," the qualities of the infant's face that are strongly appealing (large round eyes, large domed forehead, chubby cheeks, flattened face, snub nose, and smooth, soft skin). These physical characteristics induce the caregiver to stay close, cuddle, caress, smile, gaze at and talk to their babies [Morris 1994].

Brazelton and Als (1979) have described four stages in early mother-infant interaction. These stages highlight the progression of achievements of the infant and the development of reciprocity and synchrony in the relationship. The stages, outlined in Table 1, include homeostatic control, prolonging of attention and interaction, testing limits, and the emergence of autonomy. Although these original concepts were applied to the mother-infant relationship, it seems that a close father-infant relationship also follows similar development. Developmental changes in the child and caregiver-child relationship from birth to 3 years of age are outlined in Tables 2, 3, and 4 [adapted from *Zero to Three* 1997].

### First-Year Attachment Cycle

Many reciprocal interactions are infant-initiated during the first year of life within the context of the ongoing attachment cycle. This cycle begins with the infant's needs and the expression of arousal or displeasure and is completed by the caregiver's response. The infant develops trust and secure attachment through successful gratification of these basic needs and by alleviation of arousal and discomfort. (See Figure 1; adapted from Cline 1992).

The following infant and caregiver behaviors are crucial ingredients to the successful completion of this cycle and the development of secure attachment.

## Crying

One primary function of crying is to communicate discomfort to the caregiver. Wolff (1969) described four types of infant crying: hunger, pain, danger, and neurological impairment. Maternal stress level during pregnancy has been found to correlate highly with infant crying. In one study, almost half of the mothers whose infant cried extensively reported chronic and severe stress during pregnancy [Kitzinger 1989; cited in Solter 1995, p. 21]. Caregivers who respond promptly and consistently to their infant's cries have babies who cry less in frequency and duration as they grow older. Crying also serves the purpose of releasing stress-related hormones that reduces tension and arousal. Crying is an inborn stress management and healing mechanism [Solter 1995].

## Figure 1. First-Year Attachment Cycle

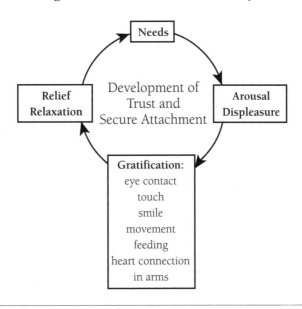

## Table 1. Stages in Early Infant-Caregiver Interaction

**1. Homeostatic control (7 - 10 days)**
- Achieve control over input and output systems; receive and shut out stimuli, control motor activity, state of consciousness, and autonomic responses.
- Caregiver must have deep sense of empathy to be in synch with infant's needs.

**2. Prolonging of attention and interaction (1 - 8 weeks)**
- Prolong interaction with caregiver; pay attention longer, utilize cues from caregiver to maintain alertness.
- Use own capacities (e.g., smile, vocalizing, facial expressions) to signal receptivity.
- Adapt to give-and-take of a synchronized relationship.
- Caregiver needs support (e.g., from spouse, kin, nurse) and must be highly sensitive to infant's cues.

**3. Testing limits (3 - 4 months)**
- Parents and infant test and stretch infant's limits; respond to information, withdraw and recover in mutual relationship.
- Prolonged state of attunement between infant and caregiver; learn more about self and other.
- Infant experiences mastery; ability to sequence controls and produce signals.
- Mother feels control over baby's responses and ability to be available and nurturing.

**4. Emergence of autonomy (4 - 5 months)**
- Baby begins to search for and respond to environmental or social cues; imitates, reaches for and plays with objects.
- Increasing sense of autonomy; increased voluntary control over environment and sense of competence.
- Enhanced cognitive awareness; aware of every sight, sound, texture, presence and absence of parents; will cry for attention.
- Object permanence begins; baby looks at spot for object after it disappears.
- Attachment feelings increase; caregivers become more important to baby.
- Parent must be able to tolerate both the attachment needs and the need for autonomy.
- Stranger awareness and anxiety begins.

## Table 2. Birth to 8 Months

1. **Development of self**
   - Explore and manipulate body.
   - Trust caregivers (can depend on caregivers to meet needs, provide a secure base for exploration, feel secure with holding and smile).
   - Comfort self (self-soothing).
   - Impact environment (shake a rattle, kick a mobile, reciprocal smile).
2. **Emotional development**
   - Express a range of emotion (pleasure, excitement, joy, fear, anger, and sadness).
   - Need caregivers to understand feelings and respond with comfort and protection.
3. **Discrimination skills**
   - Preference for attachment figures (recognize parent's voice, feel relaxed with familiar caregivers).
   - Stranger anxiety begins.
   - Learn to interact with the world (visually explore surroundings, play with parents).
4. **Physical development**
   - Body moves automatically (instinctive movements).
   - Dexterity develops (place objects in mouth, hold objects).
   - Purposeful movement (hold head up, roll over, sit, crawl).
5. **Communication and social development**
   - Communicate needs by crying, facial expressions, and body movements.
   - New forms of communication develop within a few months (different sounds, laugh, gestures to get attention, imitate sounds).
   - Reciprocal cues and signals (reach out to be picked up, divert gaze to signal overstimulation).

## Eye Contact

The caregiver-infant gaze is a primary social releaser for the development of attachment. A newborn can focus his or her eyes 7-12 inches, the exact distance needed to make eye contact in arms. Soon after birth, the infant can follow a slowly moving light and the movement of curved objects that have qualities of the mother's face. Face-to-face proximity and eye contact are synonymous with closeness and intimacy. Spitz [1965] found that infants responded with pleasure when shown a mask of a human face. When the lower part of the mask was covered, their response did not change. Covering the upper part, however, (even one eye) caused displeasure and loss of interest. He concluded that the infant's response to eye contact is instinctual. Our autonomic nervous system directs the pupils to expand slightly when viewing something positive or pleasurable. Conversely, the pupils shrink when seeing something unpleasant. The pupils cannot lie. The infant gazes into mother's eyes and receives potent messages about her emotional state and level of involvement [Morris 1994].

## Touch

All warm-blooded animals are born with an innate need to be touched and stroked affectionately. Research confirmed that the handling or gentling of mammals early

## Table 3. Eight to 18 Months

1. **Development of self**
   - Reciprocity and internalization (self-esteem results from positive and empathic message; feelings of competency and pride develop).
   - Initial stages of autonomy (says "No," expresses individuality).
   - Language development (knows own name; labeling objects and events with words).
2. **Emotional development**
   - Experience and express intense feelings (shriek with joy, hit, push when angry or frustrated).
   - Deepening attachment feelings (increased autonomy and attachment needs, shows affection and need for "secure base," frightened when attachment figure disappears).
   - Time and predictability (understands that caregiver will return after separation; feels safe with consistency).
3. **Discrimination skills**
   - Learning about choice (choosing toys, food, clothes).
   - Play and social skill development (enact simple scenes with other children; beginning to learn cooperation and sharing via adult supervision).
   - Modeling and imitation (emulate caregiver's behavior; initial stages of internalization).
   - Interact with environment (interested in how things work; increased control over objects and events).
4. **Physical development**
   - Increased manual dexterity (use crayons, stack blocks, feed self, drink from a cup).
   - Control over body and movements (sit, pull up, walk, climb stairs, run).
5. **Communication and social development**
   - Communicate through expression and actions (deliberate eye contact to get attention and express feelings; point to express desires; needs help from caregiver to learn to express feelings in acceptable ways).
   - Increased verbal skills (can use up to 10 words; employs a variety of sounds to get help).
   - Receptive to signals and cues (understands verbal and nonverbal behavior; sensitive to caregivers' tone of voice and body tension).

in life results in increased weight gain, activity, and resilience under stress [Simon 1976]. The mammalian mother's behavior of licking her young serves the purpose of cleaning and also stimulates internal systems (gastrointestinal, circulatory, immunological).

Touch for the human baby serves both physical and emotional functions. Somatic stimulation begins in labor when uterine contractions activate principle organ systems of the fetus. Human babies actually die from the lack of touch. In the nineteenth century, most institutionalized infants in the United States died of *marasmus* ("wasting away"). Institutions surveyed in 1915 reported that a majority of infants under the age of 2 had died due to failure to thrive, related to the lack of touch and affection [Chapin 1915; cited in Montagu 1986, p. 97]. Prescott (1971) found that deprivation of touch and movement contributed to later emotional problems. He also found that cultures in which physical affection toward infants was high had low levels of adult aggression, but cultures where affectionate touch was low had high adult aggression. Recent research on contact comfort between mother

## Table 4. Eighteen Months to 3 Years

1. **Development of self**
   - Seeks increased independence, but still requires clear and consistent limits from caregivers.
   - Self-identity forming through exploration and limits.
   - Develops a sense of belonging (connected with family; child care setting should reflect cultural background).
   - Internal working model solidifies (caregiver messages and emotional reactions help shape child's self-esteem).
   - Normal ambivalence regarding independence-autonomy.
   - Developing increased self-control with a framework provided by caregiver (provides a few simple and clear rules for child to follow with ongoing support; child displays sporadic impulse control).

2. **Emotional development**
   - Intense emotional reactions (pride about accomplishments; frustration and anger may be expressed through physical aggression; fears emerge—dark, monsters, people in costumes).
   - Increased control over feelings (express feelings via words and play).
   - Modeling and identification (learns to treat others by the way caregivers treat child and others).
   - Tuning into caregiver's feelings (responds to caregiver's emotional state).

3. **Discrimination skills**
   - More aware of other children (age, sex, physical differences, presence or absence from group).
   - Increased social play (moves from parallel play to interactional play).
   - Increased awareness of other children's rights (learning to share, cooperate, delay gratification, and be sensitive to the feelings of others).
   - Aware of caregiver's responses to own actions (knows when caregiver is pleased or upset).
   - Aware of and can classify similar and different objects (e.g., puts toys in groups).

4. **Physical development**
   - Increased manual dexterity (turns pages of a book, draws shapes, learning to use scissors).
   - Enhanced movement (kick and throw ball, walk on tip toes, walk upstairs).
   - Increased physical competencies (eat with utensils, dress self).

5. **Communication and social development**
   - Language and communication (increased vocabulary, creates sentences, can talk about yesterday and tomorrow).
   - Becomes frustrated when having trouble expressing self; benefits from caregiver assistance in identifying ideas and feelings.
   - Enjoys reciprocal story telling (listens as caregiver reads, participates in story telling).
   - Plays with words and concepts (enjoys songs and word games, uses objects to represent something else, acts out scenes with others).

and infant revealed interesting but not surprising findings. Low socioeconomic-status mothers were given either a soft baby carrier or a plastic infant seat to use on a daily basis. At 3 1/2 months of age, the soft carrier infants looked more frequently at their mothers and cried less; these mothers were more responsive to their babies vocalizations. At 13 months, these infants were more likely to be securely attached (83%) compared with the infant seat group (39%) [Anisfeld et al. 1990].

## Smile

Smiling is a universal human greeting that signals friendliness and nonaggression. By the eighth week, the infant begins to smile in response to seeing the primary attachment figure. The baby's smile is an instinctive response that attracts the attention of the caregiver. The smile on the face of the mother provokes feelings of safety and security in the baby. The baby's smile is a powerful signal that rewards and motivates an ongoing positive parental response. This reciprocal smile promotes secure attachment.

## Movement

Movement is another basic instinctual need for healthy development and attachment. The vestibular-cerebellar system (associated with balance and movement) is the dominant sensory system during fetal brain development. Studies on infant monkeys reared in isolation demonstrated that a mother surrogate that moved (swinging devise) prevented the development of social and affectional maladjustment [Mason & Berkson 1975]. In humans, every time mother moves, the fetus moves, naturally rocking to the rhythms and motions of mother's body. After birth, vestibular stimulation through activities such as bouncing and rocking plays a crucial role in the infant's development. Rocking slows the heart rate, promotes effective respiratory and gastrointestinal functioning, and decreases congestion. When a baby is hungry, feeding most effectively terminates crying; at all other times, rocking is the most effective soothing and calming intervention [Bowlby 1982].

Neal [1968; cited in Montagu 1986, p. 161] studied the effects of rocking on premature infants. He found that when incubators were kept in motion the infants functioned better than unrocked infants in visual tracking, auditory development, weight gain, and bodily control. Healthy parents naturally rock, bounce, and rhythmically sway their babies, which promotes reciprocity and secure attachment. Our ancestors instinctively knew this; they traveled, worked, played and slept in constant interaction with their offspring. They straddled their infants close to their bodies and provided continual stimulation, motion, and contact [Liedloff 1975].

## Feeding

In infancy, satisfaction of needs involves food and nourishment. The psychosocial experiences associated with feeding are part of the infant's emotional and relational development. The infant begins to associate food and feeding with warm skin-to-skin contact, eye contact, and soothing voice and smile. Breast feeding can become part of attachment behavior, as it is another way of clinging to the mother that is both intimate and soothing. Breast milk contains important nutrients and antibodies that nourish the newborn and strengthen his or her immune system. Colostrum in the mother's milk acts as a laxative, effectively cleaning the meconium in the newborn's gastrointestinal tract, and is rich in antibodies needed to provide immunities until the infant acquires his or her own at 6 months. As the newborn suckles on the mother's breast, the hormone oxytocin is secreted in the mother, which helps to shrink the uterus and reduces postdelivery bleeding.

The infant's brain consumes twice the energy of an adult's, and must be provided with nutrients on a regular basis, due to limited storage capacity of energy (glucose). The regularity and consistency of the feeding ritual, the quality of the food, and the care with which food is provided, greatly influence security, attachment, and later attitudes and behaviors regarding food. Research showed that children who had pleasurable mealtime experiences displayed better impulse control, concentration, ability to solve problems, and greater anticipated pleasure from others [Arnstein 1975].

## The Heart Connection

The heart is not merely a blood-pumping station; it also plays a major role in social and emotional functioning. The sound and steady movements of the mother's heartbeat are an ongoing component of fetal development. After birth, proximity to the mother's heartbeat provides familiar reassurance and stress reduction for the newborn. The heart contains neurotransmitters that directly affect the functioning of the brain. For example, the heart produces a hormone (ANF) that affects the limbic system, the part of the brain that regulates emotion. ANF also plays a key role in regulating immune system response, memory, and learning.

Research in the 1940s reported that the mother's heartbeat affected the infant *in utero* [Bernard & Sontag 1947; cited in Pearce 1992, p. 103]. Years later, researchers piped an audiotape of a human heart beat into a newborn nursery. The babies hearing the heartbeat had increased appetite, weight gain, sleep and respiration, and cried 50% less than the babies not exposed to the heartbeat [Salk 1960; cited in Verny & Kelly 1981, p. 28]. Pearce [1992] notes that if a heart cell is isolated, it loses synchronous rhythm and fibrillates until it dies. If two heart cells are placed in proximity to one another, however, they will not only survive, but will also synchronize and beat in unison. This even occurs across a spatial barrier. Infants who are placed in close heart-to-heart proximity with a primary caregiver maintain a mutual heart synchrony.

## In-Arms Holding

All components of attachment—crying, touching, movement, smiling, eye contact, feeding, clinging, and the heart connection—occur within the context of the in-arms position. Babies have been placed close to their mothers in this holding position throughout human history. This holding position provides a physical, emotional, and relational foundation for the development of secure attachment. Many children have not experienced fulfillment of the precisely evolved attachment behaviors and needs. The healing of the effects of these early life deprivations is best facilitated by utilizing the same in-arms approach. In our work with children with attachment disorder, we refer to this therapeutic framework as the Holding Nurturing Process (see Chapter 6).

## Development of Attachment (8 months to 4 years)

The first year of life involves the development of basic trust and security through consistent, appropriate, and reliable fulfillment of the infant's needs. The second year of life focuses on both needs and "wants," and the development of autonomy and self-identity. (See Figure 2, adapted from Cline 1992.) (Infants and toddlers develop at differing rates; the first- and second-year attachment cycle designations are merely reference points). During this developmental stage, the infant moves toward toddlerhood, and becomes aware of self as separate. Self-identity forms on the basis of the balance between parental limits and the child's search for independence. At 7 to 8 months of age, the infant begins to show active "goal-corrected" maintenance of closeness to a preferred caregiver. For example, the baby will both cry for and follow the attachment figure to maintain closeness. Attachment behaviors include crying, smiling, reaching, following, approaching, clinging, and protesting separation. At this same time, babies search for objects hidden from view, which Piaget [1952] referred to as "object constancy," the ability to understand that an object still exists even when out of sight or reach. This cognitive development allows the baby to use flexible behaviors to achieve the goal of proximity with the attachment figure.

Crawling also develops around 6 to 8 months; the baby will wander off but soon return to the safety of the attachment figure. Securely attached infants use their attachment figures as a safe base from which to explore. Erikson (1950) described this as the development of basic trust, a primary developmental task of the first year of life. Another sign of attachment is stranger anxiety, which occurs when the infant shows fear of unfamiliar people and places and protests separation.

The sequence of responses to separation emerges at this same time: protest, detachment, and despair. Prior to this stage, babies can often adapt to new environments and caregivers without severe disturbance. After this time, however, the baby signals extreme protest when separated from the primary attachment figure, and prolonged disruption has serious consequences for the vulnerable infant.

As the child becomes more mobile, consistent limits and discipline become a part of effective parenting. Between the ages of 8 and 17 months, toddlers have limited self-control; the parent's limit setting and discipline fosters the process of learning compliance and obedience. For example, a normal part of toddler's exploration includes biting, pulling hair, and hitting. Effective parents respond firmly and calmly, providing limits and "rules" for the child.

As toddlers grow and develop, they become more independent and autonomous, and the need for continuous closeness gives way to a need to investigate the world. By 18 months, they turn to caregivers for guidance in unfamiliar situations. This

## Figure 2. Second-Year Attachment Cycle

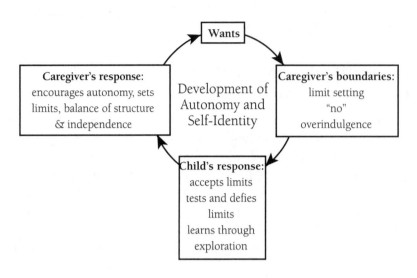

"social referencing" provides the child with an opportunity to develop morality and values. Pride emerges when the child receives parental approval and then feels good about himself or herself. Parental disapproval creates negative feelings in the securely attached child, extinguishing unacceptable behavior and leading to the development of a conscience. The child with attachment disorder is not concerned with pleasing the unavailable or maltreating attachment figure, and therefore is without healthy external limits and does not develop a prosocial conscience.

By the time babies reach their first birthday, they have rudimentary *internal working models* of their attachment relationships, based on their experience of caregiving [Bowlby 1969]. The internal working model includes perceptions about the self and expectations of the attachment figure(s); they are encoded in the child's procedural memory, based on sensorimotor experiences (preverbal memory, not conscious). Securely attached toddlers develop a positive internal working model (caregivers are trustworthy and reliable; I am worthwhile and lovable; my world is a safe and joyous place), and are emotionally and cognitively competent. Avoidantly attached toddlers are learning to cope with rejection and punishment, but not how to elicit protection, nurturance, and love. They are hypervigilant and block awareness of their anxiety, feelings, and needs. Researchers have found that the heart rates and stress hormone levels of avoidantly attached 1-year-olds significantly increased upon separation and reunion with their mothers, while their outward appearance seemed calm. Prior to the development of language, these babies are already defending against vulnerability and the expression of attachment needs and displaying rejecting behaviors towards their caregivers [Sroufe & Waters 1977; Grossmann & Grossmann 1991]. Ambivalently attached toddlers cannot make sense of their inconsistent experiences with caregivers; they cannot predict whether their attachment figures will be nurturing and protective, or hostile and rejecting. These youngsters are angry and anxious much of the time and exhibit extreme dependency. Toddlers with disorganized attached patterns have no consistent strategy to handle separation, reunion, needs, or feelings in response to their disturbed, depressed or abusive attachment figures.

During the preschool years, the ability to use language and semantic memory expand considerably. Semantic memory involves generalization or summaries regarding the meanings of recurring patterns. An example is a child pretending that her doll is mommy going to work. Episodic memory, the ability to recall specific events, also begins to develop at this time. The child has an increased ability to organize mental representations; to form detailed internal working models of attachment relationships, and to develop emotional and behavioral strategies in response, including defenses. Securely attached children can use information from all three memory systems (procedural, semantic, and episodic) and can learn that open and direct communication is most effective. Caregivers are sensitive to their needs, encourage open communication about thoughts and feelings, and validate the child's perceptions. They tolerate negative emotions, while setting clear and appropriate boundaries regarding dangerous exploration and negative behavior toward others. These caregivers facilitate a goal-corrected partnership by encouraging negotiations and constructing cooperative plans.

Avoidantly attached children are extremely defended and have learned to deny their anger, anxiety, and need for nurturance. Some caregivers are openly hostile and rejecting, while others are withdrawn and unresponsive. Either way, the child is rejected. By age 3 or 4, these children openly avoid and ignore attachment figures and do not give signals that suggest a need and desire for closeness. Children of withdrawn and depressed caregivers often become *"compulsively caregiving"*; the child tries to reassure the parents and makes few demands ("parentification"). Children of hostile and rejecting attachment figures become *"compulsively compliant"*; they are hypervigilant, monitoring the dangerous social environment, and comply in order to avoid threat and hostility [Crittenden 1994].

The internal working model of these attachment-compromised children involves denial of their need for closeness. A "false self" begins to develop [Winnecott 1965]. The child buries his or her true feelings and needs and projects an ingenuine image. Children with ambivalent attachment show inconsistent and unpredictable behaviors similar to their caregivers. They alternate between anger and neediness, show limited exploratory competence and self-reliance, and become selfish and overdependent preschoolers. They often develop a coercive pattern of behavior in order to keep the attachment figure involved and controlled. The child and caregiver become enmeshed in a coercive, angry and dishonest relationship.

A nonresponsive, neglectful, or abusive environment produces angry, depressed, and hopeless children. Most young children who are referred for mental health services have coercive-threatening attachment patterns and internal working models [Crittenden 1994]. These children have frequent and prolonged temper tantrums and tend to be loud, demanding, and disruptive. They are accident prone, emotionally and behaviorally impulsive, and want to be the center of attention, desperately seeking the attentiveness lacking in their attachment relationships. They are typically restless, irritable, and have a short attention span; they appear to have attention deficit/hyperactivity disorder (ADHD) and learning disabilities, with no neurological basis. They are "bossy," oppositional, and cannot take no for an answer. They have little frustration tolerance, demand instant gratification, and antagonize others. Keeping objects and people at the appropriate distance is difficult; they move away when they should be close and get close when they should be moving away (boundary problems). They become either victim or victimizer, being the recipient of others' abuse, or themselves being the bully.

### The School-Age Years

During the school years, children with attachment disorder become extremely manipulative, controlling, and are often diagnosed with oppositional defiant disorder and conduct disorder. Many of these children are in the process of developing narcissistic, borderline, and psychopathic personalities. By adolescence they are commonly sexually promiscuous to obtain physical closeness without emotional intimacy and become more aggressive, antisocial, and depressed. Although some turn to substance abuse, many avoid this destructive coping strategy, due to their inordinate need to be in control. Many of these teenagers displace their rage into theft, vandalism, and assaultive behaviors.

Children with attachment disorder are deprived of fundamental experiences necessary to nurture the development of the "new brain" (neocortex). Their sensorimotor and emotional development remains stuck in the lower brain center ("old brain"). The child is dominated by a basic survival drive for food, territory, sexuality, and by the emotionality of the limbic system. They lack the ego development and self-control to modulate violent impulses. In normal child development, thinking moves from concrete to abstract. Children with attachment disorder, however, remain in the realm of concrete thinking and so lack the logic and reasoning abilities necessary for planning ahead. They have little or no respect for authority, rules, and the rights of others. They seek out safe targets, weaker peers, and helpless animals in order to vent their hostility and aggression.

The experience of major loss during the early developmental years can produce children fearful of closeness and love. They feel alone, alienated from others, and possess an attitude of self-protection. They are motivated by a need for power: "If I am in control, I feel less threatened"; "I do not trust others to have influence over me." Fear of abandonment is a force that runs their lives. They do not allow anyone to be close and maintain elaborate defenses to guard against intimacy and subsequent loss.

# 4
# Personal & Social Competencies
## The Attachment Foundation

Secure attachment in the early years provides the developing child with a foundation that leads to a variety of healthy psychological and social outcomes, as discussed in Chapter 2 (developmental studies). Again, securely attached children compared to those with insecure-anxious-disorganized attachments, demonstrate advantages with the following:

- Self-esteem,

- Relationships with caregivers,

- Friendships with peers,

- Ability to control impulses and emotions,

- Cooperation and compassion,

- Independence and autonomy, and

- Positive core beliefs.

This chapter will focus on three additional areas of psychosocial functioning that are associated with caregiver-child attachment. Observations of child development and family life, as well as extensive research findings, have shown that secure attachment results in the development of the following:

- A solid and positive sense of self,

- Prosocial values and morality, and

- Resilience (the ability to handle stress and adversity well).

## Development of Self

The development of an autonomous sense of self is an early stage-salient task and is unequivocally linked to attachment. Patterns of attachment that develop as a result of the infant-caregiver relationship directly affect the child's emerging sense of self. Maltreated children and children with attachment disorder typically have extreme disturbances in self-concept, self-regulation, and the ability to function autonomously.

Children who experience a secure base with an appropriately responsive and available caregiver are more likely to be autonomous and independent as they develop. The child is able to explore his or her environment with more confidence and less anxiety, resulting in enhanced self-esteem, feelings of mastery, and differentiation of self. Contrary to the belief of some observers, children who experience consistent and considerable gratification of needs in the early stages do not become "spoiled" and dependent; they are more independent, self-assured, and confident.

### Internal State Language

Research has shown that by 28 months of age, most children are capable of using words to label their perceptions, physical states, and feelings (e.g., happy, mad, hungry). These internal state words reflect the child's developing sense of self as distinct from others and also promote behavioral and emotional self-control (e.g., the ability to express anger with words rather than assault another child) [Pearce & Pezzot-Pearce 1997]. Children with attachment disorder, however, are less able to label their internal states; they are often not aware of thoughts, feelings, and levels of physiological arousal [Beeghly & Cicchetti 1994]. There are two reasons for this. First, there is a lack of modeling in their environment; caregivers do not commonly discuss feelings in a sensible and meaningful way. Second, lack of knowing and expressing feelings (or other internal states) is a self-protective strategy. The goal is to avoid further emotional pain and negativity by withholding information [Dunn & Brown 1991].

Children with attachment disorder are often superficially charming and engaging and/or compulsively compliant. They will passively and ingenuinely comply rather than express their feelings and needs [Crittenden & DiLalla 1988]. By repeatedly avoiding the awareness or expression of thoughts and emotions, they hope to avoid additional conflict or trauma. There is a high price to pay, however; their sense of self is both underdeveloped and damaged. What remains is a superficial, "phoney," or "false self" [Winnicott 1965]. As the years pass, their self-esteem diminishes further; they become less confident and more impulsive, distractible, and unhappy [Erickson et al. 1989].

## Negative Working Model

The internal working model, first described by Bowlby [1969, 1988a], is the cognitive representation of early attachment relationships. Based on attachment patterns with primary caregivers (e.g., secure, avoidant, ambivalent, disorganized), children develop beliefs and expectations about themselves, others, and life in general: *"I am good/bad, lovable/unlovable, competent/helpless; caregivers are responsive/unresponsive, trustworthy/untrustworthy, caring/hurtful; the world is safe/unsafe; life is worth living/not worth living."* (See Table 5.) These early attachment experiences become internalized as core beliefs and anticipatory images that influence later perceptions, emotions, and reactions to others (e.g., foster and adoptive parents).

The internal working model affects how the child interprets events, stores information in memory, and perceives social situations [Zeanah & Zeanah 1989]. Pearce gives an example:

> Given different internal working models, one child may interpret another's refusal to play as a devastating rejection and evidence of personal unworthiness. Another child with a more positive internal working model may perceive and interpret such a refusal as a minor slight. The subsequent behavior of these two children may well be different (sulking or an angry outburst by the former versus readily approaching another potential playmate by the latter [Pearce & Pezzot-Pearce 1994, p. 427].

## Table 5. Internal Working Models

1. **Secure attachment**
   - *Self.* "I am good, wanted, worthwhile, competent, lovable."
   - *Caregivers.* "They are appropriately responsive to my needs, sensitive, caring, trustworthy."
   - *Life.* "The world is safe, life is worth living."
2. **Insecure attachment**
   - *Self.* "I am bad, unwanted, worthless, helpless, unlovable."
   - *Caregivers.* "They are unresponsive to my needs, insensitive, hurtful, untrustworthy."
   - *Life.* "The world is unsafe, life is not worth living."

The internal working model of children with attachment disorder includes negative self-evaluations and self-contempt. Children internalize lack of adequate care, love, and protection as self-blame, and perceive themselves as unlovable, helpless, and responsible. Negative messages communicated to the child, as well as the child's interpretation of these experiences, become a part of his or her self-image. Research has shown that this framework of negativity results in misinterpretation of social cues, including the tendency to attribute hostile intentions to others [Dodge et al. 1990]. Thus, the child with attachment disorder is conditioned to perceive threat and hostility, even when it is not there, and commonly responds with aggressive and coercive behavior, as well as a lack of empathy for others in distress [Troy & Sroufe 1987]. This results in ongoing conflict with and alienation from peers and others, further damages self-esteem, and leads to aggressive and antisocial behaviors in later years.

Modifying the negative working model is a major treatment goal with children with attachment disorder. This is extremely difficult, however, because these core beliefs become fixed, rigid, operate outside of conscious awareness, and do not often change as a result of modifying the child's environment [Alexander 1992, Flaherty & Richman 1986, Sroufe 1988]. Placing such a child in a loving foster or adoptive home may only serve to exacerbate the problem. The child will push the love away due to lack of trust, expectation of maltreatment, and an unconscious attempt to recreate prior negative attachment patterns. This negative working model is imposed on therapists, teachers, foster and adoptive parents, and siblings.

## Empathy, Morality, and Attachment

As discussed in Chapter 3, the development of pack hunting among humans facilitated the evolution of a more cooperative and sharing mentality. Small tribes and communities could only survive if people helped one another. As social animals, considering the wants and needs of others was in our evolutionary interest. Sharing with the young, weak, and vulnerable made us more altruistic. This altruism became reciprocal, forming the evolutionary basis for "good behavior" [Morris 1994].

Cooperation, caring, and empathy are learned in the secure attachment relationship. Secure attachment leads to healthy psychosocial development and is a protective factor guarding against the development of antisocial behavior. It is also associated with fostering important prosocial values, attitudes, and behavior: empathy, caring, compassion, kindness, and morality. Piaget [1965] defined morality as the tendency to accept and follow a system of rules that regulate interpersonal behavior. Morality also involves feelings of obligation to foster the welfare of others and is acquired early in life [Hoffman 1983]. The earliest signs of obedience appear in the last quarter of the baby's first year and consist of compliance to simple commands ("come here; no, don't do that"). Between 18 to 26 months, toddlers learn to be sensitive to adult standards (e.g., integrity of property, harm to others, cleanliness), and increase their ability to meet these standards [Kagan 1981]. Children can distinguish conventional rules (e.g., addressing a preschool teacher by her second name) from moral issues (e.g., bullying another child is wrong) by their third and fourth years, and are increasingly willing to offer help to others at that time [Turial 1983].

The family, of course, is most influential in the child's social and moral development, because it provides the initial learning environment. Socialization involves the transmission to the child of social and moral codes by the family or other agents of society (e.g., foster home). The child acquires, by learning and identification in the early attachment relationships, both the *content* of the parents' moral code and a *willingness* to act in accordance with those rules [Herbert 1987]. When the family does not promote secure attachment and appropriate socialization experiences, as is the case with abuse, neglect, or multiple out-of-home placements and caregivers, the child is at risk for developing not only conduct disorders, but also a more pervasive lack of morality.

How does secure attachment promote the learning of empathy and the ideals of right human conduct? Empathy and morality are learned in the context of safe and secure attachment relationships by four psychological processes:

- *Modeling* by parents or other attachment figures,

- *Internalizing* the values and behavior of parents or other attachment figures,

- Experiencing *synchronicity* and *reciprocity* in early attachment relationships, and

- Developing a positive *sense of self.*

## Modeling

First, learning prosocial or antisocial values and behavior is a function of the nature of the caregiver-child relationship and the modeling provided. Simply stated, *empathic parents rear empathic children.* Research has shown that children show signs of empathy as young as 1 year old, and, by age 2, show concern for a peer in distress [Zahn-Waxler et al. 1992]. Children with histories of secure attachment during infancy were found to be more caring towards peers and more likely to be sought out as playmates by age 3 1/2, as compared to children with insecure/anxious attachments [Waters et al. 1979]. At 4 and 5 years old, securely attached children were more caring and compassionate and had the best friendships, while avoidantly attached children were more often cruel, taking pleasure in a peer's distress [Sroufe 1983; Troy & Sroufe 1987]. These same patterns of empathy and friendships were found to continue through adolescence.

Parents who provide a balance of discipline, warmth and positive experiences, are more likely to rear children who are empathic and cooperative with others [Eisenberg & Mussen 1989]. Four- and 5-year-olds were found to display more empathy with peers when their mothers used reasoning techniques with them to teach compassion and sensitivity. In contrast, children were less empathic when their mothers used negative control practices, such as threats [Miller et al. 1989]. Adults in their 30s who showed empathy for others were found to have parents who modeled empathic care both inside and outside of the family when these individuals were youngsters [Franz et al. 1994]. Parents' modeling of empathy and altruism influences their children's lifelong altruism. A study of 162 volunteers at a Minneapolis telephone crisis counseling center found that those most likely to break their commitment and leave the agency quickly reported lower levels of parental altruism in their family-of-origin [Murray 1996]. Thus, parents who model caring and empathy are most likely to have empathic children, and empathy is one of the building blocks that contribute to prosocial morality.

Brazelton [1981] discusses the routes to "goodness and selflessness." He suggests that children behave in socially acceptable ways, even when it creates conflict with self-interest, because of a powerful fear of admonishment by caregivers. The conscience serves as a mechanism that motivates the child to avoid negative responses from attachment figures. In the early years, children accede to parental demands out of a desire for approval and fear of disapproval (e.g., losing love and affection). Thus, children reluctantly sacrifice their desires in order to feel safe and positively connected.

## Internalization

The second psychological process that contributes to developing empathy and morality is internalization. Internalization involves the learning of standards of conduct, not merely obeying rules; i.e., developing a moral inner voice. Secure attachment involves internalizing prosocial values and behaviors, such as caring, compassion, kindness, and fairness. Securely attached children have an inner voice that guides them in the direction of prosocial behavior, providing self-control over selfish and aggressive impulses [Schulman & Mekler 1994]. Children with attachment disorder have often internalized antisocial standards, such as selfishness, violence, sadistic power and control, and dishonesty. Their inner voice, based on lack of trust and prior maltreatment, does not provide a viable conscience or feeling of remorse.

During a child's first years, internalization is based on compliance: the child's desire to please the parent and the distress experienced when the parent is unhappy with him or her (e.g., "sharing is good because mommy said so.") This initial disposition towards compliance is critical for later development and is lacking in children with attachment disorder, due to their avoidant and fearful reaction to attachment figures. When internalization actually occurs, the child does not behave well only to receive a reward or avoid a punishment, but now has the ability to judge his or her own behavior. Children with attachment disorder always need external structure, because they have not developed this ability. Additionally, securely attached children can express love for their parents by following their rules ("I want to make you feel good because I care about you; you are good, therefore your rules must be good.") Children with attachment disorder do not generally experience the necessary trust and safety to feel and express love, and are inclined to act out anger through oppositional and controlling behaviors.

According to Cline [1992, 1995], children go through five predictable stages as they internalize parental values and develop a conscience. The attachment figure becomes an internalized object, the internal compass to help the child navigate through experiences in the world:

- **Stage One (12–27 months).** The child thinks, *"I want it, I'll take it."* This represents primary process thinking; no thought to consequences, consideration of danger, or understanding of the feelings of others.

- **Stage Two (2–3 years).** The child thinks, *"I would take it, but my parents will be upset with me."* Parents seem threatening and intimidating because of their size and capabilities. The child begins to show primitive causative thinking; would "take it" if the parents were not present.

- **Stage Three (3–5 years).** The child thinks, *"I would take it but my parents will find out."* The child is showing causative thinking, thinking things through, and weighing the risks of his or her actions.

- **Stage Four (6–7 years).** The child thinks, *"I would take it, but if my parents find out, they would be disapproving."* The child's behavior is now being influenced by internal control; more connected to others, caring about how they feel, wanting to do the "right thing."

- **Stage Five (8–11 years).** The child thinks, *"I want it, but I don't feel good about doing things like that."* The child's internalization is complete; his or her own moral values have developed based on attachment to parents and society, and he or she understands not only self-interest, but also the good of the group.

### Synchronicity/Reciprocity

The third aspect of secure attachment that fosters empathy and morality involves synchronicity and reciprocity: the way in which the primary attachment figure is finely attuned to the signals, needs, and emotions of the infant and developing child, and the ongoing give-and-take nature of the relationship. Children of sensitive, accepting, and cooperative mothers were found to show signs of internalizing prosocial standards and were more cooperative and self-controlled by 2 years of age [Stayton et al. 1971; Londerville & Main 1981]. The same qualities of parenting that foster secure attachment (sensitive, accepting, affectionate, and consistently available caregiving) also encourage the child to follow and internalize the parent's model. The child is "in-sync" with the parent and, therefore, learning to be aware of the feelings and needs of another person. Secure attachment implies greater awareness of the mental states of others, which not only produces a more rapid and effective evolution of morality, but also protects the child from antisocial behavior [Fonagy et al. 1997].

### Sense of Self

The route to caring for others always begins with a solid sense of self. A strong and positive self-identity, with clear boundaries between self and others, is the fourth necessary psychological process. During the second year the child typically becomes increasingly oppositional ("terrible twos"), reflecting his or her initial efforts to be independent and autonomous. When there is a solid foundation of secure attachment, this transitional phase is managed and transcended without major negative or long-lasting consequences. In Winnicott's [1965] terms, the parent provides a "holding environment"; a safe and secure context with healthy boundaries and support for appropriate forms of self-control and emotional expression. The child with attachment disorder, conversely, lacks this solid and secure foundation and has a weak and negative sense of self, with blurred or violated self-other boundaries. The negativity and defiance characteristic of the second year become pervasive and chronic, as the child assumes a controlling, fearful and punitive orientation towards others. There is no place for empathy, compassion, or kindness, as the child fights to survive in a world perceived as threatening.

There is a growing national movement to teach prosocial values to America's youth. Programs are being initiated that aim to teach youngsters to care for others and to encourage parents and teachers to do the same. For example, group homes in New York City for abused and neglected teens have begun such a program. More than 100 teens, who have severe attachment difficulties due to histories of abuse, abandonment, and multiple placements, are taught to show concern and empathy for others' feelings. Staff model caring behaviors, such as empathic listening, welcoming newcomers, and acknowledging others' emotions, and the teens are encouraged to offer comfort to peers who are depressed [Murray 1996].

## Attachment and Resilience

Why do some individuals collapse under the stresses of life, while others seem to do well coping with the same conditions? Why do some children who experience maltreatment and other disadvantages develop severe psychosocial difficulties later in life, while others with similar unfortunate backgrounds mature into normal and successful adults? Understanding the factors that contribute to vulnerability and resilience provides valuable answers.

Resilience refers to an individual's competence and successful adaptation following exposure to significant adversity and stressful life events. Vulnerability is defined as susceptibility to negative developmental outcomes under high-risk conditions. Werner [1989] identified factors that place children at risk:

• Poverty;

• Family environments characterized by discord, desertion, violence, parental substance abuse, or psychological disturbance;

- Low educational level;

- Single parent;

- Lack of family resources and support; and

- Perinatal health problems, congenital handicaps, or other biological and genetic deficiencies.

Individual and environmental "protective factors" have been identified that mediate the effects of adversity and promote resiliency. Individual protective factors in children include cognitive skills, alertness, curiosity, enthusiasm, goal setting, high self-esteem, internal locus of control (take responsibility, feel competent), and temperament (easy, uninhibited). Environmental protective factors include family-community ties, parents who set rules, show respect for the child's individuality, and foster secure attachment, and a stable family environment [Herrenkohl et al. 1994].

Studies of resiliency have consistently found that the most basic and important protective factor is the history of caregiver-child attachment. *Secure attachments are a primary defense against the development of severe psychopathology associated with adversity and trauma.* In children who have been exposed to early loss and stress, the quality of parent-child attachment is the most important determinant of long-term damage [McFarlane 1988; van der Kolk 1996]. Even when securely attached children deteriorate in the school years due to extreme adversity, they are more likely to rebound later, compared to children who were anxiously attached from early life [Sroufe et al. 1990]. Secure attachment to secondary caregivers (extended kin, fathers, mentors) can help a child overcome adversity, including an anxious attachment with mother [Egeland et al. 1988].

One of the largest interdisciplinary investigations of resiliency in vulnerable children was a 40-year longitudinal study by Emmy Werner [Werner 1989; Werner & Smith 1992]. Werner's study showed that one-third of the children who experienced perinatal stress, poverty, parental alcoholism and emotional problems, and family disruption, developed into caring and competent adults. Three types of protective factors were identified: 1) dispositional attributes, such as sociability, intelligence, communication skills and confidence; 2) affectional ties within the family that provide emotional support in times of stress; and 3) external support systems at school, church, or in the community, that provide validation, support, and a positive belief system by which to live. The researchers emphasized that "the developmental outcome of virtually every biological risk condition was dependent on the quality of the rearing environment" [Werner & Smith 1992, p. 191]. The most important ingredient in establishing a positive rearing environment is high-quality interaction between parent and child; i.e., secure attachment [Letourneau 1997].

Interventions that attempt to promote high-quality parent-child relations and secure attachment patterns are effective in enhancing resiliency in high-risk children and families. Following a home intervention program designed to improve parent-infant interaction, preterm, low birth weight infants were found to have better cognitive development and improved interaction with parents during feeding and playing [Barrera et al. 1986]. First-grade children of depressed mothers were found to have fewer behavior problems and better coping skills when high-quality mother-child interaction was fostered [Harnish et al. 1995]. Low-income, at-risk mothers and infants, provided with education and support that started prenatally and lasted until the infants were 6 months old, were found to improve the quality of their attachment relationships [Starn 1992]. Thus, although there are other factors that contribute to resiliency, such as temperament and external support systems, the development of high-quality, stable, and secure attachments in infancy and early childhood provides a foundation that is crucial to later adaptation, success, and health.

## Cultural Variations

The results of numerous studies in the United States show that about one-third of the children in middle-class families are insecurely and anxiously attached. The percentage is higher in low-income, multiproblem families. In all cultures studied (using the same assessment procedure, the Strange Situation), the results are the same; most infants (65 to 70%) show secure attachment patterns, while the remainder show some form of insecure attachment. These findings must be considered within the realm of cultural norms and variations. Does the Strange Situation, which was developed based on an American population, actually measure attachment security and insecurity in other cultures? How do the variations in the 1,300 human cultures that exist on our planet influence attachment patterns? Which aspects of attachment are universal and which are culture-specific? Even with a similar attachment pattern, to what extent do cultural and community differences result in different implications of this attachment pattern for later development? For example, the developmental consequences of avoidance for suburban Anglo American children may be different than the consequences for inner-city African American children [Colin 1996].

Ainsworth [1973] found many similarities in attachment behavior in both the United States (Balitmore, MD) and African (Ganda) cultures. Two-thirds of the babies were found to be securely attached in both populations. Also similar were the phases of attachment development and the importance of the primary caregiver as an attachment figure and a "secure base." Cultural differences were also apparent. The Ganda babies were considerably more distressed by brief separations from mother, showed more fear of strangers, and did not hug or kiss upon reunion. These differences reflect cultural variations in childrearing practices and resultant differences in infants' expectations. The Ganda babies were not used to separation (even brief) from their mothers and seldom interacted with strangers in their village. American babies were more familiar with brief separations in their home environment, were used to seeing strangers in public, and were encouraged to hug and kiss parents after an absence [Colin 1996; Karen 1994]. These studies demonstrated both the universal and culture-specific aspects of attachment.

Grossman and Grossman [1991] replicated Ainsworth's research with German families. They found that German children had similar attachment patterns as

American children. Those children who were securely attached had advantages by age 5: they had better social skills and ability to handle peer conflict and were more likely to seek out their parents when distressed. A difference was found, however, among the anxiously attached German children compared to other U.S. studies; there were fewer behavioral problems among the anxious German children. Again, cultural differences seemed to be at work, reflecting variations in parenting attitudes and cultural norms. The avoidantly attached children in the United States had mothers who were rejecting and showed an aversion to having a warm and loving relationship with their child. The German mothers were not rejecting—they cared a lot for their children and were behaving according to cultural norms that valued self-reliance and independence at an early age. When the German children were evaluated at age 10, however, those that were avoidantly attached looked like their counterparts in the United States: they had more problems getting along with peers and were less confident, self-reliant, and resilient, as compared to securely attached children. The Grossmans concluded, "The mere fact that parents are behaving in accordance with cultural norms does not necessarily spare the children any harm" [cited in Karen 1994, p. 266].

Cultural variations in childrearing practices and patterns of caregiving have been found around the world. Keefer et al. [1982] found that among the Gusii, an agricultural culture in Kenya, mothers turn away from their infants when the infants are most emotional, positive, and excited. Culturally, this looking-away pattern is normative, and the mothers are merely socializing the young according to cultural restrictions (i.e., younger individuals do not look directly at older individuals, especially under emotional conditions). This pattern is quite different from that of American middle-income mothers, who tend to make eye contact in response to their babies excitement and arousal. Takahashi [1990; cited in Colin 1996, p. 149] studied Japanese families and found that 12-month-old babies experienced an unusually high level of stress during separation (in the Strange Situations), and not a single baby showed avoidant attachment patterns. There were, however, many more babies in the resistant/ambivalent category than in the United States. These findings reflect cultural differences. Japanese children are socialized to maintain harmonious relationships; avoidant behavior is considered rude. Also, in traditional Japanese society it is rare for babies to be separated from mothers, and a close mother-child bond is encouraged throughout life.

Children reared on the kibbutzim in Israel have much different child-rearing experiences than American children. Sagi [1990] found a higher percentage of resistant/ambivalent children, which is probably a result of "multiple mothering," and the inconsistency and unpredictability of caregiving practices. Infants on the kibbutzim are monitored by hired caregivers during the day, spend only a few hours with their parents (usually around dinner time), and are responded to during the night (slowly) by another caregiver who is responsible to watch over many babies. These findings are consistent with attachment theory; resistant/ambivalent attachment patterns are often related to the child's preoccupation with the unavailable primary caregiver.

Jean Liedloff [1975] wrote about the two-and-one-half years she spent with the Yeguana, a stone-age tribe living in a South American jungle. Mothers carried their infants everywhere, the babies shared the "family bed," and were showered with love and attention. Despite little training in obedience, the children were reported to be well-behaved (compliant, friendly, nonaggressive), and grew to be self-reliant, self-confident, and caring members of the community. These culture-specific norms are in keeping with basic attachment principles and are obvious in our own (American) culture today. For example, it is becoming more common to see parents carry their babies close to their bodies in soft carriers. This practice has been found to help promote secure attachment [Anisfeld et al. 1990].

If it is true that attachment is instinctive and adaptive, based on biology and evolution, then basic aspects of attachment should be universal, found across cultures, races, and ethnic groups. The evidence suggests that there are universal attachment behaviors, but that specific behavioral patterns vary according to culture. In cultures that value distal patterns of caregiving and early independence (e.g., Northern European), avoidant patterns are more likely to develop. In cultures that encourage more contact and closeness with babies and avoid separation (e.g., Japanese), we are more likely to observe infants and children seeking contact with caregivers when under stress. In the short term, forming an insecure attachment, regardless of culture, is most likely adapative; i.e., a strategy for the child to cope with an unavailable or abusive caregiver. The general consensus, however, is that forming secure attachments early in life (i.e., keeping anger, anxiety, and defensiveness to a minimum), is probably the best formula for psychosocial well-being in any culture [Colin 1996].

# 5

# Disrupted Attachment

## Self-Regulation, Trauma, and Attachment

One of the most damaging results of abuse and neglect in children is their chronic inability to modulate emotions, behaviors, and impulses. Maltreatment affects the biological and psychological ability to self-regulate and often leads to a variety of psychosocial problems, including aggression against self and others [van der Kolk & Fisler 1994].

Secure attachment with a primary caregiver is critical if children are to learn self-control. "The primary function of parents can be thought of as helping children modulate their arousal by attuned and well-timed provision of playing, feeding, comforting, touching, looking, cleaning, and resting—in short, by teaching them skills that will gradually help them modulate their own arousal" [van der Kolk 1996, p. 185]. The reliable and appropriately responsive caregiver provides a balance of stimulation ("up-regulate") and soothing ("down-regulate") to modulate the infant's level of arousal. Neglectful and abusive caregivers, or separations and other attachment disruptions, can result in chronic over- or underarousal in infants and toddlers. Researchers found that as many as 80% of maltreated children develop disorganized-disoriented attachment patterns, resulting in numerous symptoms, including an inability to modulate emotions and impulses [Lyons-Ruth 1991].

Regulation of emotion and behavior is a crucial ingredient in healthy early childhood development; a process that caregivers and babies accomplish *together*. Signals from the infant (e.g., gazing, crying, cooing) arouse emotional reactions in the caregiver. These signals can influence what parents attend to and how they communicate in response. Conversely, caregivers influence the infant's emotions and level of arousal. Providing stimulation by playing, feeding, or encouraging active exploration, for example, is helpful for the lethargic or withdrawn infant. This "mutual regulatory process" breaks down under conditions of anxious attachment. Depressed, substance-abusing, or otherwise neglectful or abusive caregivers are not attuned to their infant's emotions and needs, leaving the baby without any necessary external regulatory support [Robinson & Glaves 1996].

A child's internal working model or core beliefs (see Table 5 on p. 47) are defined to a great extent by his or her ability to regulate emotions, impulses, and responses to external stress. The self-concept that develops in children with attachment disorder who lack self-control often leads to 1) disturbances in sense of self (e.g., sense of alienation and separateness, body image distortion); 2) inability to control impulses (e.g., physical and sexual aggression, self-mutilation); and 3) relationship

---

**Note:** The drawings in this chapter were done by clients at Evergreen Consultants as part of their treatment.

disturbances (e.g., lack of trust and intimacy, perceive others as threatening) [Cole & Putnam 1992].

A neglectful, abusive, or nonresponsive caregiving environment produces out-of-control, angry, depressed, and hopeless children by 2 to 3 years of age. Children with attachment disorder have frequent and prolonged temper tantrums, are accident prone, impulsive, and desperately seek the attention not previously experienced. They are restless, irritable, have a brief attention span, demand instant gratification, and have little frustration tolerance by the preschool years. By age 5, they are angry, oppositional, and show lack of enthusiasm. Their inability to control impulses and emotions leads to aggressive acting out and lack of enduring and satisfying relationships with peers and others.

## Maternal and Infant Depression

Depression in mothers has profound and long-lasting effects on their babies. It is estimated that 10 to 12% of pregnant women experience chronic depression, which can be directly transmitted to the fetus. Newborns of mothers who were depressed during pregnancy were more irritable, less consolable, and had less developed motor tone than newborns of nondepressed mothers [Abrams et al. 1995]. An estimated 40 to 70% of new mothers have postpartum depression caused by radical changes in hormonal levels, which can last up to three months; 30% have long-lasting and severe postpartum depression [Behavioral Health Treatment 1997]. These mothers have difficulty providing quality caregiving due to their depressed mood and diminished sensitivity to their infant's cues. If depression continues into the infant's sixth month, growth and developmental delays can occur at 1 year (e.g., slower to walk, weigh less, less socially responsive). When depression lasts through the infant's first year of life, babies show a profile of behavioral and physiological dysregulation, which can result in behavior problems and aggression at the preschool stage [Field 1995].

Research has found that children of depressed mothers have a heightened sensitivity to and sense of responsibility for other's distress. Two- and 3-year-old children of mothers with unipolar depression were more likely than children of well mothers to become upset and preoccupied when exposed to conflict or distress and were more appeasing in play with peers [Zahn-Waxler et al. 1984]. These children displayed more caregiving and comforting responses with their mothers. The depressed mothers were more likely to blame their children for their distress, expressed more disappointment in their children, and used guilt-inducing strategies to regulate the children's behavior.

More than two decades of research at the Touch Research Institute (University of Miami Medical School) has demonstrated effective solutions to maternal depression and the negative effects on babies [Field 1997]. Relaxation exercises and massage therapy both had positive effects, but the results were more dramatic for massage therapy. After four weeks (two massages of the mothers per week), the mother's anxiety levels and depression was significantly reduced [Field et al. 1996]. In another study, depressed adolescent mothers were taught to massage their babies. The infants' stress level and depression decreased, they gained more weight, and improved on scales of emotionality, sociability and soothability [Field et al. 1996].

Interactive coaching is another intervention found to be effective in improving reciprocity and sensitivity with depressed mothers and their infants. The mother is coached or guided on how to positively relate to her baby while the two play together. Two interactive patterns were identified: intrusive mothers engaged in rough handling, poked their babies, and spoke in an angry tone of voice; withdrawn mothers were unresponsive, affectively flat, and unsupportive. Coaching the intrusive mother on being less active and more sensitive to her infant's cues

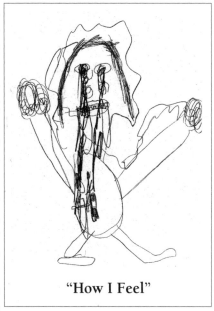

**"How I Feel"**

improved responses of the infants. A more active "attention-getting" technique was found to have positive results for the withdrawn mothers and their babies [Malphurs et al. 1996].

## The Unresponsive Infant

Some infants are not physically and/or emotionally responsive to caregivers' efforts to satisfy their needs. This lack of responsiveness is the result of numerous factors: difficult and irritable temperament, *in utero* drug or alcohol exposure, unrelieved pain associated with medical conditions, response to prenatal or postnatal stress from caregivers or environment, and genetic and/or congenital impairments or handicaps. A vicious cycle develops in the caregiver-infant relationship, as shown in Figure 3 [adapted from Cline 1992].

There are four components to this cycle:

- The infant does not respond with comfort and relaxation to caregiver's efforts to soothe and console.

- The caregiver becomes anxious, angry, insecure, and begins to lose confidence in caregiving abilities. ("What am I doing wrong?")

- The caregiver either withdraws or becomes increasingly intrusive and punitive.

- The infant responds to the caregiver's heightened stress and anxiety, becoming increasingly anxious, fearful, and unresponsive. The caregiver's negative cues and signals cause the infant to cry more, and the infant perceives the caregiver as increasingly unsafe.

A common example of the vicious cycle of the unresponsive infant is found with the colicky baby. These infants cry more than twice as much as other infants, regardless of caregiver efforts to console. Mothers of crying infants have been found

**Figure 3. Vicious Cycle of the Unresponsive Infant**

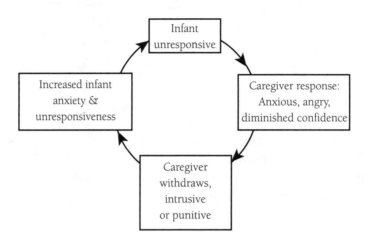

to be more anxious and tentative in dealing with their babies, while mothers of infants who cried less were more deliberate, calm, and serene. The anxious mothers reported feeling exasperated, less confident, frightened, confused, resentful, and unloving. Some reported feeling extreme hostility toward their infants [Jones 1983]. Not surprisingly, infant crying and child abuse are highly correlated. Eighty percent of parents who physically abused their infants reported excessive infant crying as the trigger for abuse [Weston 1968].

The cause of colic is unknown, and it usually ceases around 3 to 4 months of age. Some child development experts believe that colic in infants is caused by ineffectual caregiving; others believe that the ineffectual caregiving is a response to the infants' physiological condition. Either way, the vicious cycle develops, with negative consequences for both infant and caregiver. Although it is a difficult and challenging task, the caregiver must not convey agitation and anxiety to the infant who experiences chronic discomfort.

## Disorganized-Disoriented Attachment

Three organized patterns of behavior toward the caregiver were originally identified using the Strange Situation, a laboratory-based approach to studying the infant's response to separations from and reunions with the parent. The three attachment patterns were secure, insecure-avoidant, and insecure-ambivalent/resistant [Ainsworth et al. 1978].

- **Secure.** Infant is upset when mother leaves the room, but distress is not excessive; infant and mother greet one another actively and warmly upon reunion; infant quickly relaxes and returns to play.

- **Avoidant.** Infant shows little or no distress when mother leaves, and actively avoids and ignores mother upon reunion; mother also avoids, looking away from child.

- **Ambivalent/Resistant.** Infant is extremely distressed by separation, clinging on to mother and staying near the door crying; seeks contact upon reunion, but cannot be settled by mother and pushes her angrily away.

These infant responses to separation and reunion reflect the history of the parent-child relationship, the parenting style, and predict later psychosocial functioning [Ainsworth et al. 1978; Bretherton 1985].

Further research revealed an additional attachment pattern. Certain infants did not fit the original three categories; they seemed to lack any coherent, organized strategies for dealing with separation and reunion. These infants were classified as *disorganized/disoriented,* and their behavior was found to reflect seven types of reactions [Main and Solomon 1986, 1990].

- **Sequential display of contradictory behavior patterns.** Extremely strong displays of attachment behavior or angry behavior, followed suddenly by avoidance, freezing, or dazed behavior. For example, infant greets parent with raised arms, but then retreats and freezes.

- **Simultaneous display of contradictory behavior.** Infant displays proximity-seeking and avoidant behavior at the same time. For example, infant approaches parent with head averted or by backing toward parent.

- **Undirected, misdirected, incomplete, and interrupted movements and expressions.** Infant moves away from rather than toward parent when distressed or frightened. For example, infant approaches parents, but then follows a stranger; infant appears frightened of stranger, but retreats from parent and leans head on the wall.

- **Stereotypes, asymmetrical movements, mistimed movements, anomalous postures.** Infant shows repeated movement, such as rocking, hair twisting, or ear pulling; asymmetrical creeping, moving only one side of body; sudden and unpredictable movements, such as rapid arm and leg activity after sitting tense and still; uninterpretable postures, such as head cocked with arms raised for long periods of time.

- **Freezing, stilling, slowed movements and expressions.** Holding of positions, such as sitting with arms held out waist high and to sides; apathetic or lethargic movements or facial expressions, such as a dazed expression when greeting parent.

- **Direct indices of apprehension regarding the parent.** Display of extreme fear in response to parent. For example, looking frightened, flinging hands over face, running away, highly vigilant posture, when parent returns and approaches.

- **Direct indices of disorganization or disorientation.** Clear displays of confusion and disorganization upon reunion. For example, greeting stranger with raised arms instead of going to parent; rapid changes of affect, such as crying-laughing; falling when approaching parent; wandering with disoriented expression.

Therapists, social caseworkers, therapeutic foster parents, and others who work with maltreated children and disturbed families will recognize some of the previously described behaviors. Clinical experience is consistent with research findings regarding children with disorganized-disoriented attachment patterns and their family contexts. Approximately 15% of infants in two-parent, middle-class families display disorganized attachment patterns [van IJzendoorn 1995], but the incidence of this severe attachment-disordered behavior increases to a high of 82% among high-risk, maltreating families (e.g., maternal substance abuse and depression, abuse and neglect, adolescent parenthood, multiproblem family status) [Lyons-Ruth et al. 1991].

Disorganized infant attachment has been found to be associated with unresolved loss, fear, and trauma of the parent(s). These parents, who complete the Adult Attachment Interview [George et al. 1984; Main & Hesse 1990; Main and Goldwyn, in press], have been found to be "unresolved" in regards to their own attachment histories. They have not mourned losses, are frightened by memories of past trauma, may dissociate, and script their child into unresolved family drama. [Main et al. 1994; van IJzendoorn 1995]. They also actively and contemptuously devalue prior attachment figures and often abuse and/or neglect their children [Carlson et al. 1989; Crittendon 1985; Lyons-Ruth et al. 1991].

Mothers of disorganized infants typically have histories of family violence and abuse, rather than neglect alone [Lyons-Ruth et al. 1959; These mothers are "out-of-sync" with their babies, displaying confusing and mixed messages (e.g., extend arms toward infant while backing away), and inappropriate response to their infant's cues (e.g., laugh when baby is in distress) [Main et al. 1985; Spieker & Booth 1988; Lyons-Ruth et al. 1994]. Not surprisingly, these mothers show high levels of negative and downcast affect to their babies and low levels of tenderness and affection [DeMulder & Radke-Yarrow 1991].

Thus, disorganized infant attachment is transmitted intergenerationally: parents raised in violent, frightening, and maltreating families transmit their fear and unresolved losses to their children through insensitive or abusive care, depression, and lack of love and affection. The infant is placed in an unresolvable paradox: closeness to the parent both increases the infant's fear and, simultaneously, need for soothing contact. Closeness and contact with the parent triggers fear rather than safety or comfort [Main & Hesse 1990; Lyons-Ruth 1996].

This intergenerational process is conceptualized in the following way [van IJzendoorn & Bakerman-Kranenburg 1997]:

Parent's early attachment experiences
↓
Parent's attachment representations (internal working model)
↓
Parenting behavior
↓
Infant's attachment experiences

There are additional factors, of course, that influence parenting behavior. The parent's current attachment representation (internal working model, belief system) is influenced by later relationships, not only early attachment experiences. A supportive social network (friends, spouse, therapist) can ameliorate the negative ef-

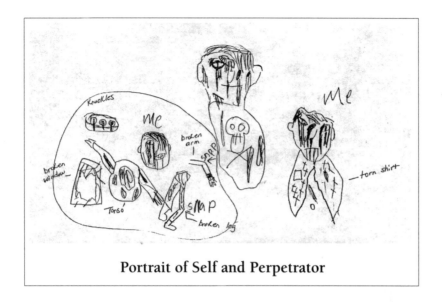

**Portrait of Self and Perpetrator**

**Drawing by Angry, Aggressive Child**

fects of early attachment trauma [Belsky et al. 1984], and a positive relationship with a secondary caregiver can help a person overcome adversity [Egeland et al. 1988]. A child's temperament and special needs also plays a role. Due to physical handicaps or highly irritable temperament, some children make it extremely difficult for parents to respond in a sensitive and warm manner to their attachment needs [Chess & Thomas 1987; Kagan 1984; van IJzendoorn 1995b].

Nevertheless, based on numerous studies, as well as vast clinical experience, intergenerational transmission of attachment patterns is considered an established

**"How I See Myself
in the World"**

fact. It is not, however, the specific traumatic events in parents' childhoods that cause disorganized attachment in the child. Rather, it is the parent's mental and emotional representation of prior attachment experiences that are most important [van Ijzendoorn & Bakerman-Kranenburg 1997].

## Aggression, Control, and Conduct Disorders

The DSM-IV [American Psychiatric Association 1994] describes three diagnostic categories of aggressive or "externalizing" disorders in children: oppositional defiant disorder (ODD), conduct disorder (CD), and attention-deficit/hyperactivity disorder (ADHD). The term externalizing refers to a core set of negativistic, defiant, and hostile behaviors (e.g., noncompliance, aggression, and tantrums, in response to limit setting; see Greenberg et al. 1997 for a complete review). By far, the largest group of children referred to mental health centers are for externalizing problems [Offord et al. 1991; cited in Greenberg et al. 1997]. Many of these children continue disruptive behavior in later years [Campbell 1991], and often repeat the poor parenting practices of their own parents [Huesman et al. 1984; cited in Lyons-Ruth 1996]. These children often show deficiencies in impulse control, emotional regulation, and problem solving [Cook et al. 1994; Moffit 1993].

Findings from the Minnesota High Risk Study, which followed a large community sample of impoverished mothers and infants from birth into adolescence, documented the relationship between insecure attachment and later conduct disorders. Insecurely attached infants, particularly those with avoidant attachment, were more aggressive and impulsive and had more conflict with peers and caregivers, during their school years [Egeland et al. 1993; Erickson et al. 1985; Renken et al. 1989; Sroufe et al. 1990]. Among high-risk families, it is clear that early avoidant attachment patterns place children at high risk for later aggression and other externalizing problems.

It is the children with histories of disorganized-disoriented attachment who are most at risk for developing severe problems, including aggression. Again, disorganized attachment refers to a lack of, or collapse of, a consistent or organized strategy to respond to the need for comfort and security when under stress (e.g., separation and reunion). Kindergarten children who were classified as disorganized in infancy were six times more likely to be hostile and aggressive toward peers, than were those classified as secure [Lyons-Ruth et al. 1993]. Infants of impoverished adolescent mothers are at risk for developing severe attachment disorder and subsequent aggression. Sixty-two percent of these infants had disorganized attachment relationships and were more likely to initiate conflict with their mothers by aggressive and oppositional behavior by 2 years of age [Hann et al. 1991]. These mothers were less affectionate and more rejecting of their child's overtures than other mothers. By the time they became toddlers, these children were aggressive, avoided and resisted their mothers, and were developing a controlling and coercive strategy to cope.

The tendency to be controlling towards caregivers and others is a foremost symptom of disorganized attachment and a constant challenge for those who care for these children. While infants and toddlers with disorganized attachment patterns are often helpless, frightened, and confused, as they enter the preschool and early school years they develop various forms of controlling behavior. The *controlling-caregiving* type is characterized by a role reversal, where the child is overly solicitous, attempting to take care of the parent. In the second category, *controlling-punitive*, the child is hostile, coercive, rejecting, and humiliating toward the parent [Greenberg et al. 1997]. Among clinic-referred preschoolers diagnosed with oppositional defiant disorder, a majority were found to be controlling-disorganized. Mothers were typically classified as "unresolved," the adult counterpart of controlling-disorganized attachment [Greenberg et al. 1991].

## The Antisocial Child

Children with a history of severe attachment disorder develop aggressive, controlling, and conduct-disordered behaviors, which contributes to the development of an antisocial personality. As early as the latency years and preadolescence, these children exhibit a lack of conscience, self-gratification at the expense of others, lack of reliability and responsibility, dishonesty, and a blatant disregard for the rules and standards of family and society.

Many of the key symptoms and traits of the adult psychopathic and antisocial personality are displayed in the child with attachment disorder [Hare 1993; Yochelson & Samenow 1976]. These symptoms include glibness and superficiality; egocentric and grandiose thinking; lack of remorse, guilt, and empathy; deceitful and manipulative behaviors; emotional shallowness; impulsivity; need for excitement; irresponsibility; not learning from experience; and lack of meaningful relationships.

All children lie occasionally to avoid punishment; the antisocial child, however, lies as a way of life. This pathological lying becomes a habitual strategy to avoid punishment and gain power and control ("I know the truth and you don't"). They often lie even when they do not have to, for no apparent purpose, which provides a sense of excitement and a feeling of having the "upper hand." These children perceive others as pawns to be manipulated and have few friendships, due to their inordinate need to control. They are superficially charming and engaging, but the longer you know them, the less you like them. They often prefer to relate to younger children whom they can control and manipulate. They secretly yearn for family connections and are jealous of others who are capable of intimacy and love, but are too fearful of closeness to reveal their needs and desires. They perceive themselves as "bad," defective, and unworthy of love.

## Maltreatment

Maltreatment of infants, toddlers, and young children (and the associated family and environmental factors) is a major cause of attachment disorder. According to the findings of the National Center on Child Abuse and Neglect (NCCAN), the problem of child maltreatment in the U.S. is increasing [NCCAN 1995]:

* Number of children seriously injured by all forms of maltreatment *quadrupled* between 1986 and 1993.

* Poverty is a major factor: children in families with annual incomes below $15,000, compared to $30,000, were 45 times more likely to suffer neglect and 60 times more likely to die from maltreatment.

* Substance abuse is another major factor: 50 to 80% of all child abuse cases involve drug and/or alcohol abuse by parents or caregivers.

* Only 28% of seriously maltreated children were evaluated by Child Protective Services in 1993, due to the inability to keep up with the sharp increases in the scope of the problem.

These increases appear to be real and not merely a result of increased awareness by professionals, the community, or the media. This is alarming because of the consequences regarding compromised and disordered attachment, as well as the cost on society. For example, children who are maltreated are 53% more likely to be arrested as a juvenile and 40% more likely to commit a violent crime [NCCAN 1995]. Maltreatment affects all children and families; no significant ethnic differences were found in the incidence of maltreatment.

Attachment theory has guided a considerable amount of recent research on abuse and neglect of young children. Studies have found maltreated children to have a high incidence of anxious and disorganized-disoriented attachment. Secure attachment is the antithesis of maltreatment, in that the caregiver's sensitivity and responsiveness to the baby's needs and signals are basic to attachment quality. In the Harvard Maltreatment Project, maltreated infants were more likely to be insecurely attached than nonmaltreated infants [Schneider-Rosen et al. 1985]. Crittenden [1985, 1992] found anxious attachment among maltreated infants and toddlers, with developmental differences. Abused children were angry at 1 year, but inhibited that anger with their mother at 2 years of age. Neglected children remained angry. By 2 years, children have already learned to avoid provoking abuse from their parents. The Minnesota Mother-Child Project, a longitudinal study of children in high-risk families, also found a high incidence of anxious attachment among maltreated children. Two-thirds of neglected babies were anxiously attached by 1 year of age, and remained so through their school years. More alarming, however, was the finding that nearly *all* the children who were emotionally neglected ("psychologically unavailable mothers") developed anxious attachment, with most classified as anxious-avoidant [Erickson et al 1989]. Disorganized-disoriented attachment, the most severe pattern of attachment disorder, was found in as many as 82% of children in high-risk, maltreating families [Lyons-Ruth et al. 1991].

What are the factors that predict which children are likely to be maltreated? Several studies provide valuable information about the antecedents of maltreatment. Since multiple factors influence quality of child care, variables of interest are grouped into *parental characteristic, child characteristics,* and *environmental factors* [Erickson & Egeland 1996]:

- **Parental characteristics**

  - Lack of understanding of the emotional complexity of the parent-child relationship;

  - Difficulty understanding the child's needs, perspectives, and developmental level;

  - Think in global, all-or-nothing terms;

  - Maltreatment and attachment disorder in their own histories of care;

  - Unresolved issues of trust, dependency, and autonomy;

  - High incidence of depression;

  - Lack impulse control, particularly under stress; and

  - Drug and alcohol abuse.

- **Child characteristics**

  - Irritable and difficult temperament;

  - Disabilities and special needs;  and

  - Prior history of loss, psychosocial problems, and attachment disorder (e.g., multiple moves in child welfare system).

Child characteristics alone do not account for maltreatment. Parents, with extra support, education, and maturity, can provide the necessary sensitivity and guidance to overcome a child's difficulty.

- **Environmental factors**

  - Poverty;

  - Violence in the marital relationship;

  - Parental unemployment, family stress and disorganization; and

  - Lack of supportive social network, especially among single parents who lack intimate emotional support.

Not all parents who experienced maltreatment in their families-of-origin abuse and/or neglect their own children. What characterizes parents who transcend their unfortunate histories and provide loving and secure care for their offspring? There are three major factors [Egeland 1988; Main & Goldwyn 1984]:

- Supportive and loving relationship with an adult during childhood (e.g., kin, foster parent, counselor);

- Supportive partner and/or social supports during parenthood; and

- Therapeutic intervention that facilitated resolution of early issues, directing anger and responsibility toward perpetrators rather than self, and providing clear account of childhood loss and trauma.

There is a great deal of support for the belief that in the majority of cases, children do not lie about abuse allegations. Children with attachment disorders, however, routinely make false allegations of abuse against parents, teachers, therapists, and others. Often their motivation is control, revenge, diversion, or even mere amusement. Their ability to appear believable, adeptness at lying, and lack of concern for others can fool the most experienced professionals. Therefore, it is crucial to have a thorough understanding of the child's background and symptomatology when assessing the validity of allegations. There are certain "red flags" that can place a child at risk for making false allegations of abuse. Children who are extremely angry about prior maltreatment and exploitation are high risk. The risk grows further if they have a previous history of making false accusations and do not want to be in their current placement.

### Neglect

Child neglect is the most frequently reported and substantiated form of child maltreatment, accounting for up to 65% of all child abuse reports. Between 1986 and 1993, the number of children physically neglected increased 163%, while the estimated number of emotionally neglected children tripled (188% increase). Birth parents are the perpetrators of neglect in most cases (91%); children are most often neglected by females (87%), because for so many a female is the only caregiver [NCCAN 1995].

There is great variability among definitions of neglect. Some definitions focus on the specific behaviors or omissions of caregivers that endanger the child's physical, cognitive, or emotional health [Zuravin 1991]. Others argue for a broader definition that focuses on the conditions of the child, regardless of the cause [Dubowitz et al. 1993]. An even broader view of neglect is suggested by Hamburg [1992], the president of the Carnegie Foundation. He indicts our society for "collective neglect," failing to provide adequate health care, child care, and policies that support families in caring for their young children [Hamburg 1992; cited in Erickson & Egeland 1996, p. 6].

Regardless of the definition, several types of neglect have been identified by health care providers and mental health professionals: *physical, emotional, medical, mental health,* and *educational* [Erickson & Egeland 1996]. Physical neglect is the most commonly identified form and includes failure to protect from harm or danger and meet basic physical needs (e.g., shelter, food, clothing). Emotional neglect involves inattention to the child's emotional needs, nurturing, or well-being. The most extreme consequence of emotional neglect is "nonorganic failure to thrive," which produces stunted growth, physical illness, and is often fatal. Medical neglect refers to caregiver's failure to provide necessary medical treatment. Mental health neglect involves refusal to comply with recommended therapeutic procedures when a child displays serious emotional or behavioral disorders. Educational neglect includes

**Child's Idea of "Having Fun"**

caregiver's failure to comply with requirements for school attendance or resistance to follow through with special recommended programs.

Studies on the consequences of maltreatment have found differences between abuse and neglect. Abused children were more aggressive, angry under stress, and showed mild developmental delays, while neglected children interacted less with peers, were passive, tended toward helplessness when under stress, and showed significant developmental delays [Hoffman-Plotkin & Twentyman 1984; Crittenden & Ainsworth 1989]. Findings from the Minnesota Mother-Child Project, a longitudinal study designed to follow children of at-risk mothers (poor, young, low education, unstable, lack of support), provided information regarding neglect. They found that emotional neglect ("psychologically unavailable caregivers") was more harmful to children than physical neglect or other forms of maltreatment. Psychologically unavailable mothers were detached and unresponsive, interacted in a mechanical manner, and showed no satisfaction or joy with their child. Nearly all the children in this group were anxiously attached at 1 year of age; at 24 and 42 months they displayed anger, noncompliance, lack of persistence, little positive affect, and steep declines on scales of development; in preschool they were negativistic, noncompliant, impulsive, highly dependent on teachers, and severely anxious; in the school years they were socially withdrawn, unpopular with peers, and exhibited internalizing problems (e.g., depression) [Erickson et al. 1989]. Mothers who were emotionally unavailable and neglectful were likely to have been neglected as children themselves, and consequently, insecurely attached to their own mothers [Crittenden & Ainsworth 1989; Belsky 1995]. Most mothers studied in the Minnesota Project who were neglected as children, neglected their own infants and toddlers. Other antecedents of neglect included disorganized and stressful home environment; tense, depressed, angry, and confused mothers; isolated families with lack of social support; low intellectual functioning of caregivers [Pianta et al. 1989].

Neglect, especially emotional neglect during the first three years, has an extremely damaging and long-lasting effect on children's functioning in the family, with peers and teachers, and in regard to coping skills and learning. Attachment theory provides a meaningful framework for understanding the sequelae of neglect [Erickson & Egeland 1996]. Children with early anxious patterns of attachment (emotional neglect) develop *negative working models*—negative expectancies and belief systems about self, caregivers, and the world in general. They expect *not* to get their needs met, so they shut down and do not even try to solicit care or affection. They expect to be ineffective and unsuccessful in tasks, so they give up. Their dependency needs are so strong they are barely able to become motivated and stay task oriented. The negative feedback they receive from others perpetuates their low self-esteem and negative expectations of self and others (vicious cycle).

## Violence

The United States is the most violent country in the industrialized world—particularly for children. Homicide is the eleventh leading cause of death for all Americans, but the third leading cause of death for children between 5 and 14 [Osofsky 1995; Children's Defense Fund 1996]. The proliferation of violence has been likened to a national epidemic, breeding more violence at an exponential rate [Levine 1996]. Nearly 1 million teenagers are victims of violent crime annually, with African American males and those living in poverty at greatest risk. Even schools cannot provide a safe haven; 105 fatalities were reported from 1992 to 1994 [Kachur et al. 1994]. One quarter of those arrested on weapons charges are juveniles [U.S. Department of Justice 1995; cited in Levine 1996]. In a Chicago neighborhood, one-third of school-age children witnessed a homicide and two-thirds witnessed a serious assault [Bell & Jenkins 1993]. Thirty-two percent of Washington, DC children and more than one-half of New Orleans children were victims of violence in their community [Richters & Martinez 1993]. Children are directly exposed to community violence. Infants and toddlers, however, are indirectly but profoundly exposed; they are "tuned into" their caregivers' fears and anxieties about violence and influenced by the adults' coping strategies [Osofsky 1994].

Infants, toddlers, and children who experience and/or witness violence in their home are seriously affected, due to the literal and psychological proximity. More than 3 million children witness parental abuse each year, including fatal assaults and physical abuse. Domestic violence is associated with maltreatment of infants; mothers abused by their male partners have higher rates of child abuse [Strauss 1993]. Physical abuse is the leading cause of death among children less than 1 year old. Two thousand children die a year—five each day—at the hands of their parents or caregivers. From 1986 to 1993, the number of physically abused children in the U.S. increased to 600,000 (a 100% increase) [NCCAN 1993].

Exposure to violence, including physical abuse, has severe and damaging consequences on many aspects of functioning: physical, developmental, cognitive/ attributional, social, emotional, behavioral, and academic [Kolko 1996]. Infants and toddlers experience the three hallmark symptoms of posttraumatic stress disorder, similar to older children: reexperiencing the traumatic event, numbing of responsiveness and avoidance of reminders of the trauma, and hyperarousal. Other common symptoms include sleep disturbance, night terrors, separation anxiety, fearfulness, aggressiveness, difficulty concentrating, and emotional detachment [Zeanah & Scheering 1996]. Young children may play out aspects of the trauma in posttraumatic play, repeating the same play sequence over and over [Terr 1990]. The following behaviors and effects on development are common for young children exposed to violence [Osofsky 1994]:

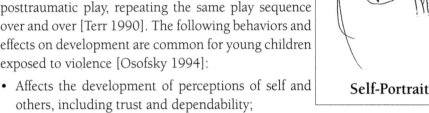

**Self-Portrait**

- Affects the development of perceptions of self and others, including trust and dependability;

- Repeated exposure leads to more severe symptoms as children grow older;

- Memory impairment due to avoidance and intrusive thoughts;

- Develop anxious and disorganized attachment;

- Play becomes more aggressive, imitating behaviors children have seen and trying to "master" the trauma;

- "Act tough" to compensate for fear, developing a counterphobic reaction;

- Appear depressed, withdrawn, or become aggressive;

- Become severely constricted in activities, exploration, and thinking, for fear of reexperiencing the trauma; and

- Difficulty concentrating in school, due to lack of sleep and intrusive imagery.

### Sexual Abuse

Sexual abuse is common in the histories of children who develop severe attachment disorder. Sexual abuse involves any sexual activity with a child where consent is not or cannot be given. This includes sexual contact that is accomplished by force or threat of force, regardless of whether there is deception or the child understands the nature of the activity [Finkelhor 1979]. Sexual activity includes penetration, sexual touching, or noncontact sexual acts such as exposure, voyeurism, or displays of explicit materials. The following information is informed, in part, by Berliner & Elliott [1996].

The exact incidence and prevalence of sexual abuse in the United States is not known. This is because sexual abuse is usually not reported at the time it occurs. Also, official child abuse statistics tend to be unreliable, because there is no national reporting system for crimes against children. We do know that rates of reported incidents of molestation of children has risen from year to year over the past 20 years. Surveys have found that 27% of women and 16% of men reported a contact sexual offense by age 18 [Finkelhor et al. 1990]. Other studies found that from 38% to 62 % of women in two U.S. cities were victimized by age 18 [Russell 1986; Wyatt 1985]. The evidence points to the fact that sexual abuse is a relatively common experience in the lives of children in this country. A recent survey reported 1.3 million children sexually abused in 1994 [Gallup et al. 1995].

Multiple episodes of sexual abuse are common, occurring in more than half the cases in nonclinical samples and in 75% of clinical samples of abused children [Conte & Schuerman 1987; Elliott & Briere 1994]. Compared to girls, boys are found to be older at the onset of victimization, and more likely to be abused by nonfamily members, women, and by offenders who are known to have abused other children [Faller 1989]. Girls are at higher risk for sexual abuse than boys by a ratio of two to one [Everstine & Everstine 1989]. Both males and females are more at risk to be sexually abused if they live without one of their birth parents, have an unavailable mother, or perceive their family life as unhappy [Finkelhor & Baron 1986]. The incidence of sexual abuse among disabled children is 1.75 times higher than nondisabled children [NCCAN 1993]. Unlike other forms of child abuse, sexual abuse does not appear to be related to socioeconomic status [Berliner & Elliott 1996].

Research indicates that children who have been sexually abused suffer from a wide range of psychological and interpersonal problems both in the short term [Beitchman et al. 1991; Berliner 1991; Kendall-Tackett et al. 1993] and in later adult functioning [Browne & Finkelhor 1986; Finkelhor 1990]. Damage occurs because sexual abuse is always nonconsensual, developmentally inappropriate, invariably alters the nature of the relationship within which it occurs, and interferes with normal developmental processes, leading to an increased risk of maladjustment later in life [Berliner & Elliott 1996]. Finkelhor [1987] synthesized the clinical issues common to sexually abused children into four "traumagenic dynamics": traumatic sexualization, stigmatization, powerlessness, and betrayal. These four dynamics were shown to be strong indicators of symptom formation in children [Mannarino & Cohen 1996].

Sexually abused children have more behavior problems than nonabused children [Cohen & Mannarino 1988; Einbender & Friedrich 1989; Gomes-Schwartz et al. 1990]. They tend to lack social skills, are more aggressive, and are more socially withdrawn than nonabused children [Friedrich et al. 1987]. They commonly suffer from somatic reactions, sleep and eating disturbances, night terrors and nightmares, bedwetting, and phobic reactions. The majority of child sexual abuse victims have been found to suffer from mild to acute posttraumatic symptoms [Burgess & Holmstrom 1984; DeFrancis 1969 ]. Researchers have found PTSD symptoms in up to 48% of sexually abused children [McLeer et al. 1988]. Particularly prevalent were the posttraumatic symptoms of fear, anxiety, and lack of concentration [Conte & Schuerman 1987].

Sexual abuse victims are four times as likely to develop a major depression during their lifetime [Stein et al. 1988]. There is a high correlation between childhood sexual abuse and dissociation, including psychic numbing, depersonalization, and disengagement [Briere & Runtz 1987; Chu & Dill 1990]. Sexually abused children are more likely to be diagnosed with depression, exhibit suicidal behavior, have lower self-esteem, greater symptoms of anxiety, and more substance abuse problems, than nonabused peers [Berliner & Elliott 1996]. Adolescents who have been sexually abused are more likely to run away from home, use drugs, and be bulimic [Hibbard et al. 1990]. Teenage mothers with a history of sexual abuse are more likely to abuse their children [Boyer & Fine 1991]. Sexual behavior problems are common among children who have been sexually abused; they display sexualized behavior more than physically abused, neglected, or psychiatrically disturbed children [Gale et al. 1988]. Cognitive functioning is affected by sexual abuse. Guilt, shame, self-blame, loss of trust, and stigmatization, are common reactions. These children often perceive themselves as different from peers, and abuse-related cognitions are common: negative self-attributes, a disbelief in self-efficacy, and a perception of self as helpless and life as dangerous and hopeless [Mannarino et al. 1994; Gold 1986].

Children are conditioned to obey adult rules and invariably feel betrayed and helpless when molested by someone in a position of trust. The child is forced into an "abuse dichotomy" when attempting to understand the perpetrator's behavior: "Either the abusive caregiver is bad or I am bad." Young children by nature are egocentric and commonly accept responsibility for the actions of others toward them. Due to the child's inherent lack of power, and acceptance of social messages ("adults are right"), he or she assumes that the abusive act is justifiable punishment for some misdeed, thus "it must be my fault and I am bad" [Briere 1989]. Consequently, these children internalize a sense of shame, guilt, and self-blame. They feel intrinsically bad, damaged, worthless, unlovable, or even evil.

Sexually traumatized children often act out sexually with other children, engage in autoerotic acts, or behave in a seductive way toward adults. This may be an attempt to gain a sense of mastery over the trauma by repetition of these events in a symbolic form. They typically engage in sexualized play that was similar to their victimization and seek to undo their feelings of helplessness by identifying with the aggressor, doing to other children what was done to them [Everstine & Everstine 1989].

## Incest

Incest is defined as any sexual contact between a child and parent, stepparent, relative, or anyone who fills the role of parent surrogate. Sexual assaults by adults in positions of trust are more traumatic than by strangers, due to the intensity of betrayal and confusion. Recent research has provided insight into the family characteristics of incestuously abusing families [Trepper et al. 1996]. The vast majority of these families are socially isolated, enmeshed, quite rigid and nonadaptable to change. Communication patterns include secretiveness, unclear and inconsistent messages, infrequent discussions of feelings, little attentive listening, and lack of conflict-resolution skills. There is limited or erratic leadership. Less than one-third of families were "father-executive" type (contrary to the popular notion that there is usually a strong, domineering father and a weak, ineffectual mother). Lack of family member role clarity is common, with undefined, shifting, and reversing roles (e.g., "parental child"). Most offending parents (78%) did not engage in nurturing activities of the victim when he or she was a baby, reflecting the lack of positive and secure attachment. More than two-thirds of offending parents used alcohol or drugs often, and used just prior to an abusive episode. Substance abuse is clearly a precipitant and a vulnerability factor. Most of the marriages (82%) were rated in overall quality as poor and characterized by emotional separateness.

Family members tend to deny aspects of incestuous abuse. Four types of denial have been identified [Trepper & Barrett 1989]:

- **Denial of facts.** The individual openly challenges the realities of the abuse;

- **Denial of impact.** The individual admits incest has occurred, but lessens the intensity of the meaning of the abuse;

- **Denial of responsibility.** The individual admits to the occurrences of abuse, but questions the offender's culpability and places blame on another person; and

- **Denial of awareness.** A family member states that if the abuse has occurred, it happened without his or her cognizance.

Offenders in abusing families most often deny the facts. Nonoffending spouses most commonly deny the impact. Victims also tend to deny the impact of abuse more frequently. Trepper concludes, "To understand incest we clearly will have to go beyond looking at the individual psychopathology of the offending parent, or even the dyadic relationship between the offender and the victim. Instead, we will need to focus our attention and research on the multiple systems variables which structure family systems" [Trepper et al. 1996, p. 15].

There are a number of mediating factors that influence the psychosocial effects of childhood sexual abuse, including specific characteristics of the abuse and family support. Children, for example, who experience a single incident of less intrusive abuse and then disclose to a supportive and protective parent, are likely to report few long-term problems. The degree of psychological trauma a child experiences is related to the amount of violence of terror associated with the event [Everstine & Everstine 1989]. Increased negative impact of sexual abuse involves penetration, violence, closer relationship to the offender, multiple offenders, longer duration and frequency [Berliner & Elliott 1996]. The younger the child, the more vulnerable he or she is to be overwhelmed and traumatized [Burgess & Holstrom 1984; Peters 1988]. The child's cognitive appraisal is one of the most important mediating factors. Greater distress is associated with higher levels of cognitive functioning (can understand the implications), blaming self, and using "wishful thinking" to cope [Spaccarelli 1994]. Family dysfunction may exacerbate the effects of abuse. Increased distress occurs when families have more conflict and violence, less cohesion and support, and more psychiatric and substance abuse problems [Conte & Schuerman 1987; Friedrich et al. 1987]. Maternal support, or a supportive relationship with another adult, is associated with decreased negative effects [Conte & Schuerman 1987]. Mothers are most likely to fail to provide support when the offender is a stepfather or mother's live-in boyfriend. Children who lack maternal support are more likely to recant the original allegation or refuse to report it [Elliott & Briere 1994].

## Ritualistic Abuse

Reports of ritualistic abuse occasionally occur when working with sexually abused children. Ritualistic abuse is one of the more controversial issues in the field of child maltreatment; there is much debate over its existence, prevalence, and the veracity of child victims' accounts [Kelley 1996]. Ritualistic abuse has been defined as abuse that occurs when some religious, magical, or supernatural connotations are used in conjunction with the fear and intimidation of children [Finkelhor et al. 1988]. Lloyd [1991] has defined it as the intentional, repeated, and stylized abuse of a child by a person responsible for the child's welfare, and is typified by such other acts as cruelty to animals, or threats of harm to the child or others. In 1994, the National Center on Child Abuse and Neglect funded a study on ritualistic abuse in the United States, and found that 31% of mental health professionals surveyed had encountered a ritualistic abuse case. They also found that 23% of protective service and law enforcement agencies had encountered at least one case of ritualistic or religion-based child abuse [Goodman et al. 1994].

Allegations of ritualistic abuse typically involve reports of forced sexual activity; physical abuse or torture; ingestion of blood, semen, or excrement; ingestion of drugs; threats of violence or death; threats with supernatural powers; satanic reference or paraphernalia; witnessing animal mutilations; and killing of adults and children [Kelley 1996]. Research has found that children who reported ritualistic abuse had greater symptomatology than children who only experienced sexual abuse [Finkelhor et al. 1988]. Reports of ritualistic abuse are consistently associated with increased impact and traumatization on victims [Briere 1988; Kelley 1989; Watermann et al. 1993].

## In Utero *Drug and Alcohol Exposure*

The impact on children, both prenatally and postnatally, of exposure to drugs and alcohol is a major public health problem and definitely a form of child abuse. Psychoactive substances used during pregnancy can affect the developing brain and cause future learning, behavioral, developmental, and physiological problems. An estimated 625,000 newborns each year are exposed to drugs prenatally; 10 to 17% of the women used cocaine during pregnancy [Jaudes & Ekwo 1997].

The increase in out-of-home placements parallels the explosion of substance abuse. A recent study found that one-third of substance-exposed infants had out-of-home placements and were extremely vulnerable to death in the first few years of life [Jaudes & Ekwo 1997]. The number of substantiated reports of maltreatment were three times higher for substance-exposed infants than nonexposed. The costs are not only emotional and physical, but also economic. The average hospital cost for delivery and care is $13,200 for a cocaine-exposed infant, compared to $1,300 for a drug-free baby [Calhoun & Watson 1991].

Fetal alcohol syndrome (FAS) is the result of excessive alcohol consumption by mothers during pregnancy, which causes physiological damage to the brain and body. Symptoms include prenatal and postnatal growth deficits, central nervous system dysfunction, specific facial characteristics, and body malformation. Children who display all the symptoms are considered to have fetal alcohol syndrome, while those who display some are diagnosed with fetal alcohol effects (FAE). Learning and behavioral disorders that result from FAS/E include poor impulse control; attention deficit disorder (with or without hyperactivity); speech and language disorders; poor short-term memory; lack of cause and effect thinking; poor personal boundaries; anger-management difficulty; poor judgment; and no connection to societal rules [McCreight 1997].

Psychoactive substances cross the placenta and the blood-brain barrier. Use of cocaine, alcohol, and narcotics during pregnancy are all associated with smaller head circumference in the newborn, indicating a potential structural effect on the brain. Infants exposed to cocaine have a higher risk of premature birth and low birth weight [Zuckerman 1994; Jaudes & Ekwo 1997]. Cigarette smoking diminishes the blood flow to the placenta and can lead to prematurity. Methamphetamine is comparable to cocaine in its negative effects on the fetus, and can cause developmental and behavioral problems in children. Heroin and other narcotics may lead to overt withdrawal in the newborn as well as developmental abnormalities [Alexander & Moskal 1997].

Prenatal and postnatal drug exposure affects development and attachment. For example, an infant or toddler with FAS/E characteristics may not be able to experience the care and nurturance that may be available from caregivers, thereby disrupting the attachment process. Children exposed to drugs *in utero* were found to have depressed developmental scores at 6 months, which continued through 24 months of age. The postnatal environment, however, has an important impact. One hundred percent of children living with drug-using mothers showed attachment disorders, including avoidance, fear, and anger toward their mothers. The majority of children (64%) of mothers who stopped using drugs after birth displayed secure attachments [Howard 1994].

### Neurobiology of Trauma and Attachment

Trauma affects children on many levels of biological functioning. Threats to the infant and young child that are of sufficient intensity, duration, or frequency, such as abuse, neglect, and anxious-disorganized attachment, trigger an alarm reaction ("fight, flight, freeze"). This instinctual response to real or perceived danger is a normal response to acute stress. Traumatic experiences during infancy and childhood, however, can trigger prolonged alarm reactions, which alter the neurobiology of the brain and central nervous system. The brain develops sequentially, with the vast majority of structural organization occurring in childhood. Thus, early life experiences have a disproportionate influence on the developing brain. Lack of critical nurturing and exposure to traumatic stress and abuse alters the nervous system, predisposing the child to be impulsive, overreactive, and violent [Perry 1994, 1995].

Traumatized children often develop symptoms of posttraumtic stress disorder, which fall into three clusters: 1) recurring intrusive recollections, such as dreams or flashbacks; 2) persistent avoidance of stimuli associated with the trauma and numbing of general responsiveness; and 3) hyperarousal, such as hypervigilance, startle response, sleep difficulties, irritability, anxiety, and physical hyperreactivity [Perry 1994].

Two parts of the primitive "old brain" (limbic system), the amygdala and hippocampus, are particularly involved with the processing of emotion, memory, and fear responses. The amygdala evaluates the emotional meaning of incoming stimuli and is the storehouse of emotional memory. The hippocampus records in memory the spatial and temporal dimensions of experience and plays an important role in categorizing and storing stimuli into short-term memory. During times of threat or danger, the amygdala reacts instantaneously, bypassing the rational brain (neocortex), and triggering an alarm reaction:

"How I Feel"

- Activating the hypothalmus, which secretes corticotropin-releasing hormone (CRH);

- Stimulating the autonomic nervous system (ANS), which affects movement;

- Raising heart rate and blood pressure, and slowing breathing;

- Signaling the *locus ceruleus* in the brainstem to release norepinephrine, which heightens overall brain reactivity, releasing dopamine that causes the riveting of attention on the source of fear [Goleman 1995; LeDoux 1992].

The amygdala is most fully formed at birth and matures rapidly in the infant's brain. Thus, traumatic experiences such as abuse, neglect, and anxious attachment, are stored in preverbal memory. These memories are intense perceptual experiences and later in life intrude on awareness in the form of hypervigilance, nightmares, hyperarousal, and anxiety.

Biochemical and hormonal reactions occur in children during traumatic stress that produce long-term changes in the mind-body system. In a series of studies on the effects of sexual abuse on young girls, researchers found three areas of physiological change:

- Higher levels of catecholamines (the neurotransmitters epinephrine, norepinephrine, and dopamine), which cause hyperarousal;

- Dysregulation of the HPA (hypothalamic-pituitary-adrenal) axis, which releases ACTH and cortisol, and prepares the body for the alarm reaction; and

- Twice the normal level of ANA (antinuclear antibody), which leads to impaired immune system functioning [Putnam 1991, 1995; DeAngelis 1995].

Perry [1994] a leading trauma researcher, reviewed numerous studies on the effects of trauma and the alarm reaction in children. Again, he reports that this reaction involves the brain, autonomic nervous system, HPA axis, and the immune system. The brainstem neurotransmitters, or catecholamines, were found to play a major role in posttraumtic stress disorder, anxiety disorders, and affective disorders. The abnormal persistence of the alarm reaction results in a dysfunctional and maladaptive set of brain activities. This process is extremely costly in terms of the energy required to trigger and sustain the physiological responses. Additionally, persistent threat can "redefine" the baseline level of the central nervous system, resulting in hypervigilance and hyperarousal.

Another leading researcher in the field of trauma, Bessel van der Kolk, reviewed the literature on the psychobiology of trauma and attachment. He writes, "Secure attachment bonds serve as a primary defense against trauma induced psychopathology ... the quality of the parental bond is probably the single most important determinant of long-term damage" [van der Kolk et al. 1996; p. 185]. He compares attachment and trauma in children in reference to physiological regulation/ dysregulation, and the instinctual neurobiological reaction in the "old brain" (brainstem and limbic system). The psychobiological effects of severe trauma, according to van der Kolk, include the following:

- Extreme autonomic responses to stimuli reminiscent of the trauma;

- Hyperarousal to intense but neutral stimuli (loss of stimulus discrimination);

- Elevated catecholamines, including norepinephrine;

- Decreased glucocorticoids, which provokes the stress response;

- Decreased serotonin levels, associated with inability to modulate arousal and increased aggression;

- Shrinkage of the hippocampus due to heightened levels of coritsol, resulting in impaired declarative memory (conscious awareness of facts or events) and skill-based memory;  and

- Activation of the amygdala and deactivation of the Broca's area during flash-backs, reflecting reexperiencing of trauma and difficulty with verbal emotional expression [van der Kolk 1996].

## Working Assumptions: The Child with Attachment Disorder

While it is common for traumatized children to display both caregiving and punitive control behavior, it is the latter form—angry, manipulative, threatening, and coercive control—that is most typical of children who are the focus of our work. Therapy with these youngsters and their parents (usually adoptive), as well as consulting with social services and therapeutic foster parents, has led us to the following working assumptions and conclusions:

- **The child's controlling-punitive orientation is a major defense linked to survival.** The child truly believes he or she will not survive without controlling and distancing others, especially caregivers. This control strategy is a form of compensation for lack of trust and internal control. Since these children have not learned to effectively regulate their own emotions and impulses, they focus on regulating and controlling their outer world.

- **A feeling of empowerment accompanies controlling, oppositional, and defiant behavior.** Parental caregiving and limit setting is perceived as a threat, rather than as an opportunity for need fulfillment or learning. All efforts to care for or help the child are filtered through the child's negative working model and are interpreted as abuse, rejection, or control. When a caregiver or therapist provides support or shows affection towards the child, the reaction is typically an increase in hostile, punitive, and controlling behavior.

- **Reciprocity in relationships is extremely limited.** These children avoid needing others, asking for help, and most forms of positive interaction. They are unable to accept praise, affection, and love. They do not believe that caregivers possess nurturing qualities, or that they themselves are worthy of love and caring. Relationships are a "one-way street"; they believe that distancing and controlling others is the only way to relate.

- **Adoptive parents, foster parents, and counselors are often at a total loss as to how to deal with these children.** Many parents are afraid of their children ("Will he burn the house down, stab me while I sleep?"), and there is typically a history of various treatment failures. Foster parents often request that these children be removed from their home. Adoptive parents routinely contemplate and follow through with relinquishment.

- **There are both historical and current family factors that contribute to the child's problems.** The child's family-of-origin was typically abusive, neglectful, violent, and chaotic, with one or both biological parents having antisocial and criminal profiles, severe depression and/or other emotional disorders, substance abuse problems, and histories of maltreatment in their own childhoods. The dynamics of their current family are also problematic. Adoptive parents are commonly angry and "burned-out," unresolved family-of-origin issues and marital distress are common, and dealing with the child is so difficult and frustrating that the parents can become rejecting and abusive. This enables the child to feel a sense of control ("I can frustrate my parents"), and replicates the "victim" scenario from earlier years.

- **Genetic and biological factors are relevant.** There is typically an intergenerational history of biologically based conditions in the birth families (e.g., unipolar or bipolar depression, severe mental disorders). These conditions contribute to extremely dysfunctional parenting practices, as well as problematic traits and symptoms in the children.

- **Parenting concepts and strategies that are recommended by mental health professionals are often ineffective.** Approaches such as time out, reinforcing positive behavior, and verbal communication, do not succeed in changing the child's negative attitudes or antagonistic behavior. Parents have lost faith in the mental health and social service systems, and feel helpless and hopeless regarding any positive outcome.

# 6

# Assessment

## Basic Concepts and Assumptions

Assessment procedures and diagnostic categories are not helpful if merely used to label a child or parent, while ignoring the strengths, coping capacities, and desire for growth and development inherent in most people. Rather, systems of classification are useful in identifying symptoms, challenges, and abilities, necessary for planning and implementing effective treatment and parenting interventions. Children's functioning is greatly influenced by the quality of their environments. A child with a particular diagnosis can behave differently depending on the level of emotional support, cognitive stimulation, form of structure and discipline, and sense of well-being or stress [Lieberman et al. 1997].

Effective assessment must be comprehensive—based on as complete an understanding of the child and family as is possible [Levy & Orlans 1995b]. There are three aspects to a comprehensive assessment:

- First, assessments are ecological; i.e., children live and develop within relationships (usually family), and families are part of larger social, community, and cultural systems. There must be an understanding of historical and current caregiver influences, as well as external social forces (e.g., extended family, child welfare system).

- Second, assessment must focus on numerous and diverse facets of the child's and family's functioning (e.g., six symptom categories are considered when assessing children; see p. 93).

- Third, assessments of the child and family involve a variety of methods and settings. Multimethods provide more information and increased reliability of findings. Behavior and functioning often vary in different environments, and it is important to observe these varying responses as a part of treatment planning (e.g., home, school, therapeutic foster home, therapy session). Therapeutic interventions may be ineffective, or even destructive, if introduced prior to a comprehensive assessment of the child and family [Pearce & Pezzot-Pearce 1977, Zero to Three 1994].

It is difficult to separate assessment and therapy: assessment is part of treatment, and treatment involves ongoing assessment. Assessment is the first stage in the therapeutic process; i.e., establishing rapport and building a collaborative alliance. For example, parents and caregivers receive support and empathy during assessment, which often reduces their anxiety, hopelessness, and guilt. Children receive limits, safety, empathy, and support, necessary to initiate the process of change and healing. Assessment occurs at regular intervals during each session and throughout the course of treatment. This model utilizes continuous feedback in order to develop optimally effective interventions: *assess → goals → intervene → reassess*.

Effective assessment is developmentally and culturally sensitive. Symptoms and behavior patterns must be evaluated in the context of normal childhood development. The developmental stage of the child during attachment trauma will determine, to a large extent, the subsequent psychosocial effects. Understanding the child's current developmental stage will help the clinician determine appropriate assessment and intervention methods. The clinician must be careful not to apply his or her own beliefs and traditions to family members from different cultural backgrounds. For example, eye contact is considered a form of intimacy in some cultures, while others consider it rude and inappropriate. Additionally, individual differences must be considered; children vary in sensorimotor, cognitive, affective, and interpersonal patterns of development.

Assessment is based on a variety of theories and paradigms: developmental, psychodynamic, family systems, and attachment theory. Since attachment disorder is basically a relationship disturbance, it is crucial to evaluate the relationship between the child and current caregiver(s). This provides valuable insight into prior attachment experiences (e.g., birth parents), as the child projects those prior patterns on to current attachment figures. The child's internal working model is also a primary assessment focus. These core beliefs and expectations regarding self, caregivers, and the world in general, formed in the early attachment relationships, influence ongoing behavior, emotion, and relationship patterns.

## Pillars of Assessment

Assessment and diagnosis of attachment disorder rests on three major pillars: early history, historical and current symptoms, and direct observation of relationship patterns. The specifics of these three pillars are described in this chapter in the sections on child, parent, and family assessment, and the six symptom categories.

Early history and symptomology provide the initial diagnosis prior to treatment, and is gleaned from the intake packet (Table 6); see Appendix A for a sample intake packet. Once treatment begins, however, direct observation of the child's attitudes and behaviors with attachment figures is primary. Direct observation of relationship patterns, as well as parental descriptions of interactions in the home, enable the clinician to focus on specific signs of attachment disorder. Table 7 summarizes important behaviors in the assessment of attachment disorder in young children [adapted from Zeanah et al. 1993]. Attachment disorder occurs as a result of a variety of factors, which can be grouped into three major categories: caregiver, child, and environmental contributions. These etiological factors, listed in Table 8, place children at risk for the development of attachment disorder.

Assessment information is collected from several sources: adult report and child self-report checklists (e.g., see Appendix A for a symptom checklist); clinical observations (e.g., parent-child interactions in therapy, child behavior in therapeutic foster home); and psychodiagnostic data (e.g., prior testing and social history).

## Table 6. Intake Packet

- Symptom checklist: completed by parents, caregivers, teachers, and/or caseworkers.
- Descriptive explanation of each symptom on checklist.
- Day in the Life: parent's narrative of child's behavior (see Appendix B for example).
- History: developmental, birth family, moves and disruptions, current family, social, and medical.
- Parents' autobiography: attachment and family history.
- Schools: current and historical issues.
- Psychodiagnostic testing: prior results, diagnoses, and recommendations.
- Psychotherapy and medication: prior and current.
- Information provided:
  - Explanation of attachment disorder and treatment program.
  - Resources and support systems, locally and nationally.
  - Bibliography.

## Table 7. Signs of Attachment Disorder in Young Children

- Showing affection
  - Lack of warm and affectionate interactions.
  - Indiscriminate affection with unfamiliar adults.
- Comfort seeking
  - Lack of comfort seeking when frightened, hurt, or ill.
  - Comfort seeking in odd or ambivalent manner.
- Reliance for help
  - Excessive dependence.
  - Does not seek or use attachment figure for support when needed.
- Cooperation
  - Lack of compliance with caregiver requests.
  - Excessively demanding.
  - Compulsive compliance.
- Exploratory behavior
  - Failure to check back with caregiver in unfamiliar surroundings.
  - Exploration limited by unwillingness to leave caregiver.
- Controlling behavior
  - Excessively bossy and punitive controlling of caregiver.
  - Oversolicitous and inappropriate caregiving behavior toward caregiver.
- Reunion responses
  - Failure to reestablish interaction after separation.
  - Includes ignoring and avoiding, intense anger, lack of affection.

The relevant areas of child and family functioning to focus on include the following:

- Presenting symptoms and problems: individual and in social context;

- Developmental history: biological, psychological, and social background; attachment history; pre-, peri-, and postnatal factors;

- Internal working model: child and caregivers (prior and current);

## Table 8. Causes of Attachment Disorder

- **Parental/caregiver contributions:**
  - Abuse and/or neglect.
  - Ineffective and insensitive care.
  - Depression: unipolar, bipolar, postpartum.
  - Severe and/or chronic psychological disturbances: biological and/or emotional.
  - Teenage parenting.
  - Substance abuse.
  - Intergenerational attachment difficulties: unresolved family-of-origin issues, history of separation, loss, maltreatment.
  - Prolonged absence: prison, hospital, desertion.
- **Child contributions:**
  - Difficult temperament; lack of "fit" with parents or caregivers.
  - Premature birth.
  - Medical conditions; unrelieved pain (e.g., inner ear), colicky.
  - Hospitalizations: separation and loss.
  - Failure to thrive syndrome.
  - Congenital and/or biological problems: neurological impairment, fetal alcohol syndrome, *in utero* drug exposure, physical handicaps.
  - Genetic factors: family history of mental illness, depression, aggression, criminality, substance abuse, antisocial personality.
- **Environmental contributions:**
  - Poverty.
  - Violence: victim and/or witness.
  - Lack of support: absent father and extended kin, isolation, lack of services.
  - Multiple out-of-home placements: moves in foster care system, multiple caregivers.
  - High stress: marital conflict, family disorganization and chaos, violent community.
  - Lack of stimulation.

- Current parents/caregivers: attachment history, psychosocial functioning, marital and other significant relationships;

- Child-caregiver relationship patterns;

- Family, community, and cultural systems; and

- Current environmental conditions and stressors.

## Attachment Disorder Classifications

The DSM-IV [APA 1994] describes two types of attachment disorders of infancy and early childhood:

- **Inhibited**, in which ambivalent, contradictory, inhibited, or hypervigilant responses occur with the caregiver (e.g., resistance to comforting), and

- **Disinhibited**, which includes indiscriminate oversociability and lack of selective attachments (e.g., excessive familiarity with strangers).

Both types refer to a markedly disturbed and developmentally inappropriate social relatedness, beginning prior to age 5. This diagnosis requires a history of pathogenic care, evidenced by at least one of the following:

- Persistent disregard of child's basic emotional needs for comfort, stimulation, and affection;

- Persistent disregard of child's basic physical needs; and

- Repeated changes of primary caregivers that prevent the formation of stable attachments.

Lieberman and Pawl [1988] clarified the clinical manifestations of attachment disorder in the context of assessment and treatment of infants and their parents in an infant mental health program. They emphasize the characteristics of the child-caregiver relationship, as well as chronic situational stresses, and describe three types of attachment disorder:

- **Nonattachment.** Infants reared with no opportunity for forming emotional connections with caregivers, which results in severe impairment in capacity to form relationships, cognitive functioning, and impulse control.

- **Anxious/ambivalent.** Infant was able to form a relationship with an attachment figure, but it was characterized by severe conflict regarding emotional and physical availability.

- **Disrupted attachment.** Considerable and damaging separation and loss with attachment figure(s), which provokes intense anxiety and long-term negative consequences for development and trust.

Zeanah, Mammen, and Lieberman [1993] suggest that disorders of attachment represent profound and pervasive disturbances in the child's feelings of safety and security. Referring to the diagnostic categories in the DSM-IV, they state, "Our clinical experiences suggest that the disorders as defined do not adequately capture the presentations of disordered attachment" [Zeanah et al. 1993, p. 337]. They propose criteria for five types of attachment disorders:

- **Nonattached.** Failure to develop a preferred attachment figure.

- **Indiscriminate.** Fails to check back with caregiver in unfamiliar settings and fails to use attachment figure as secure base when frightened. May be indiscriminately friendly and/or reckless and accident-prone.

- **Inhibited.** Unwilling to venture away from attachment figure to engage in age-appropriate exploration. May display excessive clinging or compulsive compliance.

- **Aggressive.** Anger and aggression are pervasive features of the relationship with attachment figure. May also be angry and aggressive with others and toward self.

- **Role-reversal.** Controlling behaviors toward caregiver(s), either caregiving (e.g., oversolicitous) or punitive (e.g., bossy, rejecting, hostile). Child assumes roles and responsibilities ordinarily assumed by parent.

In 1994, the Diagnostic Classification Task Force of the National Center for Clinical Infant Programs developed the *Diagnostic Classification: 0 - 3* [Zero to Three 1994]. This assessment and evaluation system was designed to serve as a guide for clinicians and researchers to facilitate diagnosis, treatment planning, professional communication, and further research. It reflects the current state of knowledge regarding attachment and developmental issues and uses a multiaxial classification system:

- **Axis I:** *Primary classification* (e.g. traumatic stress disorder, reactive attachment deprivation/maltreatment disorder);

- **Axis II:** *Relationship classification* (e.g., overinvolved, underinvolved, abusive);

- **Axis III:** *Physical, neurological, developmental, and mental health disorders* (e.g., language disorders, chronic *otitis media*, failure to thrive);

- **Axis IV:** *Psychosocial stressors* (e.g., abuse, foster placements, neglect, parental illness, violence in environment); and

- **Axis V:** *Functional emotional developmental level* (e.g., capacity for mutual attention and engagement, reciprocity, symbolic and affective communication).

Zero to Three's diagnostic classification system is based on three primary principles. The first principle is that children's psychosocial functioning develops in the context of their interactions and relationships. The second principle is that individual differences in temperament and constitutional strengths and vulnerabilities play a major role in how children experience and process life. Caregivers' responses, including their acceptance, nurturance, and skill in dealing with areas of difficulty, can transform early challenges and risk factors so that they do not handicap development. The third principle is the importance of understanding the family's cultural context regarding the child's functioning and development [Lieberman et al. 1997].

## Assessment of the Child

Child assessment focuses on symptoms, developmental history, internal working model, and current relationships, as outlined in Table 9. Attachment disorder is, in essence, a relationship disturbance. Therefore, it is necessary to understand the child in the context of historical and current family and other significant relationships.

### Presenting Problem

- The symptom checklist is completed by current caregivers (e.g., foster or adoptive parents), teachers, or others familiar with the child. There are six symptom categories: behavioral, cognitive, affective, social, physical, and moral-spiritual. (See pp. 93-105 for detailed explanation).

- Symptoms must be understood in context. What factors and events increase or decrease the child's symptoms? (e.g., acting out may escalate with mother and decrease when father is present). In which environments do symptoms occur? (e.g., compare nature and severity of symptomatology in home and school settings).

## Table 9. Assessment of the Child

- **Presenting problem:**
  - Six symptom categories: behavioral, cognitive, affective, social, physical, and moral/spiritual.
  - Environmental factors.
  - Frequency, duration, and severity.
  - Child's interpretation of problems; behavior during assessment.
  - Family systems context.
- **Developmental history:**
  - Birth parents and family; pre- and perinatal factors.
  - Postnatal experiences and developmental milestones.
  - Attachment history.
  - School history.
  - Relationship history.
  - Sexual history.
  - Strengths and resources.
  - Additional problems and concurrent diagnoses.
- **Internal working model:**
  - Core beliefs about self, caregivers, and life in general.
  - Assessment methods: sentence completion, first-year attachment cycle, inner child metaphor, drawings, psychodramatic reenactment.

- The frequency, duration, and severity of symptoms are considered. Severity is determined by categories on the Symptom Checklist (none, mild, moderate, severe). This information is used to generate a discussion with caregivers about the child's symptoms, including frequency, duration, and severity (e.g., parents' describe how often their child has outbursts of anger, how long it lasts, and the resulting level of damage and disruption for the child and family).

- The child provides his or her own perception and interpretation of symptoms and problems. Two methods used are the sentence completion task (see Appendix C) and the child-based problem list (see p. 143). The child is requested to fill out the sentence completion form during the first day of treatment. Valuable information about the child is derived by observing the way in which this task is approached (e.g., is the child honest, serious, cooperative, defiant or motivated?).

- Symptoms are explored and understood in the family context. Family members' reactions are identified (e.g., parents, siblings, and extended family members responses; family members' perceptions, interpretations, and feelings about the child). Prior attempted solutions are discussed, including the nature and outcome of previous therapeutic interventions, medications, parenting strategies, and child welfare efforts (e.g., out-of-home placements). The goals, expectations, and resources of the family are explored in detail. Are their goals and expectations realistic or unrealistic? What emotional, intellectual, social, and economic capabilities exist?

*Developmental History*

- Information about the child's biological parents and family is ascertained (when available) by reviewing social service, medical, and forensic records, and by verbal reports of current caregivers. Relevant information includes issues regarding the biological parents prior to pregnancy (e.g., psychosocial functioning, desire for the child, family background); prenatal factors (e.g., feelings about pregnancy, medical care, nutrition and health of mother, drug or alcohol exposure, support systems, stress level and emotional climate, and health of fetus); perinatal factors (e.g., preterm or postterm birth, birth experience, health of mother and infant at birth, bonding experience immediately after birth).

- Neonatal and postnatal experiences, as well as early developmental milestones, are examined. This includes the infant's temperament (e.g., level of arousal, activity, and response to stimuli); general responsiveness to caregivers; growth patterns; and eating-sleeping-elimination routines.

- The child's attachment history is reviewed in a detailed and comprehensive manner. The first three years of the child's life are crucial in reference to attachment, and the following information must be gathered:

  - Length of time with, and nature of relationship to, birth mother, birth father, and other biological family members.

  - History of placements (e.g., infant receiving facilities, foster and group homes, disrupted adoption).

  - Availability and competency of primary caregivers.

  - Attachment behaviors and indicators (e.g., separation and reunion responses, ability to give and accept affection, secure base behavior, sensitivity towards others, synchronicity and reciprocity).

  - Maltreatment (e.g., abuse, neglect, abandonment, disruptions, and moves), including the child's age; duration; details of child's emotional, cognitive, and physical response; response of significant others; and prior interventions.

  - Additional environmental and family stressors (e.g., postpartum depression of birth mother, marital-family conflict, domestic violence, divorce, death, physical and emotional illnesses of caregivers).

- The child's school history is reviewed, including behaviors, attitudes, relationships and academic performance. The nature of the child-teacher relationship is assessed; conflict with female authority figures is especially common. Relationships with peers; attentional difficulties; responses to rules, boundaries, and limits; and the child's general ability to process information and learn, are determined.

- Significant relationships are examined. How does the child relate to important people in his or her life (adoptive and foster parents, biological or adoptive siblings, extended family members, peers, social workers, therapists, guardian ad litem, and mentors)?

- Evaluation of the child's sexual attitudes and behaviors, both historically and currently, is imperative. Many of these children have been sexually abused or exposed to inappropriate and traumatic sexually oriented experiences. Information is garnered regarding prior sexual acting out (e.g., victim or perpetrator), age-inappropriate sexual attitudes and behaviors, sexualized play rituals, and self-stimulation and masturbation.

- It is important to assess and focus on the child's strengths and inner resources, not only limitations and deficits. Positive traits and characteristics identified include special abilities and interests, intelligence, sense of humor, resilience and protective factors (e.g., easy temperament, positive caregiving history, healthy adoptive parents, desire to change).

- Additional problems and concurrent diagnoses are common. In addition to attachment disorder, other diagnoses often include attention deficit/hyperactivity disorder, oppositional defiant disorder, unipolar or bipolar depression, eating disorders, and other externalizing behaviors (e.g., aggression, criminality, impulsivity).

### Internal Working Model

- The child's internal working model includes core beliefs about self, caregivers, and life in general. This internal working model serves as a blueprint for all current and future relationships. The child's specific perceptions and expectations are identified (e.g., "I am bad, defective, and deserve to be abandoned and abused; caregivers can never be trusted; I must be in control of others to survive") [Levy & Orlans 1995a]. (See Table 5 on page 47.)

- A variety of assessment methods are used to identify the child's internal working model: sentence completion, first-year attachment cycle, inner child metaphor, drawings, and psychodramatic reenactments. These methods are described in detail in Chapter 8.

## Parent and Family Assessment

Corrective Attachment Therapy is a family systems intervention. Assessment focuses on significant family influences in the child's life: psychological and biological functioning and background of the birth family and current caregivers; attachment history and parenting skills and attitudes of current caregivers; and family structure, dynamics, and quality of the marital relationship, as outlined in Table 10. Current caregivers are usually the adoptive parents.

### Parents' Attachment History

- An in-depth exploration of family background is paramount (e.g., relationship with own parents, foster care or adoptive history, relationship with siblings and extended kin, description of family dynamics and attachment patterns).

- Family-of-origin information, including specific stressors, are identified. This includes psychosocial or biological conditions (e.g., depression, aggression, sub-

## Table 10. Parent and Family Assessment

- **Parents' attachment history:**
  - Family background.
  - Additional family-of-origin information.
  - Education and employment history.
  - Assessment methods: autobiography, life script, adult attachment interview, and clinical interview.
- **Parents' current functioning:**
  - Psychosocial and physical health.
  - Marital and other significant relationships.
- **Parenting attitudes and skills:**
  - Parenting history.
  - Parenting practices with siblings.
  - Parenting practices with child with attachment disorder.
  - Parental commitment.
  - Out-of-home placements.
  - Parenting philosophies and competencies.
- **Family system:**
  - Structure, dynamics, and relationship patterns.
  - Support systems.
  - Stressors and stress management.

stance abuse), maltreatment, losses, violence in the home and/or environment, medical and emotional illnesses, criminality, parents' marital relationship, and prior therapeutic interventions.

- Education and employment history are reviewed. Educational achievements, as well as relevant life experiences, provide information about intelligence, motivation, and desire to learn and grow. Factors related to stability are identified (e.g., work history, number of relocations).

- Assessment methods used: autobiography completed prior to treatment, life script, adult attachment interview, and clinical interview.

### Parents' Current Functioning:

- The parents' psychological and physical health are disclosed and discussed. Relevant health issues may include debilitating medical conditions, clinical depression, stress and anxiety, and the impact of prior physical and or psychological traumas.

- Current and historical marital and relationship issues are ascertained. Information is reviewed regarding history of marital or other significant adult relationships (e.g., reasons for and circumstances around divorce, custody and visitation, relationship discord, and conflict resolution); current marital relationship (e.g., communication, problem-solving, and conflict management skills; dynamics and patterns; intimacy, support, stability, and satisfaction).

*Parenting Attitudes and Skills*

- A parenting history is taken, including planned and unplanned pregnancies, losses (miscarriages, abortions, infertility issues), and responses to biological, foster, and/or adoptive children entering the family system.

- Parenting practices with other children in the family are explored (e.g., strengths, problems, prior treatment). Some parents are successful with other children in their family but not so with the child with attachment disorder. This may be indicative of competent parents and an extremely difficult child, or of parents who are only effective with less challenging children. Some parents are ineffective with all their children, which may indicate either a lack of parenting skills or unresolved family-of-origin issues triggered by their children.

- Parenting successes and failures with their child with attachment disorder (e.g., types of difficulties, prior attempted solutions, maltreatment considered and/or acted out).

- The continuum of parental commitment is assessed:

  - Highly committed (for the correct reason of wanting to help the child, or unhealthy reason of meeting own needs, such as fear of failure or unresolved prior losses);

  - Ambivalent commitment (parents are burned-out, confused, frightened, and struggling with their commitment to the child); or

  - Noncommitted (parents are covertly or overtly considering relinquishment).

- Out-of-home placements are reviewed (e.g., reasons, duration, outcomes and feelings regarding placement and reintegration).

- Parenting philosophies and competencies are identified and discussed in detail:

  - Feelings toward and perceptions of the child (e.g., extreme emotional reactions including love, hate, pity, resentment, guilt, shame, and fear). Positive or negative perceptions may include seeing the child as a victim of maltreatment who must be protected and rescued, or as a threat to family safety.

  - Feelings toward the "system": parents often feel angry, frustrated, blamed, and misunderstood by the child welfare system. Parents may also blame the system unfairly.

  - View of attachment: coherent, dismissive, preoccupied, and unresolved views of attachment are associated with prior attachment experiences and influence current parenting practices. (See Appendix D.)

  - Promote secure attachment: ability to perceive their child accurately, meet individual and developmental needs appropriately, set limits, and provide a healing emotional environment.

- Discipline attitude and style: ability to provide the necessary balance of caring and structure; parents may be overindulgent, rejecting, critical, abusive, confused and lacking in self-control.

## Family System

- The structure, dynamics, and relationship patterns in the family must be identified and understood. The family system is both influenced by, and directly impacts, the emotions and behaviors of the child with attachment disorder. Assessment focuses on the following:

  - **Boundaries.** The emotional and physical barriers that enhance and protect the integrity of family members, subsystems, and the family as a unit (e.g., a demanding and aggressive child violates the physical and emotional space of siblings and parents).

  - **Subsystems.** Units in the family, determined by generation, sex, or function. The three family subsystems are parental, marital, and sibling (e.g., the mother and father in their leadership role form the parental subsystem, and in their spousal roles form the marital subsystem).

  - **Triangulation.** Detouring conflict between two people by involving a third person (e.g., a child acts out towards mother and is charming and engaging with father; father blames mother for the child's problems, and forms a coalition with the child; the parental subsystem is in conflict and, therefore, is ineffective in managing the child).

  - **Relationship skills.** Communication, problem-solving, and conflict management skills are assessed. Effective communication between parents-child and husband-wife is crucial to family functioning.

  - **Roles and rules.** Family members either create or are assigned specific roles, which determine behavior and function in the system (e.g., scapegoat, rescuer, victim, perpetrator, placator, disciplinarian). Rules are the "laws" by which the family operates and can either be realistic/unrealistic, appropriate/inappropriate.

  - **Power and control.** The healthy family system operates on the basis of a hierarchy of power and control, with the parents in the executive role. The extreme power and control needs of children with attachment disorder results in chronic and debilitating power struggles with authority figures.

  - **Intimacy.** A basic function of the family is to meet the members' emotional needs for affection, closeness, and connection. These children with attachment disorder avoid intimacy and promote a conflictual family climate in which others have difficulty meeting intimacy needs.

  - **Patterns.** Ongoing, reciprocal patterns of interaction, either positive or negative, occur in the family system. Destructive patterns must be identified (e.g., the child is oppositional and angry toward parents, parents respond with hostility and rejection, a vicious cycle of mutual negativity ensues).

- A review of family support systems and external resources is important. Support systems include extended kin, friendship networks, social service agencies, support groups, religious affiliations, and other community resources. External systems can be supportive and helpful or unsupportive and nonhelpful (diluting and disempowering the family).

- Although stress is a part of life, families who have children with attachment disorder experience extreme levels of ongoing stress. The nature of the stressors, and the way in which family members react to these stressors, must be assessed.

## Symptoms of Attachment Disorder

The symptoms of attachment disorder are divided into six categories: behavioral, cognitive, affective, social, physical, and moral/spiritual. Each of these symptom categories will be described below, with specific examples by parents (in their own words, as provided on intake forms).

Symptoms exist along a continuum, from mild to severe (Table 11). Children vary in the number of symptoms they display and in the severity of each particular symptom. Symptoms can change in frequency and duration over the course of development. Without effective treatment, the most serious symptoms of the child with attachment disorder escalate as the child gets older.

### Behavioral

Children with attachment disorder manifest a variety of antisocial and aggressive acting-out behaviors. They are often self-destructive, including self-mutilation (e.g., head banging, cutting, or burning skin), and display suicidal gestures and other self-defeating behaviors. They destroy the property of others, their own material possessions, or both. Impulsivity and physical aggression towards other children and adults is common. Aggression can be overt, such as acts of physical violence, or passive-aggressive, such as manipulative and surreptitious behaviors. Sadistic cruelty to animals, often secretive, can occur. Stealing is typical, including theft outside and inside the home. Lying is of a pathological nature; they remain deceitful regardless of concrete evidence to the contrary. A preoccupation with fire, gore, and blood sometimes occurs, as they establish an affiliation with evil and the dark side of life. They can be ingenious, devious, and "phoney," giving the appearance of sincerity, but with ulterior and self-serving motives. For example, helping professionals may assume the child's seemingly cooperative responses are sincere, when in reality, this behavior is often manipulative and controlling.

Problems regarding food and eating patterns are common, such as hoarding and gorging, and may reflect control issues and a need to fill their emotional emptiness. Children who have been sexually abused manifest inappropriate sexual behavior, attitudes, and concerns, such as victimizing others, excessive masturbation, seductive manipulation, and sexualized play. Sleep disturbances include recurrent nightmares, night terrors, disturbed sleep patterns, and wandering at night. Enuresis and encopresis are typical manifestations of anger, aggression, and control issues;

### Table 11. Continuum of Attachment

| Secure | Anxious | Disorganized | Nonattached |
|---|---|---|---|
| • comfortable with closeness and trust | • resists or ambivalent about closeness and trust | • unable to trust and be close | • unable to form emotional connections |
| • felt security | | • lacks remorse | • lacks conscience |
| • vulnerability acceptable | • moderately controlling and insecure | • aggressive and punitive control | • predatory behaviors |
| • positive working model | • negative working model (moderate) | • negative working model (severe) | • negative working model (severe) |
| • individuality/ togetherness balanced | • rejecting or clingy | • pseudoindependent | • extreme narcissism |

these children may soil in closets, clothes, and heating vents. Extreme defiant and oppositional behaviors include refusal to comply with authority, demanding and intrusive social styles, and persistent nonsense questions and incessant chatter.

## Lack of Impulse Control

Gina doesn't just open her mouth and insert her foot. She sticks her foot in her mouth when it's not even open. If she wants to do something she doesn't think, she just reacts. She never considers the consequences of her actions. She just does what the spirit moves her to do. For example, she often tries to get out of the car without looking to see if another car was coming.

## Self-Destructive Behaviors

When we brought Tony home from Romania she rocked in her crib, hit her head against the wall, pulled her hair out, and bit her hands and arms. When she walks or runs, she runs into things on purpose and falls down. She is always setting herself up to fail.

## Destruction of Property

Billy trashes his room when he is angry. He will pick up the nearest item and throw it. He has cut up my bedspread and pillow with scissors. He has put holes in the walls and has carved on our furniture. He has drawn all over his bed and has picked the wallpaper off the wall. He has mutilated pictures of himself and has broken all of his toys. He poked holes in the seats of his chairs and wrote with a marker on the carpet and sofa. He will break someone else's most precious toy, then laugh.

## Aggression Toward Others

Johnny will scream he hates us and writes on the wall that he hates us and wishes we were dead. He purposefully pushed his younger brother down the stairs. The other day he sang at the top of his lungs, "I hate you, you hate me, I am going to get my ax and chop you up." My 16-year-old daughter said to me, "Mom, do you think maybe the reason he is not nice to you and me is because we are the women figures in his life and women are who have hurt him before, so therefore he thinks if he hurts us, then he is getting back at them?" I really think she hit the nail on the head.

## Consistently Irresponsible

Sarah tells us her homework is done, but it rarely is. She puts up a big fuss when she has to do a chore and never gets it done right. All she wants to do is watch TV. She is consistently irresponsible and forgetful. She leaves behind lunch pails, backpacks, and her homework.

## Inappropriately Demanding and Clingy

Dan yells at his sisters and anyone else who doesn't do exactly as he sees fit at the moment. He wants full attention and demands that more time be spent with us, even when we give him a large amount of attention. When we have company around he can become clingy. Going to the doctor he can be clingy or when any new situation arises. He usually does it when we are busy with something or on the phone.

## Stealing

Ellen steals incessantly. She has gone through my purse many times. She stole $20 from a friend's bedroom. She also has stolen two pocket knives and was caught shoplifting. We had to resort to full body searches after she took my diamond pin to school hidden in her waistband. She also stole something off her teacher's desk. At Easter our daughters have to lock their Easter baskets in their rooms.

## Deceitful (Lying, Conning)

Keith lies to stay out of trouble, but he also lies for no reason at all. It's almost a habitual thing. He has absolutely no remorse when he gets caught lying, only for getting caught. He will hold on to his story even when you have proof in hand. When he steals candy, he comes downstairs with the chocolate on his face and denies eating candy. He is always conjuring up stories to suit his need to manipulate. We never know when he is telling the truth.

## Hoarding

We are constantly finding candy wrappers under Lisa's bed. We also find them under the couch and in corners. I recently found a half-eaten sandwich, old stale cookies, and packets of sugar between her mattress. We always give her all the food she wants and are puzzled why she has all these little stashes. Most of the time the food is never even eaten.

## Inappropriate Sexual Conduct and Attitudes

Mother reports the following information revealed by her daughter: "Sex stuff I've done to other kids. I once touched a boy's private parts. But every time I touched him I got caught and I had to have a spanking, but I never learned. I also touched a girl on her private parts, who I sometimes had over to play. There was another boy across the street who one day came over to play, and he took me behind a bush and started to touch me, but I didn't care because I was doing it back."

## Cruelty to Animals

I began to notice that Mary was very nice to the animals as long as she knew someone was watching her. As soon as she thought she wasn't being watched she would kick or hit both the dog and the cat. Then, anytime she pet them, she would pull a tail or pinch. Now, the cat is neurotic and fearful around her and the dog avoids her altogether.

## Sleep Disturbance

Robert has a very difficult time getting to sleep. He often yells for Dad or Mom several times a night. He also tosses, turns, and talks in his sleep. He sometimes gets up and wanders in the middle of the night. I once opened my eyes and there he was staring at me. It gave me a funny feeling. He also steals food during the night.

## Enuresis and Encopresis

The areas around using the bathroom are another fiasco. Tina would refuse to wipe when she had a bowel movement. She has smeared poop on the toilet seat and waited for someone to sit on it. She wets her pants almost every time her will is crossed in any way, or when she feels like she is losing control. She usually doesn't wet them enough to soak through, but just enough to make a point. She recently began to urinate on clothes in her closet and on her rug. Of course, she denies it.

## Frequently Defies Rules (Oppositional)

When I ask her to do anything, I get a look. The "look" is the most horrible expression I have ever seen on a child's face. It is mad, sad, and defiant all at once. At kindergarten she is noncompliant most of the time, running down the hall, sitting in other people's seats and screaming, "I'm the boss!" She has bit, spit on, and thrown sand at her teachers. She shows little regard or respect for most authority figures, including parents, teachers, baby sitters, and adults in general.

## Hyperactivity

Morning in our house is chaotic. Adam wakes up first and usually makes a lot of noise to wake us all up. Next, he gets out food and milk, which he often spills. The counter is left in a mess. He bumps into tables, walls, and counters, and goes from one room to the next leaving mess after mess. I give Adam his Ritalin and I have a cup of coffee. I ignore all his behavior until I've had some coffee. Once his medication kicks in he doesn't bump into things and he doesn't argue constantly.

### Abnormal Eating Habits

Michael can eat very slowly, picking at his food and the next day gulp it all down. He can eat two and three helpings at dinner and would eat continually if allowed to. He has an enormous sweet tooth. We have even caught him eating sugar right out of the sack. He steals candy often right under our nose.

### Preoccupation with Fire, Gore, or Evil

We have found a hidden pack of matches in his room. One year ago he was suspended from school for two days for setting a roll of toilet paper on fire in the bathroom. We have found burnt pieces of paper and we have noticed that his coat is singed. He has a preoccupation with violent and evil characters. We recently passed a dead dog on the road. He was fascinated by it and couldn't stop talking about how cool it was.

### Persistent Nonsense Questions and Incessant Chatter

She continually asks questions that are unimportant. When she was younger she would see me sawing wood and ask, "What are you doing?" Then she would come back and ask the same questions. At the dinner table she will go on and on talking about everything and nothing and usually not making a lot of sense. She is particularly bad when we are in the car and she has a captive audience. It drives us crazy.

### Poor Hygiene

Ken is not concerned at all about personal hygiene. He could really not care less about having pimples from not washing his face, or not brushing his teeth, or using deodorant. He hates to take a shower and wash his hair. Sometimes he will run the water in the shower and pretend he is washing his hair. He would wear the same socks and underwear everyday if he could.

### Difficulty with Novelty and Change

Blake can't stand anything new. He must have the same routines day in and day out, or we pay the price. He always needs to know where we are and what we're doing. Sometimes we think he will never grow up.

### Cognitive Functioning

A lack of cause-and-effect thinking is evident; failing to recognize and comprehend the relationship between actions and consequences. Thus, these children rarely take responsibility for their own choices and actions, and instead, blame others. Regarding cognitive style (i.e., internal working models), they perceive themselves as unwanted, worthless, impotent and "bad," perceive caretakers as unavailable, untrustworthy and threatening, and perceive the world as unsafe and hostile. They define themselves as helpless victims unable to impact their world, or conversely, as omnipotent, with a grandiose sense of self-importance as a defense against feeling helpless. Learning and language disorders are common and can occur as a result of early neurological damage (e.g., fetal alcohol syndrome, failure to thrive, physical abuse), or in conjunction with the matrix of psychosocial symptoms mentioned above.

### Lack of Cause-and-Effect Thinking

We have tried every form of acceptable discipline known to man applied diligently and faithfully. The child does not or will not learn. He knows, though! You ask him if he can tell us if he's done something wrong and he says yes and tells what it is. Then you ask him if he knows the consequences. Again, he says yes and tells you. But he still absolutely refuses to abide by the rules. It's only a matter of time before he does the same thing over again. He just does what he wants, not thinking or caring about what will happen. When playing chess with him, I can use the same moves to beat him time and time again.

### Learning Disorders

Beth is behind in her age level and her educational level. She is in a special education school, one year behind. They have told us that her problems are related to early childhood deprivation.

### Language Disorders

After leaving Guatemala, Carla's English was wonderful within six months. She can understand everything and make herself understandable. She may, however, act like she can't speak much English. She does this at school. They say she has real problems understanding. Carla will try that ploy with me when she is in trouble. She acts likes she can't figure out what you are talking about. She has admitted that she understands you. After she admits it, then she can have a five-minute conversation with you about it.

### Perceives Self as a Victim (Helpless)

Mark complains constantly that no one likes him, including his parents, other children, and his teachers. He also complains that his parents and teachers are mean to him, generally over everyday things. As an example, he will tell his mother he hates her for having to take a shower first before coming down to get his cereal, because it means he's not being taken care of if things don't go exactly his way. Whether with friends, teachers, and others, he feels he is being unfairly treated.

### Grandiose Sense of Self-Importance

He seems to think the world revolves around him, and he can't see it any other way. He always has to be in control. His wants always come first. No one else's feelings or desires count. He thinks he is an expert at everything, even things he knows nothing about. He boasts and brags, always trying to make himself seem more important.

## Affectivity

The core emotions these children experience are intense levels of anger, fear, pain, and shame. They frequently appear disheartened and depressed, generally in response to unresolved loss and grief. Temper tantrums and rage reactions are common. They are emotionally labile with frequent and unpredictable mood swings. Due to years of avoidance and denial, they are not able to identify or express their emotions in clear and constructive ways. They experience shame regarding maltreatment as well as their acting out towards others.

### Not Affectionate on Parents' Terms

If we sat down next to her and tried to put our arm around her when she was younger, she would try to get away. Hugging her is like hugging a mannequin. We still try to give her a goodnight kiss. Many times she hides her head under the covers. If you ask her for a kiss, she says "No." There is never any warmth. The only time she has ever hugged us is when others are around and she can make a show, or in inappropriate times to catch us off guard.

### Intense Displays of Anger (Rage)

He yells and screams at anyone who doesn't do what he wants them to do. His fuse is nonexistent. This is the time he often lashes out with hitting and yelling. He flies into rages if I assert my turn with the TV or insist he do his homework. He is almost totally out of control. This summer he physically attacked me three different times over trivial slights and being told "No." He has put holes in the walls and threatened me with his hands around my neck. He has even thrown a meat fork at me.

### Frequently Sad, Depressed, or Helpless

Cindy is the unhappiest child I know. She is always pouting and sulking. When asked about it she usually says it's for things like not having anything to do, yet she intensely dislikes any social interactions. I have to drag her to Girl Scout meetings or ballet lessons. She would prefer to sit in her room and watch TV to the exclusion of anyone or anything.

### Inappropriate Emotional Responses

When she becomes enraged she screams, stomps her feet, and throws objects. This occurs in public all the time, especially in restaurants. She laughs when people get shot on TV, and she laughs hysterically at juvenile TV shows. She never shows sadness in appropriately sad situations ("that's stupid"). When she gets seriously hurt, I would never know it, but if she has a minor injury she cries and screams.

## Marked Mood Changes

Lisa can have different personalities from one moment to the next. She can be a normal happy child and then something will set her off and she will act like "Rosemary's Baby." She can be in a good mood at school and then see me when I pick her up and change into a bad mood. I never know what to expect from Lisa. Each new day is a new challenge.

### Social Behavior

Chronic noncompliance is manifested interpersonally as control battles, defiance of rules and authority, and inability to tolerate external limits. Thus, these youngsters create frequent conflict with caregivers, teachers, siblings, and peers. They relate to others in a manipulative, controlling and exploitative fashion, lacking the ability to connect with genuine intimacy and affection. Lacking trust in others (a direct result of unavailable, unreliable, and hurtful caregivers in the early years), they overcompensate in the direction of pseudoindependence. They are superficially engaging and charming, indiscriminately affectionate with strangers, and lack long-term meaningful relationships. Lack of eye contact is apparent when interaction is perceived as intimate, but they maintain eye contact for purposes of seduction or control. Typical social roles developed and maintained include victim (helpless, powerless) and/or victimizer (perpetrator, bully). Blaming others for their own mistakes and problems, and taking little or no responsibility for their actions and choices, further alienates and frustrates others.

## Superficially Engaging and Charming

When Marta came off the plane from Columbia she cried for about 15 minutes and then she became everyone's darling. She gave big hugs and kisses to all of the waiting relatives. She showed no apprehension at all. When people are around she immediately launches into her friendly adorable routine. She walks down the street and starts a conversation with everyone she encounters. She has said, "I love you" to people she hardly knows.

## Lack of Eye Contact for Closeness

He seldom ever looks people in the eye unless asked to do so, and still has difficulty even then. Whenever his behaviors is unacceptable and we tell him, down goes the head to avoid eye contact. On the other hand, he can flat out lie to you, staring you right in the eye.

## Indiscriminately Affectionate with Strangers

Ken will go to anyone. When we first adopted him he went up to strangers and hugged them. When he meets people on his terms he is extremely friendly and talkative. He will say "I love you" to anyone on the street.

## Lack of or Unstable Peer Relationships

Everyday Jessica's best friend changes. A perfect stranger can be her best friend. She lies to them, blames them for things she has done, steals from them, and quarrels with them. They never last very long. Her best friends are kids three to four years younger than her. We hear her bossing them, telling them how a game is to be played. When things don't go her way, she makes new rules. It seems like the only friends she can keep for any length of time are the underdogs, the kids who nobody else likes because they do bad things, or the ones that have the worst family problems.

## Cannot Tolerate Limits and External Control

Sheila hates authority of any kind. She does not follow instructions well and has a difficult time obeying rules. She doesn't take guidance from parents, teachers, or other adults. When asked to throw something in the kitchen trash, she will put it in the wastebasket in the living room. She complies with the intent, but has to change the conditions, if only in a slight way, just to be in control.

## Blames Others for Own Mistakes and Problems

If he loses something he blames me. If he bumps into someone, they bumped into him. He won't ever take the blame for anything. He will make up any excuse, no mater how ridiculous to avoid blame. If he hits a wrong note, it's because something is wrong with the instrument. If he misses an assignment deadline, it's because the teacher never told him it was due.

## Victimizes Others (Perpetrator, Bully)

He doesn't give other children their space. He will get up into their face and will bully them for no reason. It doesn't matter how big they are. He often tries to control the children around him by pushing them, hitting them with his backpack, or bossing them around. He is also verbally manipulative to both children and adults.

## Victimized by Others

She sets herself up to be victimized by everyone. Other kids will hurt her or blame her for things and she says nothing. She has even confessed to things and then we find out that someone else really did it. She will purposefully lose a privilege and then feel sorry for herself as the helpless martyr.

## Lacks Trust in Others

Katie doesn't trust that I will take care of her even after seven years. She is afraid that I won't be there for her. When I leave town, she gets mad for days, before I go and when I return. She will lie, steal food, and refuse to do anything for the family. She just doesn't trust that anyone will be there for her.

### Exploitative, Manipulative, Controlling, and Bossy

At home, Allison is just awful. She is angry, defiant, and mean. The first time Grandma watched her she was fine. I was shocked. The next night Grandma looked awful. She said Allison was the most bossy child that she had ever seen, She commented that she acted like she was 40 instead of 4. Allison says that it makes her mad that we are the bosses. She wants to be the boss. She is angry that we are the parents. She wants to be the parent.

### *Physical*

Anger, grief, fear, and emotional pain are stored and expressed in the bodies of children with attachment disorder. They are typically stiff, chronically tense, and physically defended against closeness and contact. Chest muscles are particularly rigid as a reaction to the suppression of anxiety and fear, which results in shallow and restricted breathing. Tension in the throat and facial area blocks the impulse to cry. They pull back their shoulders, distancing themselves from others. Some appear robotic in nature, with minimal facial expression and a vacant stare in their eyes, their bodies expressing emotional repression and avoidance of others. Problems with personal hygiene are common. They take little pride in their appearance and living quarters, often refusing to shower, brush their teeth, and maintain a clean environment. They are often accident prone, and experience many physical injuries. Minor injuries are magnified and dramatized in order to receive attention through manipulation and control. Serious injuries, conversely, are underemphasized and kept secret, in an effort to avoid vulnerability and helping responses from caregivers. They are tactilely defensive; rigid body armor is a defense against human contact and a somatic reaction to prior trauma. Genetically, their family history is characterized by numerous biologically based problems, such as clinical depression, substance abuse, aggression, and severe psychological disturbance.

### Poor Hygiene

Sheila swears that she brushed her teeth, but when I check, I find that her toothbrush is totally dry. When told to wash her hair, she just stands in the shower, not even wetting her head. Her hair looks just as greasy as when she went in. She sometimes sleeps in her clothes, and wears the same smelly things for days.

### Chronic Body Tension

When you hug Chelsea, it's like hugging a 2 x 4. She always seems tense. She sits straight and stiffly, and she only tightens up more if you get close. You can hardly tell when she's breathing. She kisses like stereotypical Hollywood types (hug-hug, kiss-kiss, let's do lunch). There's never any warmth.

### Accident Prone

When he walks or runs, he falls down many times. He is always pushing or bumping into his brother. He always says, "It was an accident." He used to turn over furniture and make the pictures on the wall crooked when he was angry. If there is anything special to any other family member, you can be sure that he will accidentally break it.

### High Pain Tolerance/Overreaction to Minor Injury

Jim was in the backyard playing with his younger brother. He fell and broke both bones in his arm. He didn't even cry. It wasn't until I said, "Oh my God, your arm is broken" that he reacted at all. On the other hand, when he had a small splinter in his finger, he screamed like someone was killing him.

### Tactilely Defensive

When Lucy first came to our home I tried to hold her and stroke her cheek. She screamed and pulled away and said "Don't touch me, you're hurting me." It took six weeks before I could even approach her. She still avoids any physical contact or affection.

### Genetic Predispositions

Danny's biological father has been in jail off and on his entire life and his mother was always depressed. I'm told that he was physically abusive to his mother, and later to his sister and animals. Danny has never met his father, but the apple sure doesn't fall from the tree. He acts just like his dad. He has even said, "I'm going to grow up just like my birth dad because he has power, he hurts people."

### *Spiritual/Moral*

Spiritual health can be defined in various ways: a state of well-being, not just the absence of disease; the quality of being at peace with oneself and in harmony with the environment; a sense of empowerment, personal worthiness and control; feeling connected to one's deepest self, to others, and to all regarded as good; a sense of meaning, purpose, and hope [Hafen et al. 1996]. Combining various concepts, one researcher identified four aspects of spiritual health:

- A *unifying force* that integrates physical, mental, emotional and social health;

- A focus on a *meaning in life*, which serves as a powerful inner drive for personal accomplishment;

- A *common bond* between individuals, enabling us to share love, warmth, and compassion with others, and to be unselfish while following a set of ethical principles; and

- Based on *individual perceptions and faith*, acknowledging some power or force behind the natural working of the universe [Banks 1980; cited in Hafen et al. 1996, p. 380].

Children with attachment disorder generally have few of the above qualities. Spirituality is about a relationship. These children are incapable of intimate and enduring relationships, do not feel a sense of goodness and self-worth, and act on the basis of self-interest. They feel separate and disconnected from all personal relationships, including a spiritual relationship.

Since children with attachment disorder reject parental authority, it is not surprising that they also reject the concept of an "ultimate authority figure." Rather than perceiving a higher power as loving and benevolent, they either view God as "bad" and punishing (a projection of their own negativity), or see themselves as unworthy of God's love. They often blame God for their troubles and feel "it does no good to be good."

Early maltreatment and compromised attachments have left these children with "scars on their souls." They are not in harmony with spiritual ideals and purposes. Faith, forgiveness, compassion, and unselfishness are alien to them. Rollo May [1972, p. 23] writes, "When children are not loved adequately they develop a penchant for revenge on the world, a need to destroy the world for others as much as it was not good for them."

As previously described, children with attachment disorder lack moral and ethical development. They experience little or no remorse, lack compassion and empathy, and have a poorly developed conscience. They do not develop a sense of family, community, interdependence, and the desire to cooperate with others, which is deeply rooted in our evolutionary past. Although they know the difference between right and wrong, they prefer to choose wrong, with no thought of consequences, no concern for others, and no personal accountability for their actions.

### Lack of Meaning and Purpose

One day Joey told me that if his birth father was going to abuse him for the first three years of his life, then he was going to be placed in foster homes forever, what's the point—what's the use—he doesn't understand why he was born!

### Lack of Faith, Compassion, and Other Spiritual Values

Andy sometimes seems to enjoy watching others being hurt. He will destroy people's things without the slightest concern. He treats his friends poorly and then is surprised when they reject him. When he is angry, the coldness in his eyes is scary. He doesn't seem to care about anyone, including himself.

### Identification with Evil and the Dark Side of Life

We are involved in the ministry. Tara does everything in her power to embarrass us and has even told our congregation "When you pray to God, I pray to the devil." She even drew pictures of the devil in the hymnals. She has said, "If there was a God, I wouldn't be like this. God would never let me be abused." She also has said, "If there is a God, he must be bad."

### Lack of Remorse (Conscience)

It seems he doesn't care who he hurts, even his brother. He seems to delight in watching others be in pain. If someone gets hurt, he will laugh. He will steal from other kids or call them hurtful names without the slightest care. He will say he is sorry, but he never really means it. He is just sorry he got caught. He truly does not care about right or wrong. If he wants to do something, he thinks it's OK to do it, right or wrong, as long as he wants to do it or thinks he can get away with it.

## Special Assessment Considerations

Symptoms of attachment disorder occur along a continuum (Table 11), from mild to severe, as a result of the followings factors:

• Developmental stage at the time of disruption;

• Length of time of disruption;

• Nature and quality of attachment prior to disruption;

• Nature and quality of attachment experiences following disruption;

• Constitutional factors, including genetic background and temperament; and

• Protective factors, including support from extended family and positive out-of-home placement.

Children with moderate to severe attachment disorder typically display the following symptoms: impulsive, angry, and aggressive; controlling, manipulative, and bossy; unable to form genuine and loving relationships; lying and stealing; lack of empathy and remorse; and self-contempt and poorly defined sense of self. Children with severe attachment disorder sometimes exhibit cruelty to animals and a preoccupation with fire, including fire setting.

### Cruelty to Animals

Cruelty to animals is one of the most disturbing manifestations of attachment disorder. It ranges from annoying family pets (e.g., tail pulling, rough play, kicking) to severe transgressions (e.g., strangulation, mutilation). These children lack the capacity to give and receive affection with pets, lack the motivation and sense of responsibility necessary to provide appropriate care, and are not able to empathize with the suffering of animals. They often delight in venting their frustrations and hostilities on helpless creatures to compensate for feelings of powerlessness and inferiority.

Margaret Mead [1964] suggested that childhood cruelty to animals is a precursor to adult antisocial violence. Researchers found that the combination of cruelty to animals, enuresis, and fire setting predicted later violent and criminal behaviors in adults [Hellman & Blackman 1966]. Researchers at Northeastern University found that children who abuse animals are five times more likely to commit violent crimes as adults. The FBI's Behavioral Science Unit found that a majority of multiple murderers admitted to cruelty to animals during childhood [Cannon 1997].

Parental abuse of children was the most common etiological factor found in cruelty to animals [Tapia 1971]. Erick Fromm [1973] noted that children who are sadistic are usually themselves the victims of cruel treatment. Schowalter [1983] concluded that cruelty to animals represents a displacement of aggression from the child to a helpless animal. Cline [1992] suggests that a pet in the home of a child with attachment disorder is an endangered species. We have found that animal harassment and abuse is often undetected by the parents. The child can be remarkably surreptitious in his or her offenses. Unknowing parents are at a loss as to why the family's gerbils and parakeets mysteriously die.

### Attraction to Fire

Fire provides a particular appeal for some children with attachment disorder. Its attributes of power and destruction are attractive qualities to the child who is filled with rage and feels powerless. The child's fire-setting behaviors are extremely disconcerting to caregivers. The child senses this fear and apprehension, and then uses this to his or her advantage in order to gain a sense of further power and control.

Fire-setting episodes are rarely impulsive acts, but are more likely to be carefully considered and planned. Some children establish elaborate alibis in a moment's notice, while others show little inclination to "cover up" their actions. Fire-setting behaviors vary in degree from simple fascination and/or occasional lighting of matches, to more serious actions, such as setting fire to a home. The more serious the nature of the premeditated fire, the more seriously disturbed the child. Society is beginning to recognized the magnitude of this problem. Juveniles now account for the majority of all arson arrests; children and teens accounted for 55% of arson arrests in 1994. One third of those arrested were under 15 years old, and 7% were under the age of 10. No other serious felony has such a high rate of juvenile involvement [Estrin 1996].

## Differential Diagnosis

Attachment disorder shares a particular affinity with attention deficit/hyperactivity disorder and bipolar disorder. ADHD is estimated to occur in between 3% to 6% of school-age children (1.5 to 2.5 million). ADHD involves behavioral and learning difficulties relating to inattention, impulsivity, and hyperactivity. The exact causes of ADHD are unknown, but research indicates there is a physiological component. Environmental and social factors, such as quality of parenting, diet, and toxins affect ADHD, but are not causal factors [Bain 1991]. The correlation of ADHD and reactive attachment disorder has been placed at between 40% and 70% of abused, neglected, and adopted children. ADHD is vastly overdiagnosed in this population [Alston 1995].

Children with attachment disorder also frequently suffer from bipolar disorder. Bipolar refers to a genetically linked affective disorder characterized by both manic and depressive mood episodes. These mood swings can range from overly expansive and irritable, to sad and hopeless, with intervening periods of normal mood. Symptoms of bipolar disorder were thought to show up in adolescence or early adulthood. Young children with bipolar disorder often do not display intense mood shifts, but rather less dramatic variations in behavior that can easily go undetected.

Consequently, bipolar disorder is infrequently diagnosed in children. For a comprehensive symptom comparison between ADHD, bipolar disorder, and attachment disorder, see Appendix E.

# 7
# Corrective Attachment Therapy

## Basic Theoretical & Treatment Issues

### Structure of the Healing Process

It is imperative to have an organized and systematic framework when working therapeutically. This framework helps the therapist develop clear goals, stay focused, and move consistently toward desired outcomes. There are a variety of frameworks that have been conceptualized by practitioners working with maltreated children and adults. Herman [1992] recommends the following three phases during the process of treatment with traumatized adults: 1) regaining a sense of safety, 2) remembrance and mourning, and 3) reconnection with ordinary life. Pearce and Pezzot-Pearce [1997] use a three-stage approach to reformulate the meaning of maltreatment for children: 1) building mastery, 2) reconceptualizing meaning, and 3) developing positive self-esteem. Gil [1996], in her work with abused adolescents, proposes numerous steps in the structured processing of trauma, which serve two basic goals: 1) reinterpretation and integration, and 2) resolution and closure so that the individual feels more in control. Recovery from posttraumatic stress disorder follows three stages [Brown & Fromm 1986]: stabilization, integration of memories, and development of self. Brohl [1996], in discussing the healing process for traumatized children, also conceptualizes three stages: confusion, reorganization, and integration.

Regardless of the specific classifications used to describe the process of healing and change, there are a number of benefits to having a framework:

- Organizes otherwise complex information and experiences; attachment disorder affects *every* aspect of functioning.

- Makes it easier to stay goal oriented, reducing the possibility of becoming unfocused and overwhelmed; specific goals and methods are connected to each step or stage.

- Provides a "framework for freedom"; the therapist can spontaneously and empathically be in the relationship with the child or other family member knowing there is a secure base.

- Affirms the developmental nature of healing; treatment is a process that builds upon prior accomplishments step-by-step.

- Enhances hope and optimism, as both the therapist and family members sense positive movement toward attainment of goals.

- Necessary when teaching mental health professionals how to provide effective treatment.

The treatment framework proposed by the current authors is divided into three phases—*revisit, revise, revitalize*—each with specific rationale, goals, and methods. Before discussing these specifics, however, it is important to enumerate the theoretical foundation and basic principles upon which this framework is built.

## Basic Principles

- **Systems model.** The child, parents, and other family members must be understood in the context of the systems that influence their lives. The focus is on prior and current family systems, and external systems such as social services, extended family and social networks, and community resources. The systems model concentrates on the behavior of family members as they interact in ongoing and reciprocal relationships, and on the family as it interacts with external social influences. For example, family members affect one another—each person's behavior serving both as a response and a trigger. A child who enters an adoptive family with an attitude of hostility may trigger an angry and punitive response from adoptive parents. This parental response reinforces the child's belief that all caregivers are hostile and rejecting. Hostility and rejection become mutually reinforcing in this child-parent relationship. Thus, interventions must focus on both the individual and the social systems in which he or she functions.

- **Collaborative treatment team.** A multidisciplinary treatment team is utilized, consisting of a primary therapist, co-therapist, therapeutic foster parent(s) (when necessary), medical consultant, and follow-up therapist (when possible). Although the parents are themselves the focus of treatment regarding individual and/or marital issues, they are empowered as members of the treatment team regarding parenting practices. A supportive and collaborative team is paramount when working with difficult, treatment-resistant children and their families. Children with attachment disorder are extremely challenging, and their parents are typically frustrated, demoralized, and have lost faith in the helping system. The therapist can remain focused on goals, and the child is unable to triangulate, within the structure of a unified treatment team.

- **Integrative and holistic.** Assessment and intervention occur on all relevant levels of the human experience—emotional, cognitive, social, physical, behavioral, moral, and spiritual. This orientation assumes that all of these dimensions are interconnected. Behavioral change leads to alterations in meaning and beliefs; conversely, cognitive changes produce alterations in actions and choices. Mind affects body and body affects mind.

- **Didactic and experiential.** Treatment is both psychoeducational and experience based. Information is provided to family members in order to improve coping skills (e.g., anger management and conflict resolution); parenting skills (e.g., understanding child development, discipline, and consequencing); and related areas of individual and family functioning. The process of change and healing is primarily experiential, requiring direct participation and genuine involvement on the part of the child, family, and therapists.

- **Developmental focus.** The developmental stage of the child at the time of attachment trauma determines, to a great extent, the psychosocial consequences. Also, the symptoms of attachment trauma change as development unfolds. Thus, treatment must be sensitive to age- and stage-related issues. Follow-up therapy is provided over time to deal with developmentally provoked symptoms and challenges. The process of treatment is sequential and developmental. A therapeutic foundation is built, and change occurs progressively as goals are attained, skills mastered, and experiences are integrated.

- **Culturally sensitive.** Behavior, as well as the personal meaning of events, varies depending on cultural background and tradition. The therapist must be aware of the cultural orientation of the child and family, and be careful not to project his or her own cultural biases, perceptions, or beliefs on those individuals. The therapist communicates acceptance and respect for the cultural beliefs and traditions of each family member.

- **Resource model.** Therapy is strength and competency based. All family members have resources and strengths that must be identified and encouraged. It is helpful to focus on "what is right" and build upon that, not only on "what is wrong." For example, although it is necessary for children to deal with prior traumatic experiences as part of the healing process, it is equally important to build on the child's strengths and teach skills that foster a sense of mastery and hope. The therapist is aware of his or her own tendencies to become frustrated, overwhelmed, and pessimistic. Remaining positive, using a language of hope, and communicating an expectation of success, are helpful. Therapists' use of humor also helps to maintain perspective and avoid the pitfalls of negativity.

- **Change- and goal-oriented.** The primary goal of treatment is positive change—new choices, perspectives, options, behaviors, coping skills, and relationships. Every aspect of treatment is oriented towards the growth and evolution of the child and family. It is crucial to have a conceptual framework that defines the process of change. Our theoretical framework is *revisit, revise,* and *revitalize.* This framework provides a structure for determining therapeutic goals and methods during the course of treatment. Specific goals for the treatment of child and family are determined. A four-step model guides treatment interventions: *assess → set goals → intervene (method) → reassess.* All interventions are based on specific goals for the child, parents, family system, and larger social network (e.g., extended family, community, and agency support).

- **Theory- and research-based.** Treatment is based on a variety of theories and paradigms. The underpinnings of the current model are trauma theory (posttraumatic stress disorder, neurobiology of stress and trauma); family systems theory (dynamic, structural, strategic approaches); attachment theory and research (internal working model, developmental research, disorganized-disoriented attachment, parent-infant bonding); experiential therapy (affective expression, process orientation); cognitive-behavioral treatment (cognitive rescripting, developing coping skills); and psychoanalytical theory (object relations).

- **Flexibility and adaptation.** The proposed three-stage model is merely a guide, a framework developed to make sense out of a complicated process. Actual treatment rarely follows such a predictable and linear sequence of events. The therapist must be flexible and spontaneous in knowing when to be directive or nondirective, respect or transcend defenses, confront or support, revisit past or orient toward future, follow structure or let go.

## The Sequence of Treatment

The treatment process involves ongoing reassessment. Each phase of therapy—revisit, revise, revitalize—follows a sequential format, incorporating the following clinical tasks and activities: *assess → goals → intervene → reassess*.

- **Assessment.** Initial assessment begins by reviewing the intake packet (Table 6) and speaking with parents, therapists, and caseworkers over the phone (families accepted at Evergreen Consultants are often from out of state). Assessment continues in the beginning of treatment with the child, parents, other family members, and hometown therapist. (Refer to Chapter 6 for a comprehensive review of assessment).

- **Goals.** Specific goals are established for the child and family based on evaluation and assessment (See page 122 for a list of goals).

- **Intervene (methods).** A variety of systematic procedures and interventions are introduced in order to facilitate positive change. Therapeutic methods *must* be based on clinical goals.

- **Reassess.** The therapist evaluates the results of interventions. Therapeutic outcomes occur on many levels: emotional, behavioral, cognitive, social, physical, moral/spiritual. The therapist asks the following question: "How did the child and parents respond to the specific intervention?" Based on a positive response, the therapist proceeds. Based on a negative response (e.g., resistance, severe anxiety, new information), a different therapeutic direction may be considered.

## Corrective Attachment Therapy

The treatment process recapitulates the physical, emotional, and interpersonal characteristics of secure parent-child attachment. That is, the ingredients found in parent-child relationships leading to secure attachment must also be available in the therapist-child relationship, which requires these necessary ingredients:

- **Structure.** The therapist provides a framework with limits, rules, and boundaries, similar to the clear and consistent structure provided by the sensitive and appropriately responsive ("healthy") caregiver. The structure is consistent and predictable, yet flexible, and changes in accordance with the child's developmental needs. For example, the therapist informs the child of the rules of therapy and/or the therapeutic foster home, and together they establish an explicit contract. The contract defines the responsibilities of the child and of the therapist, and the goals they hope to achieve.

- **Attunement.** The therapist is sensitively attuned to the child's needs, feelings, and internal working model. Based on a precise understanding of how the child thinks and feels, the therapist provides the message: "I know what you need in order to feel safe, and I will meet your needs." For instance, it is understood that the child's hostile and controlling demeanor is actually a defensive strategy designed to protect him or her from feelings of vulnerability, insecurity, and fear.

- **Empathy.** Just as the healthy parent cares deeply about his or her infant and child, the therapist conveys a heartfelt level of caring and compassion. The therapist remains proactive, empathic, warm, and caring, rather than reacting negatively to the child's overtly hostile or distancing behavior. The message conveyed is: "How sad that those terrible things happened to you; I'm sorry that you were treated that way; I understand what you feel and how much pain you must be in."

- **Positive affect.** Parents who foster secure attachments generally experience and exhibit positive emotional responses as they interact with their children. They become irritable and impatient on occasion, but are able to maintain their composure and model healthy coping styles. The therapist also maintains a positive demeanor, particularly when the child is acting out (e.g., verbal abuse, distancing, defiant). This prevents the reenactment of dysfunctional patterns, such as when the child directly or unconsciously "invites" a caregiver to be rejecting, angry, or abusive. The message to the child is: "I will not allow you to control our relationship in unhealthy and destructive ways." This provides modeling of positive affect, as well as appropriate boundary setting.

- **Support.** Parents of securely attached children provide a scaffold of support; i.e., a framework that props up or supports the child as development unfolds: the infant is held in the parent's arms, the toddler explores the environment but checks back with the parent for reassurance, and the preschooler plays independently with friends while still under the watchful eye of the parent. The therapist also provides a scaffolding of support tailored to the developmental needs and capabilities of the child. During the initial phase of treatment, the therapist emphasizes rules, expectations, and natural consequences. As therapy progresses, the focus shifts to reinforcing and celebrating the child's independent achievements.

- **Reciprocity.** A positive reciprocal relationship is one in which there is mutual influence and regulation. The securely attached child achieves a "goal-corrected partnership" with his or her parents, characterized by a sharing of control, ideas, values, feelings, plans, and goals. This parent-child alliance, achieved by approximately 4 years of age, is based on the successful completion of earlier stages of attachment. Marvin [1977] developed the "cookie test" procedure to access a child's ability to inhibit his or her own impulses for the benefit of the relationship:

  *Mother shows the child a cookie, tells her she can have it only after mother finishes a chore, places the cookie in sight but out of reach, waits three minutes, then gives the cookie to the child.*

Only 19% of 2-year-olds could wait (they cry, reach for the cookie, grab mother's leg in protest). Most securely attached 3- and 4-year-olds, however, were able to wait the three minutes. They could inhibit their impulses, taking the mother's needs and feelings into consideration. Children with attachment disorder, regardless of their age, fail the cookie test. They have not achieved the state of a goal-corrected partnership due to prior insecure and pathological attachment experiences.

The therapist guides the child toward a reciprocal relationship based on mutual respect and sensitivity. This begins with the establishment of a foundation for secure attachment (safety, protection, and basic compliance to a healthy caregiver). The child begins to learn to balance his or her own needs with those of others.

- **Love.** Secure attachment is synonymous with love; the ability to feel a deep, special, and genuine caring for and commitment to another human being. Children with attachment disorder are generally incapable of experiencing and demonstrating love toward themselves and others, because they lack the early attachment relationships necessary to create that feeling. Attachment therapy provides that relationship context and in doing so, guides the child to a place where love is suddenly an option. During the course of successful treatment, a child will commonly say for the first time, "I am feeling love in my heart."

This open expression of loving feelings occurs with parents holding their children "in arms," eye-to-eye, face-to-face, heart-to-heart. Children, however, will only feel safe in experiencing and expressing love if the parent(s) are available to receive that love. Thus, therapy also helps the parents become emotionally available.

## Holding Nurturing Process

This section will describe the rationale, goals, and functions of the Holding Nurturing Process (HNP), utilized as a therapeutic context with severely traumatized children with attachment disorder. As is the case with most clinical interventions, the HNP cannot be understood outside of the therapeutic milieu in which it occurs, or without considering the skillful implementation of the experienced, trained, and sensitive therapist. *The HNP is not a method or technique—it is a relationship context in which other methods are employed* (e.g., cognitive rescripting, teaching prosocial coping skills). The HNP is characterized by the safety and empowerment of the child. The therapist, in a position of authority, must provide a balance of structure and nurturance and respect the child's individual needs and choices. It is imperative to avoid establishing a complementary relationship of coercion and compliance, characteristic of prior unhealthy attachment relationships.

*Goals and Functions*

### HNP Promotes Attachment Behavior

The HNP creates an "in arms" experience that promotes secure attachment behavior. This is done in the infant-nurturing position on a comfortable sofa, face-to-face and eye-to-eye. It stimulates infant and parent attachment behaviors practiced by most cultures throughout the world. These species-specific behaviors have changed little over the past 100,000 years.

An important feature of attachment behavior is the eye contact, touch, and movement that occurs in the "in arms" position. Secure attachment forms when a consistent and appropriately available caregiver provides the infant/child with limits, love, eye contact, positive emotional responses, nurturing and safe touch, gentle movement, stimulation, and soothing. The mother and baby create a mutual regulatory relationship that includes reciprocity, synchronicity, pleasure, and safety. Children who experience maltreatment and multiple relationship disruptions miss this necessary mother-baby attachment context; i.e., they have not experienced fulfillment of many of these precisely evolved attachment-oriented needs. The HNP, in which the child is in the arms of the therapist and/or primary caregiver, simulates the original attachment relationship. The healing of the effects of these childhood deprivations can be best facilitated by utilizing this same "in arms" approach.

Biologically based attachment behaviors, although instinctual, must be activated by signs or signals from caregivers. These environmental triggers are referred to as social releasers. Social releasers that activate attachment behavior include eye contact, smile, gentle and firm touch, movement, and the provision of a safe and secure environment. In the HNP, the therapist and/or caregiver activates previously dormant attachment needs, feelings, and behaviors. This process also stimulates the old brain (brain stem and limbic system), the part of the brain that regulates attachment behavior, maternal instinct, self-preservation, and stress-related responses.

## HNP Reduces the Effects of the "Alarm Reaction" Caused by Maltreatment

The HNP reduces the effects of the severe and chronic stress response associated with maltreatment. Abuse, neglect, and traumatic disruptions in the caregiver-child relationship cause a portion of the limbic system (amygdala) in the brain to trigger the release of stress hormones. Norepinephrine increases the brain's overall reactivity, making the senses more alert. Dopamine mobilizes the body for action (fight or flight), increasing heart rate and blood pressure, and rivets attention on the source of the fear. This alarm reaction is designed to trigger automatically when danger or threat is sensed. Maltreated children, however, experience a chronic alarm reaction, resulting in symptoms of posttramautic stress disorder (hyperarousal, intrusive recollections, compulsive avoidance).

The Reticular Activation System (RAS) is a switching device between the old brain and the new brain. When we are emotionally charged or sense danger, the RAS shuts down energy to the cerebral cortex, allowing training and instinct to dominate. When we are calm and relaxed, the limbic system shuts down, allowing our higher brain center characteristics of creativity and logic to return. Maltreated children with attachment disorder perceive their emotional and physical survival to be constantly threatened. They are in need of a therapeutic environment that reduces their biological level of stress and fear. The HNP provides a context in which the child can be calmed, soothed, and relaxed, thereby reducing the release of stress-induced hormones. The child is better able to process information, pay attention, and utilize the neocortex for learning and change.

## HNP Promotes Self-Regulation

A primary parental function is to teach the child to self-regulate; i.e., to modulate and control emotions, impulses, and behavior. Initially, the attachment figure regulates the infant's arousal level by providing attuned and sensitive caregiver responses (e.g., soothes when overstimulated, stimulates when bored or lethargic). Over time, the securely attached child internalizes the parent's lessons and achieves self-regulation. Children with attachment disorder, however, do not learn this important lesson, and consequently display such symptoms as aggressive and sexual impulsivity, chronic hyperarousal, difficulty concentrating and staying on task, and inability to control emotions (e.g., temper tantrums).

The HNP provides a milieu in which the therapist facilitates the development of the child's self-control. In the safety and security of the "in arms" relationship, the therapist can choose to soothe (down-regulate) or stimulate (up-regulate) the child. Eventually, the child learns to manage his or her own internal reactions. For example, a child can be safely held "in arms" through a temper tantrum, learning to talk about anger and frustration as an effective coping skill. The child begins to learn self-control and to appreciate a newfound sense of mastery over previously out-of-control emotions.

## HNP Provides Necessary Structure

The HNP provides the structure necessary to meet the fundamental limit-setting needs of oppositional, angry, acting-out children. Children with attachment disorder are typically diagnosed with oppositional defiant disorder and, later, conduct disorder. They are "bossy," manipulative, and defiant, and require clear and consistent external boundaries. The HNP engenders a feeling of safety and security for children who are deficient in internal control. They are extremely anxious regarding their own angry and aggressive impulses, fearful of hurting others and/or themselves. The firm yet nurturing context of the HNP is reassuring. They begin to feel safe and secure with a caring, limit-setting, helpful adult.

Bath [1994] reviewed the therapeutic aspects of various physical containment methods with children. He concluded that even when the goal was to contain aggression safely, "its careful application can strengthen the relationship between child and caseworker and enhance the child's capacity to trust" [Bath 1994, p. 46].

## HNP Facilitates Corrective Experiences

Children with attachment disorder have an inordinate need for punitive and/or coercive control of others. This control orientation precludes the development of a positive rapport and working alliance, often resulting in treatment failures. The firm yet caring structure of the HNP diminishes the child's ability to manipulate or control the therapeutic process, which facilitates the development of respect and trust.

These children are extremely emotionally defensive. Although they experience sadness, worthlessness, rejection, and fear, they generally only allow the direct expression of anger. They feel empowered by demonstrations of anger and aggression. The HNP allows the child to identify, explore, and express a wide range of emotions. Chronic defenses are transcended in an atmosphere of safety and security, leading to favorable emotional and social outcomes.

The HNP reduces the reinforcing of negative behavior patterns. Children with attachment disorder are often reinforced for aggression and destructiveness. For example, they learn at an early age that anger works: if others retreat in response to their anger, they believe they have won; if others escalate in response to their provocation, they also believe they have won, because they have engaged others "on their terms." Certain caregiver and/or therapist responses, such as anger, helplessness, or emotional distance, serve to empower the child's negative patterns. In the HNP, however, acting-out behaviors are drastically reduced, and negative behaviors are not reinforced. Prosocial choices and actions are encouraged and learned.

The development of a new belief system (internal working model) is a primary goal of treatment. Children with attachment disorder operate with negative core beliefs: "I am worthless, defective, unlovable; caretakers are unsafe, unavailable to meet my needs; I must control others to survive." This negative working model develops as a consequence of pathological parent-child experiences (e.g., abuse, neglect, abandonment). The therapist-child relationship established in the HNP provides curative messages to the child. The child begins to internalize a model of authority and caregiving that is based on qualities of secure attachment.

The oppositional orientation of the child with attachment disorder results in chronic power struggles and control battles. The physical and emotional proximity, firm yet caring approach, and thorough understanding of the child's *modus operandi*, substantially reduces these power struggles. The child begins to feel safe with a therapist in a position of authority, and now has an opportunity to relate in a new way (affiliative, cooperative) in contrast to the old way (resistant, defiant).

The HNP provides a safe context to address and work through traumatic, painful, and frightening experiences. Children with attachment disorder have typically managed to deny, avoid, displace and/or dissociate from prior trauma, despite many prior treatment efforts. In our experience, working with children using the HNP leads to the establishment of a deep rapport, a sense of trust, appropriate risk taking, honest disclosure, emotional genuineness, openness to change, and receptivity to the therapist. Healing occurs when experiences that were previously frightening and adverse are dealt with in the safety, security, and acceptance of the "in arms" relationship.

Touching and being touched are fundamental to the human experience. Unfortunately, children with attachment disorder, as a result of physical and/or sexual abuse (traumatizing touch) or neglect (insufficient touch), are typically tactilely defensive and afraid of closeness and touch. In the HNP, the therapist is physically close to the child and is able to provide corrective touch—safe, caring, and nurturing. As therapy progresses, the child learns the difference between "bad touch" and healthy touch. Anxiety associated with physical closeness and touch decreases, and the child begins to feel comfortable and safe.

# Therapeutic Style

There are a wide variety of styles and demeanors displayed by therapists. Stylistic differences include intellectual-emotional, distant-engaged, proactive-reactive, didactic-experiential. Certain therapeutic styles are more effective with some populations, while different styles are more effective with others. In working with children with attachment disorder and their families, we have found that the most effective therapeutic style is *proactive, engaged,* and *experiential.* The components of effective therapeutic style and structure are listed below.

## Interviewing versus Reciprocity

The therapist who employs an interviewing style maintains an objective clinical distance. The goal is to obtain information by receiving answers to questions. The therapist who employs a reciprocal style becomes deeply involved and engaged with the child, in addition to obtaining information. Reciprocity between parent and child is a basic ingredient in the development of secure attachment. Thus, reciprocity in the therapist-child relationship is a basic ingredient in correcting attachment disorder. The reciprocal relationship with the child occurs on four levels:

- **Physical.** Eye contact, safe and nurturing touch, firm and caring structure of the in arms position, promote a positive physical connection.

- **Emotional.** Empathy, compassion, warmth, and caring are communicated to the child to set a curative and secure emotional tone. Feelings are encouraged and must be expressed in nondestructive, acceptable ways.

- **Intellectual.** Understanding the etiology and current manifestations of attachment disorder creates a deep connection; the therapist can have genuine empathy for the child's mind set, personal interpretations, and psychosocial sequelae. Children's sense of safety increase when they feel understood.

- **Interpersonal.** The relationship established is characterized by firm and caring authority, appropriate boundaries, mutual respect, and genuine involvement. The therapist provides a healthy role model of managing emotions, setting limits, and sensitivity to others, which was lacking in early attachment relationships.

## Proactive versus Reactive

Parents and helping professionals commonly express frustration regarding their inability to develop an alliance and rapport with children with attachment disorder. Yet a positive rapport and collaborative alliance are crucial to the success of therapy. Therapeutic styles can be either reactive or proactive. Therapists with a reactive style may feel helpless, angry, and frustrated, become rescuing or rejecting, and engage in nontherapeutic control battles. The therapist utilizing a proactive therapeutic style guides the child to mastery and success by maintaining a firm, consistent, and curative structure. The therapist sets the tone, determines the pace, and circumvents debilitating power struggles.

### Orchestrating the Tempo and Emotional Tone

The pace or tempo of music creates different moods: to build excitement, the tempo is increased; to create calm and a feeling of relaxation, the tempo is decreased. Variations in therapeutic style and demeanor promote similar changes in mood, emotion, and physiology. The therapist "ups the tempo" by modulating the tone and rhythm of his or her voice and communicating animation through facial expressions and eye contact. This is similar to the way a parent activates or "up regulates" an infant or toddler. Physical activity (e.g., kicking technique; see p. 132) also is a form of activation, simulating the infant's instinctual strategy to discharge tension. The goals of activation are acknowledging and expressing feelings; transcending such defenses as denial, avoidance, dissociation, and resistance; promoting active involvement and engagement with the therapist for children who are passive, withdrawn, or depressed; and initiating the first stage in the process of attachment and healing (tension-discharge-relaxation). The therapist also employs humor and conveys excitement to stimulate and activate the child. An experience of positive connection occurs when the therapist and child share a humorous and lighthearted moment together. Parental excitement (e.g., parent conveys joy to the child who accomplished a task) is a natural component of secure parent-child attachment. The therapist genuinely feels and conveys excitement to the child in order to reinforce positive choices and celebrate achievements.

The therapist "slows the tempo" by a soft, slow tone and rhythm of voice, gentle and soothing touch, and an accepting, empathic, patient attitude. This is also similar to the manner in which parents "down regulate" or soothe their young children. The goals of calming and relaxing the child therapeutically include reducing impulsivity and hyperarousal of the anxious and traumatized child, promoting a sense of comfort and safety, processing and integrating therapeutic experiences, and facilitating a secure and trusting connection, as the child discharges tension and relaxes with a therapist perceived as safe and protective.

## Managing Resistance

Children with severe attachment disorder are angry, oppositional and defiant, mistrustful, contemptuous of authority, and lack genuine and caring relationships. It is not surprising, therefore, that they are extremely resistant to therapy and therapeutic relationships. The majority of families that enter our treatment program have experienced a number of prior treatment failures. There are two basic patterns of resistance:

- **Active resistance.** The child overtly opposes, challenges, and avoids participation. These children can become physically and verbally aggressive, hostile, punitive, and coercively controlling. These resistive behaviors and attitudes are direct, transparent, and blatant.

- **Passive resistance.** The child's resistance is covert, often subtle, and more challenging to manage therapeutically. These children are commonly superficially compliant and solicitous, self-pitying, "helpless," and employ a variety of methods to manipulate and control (e.g., act "dumb," forget, leave tasks incomplete, not follow rules, respond slowly to questions and tasks).

There are a variety of therapeutic responses and strategies that we have found to be effective in managing and reducing resistance:

- **Remain proactive.** Therapist sets the tone for the relationship and the treatment process.

- **Neutral emotional response.** Therapist avoids negative emotional responses (e.g., anger, shock, punishment); does not get "triggered" by the child's attitudes and behaviors.

- **Avoid control battles.** Resistance has no power or influence when it "falls on deaf ears." The therapist does not engage in most control battles and power struggles. When the therapist chooses to engage in an issue of power and control, he or she must do so with firm and clear authority.

- **Doing more of the same.** Prescribing the symptom or current behavior "takes the wind out of the sails." For example, a therapist may encourage an oppositional child to look into his or her eyes and say loudly, "I don't want to do it your way"—the child is now complying with the therapist's request.

- **Acknowledging choices and consequences.** The child is given the message that resistance is a choice and has certain consequences. For example, a child may be told that he or she is free to choose to be noncompliant in therapy, and a dialogue ensues regarding all the possible consequences of that choice.

- **Convey commitment and perseverance.** These children have learned to "wait the other person out"; i.e., realizing they have succeeded in getting their way because others became frustrated, confused, or hopeless in dealing with them. The therapist gives the message, "I will persevere with you no matter how long it takes."

- **Do not resist the resistance.** The therapist allows the child to express resistance while remaining calm and projecting an air of indifference regarding the behavior (not the child). For example, the therapist may dialogue with a co-therapist (third-party conversation) about the child's resistant behaviors in a nonchalant way, which eliminates the power of resistance.

- **Identifying underlying emotions.** Resistance is generally fueled by fear and anxiety. Acknowledging and displaying genuine concern and compassion for the child's underlying fears of abandonment, abuse, and loss, switch the focus from superficial manipulation to meaningful emotions.

- **Providing empathy.** The therapist communicates the message, "I understand why you do not want to participate in therapy; if I had a background like yours, I would not trust anyone either; how sad that you were taught to be afraid and mistrustful." Children feel understood and validated and often reduce their defensiveness and resistance.

- **Positive frame.** The therapist encourages, validates, empowers, and guides the child to success and rapport. The message conveyed is, "I know you can do this; you can be a winner, not a quitter."

- **"Firing" the child.** It is often helpful to "fire" a child from therapy for a brief period of time. The message conveyed is, "You are not really working hard and maybe this kind of therapy is not for you." The tables are now turned; the therapist does not try to convince the child to participate; rather, the child has to earn therapy back—convince the therapist why he or she should reconsider. When faced with the consequences of their resistant attitudes and behaviors, children begin to experience inner conflict. Rather than expending energy on resistance, they begin thinking about the importance of change. A shift occurs from resistance to self-motivation.

## Contracting

Contracting with the child and parents is a basic and crucial component of the initial stages of treatment and also occurs throughout the treatment process (recontracting). Therapeutic contracts are generally verbal agreements regarding specific desired outcomes. Therapeutic contracts are established between therapist and child, therapist and parents, and parents and child

The child contracts with the therapist, for example, to follow the rules of therapy, learn to express feelings verbally, and to develop trust. The parents, for example, agree to learn effective parenting skills, reduce resentment toward their child, address their family-of-origin issues, and form a united team with the therapist. Parent-child agreements focus on expectations and consequences for the child's behavior, such as the necessity to learn to trust, cooperate, and be sensitive to others in the family. There are four benefits to therapeutic contracts:

- **Increases motivation.** There is a direct correlation between the strength of the treatment contract and the desire, commitment, and motivation to change [Levy & Orlans 1995a]. Contracting promotes the child's and parent's active involvement and ownership in treatment.

- **Provides structure.** Contracts are established regarding the goals of treatment and the general framework of treatment [Hughes 1997]. Specific goals regarding the child, parents, and family system are identified and agreed upon. Aspects of the therapeutic framework, such as "rules," expectations, and treatment format, are established. The roles and responsibilities of each participant (child, parents, and treatment team) are defined.

- **Promotes positive relationships.** Therapeutic contracts are relationship agreements that establish a "collaborative framework" for treatment [Heinssen et al. 1995]. They focus on a willingness to accept, comply with, and accede to behaviors and goals within the context of a relationship. Agreements between the therapist and child, for example, provide a context in which trust, reciprocity, and honest communication can occur. This forms the basis for a "goal-corrected partnership." When the child forms agreements with the therapist, he or she is saying, "Yes, I will," instead of the oppositional response, "No, I won't." As the child maintains his or her agreements, there is an increase in caring and sensitivity towards the needs and feelings of another person. Parent-child contracts provide the opportunity for caregivers to praise the child for maintaining an agreement, and begin a positive cycle of interaction.

- **Facilitates accountability and self-esteem.** Therapeutic contracts provide a vehicle to address accountability. When the child does not maintain his or her agreements, the therapist confronts and challenges the "breaking of the contract." Conversely, the therapist offers praise and approval to the child who maintains agreements. This reinforces the child's honesty and positive responsiveness in the relationship, and initiates the process of enhancing self-esteem. As the therapist attributes the child's success to his or her own efforts, feelings of inadequacy and negative self image are reduced; i.e., the child is now perceiving him or herself in a positive light.

Therapeutic contracts must be age- and stage-appropriate, based on the emotional, cognitive, and developmental capabilities of the child. The contracts are exclusively with the parents when treating children under the age of 5. Contracting is an ongoing therapeutic process. Agreements are discussed and evaluated in every session, and recontracting occurs as needed. Contracts are established on the basis of various therapeutic tasks and interventions. For example, the "rules of therapy" and the "child's list of problems" provide a vehicle for goals and contracts to be defined (see case examples on pages 139-146). The stages, objectives and responsibilities of therapeutic contracting are outlined in Table 12 [adapted from Heinssen et al. 1995].

## Therapeutic Goals

Effective therapy is contingent on the establishment of clear and concrete goals. Goals must be framed positively ("desired outcomes"), stated in specific behavioral terms, and be realistic and achievable. A sense of ownership regarding goals increases motivation for children and parents. Therapeutic goals for children, parents, and attachment are listed below:

*General Treatment Goals*

- Develop a therapeutic context that facilitates a constructive working alliance with the child and parents.

- Clarify parents' (or primary caregivers') level of commitment to the child.

- Encourage family members to identify their expectations and attitudes about therapy and, if pessimistic and limiting, to consider new possibilities.

- Encourage parents and child to personally invest in the treatment process; this promotes a genuine desire to change (contracting).

## Table 12. Therapeutic Contracting

1. **Define problem**

   *Goal:* Understand the nature of the problem and believe that it can be solved; therapist characteristics of empathy and optimism create atmosphere of hope and collaboration; stress child's and parents' active role in treatment as well as responsibilities of both family and therapist.

   *Therapist's responsibilities:* Provide a framework for understanding problems; create a safe atmosphere ("secure base"); introduce idea of collaboration; focus on problem solving that is achievable.

   *Child's and parents' responsibilities:* Develop an understanding of problems and need for treatment; develop a sense of ownership of ensuing treatment plan; agree to roles and responsibilities.

2. **Reframe problems as goals**

   *Goal:* Reduce perceptions of helplessness and hopelessness by establishing realistic goals. For example, treatment goals for the child with attachment disorder include enhanced self-concept, reduction of self-destructive behavior, increased trust, reciprocity, and emotional closeness with parents.

   *Therapist's responsibilities:* Mobilize child's and parents' cognitive and emotional resources by encouraging attainment of short-term goals (e.g., child's positive attitude and choices in session and in the therapeutic foster home).

   *Child's responsibilities:* Elaborate core beliefs (i.e., negative working model), emotional responses, and behavioral symptoms; commit to goals and "rules" of therapy.

   *Parents' responsibilities:* Collaborate with treatment team; openness to learning, dealing with personal issues, and receiving support.

3. **Psychosocial change**

   *Goal:* Specific tasks in session and at the therapeutic foster home are defined; "small victories," as each task is successfully completed, increase belief in competency and counteract feelings of helplessness (victim mind-set); create a "success momentum."

   *Therapist's responsibilities:* Propose methods and tasks for the child (e.g., first-year-of-life attachment cycle, inner-child metaphor, "rules" at foster home, direct verbal communication); explain reason for each method and task; provide support and positive reinforcement following accomplishment; address family issues (e.g., marital conflict, family-of-origin issues of parents, sibling conflict).

   *Child's and parents' responsibilities:* Express a personal commitment to goals, or express in honest way reluctance to work on goals; establish daily goals that are concrete, observable, and attainable; discuss and evaluate attainment (or nonattainment) of goals.

- Provide information about attachment disorder and the treatment process to reduce anxiety and educate.

- Increase expectation of success and sense of hope.

### Therapeutic Goals for Child

- Contain and reduce acting-out behavior.

- Identify and express emotions verbally in face-to-face interaction.

- Address prior attachment-related trauma in a direct and honest manner with the therapist and primary caregivers.

- Experience positive (safe, genuine, nurturing) interaction and attachment with significant others (therapists, caregivers, siblings).

- Direct anger and responsibility for maltreatment towards perpetrators, rather than towards self or current caregivers.

- Identify the source of his or her negative working model, understand the current manifestations, and develop a belief system that includes positive self-regard and a realistic perception of others.

- Interrupt the vicious circle of negative relationship patterns by experiencing trusting, supportive, and nurturing interactions.

- Reduce the emotional charge of past traumatic events and memories by dealing with those traumas in new and effective ways (empowerment, mastery, desensitization).

- Acknowledge and express a range of difficult emotions (anger, fear, sadness, pain, guilt, shame) in a direct and genuine manner with positive personal and interpersonal consequences.

- Take responsibility for one's own actions and decisions; learn to solve problems and make prosocial choices.

- Relinquish the extreme control orientation; rather than equating survival with vigilance and control, learn to allow safe and trusting relationships.

- Learn how to trust and whom to trust.

- Experience a constructive grieving process regarding the loss of attachment figures.

- Develop positive regard (trust, respect, caring) towards one's self; reduce self-contempt associated with the negative (internalized) self.

### Therapeutic Goals for Parents

- Develop a collaborative alliance with the treatment team.

- Explore family-of-origin issues and attachment histories.

- Improve communication and problem solving in their marital relationship; maintain a united and supportive team.

- Learn effective parenting attitudes and skills.

- Create a secure base for child.

- Develop and maintain support systems.

### Corrective Attachment Therapy Goals

- Enhance secure attachment behavior in parent-child relationship (eye contact, positive affect, nurturance, safe touch, need fulfillment, affection).

- Develop a reciprocal, goal-corrected, parent-child partnership; sharing of control, ideas, values, emotions, plans, and goals.

- Increase attunement, empathy, support, and positive affect from parent to child.

- Create a parental framework and structure with developmentally appropriate limits, rules, and boundaries.

- Enable parents to function as a "secure base" for child.

- Facilitate signs of secure attachment with parents:

    - Warm and affectionate interactions,

    - Seek comfort when in need,

    - Rely on for support and help,

    - Cooperative and compliant,

    - Check back in unfamiliar or threatening surroundings, and

    - Experience closeness and display relief after separation and upon reunion.

# 8

# Corrective
# Attachment Therapy
## Revisit, Revise, & Revitalize

## Revisit

The first stage of the healing process involves revisiting prior significant attachment and trauma experiences (e.g., separation, abandonment, abuse, neglect, multiple placements, and violence in the home). Many theorists and clinicians who deal with maltreated children with attachment disorder acknowledge the need to revisit early life events in order to identify emotional, cognitive, social and physical sequelae [Crittenden 1992b; Friedrich 1990; Gil 1996; James 1994; Pearce & Pezzot-Pearce 1997; Terr 1990]. Through the process of revisiting, the therapist gains valuable diagnostic information and understanding of the child's internal working model, emotional responses, and interpersonal patterns. The basic question is: "What was this child's unique response to prior life events, and how does this affect current and future attachments?" This stage focuses on four elements:

- Personal meaning and interpretation,

- A detailed review,

- Acknowledging and expressing affect, and

- Managing defenses.

### Personal Meaning and Interpretation

It is necessary to understand the child's subjective and idiosyncratic meaning of events; i.e., the child's personal understanding and interpretation of what happened. As discussed in Chapter 4, internal working models and core beliefs are formed in the early stages of life and become templates through which the child subsequently perceives self, others, and life in general. These core beliefs become a child's point of reference, a standard by which he or she measures all later experiences. The securely attached child develops a belief system with a positive orientation toward self ("I am good, worthy of love, competent"); caregivers ("they are trustworthy, safe, loving, and responsive to my needs"); and humanity ("people are basically good, life is worth living"). The belief system of the child with attachment disorder is oriented negatively toward self ("I am bad, unworthy of love, impotent"); caregivers ("they are untrustworthy, threatening, unloving, and unresponsive to my needs"); and humanity ("people are basically bad, life is not worth living").

What one believes to be true, based on early experiences, to a large extent governs emotions, actions, and choices. Attribution theory suggests that children construct beliefs about how and why things happen; i.e., different causal explanations or types of attributions [Kelley 1973; Peterson et al. 1993; Seligman et al. 1984]. The meaning the child assigns to important life events significantly determines subsequent psychosocial functioning and adaptation. For example, maltreated children routinely attribute blame and responsibility to themselves ("It was my fault that I was abused," "I must be bad because I'm treated bad"). Research has shown that subjective factors (i.e., personal meaning and perception) accounted twice as much as objective factors (e.g., injuries, force) to the severity of psychological distress in children who experienced violence and abuse [Weaver & Clum 1995; cited in Pearce & Pezzot-Pearce, 1997, p. 55].

The concept of learned helplessness also explains how children perceive themselves as inadequate, powerless, and defective, due to their inability to respond effectively during threatening and traumatic situations [Seligman 1993]. Our core beliefs become self-fulfilling prophecies; we draw situations to us that validate our beliefs. For example, the child with attachment disorder consciously and unconsciously creates social scenarios that justify and support his or her negative working model ("I will push you away until you reject me, which then reinforces my belief that I am not lovable"). Figure 4 depicts the vicious cycle of the child with a negative working model.

### A Detailed Review

The child is guided through a verbal accounting of events, the context in which events occurred, personal meaning, affective and somatic responses, and imagery. Honesty is encouraged to reduce denial, distortion, and dissociation. The child acknowledges and shares thoughts and feelings about painful events with the therapist. Timing, however, is crucial. This sharing must occur in the context of a safe and secure therapeutic relationship. All of the previously discussed elements of the HNP (healthy limits, eye contact, clear boundaries, safe touch, and secure base) create a therapeutic environment in which this honest sharing occurs. This detailed account includes the following components:

- Child's perceptions of events,

- Emotional and somatic reactions,

- Associated imagery and memory, and

- Responses of significant others.

There is a universal belief in the value of "truth telling" as part of a healing ritual [Herman 1992]. As the child shares his or her story honestly, often for the first time, in the accepting and empathic eyes of the therapist (and later the parent), a meaningful connection is created. Further, telling and retelling the story desensitizes the negative emotional charge associated with traumatic events. The acceptance and validation received from the therapist in the "in arms" experience also reduces the child's shame and guilt. Truth telling in the Holding Nurturing Process involves the following:

## Figure 4. Vicious Cycle of the Acting-Out ("Bad") Child

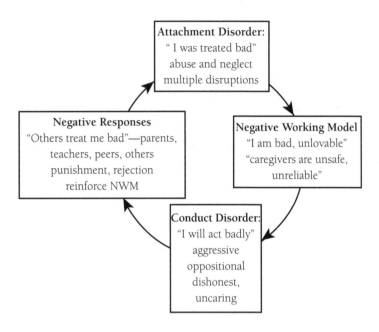

- Honest, often for the first time;

- Meaningful connection created "in arms";

- Desensitizes negative emotional charge; and

- Reduces shame and guilt.

### Acknowledging and Expressing Affect

More than 100 years ago, Breuer and Freud wrote, "Recollection without affect almost invariably produces no result" [cited in Herman 1992, p. 177]. The controversy over the efficacy of addressing affect and encouraging catharsis has existed for all these years. Some clinicians view catharsis as a necessary part of the therapeutic process [Moreno 1977; McGuire 1991; Nichols 1986], while others consider it unnecessary [Binstock 1973; Lewis & Bucher 1992]. Our clinical experience has demonstrated that, "if you can feel it, you can heal it." The release of repressed emotions that could not be safely expressed earlier (i.e., during traumatic events), is validating and empowering for the child. Again, the therapeutic context is crucial. The safety of the therapist-child relationship provides a "secure base" from which to explore painful and frightening emotions and memories.

### Managing Defenses

Defense mechanisms such as idealization, projection, displacement, dissociation, denial, and splitting are designed to protect the child from overwhelming and intolerable feelings and memories of traumatic experiences. Although these defenses are adaptive for survival, they have damaging long-term psychological consequences. For example, overidealizing an abusive or neglectful mother allows the child to avoid and deny the painful reality that she provided insufficient nurturance, love, and protection. Denial saves the child from having to experience the grief and rage that accompanies facing the truth. Dissociation is an automatic response that protects the child during trauma; the child splits off from the experience, no longer having to feel the pain, fear, or humiliation of the moment. Displacement enables the child to project onto foster or adoptive parents the feelings and perceptions that he or she actually has toward maltreating biological parents or others.

Defenses are acknowledged, confronted, and challenged in the safety of the HNP. This safe context enables the child to reduce defenses while telling his or her story and sharing emotions. This results in enhanced trust and a sense of mastery and empowerment.

## Revise

The second stage in the therapeutic process is revision. The focus now becomes both developing and revising: *developing* secure attachment patterns that were never previously established, and *revising* disturbed attachment patterns that were created early in life. All previous interventions have provided a foundation for assisting the child and parents to achieve the following goals:

- Construct new interpretations;

- Deal effectively with emotions;

- Develop secure attachments;

- Learn prosocial coping skills;

- Create mastery over prior trauma and loss;

- Develop a positive sense of self;

- Enhance self-regulation; and

- Address family systems issues (family-of-origin work with parents, marital issues, parenting skills, mobilizing community resources).

There are several basic issues to consider during this phase of treatment. First, during therapy it is difficult to separate cognitive, emotional, and social change. There is an ongoing process of weaving interventions that focus on various components of change. Second, cognitive rescripting (i.e., challenging the child's negative working model) is only effective when combined with positive emotional change. The emphasis must be on changing both thoughts and feelings, since one affects the other, in an ongoing and reciprocal manner. Third, the climate and context in which these changes occur is crucial. The therapist functions as a "secure base" for the child, providing safety, predictability, empathy, guidance, and support. It is common knowledge among mental health professionals working with maltreated and traumatized children that a major goal is always empowerment of the "victim." The therapeutic environment must provide a safe context for appropriate risk taking, honest disclosure, and emotional release, which leads the child from helplessness to empowerment and from inadequacy to mastery.

### Personal Meaning and Interpretation

The modification of the child's negative working model and maladaptive core beliefs is accomplished in a four-step process:

- **Identify and acknowledge beliefs.** Common beliefs of the child with attachment disorder are: *"I don't deserve love, I am helpless, I cannot trust anyone, I must control others to survive."* These beliefs are initially identified during the discussion of the first-year-of-life attachment cycle.

- **Therapist challenges negative working model.** Employing a variety of treatment methods (first-year-of-life attachment cycle, psychodramatic reenactment, inner-child metaphor, parent/child dialogues, and discussion of prior behavior) the child's belief system is questioned and challenged.

- **Child challenges negative working model.** Children with attachment disorder deny, blame, and idealize in an attempt to avoid painful realities. For example, a child will place a previously abusive or neglectful parent "on a pedestal," rather than face the truth about being unloved. Children must "own" and acknowledge the truth about their current belief systems before they can change it.

- **Repetition and rehearsal.** Acknowledgment and change requires many repetitive therapeutic experiences and numerous rehearsals of new ways of thinking. Repetition is particularly crucial with these children due to chronic denial and avoidance.

## Emotional Change and Healing

The word emotion comes from the Latin *ex movere*, which means "to move out of." Emotion literally refers to an impulse toward outward expression. As a result of the loss of primary attachment figures, maltreatment, multiple relationship disruptions, and repeated moves, children with attachment disorder experience intense negative emotions. The primary distressing emotions are anger, fear, sadness, and shame, which remain unresolved, stored in the body-mind system, and continually influence daily choices and behaviors. The treatment process must help the child develop masterful management over previously overwhelming feelings.

### The Emotional Body

Our bodies and minds are inseparable. Research in the field of psychoneuroimmunology has revealed an undeniable connection between physical and mental functions and its relationship with health and disease [Borysenko & Borysenko 1994]. Anger, fear, sadness, and shame are not merely emotions, they occur and are stored on a somatic level; i.e., in the body. These feelings do not vanish as a result of intellectual understanding. Although cognitive mediation is a necessary part of treatment, traumatically charged emotions must be directly addressed on a somatic level. For example, people experience emotions in their bodies: we "burn" with anger, "shake" and are "pale" with fear, become "heavy hearted" and "choked" with grief.

We are biologically programmed to experience and release emotions physically. Among certain primitive cultures, for example, lengthy dancing rituals facilitate the release of grief and loss, thereby avoiding physical and emotional repression. Infants instinctually express both painful and pleasurable emotions via physical action: kick their legs, wave their arms, arch their backs, move their heads from side to side, and erupt in piercing screams. Children with attachment disorder experience trauma, including painful emotion and memory, in their bodies. During treatment children are encouraged to express their feelings naturally (e.g., cry, kick, and yell) in a safe and secure environment.

The therapeutic technique of *kicking* taps into a child's natural tendency toward physical expression of emotions. While in the HNP, the child is asked to kick his or her legs up and down with heels touching the couch, as if swimming. Kicking serves several functions. For the child who is either depressed or detached, this technique activates emotional arousal. For example, a child who is dysphoric (sad, lethargic, disengaged) becomes physically and emotionally activated and increasingly involved in the therapeutic process. The sympathetic adrenal system is mobilized, and the muscles are primed for active expression. Conversely, this technique reduces levels of overarousal in hyperactive and severely anxious children. For example, children with symptoms of posttraumatic stress disorder (hypervigilant, intrusive recollections, chronic avoidance) experience a safe and nondestructive release of anger and aggressive impulses. Additionally, a physical activity such as kicking triggers the release of endorphins, which are naturally occurring hormones that promotes relaxation and a sense of well-being.

An instinctual response to fear and threat is to hold your breath. Another effective body-oriented technique is to encourage the child to breath deeply and fully. Deep breathing cleanses carbon dioxide from the body, and increases oxygen supply and available energy. It also promotes the release of genuine and deep-seated emotion.

Visualization techniques are also useful to help children identify and express their emotions. For example, the therapist asks the child the following questions: *"What color is your heart? Is it hard or soft? Where in your body do you feel your anger, sadness, fear, and shame? What physical action would match the emotion you are feeling?"* The child's response is diagnostic of his or her emotional state: *"My heart is black and hard as a rock. My stomach hurts and I have a headache. I feel like punching someone."* As therapy progresses the child's response is diagnostic of positive change in emotional states: *"My heart is pink and becoming softer. I feel more relaxed and my stomachache went away. I need lots of hugs."*

### Catharsis

Cathartic release of emotions has been found to be helpful for grieving losses [Scheff 1979], treating posttraumatic stress disorder and sexual abuse [Allen &

Borgen 1994], and in reducing and managing anger [Chandler 1993]. However, catharsis is useful in the treatment process only when integrated with other therapeutic techniques, when occurring within the context of a safe and healing relationship, and when combined with a cognitive component (e.g., cognitive rescripting).

Traumatic memories of infants and young children are organized on a nonverbal, sensory-based level (visual images; olfactory, auditory, or kinesthetic sensations; intense waves of feelings) [van der Kolk 1996]. Emotional experiences and strong, affectively charged memories are disconnected from language and rational thought. Though many of these incidents occurred before conscious memory, the feelings provoked are not forgotten. Cathartic methods provide access to these sensory-based memories.

The child with attachment disorder is a hostage to powerful emotions. Rage, fear, and unresolved emotional pain dictate his or her choices and actions. These children spend a great deal of time and energy in service to these emotions rather than the emotions being in service to them. Prior traumatic experiences have taught them to deny, avoid, repress, or dissociate from emotions. They must be taught to experience, process, and express emotions in a constructive way. A crucial part of this process involves emotional release, which is effective under the following conditions:

- The child expresses affect within the context of a corrective relational experience; i.e., the child internalizes acceptance, empathy, and support from the therapist.

- Shame is reduced as the child releases intense emotions, eye-to-eye, face-to-face, in an accepting environment.

- The therapist models constructive expression of his or her own affect; i.e., does not react to the child's emotions with anger, anxiety, or shock. Important messages are conveyed: "You are safe with me because I can handle your intense feelings. I will teach you how to handle your emotions, and also show you by my example."

### Tension-Discharge-Relaxation Cycle

There is a natural tendency in all living organisms to follow a cycle of tension, discharge, and relaxation (see Figure 5). When a child releases anger and/or emotional pain in the HNP the result is calmness, relaxation, and a new level of emotional openness and vulnerability. Defenses are diminished and the child is more capable of giving and receiving love and affection. At this point, parent-child intimacy and secure attachment is possible.

The tension-discharge-relaxation cycle is identical to the first-year-of-life attachment cycle in structure and function. In the first-year attachment cycle, the infant's level of tension increases due to needs and discomfort. This tension is discharged via physical release and signaling (crying, sobbing, kicking). The infant relaxes as the reliable and responsive caregiver provides need fulfillment and safety. This is the time that attachment is most likely to occur.

## Figure 5. Tension-Discharge-Relaxation Cycle

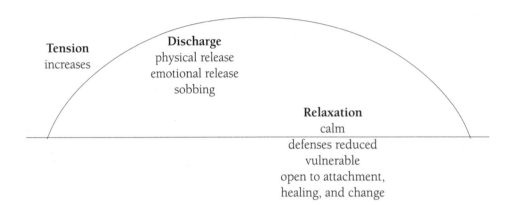

A similar process occurs therapeutically. The child's level of tension increases while confronting issues in the context of the HNP. This tension is discharged via physical and emotional release (sobbing, screaming, kicking). The child relaxes as the supportive and empathic therapist provides encouragement and safety. This is the time that the child is most open to positive change and attachment. Progress can be made with cognitive rescripting (modifying negative core beliefs) and emotional healing. Additionally, secure attachment between parent(s) and child can be facilitated at this time of emotional availability, reduced defensiveness, and relaxation.

Sobbing, continuous and deep crying, is unique to the human species, and is a basic form of release of tension resulting from emotional pain. "The process of mourning is ineffective to discharge the pain of loss unless it includes sobbing deeply" [Lowen 1988, p.185]. Nature has not only provided sobbing as a mechanism to discharge physical tension, but also as an entree to human connection. Sobbing typically follows the child's release of anger in the context of the HNP. As sobbing occurs, the child becomes increasingly more calm, vulnerable, and open to secure attachment.

### Mourning Losses

It is difficult but essential to confront losses of significant attachment figures in the child's life. Children with attachment disorder experience a variety of losses:

- **The loss of a primary attachment figure.** Child is removed from abusive or neglectful parents by social services;

- **The loss of a subsequent attachment figure.** Child must leave foster parent(s);

- **The experience of multiple losses.** Child who moves through a variety of foster homes or other out-of-home placements; and

- **The loss of never having a biological attachment figure after birth.** Child who is born drug exposed and immediately placed in foster care.

Children with attachment disorder typically avoid or deny their grief about losses by being chronically angry, controlling, or aggressive. Also, fantasies of revenge or ingenuine "forgiveness" are designed to avoid grief, sadness, and shame. Through the use of various therapeutic vehicles (inner-child metaphor, first-year cycle, psychodramatic reenactment, photos, and life books) the child can express his or her grief directly and honestly.

## Compliance

Children who are securely attached develop basic compliance in reference to the rules, standards, and expectations of their caregivers. This is the first step in the process of internalizing parental values and the development of morality and conscience. Since the context of secure attachment was unavailable for children with attachment disorder, they did not develop basic compliance with authority figures. Consequently, they became controlling, oppositional, "bossy," and engage in power struggles in relationships. Foster and adoptive parents, teachers, siblings, and peers, commonly report that these children are extremely difficult to get along with.

The attachment therapist provides the conditions associated with early phases of attachment (nurturance, structure, support, and attunement) in order to help the child learn basic compliance to authority. The therapist has to be willing and able to take control of a child who is personally and interpersonally out of control. The therapist, utilizing the Holding Nurturing Process, facilitates multisensory compliance: verbally, visually, somatically, and emotionally. The child's verbal responses, eye contact, body position, and feelings of safety and security, all reflect an increased level of compliance with the therapist. Desensitization occurs when the child's level of anxiety decreases as he or she experiences letting go of control with a safe adult. The following is an example of the development of compliance while in the holding nurturing position.

**Therapist:** "Do you want to know the rules of therapy?"

**Child:** "Yeah."

**Therapist:** "OK, you need to look in my eyes, turn towards me, and ask me the rules."

**Child:** (turns toward therapist, gazes into eyes) "Dr. Levy, would you tell me the rules?"

**Therapist:** "Sure, I would be glad to tell you the rules."

It is imperative to avoid becoming embroiled in power struggles with noncompliant children. *Paradoxical interventions* ("prescribing the symptom") are effective in avoiding such control battles and shifting the responsibility to the child. The more oppositional and controlling the child, the more effective these techniques are. The following example depicts an interaction with a highly resistant, angry, and oppositional child.

**Therapist:** "Do you want to know the rules of therapy?"

**Child:** "I don't care about your rules and I don't even want any therapy."

**Therapist:** "Wow, I can understand why you wouldn't want therapy, it never worked for you before. Maybe you should stay the way you are forever."

**Child:** (pauses, surprised, doesn't know what to say) "You're right, I don't believe in this therapy crap."

**Therapist:** "Gee, I'm sorry it didn't work out for you."

**Child:** "Yeah, nothing ever works out for me."

The example above demonstrates how the therapist circumvents a power struggle by combining empathy (*"I understand…"*) and paradox (*"maybe you should stay the way you are forever"*). A shift occurs; rather than fighting with the therapist for control, the child begins sharing his hopelessness, pessimism, and sense of failure. The child is communicating honest emotions rather than battling for power and control. The door is now opened for constructive and productive work in therapy (new choices, increased compliance, contracting).

## Trust

A hallmark of attachment disorder is lack of trust in caregivers and self. The child's core belief (negative working model) about caregivers is *"I cannot trust that caregivers will keep me safe, fulfill my needs, or love and value me."* The child's core belief about self is: *"I cannot trust that I will ever be safe; my needs are not valid; I do not trust that I am capable, lovable, or worthwhile."* Children with attachment disorder begin therapy not trusting the therapist, their current caregivers, or their ability to improve.

A salient developmental task of the first year of life is to develop basic trust in the context of a secure attachment relationship. Infants who are securely attached learn that helplessness and vulnerability are tolerable physical and emotional states. They trust their caregivers to provide safety, protection, and need fulfillment. The infant and toddler with insecure, disorganized attachment learns that helplessness and vulnerability are not tolerable states. Insufficient or nonexistent parental care results in a lack of trust and high levels of anxiety associated with helplessness. As development unfolds, the child becomes increasingly more angry, controlling, and oppositional, to defend against feelings of intense helplessness and vulnerability.

The first step in the therapeutic process is to assist the child in acknowledging his or her lack of trust. The following dialogue exemplifies the beginning stages of trust development, employing the "story of attachment during the first year of life" (see Case Example on p. 139).

**Therapist:** "Did your birth mother take good care of you and meet your needs?"

**Child:** "No, she wasn't around very much, and anyway she was drunk a lot."

**Therapist:** "So did you learn to trust her, and did you learn to trust that adults would take good care of you?"

**Child:** "No, I don't trust anybody."

**Therapist:** "Is that why you don't trust your forever mom and dad (adoptive parents)?"

**Child:** "I guess so."

**Therapist:** "Did you ever know this before—why you don't trust anybody?"

**Child:** "No, I never did know."

**Therapist:** "Look into my eyes and tell me you don't trust me or anybody."

**Child:** (looks directly into therapists eyes) "I don't trust you, Mike."

The child, in the example above, is allowing honesty and vulnerability with the therapist in the safety of the holding-nurturing context. She is honestly sharing her lack of trust in caregivers, eye-to-eye, "in arms." The key ingredients of early secure attachment, as discussed previously, are now available in the therapist-child relationship, and the child begins the initial stage of trust development.

## Prosocial Coping Skills

Children with attachment disorder have internalized antisocial values, belief systems, and patterns of relating: dishonesty, coercion, aggression, mistrust, betrayal, selfishness. Treatment must provide an opportunity to learn prosocial coping skills so that they can function successfully in families and in society. These children lack the ability to identify and manage emotions, communicate honestly, regulate impulses, and to solve problems effectively. Teaching prosocial coping skills not only reduces acting out, but also builds self-confidence and self-esteem. The child feels a sense of mastery as he or she learns to curb impulses, control anger, and solve problems effectively. Further, the child receives positive feedback from others (parents, siblings, friends, teachers), which reinforces positive behavior and enhances self-esteem.

### Communications Skills

Research has shown that maltreated children with attachment disorder are least likely to identify and understand their feelings, compared to children with other psychosocial disorders [Beeghly & Cicchetti 1994]. Thus, the first step is to help the child "know" what he or she is feeling. The child is asked to chose among four feelings ("are you feeling *mad, sad, scared,* or *glad*")? Next, communication skills are taught in the context of the HNP: empathic listening, "eye-to-eye, face-to-face" verbal sharing of thoughts and feelings. The child is encouraged to practice honest verbal communication, rather than acting out emotions physically and socially.

### Self-Control

The ability to regulate and control one's impulses, emotions, and level of arousal is learned in the context of the secure attachment relationship during the first three years of life. A child with attachment disorder failed to master this stage-specific task, due to the lack of healthy role models and internalization. The therapist provides a model and encourages the child to practice self-control skills: think before taking action, time out to calm down, positive self talk, verbal expression of feelings, asking for feedback and help, monitoring the body for cues of tension and emotions, mind-body relaxation techniques.

Anger management skills are particularly important to learn, as these children act out in aggressive and violent ways (e.g., temper tantrums, assaultive behavior, destruction of property). They rationalize their loss of control with no regard for the feelings of others. The therapist teaches the child self-control skills:

- Identify anger prior to acting impulsively;

- Express the anger verbally and nonabusively;

- Develop and maintain agreements (contracts) regarding nonviolence; and

- Practice these skills in various settings (treatment, family, school, peers).

### Problem Solving

Children with attachment disorder are unable to manage conflict (internal or interpersonal) and solve problems because of chronic emotional turmoil and their refusal to reach out for help. Thus, learning to solve problems effectively involves both the ability to utilized internal resources and to turn to others for guidance and support. Children learn these skills and practice them in various settings:

- Identify a specific problem;

- Brainstorm possible options and solutions;

- Communicate with a "trusted" significant other about alternatives;

- Make a list of pros and cons, choices, and consequences; and

- Evaluate the results of the particular solution chosen.

## Therapeutic Methods

A number of therapeutic methods, described in detail (with case examples) below, provide the structure to achieve treatment goals:

- First-year-of-life attachment cycle,

- Child's self-report and list,

- Rules of therapy,

- Review of historical information,

- Inner child metaphor, and

- Psychodramatic reenactment.

### First-Year Attachment Cycle

This intervention is used in the initial phase of treatment and includes an explanation of the attachment cycle that occurs in the first year of life. A salient psychosocial task during the first year of life is the development of basic trust in reliable and appropriately responsive caregivers. This therapeutic intervention focuses on the correlation between need fulfillment, basic trust, and the establishment of secure attachment. The goals of the first-year-of-life attachment cycle intervention include the following:

- To educate the child about early attachment experiences and their psychosocial consequences. This provides a cognitive frame; the child develops an understanding of his or her thoughts, feelings, and behavior, both historically and currently.

- To provide the message to the child: "I understand you and can help you; lack of good care was not your fault; you have responded in an adaptive and understandable way to unfortunate circumstances (abuse, neglect, abandonment)." This is a positive reframing and normalizing experience for the child.

- To set the stage for cognitive-affective revision, the development of positive regard for self and others, and the working through of emotional trauma.

- To initiate a therapeutic relationship, based on genuine engagement, cooperation, and empathy.

Using a diagram (see Figure 1 on p. 35) and discussion while in the HNP, the attachment cycle is explained, with variations in age-appropriate language, as follows:

> The first-year-of-life attachment cycle involves four stages: need, arousal, gratification, and trust. The infant is helpless, has very basic needs, and must depend on caregivers to meet those needs. (The child is asked to describe a baby's needs.) The infant signals that he or she has needs and/or discomfort via arousal (cry, scream, kick). The reliable and responsive caregiver gratifies those needs (nourishment, eye contact, smile, touch, rocking), which leads to secure attachment and the development of basic trust. When the caregiver does not gratify the baby's basic needs (or there is no consistent caregiver available), insecure attachment occurs; i.e., the infant does not learn to trust self or caregivers.

The child is told about the consequences of insecure attachment: anger; inability to trust and be emotionally close; discomfort with touch; perceives self as defective and caregivers as unsafe; inordinate need to control others ("bossy," manipulative); and lacks self-control. The child is asked to evaluate him or herself in reference to these prior traits: *What happened in your early family life? Were your needs met? Did you learn to trust caregivers?*

## Case Example: First-Year Attachment Cycle

Angie was sexually abused by her alcoholic birth father from ages 5 through 12. She had virtually no attachment to her birth mother. She entered the foster care system when she was 12. She became pregnant at age 15 by a 32-year-old man who took no responsibility before or after the birth of her daughter, Annie. Annie was born drug exposed, and was placed immediately with her 87-year-old great-grandmother. She could not be soothed, screamed every night for two years, and had a variety of "caregivers" who helped the great-grandmother. She was reunited with birth mother at age 2; for seven months she suffered severe neglect and sexual abuse (mother's boyfriend was a registered sex offender). Social Services placed Annie in a foster home where she remained for several years; the foster parents planned to adopt her, but relinquished after deciding she was too aggressive and disturbed. After two brief additional foster placements, Annie, age 6, was placed with the current parents on a foster-adopt arrangement.

Annie was 7 years old at the time of treatment. Her current parents reported that Annie displayed the following symptoms: cruelty to animals, violence and aggression, self-mutilation, enuresis and encopresis, constant lying, lack of remorse, and behaviors that were manipulative, oppositional, controlling, and sexually provocative. The parents were frustrated and demoralized. The mother was experiencing health problems, was angry and "numb," and resented her husband for not supporting her and understanding Annie's problems. The father was angry at both his wife and Annie and had considered leaving the marriage. They reported that prior therapy attempts had failed because Annie constantly lied.

**Therapist:** "This is called the circle of the first year of life. Can you look into my eyes and tell me what it is called?"

**Annie:** "The circle of the first year of life." (maintains eye contact on the second try)

**Therapist:** "I'll draw a circle. Here it is. Not perfect, a little crooked."

**Annie:** "No one's perfect, except the Lord!"

**Therapist:** "OK. There's the four parts of this circle." (draws four lines on the circle) "It begins when a baby is born. What can a baby do?"

**Annie:** "They can't do nothing."

**Therapist:** "That's right, babies are very helpless. But they do have needs. What do little babies need?"

**Annie:** "Food."

**Therapist:** "That's right, food. What else?"

**Annie:** "Love."

**Therapist:** "Yes, love; what else does the baby need?"

**Annie:** "A home."

Annie, previously resistant and agitated, is now calm, engaged in the task, and even enjoying herself (laughter). She seems interested in the first-year-of-life story. The therapist and Annie make a list of babies' needs: "food, love, a home, milk, eye contact, touch, movement (rocking), care, smiles from caregivers." The therapist explains the importance of eye contact, smiles, loving touch, and other caregiver-baby behaviors, as they relate to secure attachment. Annie is attentive.

**Therapist:** "So how does the little baby tell the mother or father she has needs when she can't talk?"

**Annie:** "Cry."

**Therapist:** "That's right. Is it a little cry or a big cry?"

**Annie:** "A loud cry!" (screams out in a loud babylike cry)

**Therapist:** "Very good. You sound just like the baby who has many needs." (Annie smiles, enjoying the "game.")

The therapist explains that babies use various signals of arousal (crying, screaming, kicking, facial expression) to let caregivers know they have needs and/or discomfort. Annie participates eagerly in the dialogue.

**Therapist:** "Now, let's say the baby has a really good mom or dad, who comes along and takes care of the baby's needs. What does that mom or dad do?"

**Annie:** "Feeds it."

**Therapist:** "Yes, and rocks, holds, gives loving touch and eye contact and smiles. What do we call this: can you sound it out?" (writes *gratify* on paper)

**Annie:** "G-R-A-T-I-F-Y."

**Therapist:** "Very good. You sure have a smart brain. Gratify means to take care of, to meet the baby's needs."

Annie maintains good eye contact with the therapist during this dialogue, but seems to be getting more agitated and anxious. Emotions and memories may be provoked by the discussion of caregivers.

**Therapist:** "So, the baby has needs, expresses those needs by crying and other signals, the mom or dad take good care of the baby. What does the baby feel towards that mom or dad?"

**Annie:** "Cared for?"

**Therapist:** "That's right, what else does that baby feel?"

**Annie:** "Happy."

**Therapist:** "Yes, what else?"

**Annie:** "Loved."

**Therapist:** "That's right. Is that baby feeling safe?"

**Annie:** "Yeah, safe."

**Therapist:** "And there is a special feeling that the baby has toward the person who is taking good care of her. I'll write it down. Can you sound it out?" (writes *trust* on paper)

**Annie:** "T-R-U-S-T."

**Therapist:** "Very good! That baby learns to trust the mom or dad who takes care of her in a good and loving way."

The therapist explains that baby learns to trust caregivers, self ("my needs are OK"), and the world in general ("life is good; I feel safe"). The therapist also explains how trust leads to the perception of caregivers as safe, reliable, and loving. Annie is still engaged and responsive.

**Therapist:** "Now, how did this circle work out for you when you were a little baby?"

**Annie:** "I wasn't taken care of. I had to crawl in crap. There was cat crap all over the house."

**Therapist:** "How do you know this? Do you remember or did someone tell you about it?"

**Annie:** "My mom told me." (referring to current pre-adoptive mother)

**Therapist:** "Yes, it is true. Let's talk about what else happened to you and how it made you think and feel. You had a birth mom, right?"

**Annie:** "Yes, Angie; she threw me away. She put me up for adoption."

**Therapist:** "Angie was only 16 years old when you were born. She didn't take good care of herself when you were in her tummy, and after you were born."

**Annie:** "She took drugs."

**Therapist:** "Yes. And you had to go to your great-grandmother's house a lot. She was old but tried to take care of you. What do you think you were feeling and learning back then?"

**Annie:** "I don't think I ever learned how to trust." (begins to cry) "I don't trust at all."

A dialogue ensues regarding lack of trust in and anger towards caregivers. Annie admits that her anger and mistrust toward pre-adoptive parents is really meant for her birth mother. She begins to talk about her feelings ("mad, scared, sad") and self-contempt ("I feel like a bad baby"). The parents (observing on a TV monitor in another room) were pleased, and later reported that Annie had not been cooperative or verbally responsive in prior therapy.

## Case Example: First-Year Attachment Cycle

Megan spent the first 3 1/2 years of her life in a Romanian orphanage, where she was the victim of physical abuse, neglect, and multiple caregivers. She assumed the role of caretaker with other children as a survival strategy. An American couple adopted her at 3 1/2; she began to act out aggressively as soon as she arrived at their home. The family started our program when Megan was age 10, following several prior unsuccessful treatment attempts.

**Therapist:** "What does a baby need?"

**Megan:** "A bottle, warmth, attention, diapers, and a blanket." (appears interested and attentive for first time during treatment)

**Therapist:** "That's right, and let's talk about what else babies need and then what happens."

Megan and therapist engage in a half-hour dialogue about the attachment cycle: needs → arousal → gratification → trust. Megan is engaged in the conversation, cooperative, and emotionally genuine.

**Therapist:** "So, did you learn to trust good caregivers?"

**Megan:** "No, I was in the orphanage. I didn't trust anyone."

**Therapist:** "You were a normal little baby with needs. Who took care of you?"

**Megan:** "No one." (cries)

**Therapist:** "What did you learn?"

**Megan:** "I learned to lie."

**Therapist:** "If you could not trust adults to take care of you, what did you do?"

**Megan:** "I wanted to be bossy."

**Therapist:** "You couldn't even be a little girl? How did that make you feel?"

**Megan:** "Sad." (cries, genuine sadness for first time)

Megan began to sob and talked about holding in her sadness for a long time. Next, she talked about being afraid ("someone will hurt me") and compensating for fear via aggression.

**Therapist:** "You have lots of scared feelings too?"

**Megan:** "Yes." (maintaining good eye contact)

**Therapist:** "What do you do with all that scared?"

**Megan:** "Hurt people; I let it out on other people. That's not good!"

The first-year-of-life attachment cycle exercise was an effective vehicle for Megan to become genuinely involved and emotionally available in the initial stage of treatment. Information gleaned from this experience was integrated into a treatment contract (e.g., learn to be less "bossy," more honest about feelings, verbal communication rather than aggression).

### Child's Self-Report and List

An initial intervention with the child in the context of the HNP is to ask how he or she perceives personal and family problems. The therapist and child develop a "list of problems" based on the information that the child provides. The goals of this therapeutic task include the following:

• Sending the message to the child: "I value and want to hear your ideas and opinions."

- The child and therapist working together cooperatively, which sets tone for honesty and reciprocity in the therapeutic relationship.

- Emotions are often provoked as the child discloses perceived problems. The therapist's empathic response provides comfort, encourages further disclosure, and creates a climate conducive to a "secure base" for the child.

- The therapist's interaction with the child provides a model for the parents, as they observe from another room (one-way mirror or closed-circuit TV). The parents become more optimistic as they see their child interacting in an honest and cooperative manner.

### Case Example: Child's Self-Report and List

Adam, age 7 1/2 at the time of treatment, spent his first two years in Russia with his birth mother and experienced physical abuse, neglect, and negligible attachment. Although he has been in the adoptive home for five years, he has refused to form attachments to the parents. Despite prior therapy, he continued to be rageful, oppositional, destructive, deceitful, cruel to pets, self-destructive, and displayed no remorse.

**Therapist:** "We will make a list. What's your number-one problem?"

**Adam:** "Telling the truth."

**Therapist:** "Telling the truth or telling lies, which is your problem?"

**Adam:** "I tell lies."

**Therapist:** "OK, what's your next problem?"

**Adam:** "Can you do some with me?"

**Therapist:** "Sure, but first I want you to tell me your ideas, OK?"

**Adam:** "OK. Forgetting, I keep forgetting things."

A reciprocal relationship is developing. The therapist invites Adam to honestly disclose his perceptions; Adam asks for the therapist's help ("Can you do some with me?"). Eventually, Adam lists 12 problems that his parents verified as accurate:

*Telling lies.*

*Forgetting things.*

*Picking on sister and brother.*

*Don't ask for help.*

*Cheating.*

*Bossy.*

*Don't mind Mom and Dad.*

*Lots of mad, sad, scared.*

*Stealing.*

> *Break things.*
>
> *Hate and torture myself.*
>
> *Torture my family.*

The goals were achieved: Adam was honest, worked cooperatively with the therapist, and began to experience and share genuine emotions as he discussed his problems. Again, the parents felt more optimistic as they observed their child's efforts. The "list" was translated into a treatment contract and served as the foundation for subsequent therapy.

### Rules of Therapy

The child is told the rules of therapy while in the HNP. Each rule is explained and discussed. Rules become contracts for specific behavior on the part of the child and the therapist. Rules also provide structure, necessary for developing a feeling of safety and security. Listed below are the rules of therapy:

- **Eye contact is essential in all therapist-child dialogues.** Eye contact is a crucial component of secure attachment.

- **Much of therapy occurs "in arms."** We demonstrate the HNP to the child and explain why we use this procedure.

- **"We will not work harder on your life than you."** The child is told that the treatment team will work hard to provide help, but it is the child's responsibility to work the hardest. A discussion ensues about personal responsibility and the desire to change.

- **The Three Rs.** We share our philosophy that all children are expected to be respectful, responsible, and resourceful.

- **"I don't know" is not an acceptable answer.** Children generally say, "I don't know" as an avoidance technique. Two alternative responses are acceptable: the child can ask for help from the therapist; children with attachment disorder have difficulty asking for help, or the child can offer his or her best guess, which encourages introspection and resourcefulness.

- **Verbal responses must be expressed in a timely fashion.** A form of interpersonal control and passive aggression is making others wait for a response. Instead, we encourage quick, eye-to-eye, honest disclosure.

- **No physical violence.** Most of these children have been physically abused and/or witnessed violence. Consequently, they act out abusively and aggressively. They are encouraged to express their anger verbally. A mutual contract is established between the therapist and the child, to protect both from harm.

### Case Example:  Rules of Therapy

Adam, age 7 1/2 (previously described in the Case Example on p. 144) was told the rules of therapy during the first treatment session:

**Therapist:** "Are you ready to hear the rules of therapy?"

**Adam:** "OK."

**Therapist:** "If I tell you the rules, will you want to follow them? Because I hear that you usually don't follow rules."

**Adam:** "Yeah, I will."

**Therapist:** "Great, so look in my eyes and say, 'Dr. Levy, please tell me the rules.'"

**Adam:** "Dr. Levy, please tell me the rules." (good eye contact, strong voice)

Reciprocity and contracting have begun. Initial stages of rapport building occurs in therapist-child relationship. Adam is compliant and relaxed in the safety of the HNP.

**Therapist:** "First rule, good eye contact when we talk together. Do you know why that's important?"

**Adam:** "It's not polite if you don't look in someone's eyes?"

**Therapist:** "You're right, but there are other reasons too. I'll tell you more about eye contact later, when we talk about how babies feel close and safe with moms and dads. Did you feel safe when you were a baby?"

**Adam:** "In Russia?"

**Therapist:** "Yes, in Russia."

**Adam:** "I don't remember who my Mom was." (starts to cry, becomes agitated)

Going over the rules became a springboard for the identification and expression of emotions (sad, mad, scared) and of Adam's negative core beliefs. Contracts were developed that specified therapeutic and family goals. A positive therapeutic relationship was established. The parents were more hopeful and optimistic as they observed the interaction. Due to prior treatment failures, they were feeling hopeless and considering relinquishment.

### Review of Historical Information

As noted in Chapter 6, historical information is reviewed as a part of assessment and treatment planning. It is also therapeutic to review with the child relevant documents, such as social history, social service records, police reports, life books, and photographs.

Although some mental health professionals believe this is threatening and may retraumatize the child, our experience does not confirm this. We have found that honest and open discussion of the specifics of maltreatment and compromised attachment is crucial to the healing process, and that most children are capable of effectively dealing with these issues with proper guidance and support.

The goals of reviewing historical information together include the following:

• Reduces avoidance and denial regarding the child's traumatic early history,

- Revises misinterpretations of prior events,

- Creates a positive rapport and collaborative therapeutic alliance, and

- Provides a springboard to address the child's emotions, memories, and interpretations necessary for later therapeutic progress.

## Case Example:  Letter

Eric was 10 months old when social services removed him from his 16-year-old birth mother due to neglect. He was placed in a foster home, but after two years he was moved to another foster home because of his aggression and self-mutilation. He was adopted at age 5, continued oppositional and aggressive behaviors, and would not attach to adoptive parents. He began our program at age 10, after three prior unsuccessful treatment efforts, including hospitalization and a group home.

Eric was minimally cooperative and engaged in the therapy process until he (and the therapist) read a letter written years earlier by his first foster mother. The mother wrote, "He was out of control, picked his nose until it bled, then smeared the blood on our walls. I just couldn't keep him anymore." Eric began to sob as he and the therapist read the letter together. He talked about hating his birth mother for "giving me up," and hating himself because "I'm not a keeper." He began to work hard in therapy, and later apologized to his adoptive parents for "taking my anger out on you."

## Case Example: Photo

Ashley, age 7 at the time of treatment, was the victim of abuse (physical and sexual), neglect, and multiple disruptions. She was removed by social services from her drug-abusing birth parents at age 3, placed with an aunt, then in a shelter and foster home. She was adopted at age 6 and continued to act out aggressively and sexually, including behaving violently towards a younger sibling.

Ashley was resistant for the first several days of therapy; she would laugh, close her eyes, and refuse to talk. On the third day, she was shown a photo of her birth parents, while in the HNP. She expressed anger, then sadness ("they gave me away"), and began to talk genuinely about being abandoned. Eventually, she said to her adoptive mother, "I'm afraid you will give me away too." As her mother held her close, they cried together. This initiated the process of attachment between mother and daughter.

## Case Example: Social Service Records

Danny, age 10 at the time of treatment, was severely neglected by his substance-abusing birth mother and grandmother. His birth father had abandoned the family. Danny was also physically abused and witnessed violence in the home during "parties." He had three foster placements and two failed adoptions prior to entering the current adoptive family at age 6. Danny was diagnosed with oppositional defiant disorder and attachment disorder; he was manipulative, dishonest, angry, and refused to form an attachment to his adoptive parents.

The therapist and child read social service reports together, while in the HNP:

**Therapist:** "These were complaints to social services from people who didn't like how your birth mother treated you. This was the first of many complaints in September 1981. How old were you then?"

**Danny:** "I was only three months old."

**Therapist:** "So bad treatment started when you were three months old?"

**Danny:** "Yes."

**Therapist:** "It says here that your birth mother would go out partying and leave you with your grandmother, who was drinking and did not take good care of you."

**Danny:** "Can I see?" (looks closely at the report)

**Therapist:** "It says that your birth mother left you from Monday morning until Wednesday night."

**Danny:** "Jeez!"

**Therapist:** "What does a three-month-old baby need?"

**Danny:** "Love."

**Therapist:** "From who?"

**Danny:** "My mom."

**Therapist:** "Of course; all babies need their mom."

**Danny:** "I was three months old and my mom was dumping me already!"

**Therapist:** "What a start you had. How did that make you feel about yourself?"

**Danny:** "I felt like people dumped me all the time, like I was a piece of garbage."

Danny is deeply involved in the dialogue provoked by the social service records. His negative working model ("I felt like a piece of garbage") is surfacing, and he is honest and open with the therapist. Parents later reported being surprised by his level of honest disclosure and vulnerability.

**Therapist:** "Here it says that your birth mother was intoxicated, gave you watermelon filled with liquor, and you received a severe sunburn in a park. She was told to get counseling in order to keep her children. She either missed her appointments or came to counseling drunk. What does that tell you?"

**Danny:** "Alcohol and drugs were more important than me." (starts to cry)

**Therapist:** "So what happened?"

**Danny:** "They took me away."

Danny is facing the reality that birth mother made a choice; she chose drugs and alcohol rather than her child. This initiates the process of cognitive rescripting ("I was not a bad baby; my mother made bad choices"), and sets the focus on choices and consequences.

**Therapist:** "What are you thinking and feeling about this information? How has this affected your life?"

**Danny:** "I have been acting like her; saying I don't have to do things and I don't want help!"

**Therapist:** "If you continue to make these kind of choices, how will your life work out?"

**Danny:** "I'll end up just like her, or in jail."

**Therapist:** "Is that what you want for your life?"

**Danny:** "No."

**Therapist:** "What do you want to do about this?"

**Danny:** "I better get to work." (crying, gazing at therapist)

This intervention accomplished several goals: his negative working model and genuine emotions surfaced, a positive therapeutic relationship developed, a contract was established, and he was motivated to work hard in therapy.

### Inner Child Metaphor

A metaphor is the application of a word or phrase to something that it does not apply to literally, in order to indicate a comparison with the literal usage. Although there is no literal "inner child," this concept provides an effective framework to therapeutically address early life perceptions and emotions. Other clinicians have described and utilized this concept. It has been referred to as the divine child [Jung 1969]; true self [Miller 1983; Winnicott 1985]; child within [Whitfield, 1987]; and the real self [Horney 1959; Masterson 1985; cited in Whitfield, 1987, p. 1].

The child, while in the HNP, is gently guided back to an earlier time in life, and is encouraged to visualize him or herself as that little baby or child. The goals of revisiting the inner child include the following:

• To facilitate the identification and understanding of early life experiences, when belief systems were first developed and powerful emotional experiences shaped the child's life. Future perceptions, behaviors, and choices emerge from this basic foundation.

• To provide a vehicle for the healing of prior attachment trauma.

• To promote the development of the social skills and emotional capacity necessary for healthy attachment and relationships.

• To enable the child to learn to relate positively to self, leading to increased self-esteem, positive self-regard, and a positive working model.

The therapist-child dialogue includes all or some of the following questions and topics:

*"Picture the little girl. How old is she? What is she doing? What is she thinking and feeling?"* This dialogue facilitates a child-directed sharing of thoughts, feelings, and memories. Children typically find this experience interesting and become emotion-

ally engaged. They commonly identify feelings of sadness, fear, loneliness, helplessness, anger, and shame.

*"What does this little girl need?"* The child commonly responds by identifying the needs of the little girl (e.g., "She needed someone to hold and protect her"). Children with attachment disorder have learned to discount and dissociate from their emotional needs. This portion of the therapy process enables them to acknowledge and "own" their basic needs.

*"Tell the little girl what she needs."* We now introduce a small stuffed animal (warm, fuzzy bear) to symbolize the little girl. This shift from a visualization paradigm to the use of an external symbol facilitates further concrete expression of thoughts and feelings in a less threatening manner. The child is asked to speak directly to the "little girl" (stuffed animal). Children ordinarily share statements such as, "You need love, to be held and protected, you need a mommy, you need someone to take care of you."

*"What does that little girl want to say?"* (to mommy, daddy, or other caregivers). *"Can you pretend you are that little girl? What is she is thinking and feeling?"* Children find it easier to share perceptions and emotions associated with early loss and trauma by putting a "voice" to the "little girl." Common responses are: "I'm afraid of you; I hate the way you treat me; you don't take care of me."

*"Have you taken very good care of this little girl?"* The response to this question reveals the child's self-contempt and the vicious circle of attachment disorder. ("My caregiver mistreats me; I feel defective and unlovable; I hate myself; I treat others badly; others mistreat me.") The child is encouraged to display nurturing, supportive behaviors towards the "little girl" in order to teach self-acceptance and self-love, thereby breaking the negative cycle and promoting the development of a positive working model. The child's ability to identify and meet the needs of the "little girl" reflects the extent to which her negative working model is changing. The goal is to change from a negatively internalized self ("I am bad and do not deserve love") to a positively internalized self ("I am good and I do deserve love").

*"Can she forgive you for not taking good care of her?"* The response is diagnostic of the child's capacity to mitigate self-contempt. The therapist informs the child, "You were treated badly and you learned to treat yourself badly." Self-empathy and self-forgiveness are encouraged over time.

*"Who is in control of your life if you continue to treat yourself badly?"* This question elicits the paradox of control. These children are motivated by a profound need to control, yet their choices and actions are driven by prior events and relationships (lack of self-control). The basic message to the child is: "If you continue hating yourself, the perpetrators are in control of your life."

*"How does life work out for her?"* The therapist instructs the child to give the "little girl" a detailed accounting of her life up to this point in time, emphasizing the information gleaned from therapy. This exercise provides a vehicle for the child to synthesize and integrate therapeutic experiences, and is diagnostic of his or her capacity for awareness, disclosure and cooperation.

*"Do you know anyone else who can help you love this little girl?"* Children consistently respond by identifying their current caregivers (e.g., adoptive mother or fa-

ther) as an appropriate source of love and protection. This represents a shift from pushing the caregiver away to inviting the caregiver into their life. Children express this change concretely by inviting the mother into the session and asking her for help ("Mom, will you help me learn how to love my little girl?"). The mother is instructed to place the child and "little girl" into the "in arms" position, and to provide a healthy model of affection, support and comfort. This enhances positive mother-child attachment as well as the bond between the child and her "little girl" (positive internalized self). Mothers (and fathers) who were previously angry, defensive, and emotionally unavailable to their child, can now experience the giving and receiving of affection. The parent(s) and child are connecting in a safe, secure, trusting, and intimate manner, often for the first time.

*"Do you wish this could have been your mom from the beginning?"* This question serves as a springboard for enhancing mother-child attachment. Mutual acceptance and affection increases intimacy, trust, and secure attachment. The mother is asked a similar question ("Do you wish you could have been this child's mother from the beginning?"). Mother now has the opportunity to tell the child her thoughts and feelings about the child's prior trauma and how she is wanted and loved.

This portion of the session ends with approximately 30 minutes of positive attachment (eye contact, positive affect, holding) between mother and child. Mother typically gives her child a "bottle" filled with juice or milk to further simulate early secure attachment. Mother-child and father-child attachment exercises are repeated many times during treatment. Repetition and rehearsal are crucial to the process of change for parents and children.

## Case Example: Inner Child Metaphor

Kelly and her siblings lived with their maternal grandmother, an active alcoholic, for the first four years of her life. Kelly's birth mother was in prison for drug-related offenses and child molestation; her birth father was unknown. Kelly was neglected, physically and sexually abused, and both witnessed and was the victim of violence. After one year of foster care, she was adopted (age 5), and for the next five years acted out through temper tantrums, oppositional behavior, lying, stealing, not making friends, destroying property, showing no remorse, and forming no attachments. Prior treatment efforts were not successful, and the parents were considering relinquishment. She began our program at age 10.

Kelly's negative working model was revealed as the inner child metaphor began:

**Kelly:** "I don't want to talk to her; I don't want to take care of her." (referring to the stuffed animal representing Kelly as a baby)

**Therapist:** "Can you tell the baby why?"

**Kelly:** "I wasn't taken care of, so I won't take care of you. I take care of myself, so you should take care of yourself."

Kelly's self-contempt, which she developed by internalizing the abuse and neglect, was identified and expressed:

**Therapist:** "How mad have you been towards little Kelly; a 1, 5, or 10?"

**Kelly:** "A 10."

**Therapist:** "Look at her and tell her."

**Kelly:** "I'm really mad at you, little Kelly." (yells)

**Therapist:** "Tell her how you have been feeling towards her."

**Kelly:** "I hate you!" (screams)

**Therapist:** "Is that true, you've been hating little Kelly?"

**Kelly:** "I hate you because you're a rotten kid; I've been hating myself for a long time." (cries)

Cognitive rescripting now begins; an opportunity for Kelly to change her interpretation of prior events and attribute responsibility for maltreatment to the hurtful adults, rather than towards herself:

**Therapist:** "Can you tell little Kelly what she was thinking back then?"

**Kelly:** "Little Kelly, you thought you were bad and that you didn't deserve love."

**Therapist:** "You thought you were bad because bad things were happening to you?"

**Kelly:** "Yes, I thought I was a bad kid." (cries)

**Therapist:** "It wasn't your fault, but when you were very young, you couldn't figure that out. When babies are loved they feel lovable and good. But if they are treated bad, they feel like they don't deserve love, and feel bad about themselves. Tell little Kelly the truth as you know it to be now, as a big girl."

**Kelly:** "You did deserve love, because you were just being a baby, but your Mom didn't come to help you. You thought you were bad, but you weren't." (cries)

Kelly is now ready to experience positive feelings towards herself (self-acceptance, support, and love), rather than self-contempt and self-blame:

**Therapist:** "You have been treating little Kelly badly, do you want to keep doing that? This is your chance to change."

**Kelly:** "I want to treat her good now."

**Therapist:** "How can you show little Kelly you are caring for her?"

**Kelly:** "I can give her a hug." (wraps the "baby" up in her arms, hugs her tightly, gently strokes her leg)

**Therapist:** "Feel your love going into the baby's heart; what is the baby feeling?"

**Kelly:** "She's feeling safe and happy; I'm giving her a real hug." (Kelly appears relaxed and calm.)

At this point the therapist recommends that Kelly tell the story of "little Kelly" to her mother. Mother and child dialogue about the early life experiences, how Kelly was hating herself and her birth mother, and the positive changes now occurring.

## Psychodramatic Reenactment

Children, in general, are less apt to verbally express cognitions and emotions and are more likely to demonstrate internal states through action and behavior. This is the principle behind play therapy; increasing motivation, involvement, and self-expression through action-oriented tasks. Children with attachment disorder are emotionally and socially detached, avoiding the painful realities of their past and current lives. Psychodramatic reenactment reduces the child's denial and detachment, while encouraging genuine participation.

During psychodramatic reenactment, treatment team members role play individuals and scenarios from the child's life to "revisit" and work through prior attachment trauma. The goals of this intervention include the following:

- To enhance genuine involvement in the therapeutic process via an action-oriented activity.

- To encourage the child to experience and express the perceptions, emotions, and behavioral responses associated with early life attachment-related and traumatic events.

- To discuss the thoughts and feelings associated with early trauma and loss in a safe and secure therapeutic context.

- To achieve a corrective and curative experience, involving alternative ways of perceiving self and others, managing emotions, and responding behaviorally.

- To promote a healing experience that leads to emotional resolution and enhancing the child's sense of mastery and self-identity.

It is important to thoroughly prepare children and parents for these emotionally challenging experiences. A contract is established with both the child and parents; they are informed of what to expect during the exercise and asked if they are willing to participate. Psychodramatic reenactment is an effective therapeutic method that enables the child to confront and begin to resolve traumatic emotions and memories, revise maladaptive perceptions of events, feel increased competence, and connect in a secure and trusting way with his or her parents. The child has an opportunity to perceive the parents as protective and caring, rather than threatening and untrustworthy. Parents are able to take concrete and positive action to help, protect, and defend their vulnerable child, which diminishes their feelings of helplessness and pessimism.

Preparation for psychodramatic reenactment involve three components:

- **Prepare the child.** The therapist explains why this exercise is recommended and what will happen. This reduces the child's anxiety and enable him or her to feel a sense of control. A verbal agreement (contract) is established if the child gives permission.

- **Prepare the parents.** The therapist gives a similar explanation to the parents, and the roles and responsibilities of each participant are defined. This reduces the parents' level of anxiety regarding the safety of their child and helps to clarify their own emotions. A contract is established.

- **Set the stage.** The child gives a detailed description of a prior traumatic situation, including feelings, perceptions, body sensations, reactions of significant others, and consequences. The child is given the role of "director," telling participants how to play the roles of others in the reenactment. This helps the child feel empowered and enhances genuine involvement and motivation. Child and parents are encouraged to "be real," to allow genuine emotions and reactions.

### Case Example: Psychodramatic Reenactment

Sara, age 10, was physically abused and neglected when under the care of her drug-addicted birth mother during the first three years of her life. In the psychodramatic reenactment, a therapeutic assistant played the role of the mother's physically abusive boyfriend. In phase one, the "boyfriend" enters the treatment room and pretends to physically threaten Sara:

> **Boyfriend:** "I'm going to throw you against the wall."
>
> **Therapist:** "What are you thinking and feeling now, Sara?"
>
> **Sara:** "I'm scared he's gonna kill me and no one is here to help me."
>
> **Therapist:** "That must have been awful to be so alone and scared. Do you have anyone in your life now who would protect you?"
>
> **Sara:** "My Mom and Dad (adoptive) would never let anyone hurt me."

In phase two, the "boyfriend" once again pretends to threaten Sara, but this time Sara's adoptive parents storm into the room and shout at the "boyfriend."

> **Parents:** "You get out of here. Leave our daughter alone. We won't let you hurt her anymore!"
>
> They then embrace Sara and hold her on their laps.
>
> **Sara:** "I really know you guys will protect me and I'm learning to trust you more."

Twenty to 30 minutes of "positive attachment time" follow the reenactments. During this time, parent(s) and child integrate and enjoy the positive emotional experience of secure attachment (increased trust, safe and relaxed closeness, positive affect).

### Case Example: Psychodramatic Reenactment

Lauren was 3 1/2 years old when social services placed her in a foster home due to neglect and abuse. Her birth parents had been in and out of jail for drug-related and other criminal offenses. Her mother had been neglectful; her father was violent toward his wife and had physically and sexually abused Lauren. After a second foster home placement, she was adopted at age 5. Treatment began at age 7 1/2; she was aggressive, oppositional, depressed, and isolated from the family.

The psychodramatic reenactment focused on several scenes from the child's memory, confirmed by social service records and the adoptive parents' knowledge of events. These scenes included the birth mother yelling at Lauren and then expressing love and caring (inconsistency); the birth father hitting the mother in front of Lauren; birth father giving Lauren a bath (sexual abuse) and locking her in the bathroom; and the social worker taking Lauren away as the parents were taken to jail.

Lauren was able to express genuine affect regarding events: "I though I was going to die, or Mommy was going to die. Daddy had a knife. I was really scared"; "I was locked in the closet and bathroom. It was dark and I was scared." Asserting herself led to empowerment; she was able to communicate strength and personal boundaries to "birth father" ("Stop it, you're hurting me), and attribute appropriate responsibility to "birth mother" (I'm not a bad little girl, you are being a bad mom").

Lauren was able to be closer and more vulnerable with adoptive parents following the reenactment, as they processed the experience "in arms." She spoke to her parents about never feeling safe before and using aggression to protect herself. The parents began talking about prior losses in their lives, and decided to work more on those issues in therapy the next day. The parents reported that they had never seen Lauren this honest, open, and intimate.

## Revitalize

The final stage in the therapeutic process is *revitalize*. During the first two stages of Corrective Attachment Therapy, the focus is on revisiting and revising the past. This final stage is oriented more towards the present and the future. The key components of revitalization are discussed below:

### Redefining Self

The child who has successfully dealt with prior attachment trauma is able to develop a new and increasingly more positive identity. People and events from the past are placed in perspective, and the child is able to function without feeling overwhelmed or devastated by traumatic memories. Discussing the past no longer provokes intense negative emotions and physiological reactions. The old self has been mourned, and a new sense of self is emerging—new beliefs, relationships, coping skills, and a sense of hopefulness. Helplessness and isolation, the core experiences of the old self, are replaced by empowerment and connection with others [Herman 1992]. The child no longer feels compelled to consciously or unconsciously reenact pathological patterns; new choices of thinking, feeling, and interacting are now available. The child is capable of trust, affection, empathy, and reciprocity in his or her relationships with family and others. The old need for power and control over others, to compensate for feelings of fear and helplessness, are replaced by a sense of personal competency and power. Pseudoindependence is transformed into genuine autonomy and self-reliance. As the child allows attachment needs to be fulfilled (intimacy, interdependence, trust, safety), he or she develops a stable sense of self.

Secure attachment is a protective factor, creating resiliency in the face of adversity. The child now has an emotional storage bank from which he or she can draw during stress. The child becomes equipped to cope effectively with emotions, relationship conflicts, developmental milestones, and the challenges of life.

## Family Renewal

Revitalization of the family occurs on two levels: relationships within the family and interactions between the family and others. Family members experience safety, enhanced trust and intimacy, effective communication, improved problem solving and conflict-resolution abilities, clear and respected boundaries, and a sense of cohesiveness and felt security. The family climate of hopelessness and heaviness is replaced by optimism, excitement, and playfulness. Family members can have fun and enjoy each others' company.

The parents are feeling more positive in both their marital relationship and parenting role. Marital communication, conflict management, and emotional closeness are enhanced. They are functioning as a united team and feeling increased confidence in their ability to parent effectively. Sibling relationships also improve with increased trust, safety and respect.

The family is able to utilize and benefit from such outside resources as support groups, extended kin, religious affiliations, and recreational opportunities. The family shifts from fear, isolation, and crisis management, to interactions within their community that are fulfilling and validating.

## Moral and Spiritual Evolution

Disconnection from self and others is converted into self-love and the ability to form loving relationships. As the child and family members let go of fear, resentment, and the self-protective need to survive under threatening conditions, minds and hearts are now open to uplifting emotional and spiritual beliefs and values: compassion, forgiveness, empathy, faith, charity, joy, peace, contentment, love, and harmony.

Forgiveness is considered to be an important step in the healing process. Forgiveness involves compassion of the heart in order to understand the forces that were acting on both ourselves and others that hurt us [Judith 1996]. Corrective Attachment Therapy facilitates a variety of forgiveness experiences:

- Self-forgiveness,

- Child forgives birth parents for maltreatment and abandonment,

- Adoptive parents and child forgive one another,  and

- Siblings and child express forgiveness for each other.

Forgiveness can be defined in both psychological and spiritual ways. In our work with children with attachment disorder and families, forgiveness occurs when one is no longer controlled by negative emotions. This occurs through a four-stage process:

- Experience and express anger directly. Remaining angry, consciously or unconsciously, prevents both grieving and forgiveness.

- Genuinely acknowledge and experience grief as it relates to the loss of a specific person.

- Coming to terms (accepting) the loss without distorted perceptions or unrealistic fantasies.

- Integrate prior losses into one's life. Moving towards the future with new personal resources, skills, meanings, and positive relationships.

Recent studies have demonstrated the beneficial psychological and physical effects of forgiveness. A 1996 study of divorced mothers found that the women who forgave their ex-husbands were less anxious and depressed and became better parents than those who could not forgive. Other research has shown that people who scored high on forgiveness scales had significantly lower levels of blood pressure, anxiety and depression, and higher self-esteem [Briggs 1997].

**Case Example: Forgiveness Ritual**

Jackie's birth mother was 16 years old when she was born. Her birth father was unknown. She was placed in a foster home immediately after birth and reunited with her birth mother at 3 months of age. For the next 2 1/2 years, there were a series of disruptions and reunifications. At 3 years of age, the birth mother's parental rights were terminated and Jackie was placed for adoption. Jackie was 11 years old at the time of treatment.

At the end of a two-week Corrective Attachment Therapy program with Jackie and her adoptive parents, a "magic wand" forgiveness ritual was introduced. During the course of treatment, Jackie dealt with her anger and grief regarding neglect and abandonment from her birth mother and was now ready to begin the process of forgiveness.

> **Therapist:** "Let's pretend for 10 minutes that I have a magic wand, and you can now speak openly and honestly to your birth mother who will listen and understand. What do you want to say to your birth mother?"

> **Jackie:** (speaks to co-therapist who is role playing the birth mother) "Why did you give me up? Why didn't you take care of me and love me?"

> **Birth mother:** "I was very young, scared, and alone. I didn't know how to take care of a little baby."

> **Jackie:** "I've been hating you all these years and hating and blaming myself."

> **Birth mother:** "It wasn't your fault, you deserved to be loved. I just couldn't do it."

> **Jackie:** "Now, after this therapy, I understand you didn't get what you needed either, when you were young."

> **Birth mother:** "Can you ever forgive me for not being there for you?"

**Jackie:** "Now that I have gotten rid of a lot of my mad and sad, maybe I can start to forgive you."

Following the dialogue between the child and "birth mother," the adoptive mother discussed Jackie's feelings with her "in arms." The adoptive mother was supportive of Jackie's desire to forgive birth mother. This intervention initiated a process of forgiveness and also strengthened the attachment between Jackie and adoptive mother.

## Contraindications and Concerns

The therapeutic Holding Nurturing Process (HNP) described in this book is appropriate for children who are severely attachment disordered and not amenable to conventional therapy approaches, due to their extreme control orientation and inability to form a constructive, trusting therapeutic rapport. Children who are accurately diagnosed with serious attachment disorder typically benefit from the safety and security of this process when it is used correctly. Therapists must be nonpunitive, provide considerable support, empathy and validation, and be confident and personally comfortable with this approach. Therapists must also be emotionally clear and neutral and have substantial awareness of their own issues and areas of sensitivity. This process should not be employed without a careful client screening process or without specialized clinical training and supervision.

It is necessary to have a therapy environment conducive to the treatment process described. A treatment and observation room separated by a one-way mirror, or a separate room with a TV monitor, allows parents, therapists, and treatment parents to observe. Further, it is crucial to have sufficient time allocated to accomplish clinical goals and resolution, both on a daily and weekly basis. Lastly, a supportive and knowledgeable treatment team is essential. There are a number of qualities the therapist must possess for effective Corrective Attachment Therapy, which are listed in Appendix F.

# 9

# Corrective Attachment Therapy

## The Family System

## Basic Principles

Much of attachment theory and research has focused on the mother-child relationship. This is a simplistic and limited view; attachment occurs within the broad emotional network of the family system, including the role of father, siblings, extended kin, and external social systems. The basic principles of a systems approach, *context, circularity* and *organization,* are outlined below:

- **Context.** No family member (or relationship) can be understood outside of the context in which he or she functions. Thus, mother-infant attachment patterns can only be understood within the network of all other family relationships (e.g., husband-wife, father-infant, parent-grandparent) and extrafamilial systems (e.g., extended kin, cultural context, social programs).

- **Circularity.** Traditional models in the mental health field were based on the belief that relationships are "linear"; i.e., there is a cause and effect. The systems model presumes that relationships are "circular"; i.e., based on ongoing, reciprocal, interactive patterns, in which each family member's behavior serves as both a trigger and a response. A clear example is the reciprocal nature of mother-infant attachment behavior (see Chapter 3).

- **Organization.** Family systems are organized around rules, roles, boundaries, and subsystems. For example, subsystems in the family include spouse subsystem, parental/executive subsystem (parent-child interactions), sibling subsystem, and other subsystems (e.g., alliances with extended kin). Each of these subsystems has its own set of operating rules, communication patterns, and boundaries that separates it from other subsystems. In well-functioning families, for instance, a child may be appropriately excluded from the spouse subsystem ("this is mommy and daddy's time to be together"). In contrast, a dysfunctional family may allow a child to have too much power and control ("we will allow you to intrude on our time and space").

It is important to evaluate and understand the context of the whole family, as well as external supports, when considering attachment security or disorder. Byng-Hall [1995a] describes a "secure family base," and delineates several family situations that undermine such family security:

- **Loss of attachment figure.** Actual loss, or fear of losing an attachment figure, such as prior abandonment or separation.

- **Capture.** A family member "captures" the attachment figure; e.g., an insecure father takes control of the mother, preventing a child from attaching securely.

- **Turning to an inappropriate attachment figure.** Due to the lack of availability of an appropriate attachment figure, a family member relies on another who is inappropriate; e.g., a mother relies on a child for need fulfillment and security, due to an absent partner.

- **Relationship conflict.** Conflicts regarding power and authority between caregivers or caregivers and children undermine a secure family base; e.g., an abusive parent becomes both a source of danger as well as the protective attachment figure for the confused child.

- **Reenactment of loss and trauma.** Parents and caregivers are unable to respond appropriately to a child's attachment needs when they are unresolved about their troubled past; e.g., a parent may repeat patterns of maltreatment learned in his or her family of origin.

## Family Systems Influences

The family systems approach to attachment focuses on three major influences: marital relationship, attachment histories of caregivers, and extended social networks. Each of these areas of influence is described below.

### Influence of Marital Relationship on Parent-Child Attachment

The process of attachment occurs within the dynamic and emotional setting of the parents' or caregivers' relationship to a significant other (spouse or partner). Many studies show that the quality of the parents' relationship influences the security of the child's attachment [Amato 1986; Belsky et al. 1984, 1991; Brody et al. 1986; Dickenson & Parke 1988; Goldberg & Easterbrooks 1984]. Mothers living without a husband or boyfriend were found to be more likely to have babies with deteriorating attachment; i.e., the babies were securely attached at 1 year of age, but became insecurely attached by 18 months [Egeland & Farber 1984]. Another study found that mothers felt more confident and competent in the maternal feeding role with their 1-month-old infants when husbands had high esteem for their wife as a mother; tensions and conflict between husband and wife were negatively associated with maternal feeding competence [Pedersen et al. 1978].

Father-child attachment is influenced in a similar way by the emotional field. Fathers who witness the birth of their infants are much more likely to be "engrossed" with their babies and supportive of their partners [Greenberg & Morris 1974]. A body of research accumulated recently indicates that poor marital quality has a more negative impact on father-child relationships than on mother-child relationships [Cummings & O'Reilly 1997]. Conflict between parents, in general, is most consistently linked with children's adjustment problems. Adults' conflicts, particularly physical aggression, have negative effects on children's emotional, social, and physical functioning, including increased aggressiveness towards peers, which disrupts the process of attachment in the early years [see Cummings & Davies 1994, for review].

Further, as has been discussed in Chapter 5, mothers who are depressed are more likely to have infants and toddlers who are insecurely attached. A supportive relationship with a husband or partner significantly reduces depressive symptoms in mothers, while lack of support and the stress of marital conflict increases their risk of depression [Beach & Nelson 1990].

## Intergenerational Transmission

Patterns of attachment are transmitted over generations. The parents' attachment histories influence their current relationships and parenting practices. "A child attaches not only *to* his or her primary caretakers, but also attaches *through* the primary caretaker(s) to the entire emotional field" [Donley 1993, p. 11]. Thus, there is a high correlation between the child's patterns of attachment and the experiences the parents had in their childhoods. Parents who can make sense of their childhood experiences in an honest, responsible, and realistic way ("coherent" story), are more likely to have securely attached children. Parents who are dismissive, preoccupied, or unresolved in reference to childhood attachment difficulties ("incoherent" story) are likely to have children with insecure/anxious attachment [Main et al. 1985]. Parents with unresolved traumatic experiences (e.g., abuse, abandonment, severe parental psychopathology) more often have children with the most dysfunctional attachment pattern; i.e., disorganized-disoriented attachment [Main & Hesse 1990]. These parents have not mourned the loss of prior attachment figure(s), remain anxious and unresolved about past trauma, and may even dissociate to avoid their pain. They transmit fear and anxiety to their children, inhibiting the establishment of secure attachment.

Parents who have troubled and unresolved attachment histories often do not relate to their infants and young children in a genuine and meaningful way, but rather, they *script* their children into some past drama from their family of origin (or other childhood experiences, such as foster care placements). Parents may have conscious or unconscious scenarios from childhood that they repeat or reenact with their own children ("replicative script"). For example, abuse or neglect from childhood is repeated in the next generation ("cycle of abuse"). Parents may react to uncomfortable childhood experiences by attempting to be different with their own children ("corrective script"). A parent who was abandoned in childhood becomes an overindulgent and overprotective parent with his or her own children.

Object relations theory refers to this process of scripting as *projective identification*, in which one family member causes another to take on a role that he or she has disowned. Again, the parent with a history of abuse may project negative attributes on to his or her child, reflecting unresolved pain and loss. Stern (1985) calls this *selective attunement*; the child is not perceived as a separate and unique being, but becomes molded to fit the parent's fantasies. The parent responds selectively to the infant's or young child's emotions and behavior; e.g., "happy moments are acceptable, but distress and anger are not." This not only prevents the child from forming healthy attachments, but also hinders the child's ability to learn to manage emotions and damages his or her emerging sense of self [see Byng-Hall 1995b, for review of family scripts].

### Extended Social Network

Many factors external to the primary parent-child relationship affect attachment, such as extended family kinship network; community support systems (e.g., church, school, neighborhood programs); and social service agencies that influence family life. Parents who perceive their neighbors as friendly and supportive, for instance, are more likely to have securely attached children [Belsky et al. 1989]. Other studies show the importance of social supports for family and attachment [Crockenberg 1981; Belsky & Vondra 1989; Colapinto et al. 1989]. Family support programs are vital in helping and supporting high-risk families and children. Home visiting, for example, in which the professional and parent develop a "partnership" in order to foster secure attachment and healthy childhood development, is a primary means of service delivery in many of these programs [Klass 1996]. High-risk families can be helped by education, prevention and early intervention programs, which focus on promoting secure attachment patterns. Social service programs, however, can also have a "diluting effect" on the family, in which "the regulatory intervention of a social service agency in the life of a family tends to loosen connections among family members" [Colapinto 1995, p. 61]. The goal of social programs must always be to nurture, strengthen, and empower the family in a positive direction.

## Fathers

Until quite recently in human evolution, infants remained close to their mothers because of the necessity of breast feeding for survival. The major role of the father was to protect the family from external threats. Cultural anthropologists who study primitive hunter-gatherer societies offer evidence of this gender-role adaptation; close relationships between fathers and infants were found in only three of the 80 nonindustrial cultures surveyed [West and Konner 1976; cited in Colin 1996, p. 167].

More recently we have come to realize that fathers are capable of caring for and attaching to their children. Mothers possess qualities that place them in the role of primary attachment figure, such as breast feeding ability and secretion of hormones during pregnancy and after birth that promote caregiving. Gender role socialization and expectations also encourage mothers to care for their young more than fathers. Nevertheless, research and observation clearly show that fathers are important attachment figures and crucial members of the family system.

Mothers are biologically, hormonally, and emotionally programmed to bond. This does not mean that the father's role is unimportant. Although fathers are not as biologically and culturally primed, they are capable of the same "motherly" behaviors as women. The sight of their newborn triggers a similar range of loving behaviors, including protection, giving, and responsiveness to the infant's needs. Human fathers stay with their offspring and care for them more than any other primates. Studies show that the more the father is involved in the pregnancy and delivery, and the sooner he holds the child after birth, the more absorbed and interested he is in continuing a positive involvement [Greenberg & Morris 1974]. The father's self-confidence increases as he handles the baby, and as his parenting instincts emerge so does his level of commitment.

Despite the growing awareness of the importance of active and involved fathers, the problem of absent fathers is increasing and producing long-term damage to children. Consider the following:

• In 1986, the United States became the leader in fatherless families, passing Sweden. Between 1950 and 1996, the percentage of children living in mother-only families climbed from 6 to 27%.

• 18% of European American children, 28% of Hispanic children, and 53% of African American children in the United States live with their mothers only.

• More than 1 million American babies (1 in 4) are born each year to unmarried mothers, most of whom are in households without fathers.

• 35% of children living with mothers *never* see their fathers; 24% see their fathers less than once a month [Crowell & Leepers 1994; Hutchins 1995].

There are a number of negative effects of father absence on the family and in reference to the psychosocial adjustment and development of children, as reviewed by Lamb (1997). First, there is the absence of a co-parent; i.e., two partners to help with child care, participation in decision making, and giving the mother a break from the demands of parenting. Second, there is the economic stress that accompanies single motherhood; the income of single mother-headed households is lower than any other family group [Peterson & Thoennes 1990]. Third, a high degree of emotional stress is experienced by single mothers who feel isolated and alone, and by children who are affected by perceived or actual abandonment. Last, children suffer as a result of hostility and destructive conflict between caregivers (e.g., predivorce and postdivorce marital conflict). Children living with their mothers are often exposed to violence and conflict between parents (current or historical). Overt hostility between parents is associated with child behavior problems, including childhood aggression [Cummings 1994; Grych & Fincham 1990]. Thus, father absence is harmful to children and families, not only due to the lack of a gender-specific role model, but because the emotional, social, and economic aspects of a father's role are not fulfilled.

Compared to mothers, fathers today still are significantly less involved with their babies. When fathers do get involved, it is often as playmates, rather than as primary attachment figures. Mothers were found to play more with their babies when they are 15 months of age, but fathers were playing more when babies are 30 months old [Clarke-Stewart 1978]. Young children who play regularly with their fathers have better peer relationships and display greater social confidence. However, fathers who are insensitive to cues of overstimulation (e.g., play too rough) have children who are intrusive and insensitive with their peers [Parke 1990].

When men do care for their children, they tend to interact with, nurture, and generally rear children competently, but differently from women. *Not worse, not better, but differently* [Pruett 1997]. Mothers typically hold their infants in a relaxed and quiet manner, whereas fathers more often activate or stimulate their infants prior to holding them close. Again, this trait leads to more playful and novel interaction over time [Parke 1990]. Fathers encourage their babies to solve physical and intellectual challenges, even past the signs of frustration. Mothers encourage exploration but are more apt to help the child once frustration is apparent [Biller & Meredith 1974].

Research and family observation (and fathers who know) clearly reveal that fathers are important and highly valued attachment figures in many families. Pedersen [1980] found that the more actively involved a 6-month-old baby had been with his or her father, the higher the baby scored on infant development scales. Paternal involvement was also found to significantly reduce the effects of long-term vulnerability for at-risk, premature infants [Yogman 1989]. Laboratory procedures designed to assess separations and reunions, found that father's presence had similar effects on babies and toddlers as the mothers, just less intense: Babies *cried* when the mother or father left, but cried less for father; they *explored* and *played* less during the absence of either parent, but less so when the mother was gone; they would *cling* to mother and father on reunion, but less intensely to father. The children clearly related to their fathers as attachment figures who served as a secure base [Kotelchuck 1976].

Infants observed in the home, ages 7 to 13 months, showed no preference for mothers over fathers on most attachment measures (e.g., proximity seeking, touching, crying, signaling desire to be held, protesting on separation, greeting on reunion) [see Lamb 1997, for research review]. When infants are distressed, however, they consistently prefer their mothers, supporting the notion that children arrange their attachments in a hierarchy. Finally, the distribution of infant patterns of attachment to mothers is basically the same as for fathers (65% secure, 25% avoidant, 10% resistant) [Main and Weston 1981]. While one secure attachment was better than none, children found to be securely attached to both parents were most competent and confident, and displayed more empathy [Main & Weston 1981; Easterbrooks & Golderg 1991].

Karen writes, "Although fathers are usually secondary caregivers, they are not merely secondary mothers" [1994, p. 204]. They provide valuable stimulation, playfulness, and serve as a stepping-stone to the outside world, where people are commonly not "in-synch" and attuned. They facilitate the child's ability (especially sons) to move outside the mother's orbit. They provide role models for their sons and invaluable models to daughters regarding a relationship to male figures. Lamb [1997, pp. 13–14) in his book on the father's role in child development, offers a number of salient conclusions based on 30 years of research and observation in the field:

- Fathers and mothers influence their children in *similar ways;* warmth, nurturance and closeness are associated with well-adjusted and healthy children whether the caregiver is a mother or father.

- Characteristics of individual fathers (e.g., masculinity, intellect) are much less important than the *quality of the relationship* established; children who have secure, supportive, reciprocal, and sensitive relationships with their fathers (or mothers) do better on every measure.

- The amount of time fathers and children spend together is less important that the *quality* of their time together.

- The *family context* is often more influential than individual relationships; the father-child relationship must be viewed within the broader family context (e.g., father's relationship with partner or spouse and with other children; how significant others perceive and evaluate the father-child relationship).

- Fathers play *multiple roles* in the family—nurturing parent, protector, disciplinarian, breadwinner, emotional partner, playmate. Fathers affect their children's development and adjustment based on their success in all of these roles.

- A father can only be understood within the standards of his *sociocultural context*; his role varies according to individual, familial, and cultural values.

## Siblings

Sibling relationships serve an important function in the emotional and social development of children. Siblings actively shape one another's lives and prepare each other for later experiences both within and beyond the family. Many crucial lessons children learn about sharing, competition, rivalry, and compromise are learned through their negotiations with siblings [Lobato 1990]. Sibling relationships also provide an arena in which children learn about intimacy, empathy, and love.

Conflict is inherent to all sibling relationships. Sibling conflicts, however, are amplified and multiplied in the family with a child with attachment disorder. These difficulties and disagreements go beyond "normal" sibling squabbles. The infant who had consistent and appropriate need fulfillment becomes secure and has a higher tolerance for sharing attention, affection, and possessions with siblings. Early unmet needs and insecure attachment, conversely, leave children feeling chronically fearful, jealous, demanding, and self-absorbed. They reject parental love, yet resent their siblings who are "easier" to love. Sibling relationships and conflicts are characterized below:

- When parents acquiesce to the demands of their child with attachment disorder, siblings perceive this as favoritism and a double standard. They may resent their parents, imitate the negative behavior to gain attention, or distance themselves from the family to avoid stress and conflict. Siblings often experience resentment when "special needs" children in the family are indulged or permitted to engage in behaviors unacceptable by other family members [Meyer & Vadasy 1994].

- Siblings are commonly ambivalent. They want to love, support and accept their brother or sister, yet they feel angry and mistrustful. This often results in feelings of guilt and shame.

- Siblings may feel shortchanged due to the disproportionate time and energy the child with attachment disorder receives from parents. The parents or caregivers generally feel desperate, hopeless, and exhausted, having little or nothing left over for their other children. Siblings feel neglected and isolated.

- Siblings perceive the family as "marked." They are often embarrassed at school by the acting-out behavior of their brother or sister who has attachment disorder, and avoid bringing friends to their home. They feel ashamed and embarrassed about the ongoing battles among family members and resent the need to restrict social activity.

- Siblings often adopt or are assigned the role of "parental child." They become overly responsible as a result of their desire to protect their overwhelmed parents and to compensate for their sibling's lack of responsibility. They routinely avoid expressing their anger and discontent, assuming that their parents have "enough to deal with."

### Case Example: A Sibling's Frustration

A sibling of a child with attachment disorder writes:

> Wendy makes me mad because she screams so much, and we're always hiding everything. She demands total attention and you can't disagree with her, because if you don't always watch her or agree, she will go crazy. She will make a mess and try to hurt you until she gets what she wants. I can't bring friends over because she hits them and embarrasses me, and because she goes wild and screams and cusses and hits them in bad places. It is also embarrassing in public, like going out to eat because she's loud and all the bad language. I don't want to ride in cars with her because my head aches with her awful behavior and screaming. I can't do anything fun with her or anything at all because she can't be still and under control unless everything goes her way. She's more a pain than anything else.

### Case Example: Younger Siblings

The most frequent victims of aggression from the child with attachment disorder are women, smaller children, or helpless animals. Younger siblings becomes convenient targets for their angry wrath. A mother writes:

> Darlene and Caroline are the family members who feel threatened by John, because they are the ones he abuses. Darlene gets most of the verbal abuse with some physical (a kick or punch). Caroline gets most of the physical abuse (kicks, punches, and bites), because she is the little sister. John threatened Darlene once with a butcher knife, but Bud wrestled it away before his threats got too menacing.

## Family Systems Intervention

Family systems principles provide the foundation for Corrective Attachment Therapy. It is necessary to understand the child within the context in which he or she functions—the family. The family systems approach focuses on assessing and changing relationship patterns. Family relationships are reciprocal and circular, with the behavior of each family member serving as both a trigger and response for one another. These ongoing patterns of interactions maintain the family system and often the behaviors and symptoms of family members.

Children with attachment disorder enter a family with a variety of prior psychosocial patterns and symptoms. For example, when a child with a history of maltreatment, several out-of-home placements, and anxious and/or disorganized attachment, is adopted into a family, the focus becomes not only the child's history of problems, but also the constellation of family-related issues: parents' attachment histories, marital relationship issues, sibling issues, parenting attitudes and skills, relationship patterns and dynamics, and external social systems.

## The Traumatized Family

Families who enter treatment are commonly demoralized, angry, and "burned out." The parents were often intellectually and emotionally unprepared when they adopted the child with attachment disorder. After several years of having the child in their home, high levels of stress and ongoing negative patterns of relating have produced a climate of hopelessness and despair. Treatment failures are common, including a variety of ineffective therapeutic interventions and parenting approaches.

Parents have often been blamed by mental health and social service professionals who lack an understanding of attachment disorder. Helping professionals may assume that the child's acting out is entirely a result of ineffective parenting, without identifying the child's prior attachment difficulties. Symptoms of posttraumatic stress disorder are routinely observed in the parents, the siblings, as well as the child with attachment disorder.

Some parents who adopt special needs children are psychologically capable of meeting the challenge. Others, however, have histories of dysfunctional family relationships, as well as current individual and marital difficulties. In these cases, treatment must focus, in part, on the parent(s) issues to avoid scapegoating the child. The therapist must walk a tightrope to maintain a delicate balance. On the one hand, provide empathy and support to parents who are feeling disgruntled, hopeless and blamed. On the other hand, confront the parents' own issues to effect necessary change.

## Power and Control

Families whom we treat are characterized by both a control-oriented child and parents who lack the information and skills necessary to effectively deal with their child, resulting in chronic power struggles. Positive changes for the child and parents become the focus. The therapist creates a climate of healthy limits, boundaries, and structure for the child by providing rules, contracts, and clear expectations. The dynamics of power and control shift, as the child's control strategies become ineffectual with a firm and confident therapist. Over time, the child learns to feel safe with external limits. This is crucial modeling for the parents, who become more hopeful by observing strategies that are effective with their child and increasingly motivated to learn new parenting attitudes and skills. During the course of treatment, the therapist spends considerable time educating the parents about attachment disorder and rehearsing effective parenting approaches.

## Case Example: Father-Daughter

Megan had been chronically dishonest and controlling in the family, at school, and in prior therapy attempts. She would physically threaten and hurt her younger siblings, then lie about feeling remorse. One week into therapy (seventh session), she conversed with her father, in arms, and was honest for the first time.

**Father:** (Megan starts to cry as soon as she looks into father's eyes.) "Why are you crying?"

**Megan:** "I told you a lie." (sobbing)

**Therapist:** "Can you look into your father's eyes and tell him what the lie was?"

**Megan:** "When I told Katie and Sam (adoptive sibs) I was sorry for hurting them, I lied."

**Father:** "So you're not sorry; you don't really feel sorry for hurting them?"

**Megan:** "I said it, but inside I don't really mean it. I'm sorry deep down, but I won't let it come out."

**Father:** "What's holding it in, sweetie?"

**Megan:** "The bad part of me." (sobs, buries head in father's chest)

**Father:** "Do you want to feel bad about the things you've done to your brother and sister?"

**Megan:** "I want to feel bad; but I'm not sure I really do."

**Father:** "Why do you lie so much?"

**Megan:** "I feel safer when I lie, like I have some control over things, like I have a secret and you don't know what it is."

**Father:** "I'm so glad to hear you say that. Thanks for being honest now. I'm proud of you, I love you." (They hug one another, Megan sobs.)

During this session, the father later reported, Megan let go of "needing to be in control" for the first time. Her aggression and dishonesty had been control strategies.

## Triangulation

Children with attachment disorder are experts at "working one against the other." For example, a child may form a coalition with one parent against the other, or with a counselor against the parents. This is one of the child's strategies of manipulation and control. The structure of treatment prevents this triangulation. The treatment team and parents create a strong and unified *collaborative alliance,* while the parents are also helped to develop and maintain a unified parental team. An emphasis is placed on the parents' learning communication and problem-solving skills so that they can be "on the same page." It is also important that treatment team, parents, and external systems (e.g., social services) are united and working towards common goals.

One mother writes:

It is impossible for me to put into words the effect this child has had on our marriage. She intentionally causes arguments between me and my husband. The bad thing is we know that she is doing it and we try not to let it happen, but sometimes she has done it before we even realize what is going on. I know this sounds hard to believe for a four-year-old child, but she does it. After she has gotten my husband to do whatever it is that she wants him to do, she gives me the most superior look. It just blows my mind.

## Case Example: Triangulation

Severe marital conflicts occurred following the adoption of Annie. She would be hostile, controlling, and aggressive towards her mother, yet charming and cooperative with her father when he came home from work. The father blamed his wife for Annie's problems, the wife felt betrayed by her husband; Annie had managed to triangulate the parents.

Annie had successful sessions with her (adoptive) mother, including honest dialogues, contracting in reference to prosocial coping skills, and positive attachment time. Next, positive father-daughter connecting was needed. The mother, however, was still angry at her husband for prior lack of support, and she lacked confidence in his parenting abilities. The therapist asked the mother to observe and then facilitated a father-daughter in arms dialogue.

**Father:** "How are you feeling right now?"

**Annie:** "I don't feel love inside right now."

**Father:** "You don't feel love inside? How come?"

**Annie:** "I don't know."

**Father:** "Well, Dad feels a lot of love inside. I love Mom, I love you." (holds Annie gently, looks into her eyes, begins to cry)

**Annie:** "Oh, well, you must feel warm inside. I learned that when you feel love you feel warm inside."

**Father:** "Oh yes, definitely. Definitely warm inside. And I feel happy that you are working hard in therapy."

**Annie:** "Me too. I feel good I'm getting better." (She puts her head on father's chest and hugs him tightly; they hug for several minutes.)

**Therapist:** "Annie, can you look in your dad's eyes and tell him how you have been treating him and mom before you came here?"

**Annie:** "I wasn't treating you very good. I said mean things and disobeyed." (starts to cry)

**Therapist:** "Can you tell your father why you are crying?"

**Annie:** "I had a lot of bad thoughts, I'm sorry the way I've treated you and Mom." (Father gently wipes her tears.)

Father and Annie dialogued for almost one hour. Annie shared her "bad thoughts" ("I wanted to hurt you"); fears ("I was afraid you would abuse me too"); and displayed remorse ("I'm sorry"). Father was firm yet loving, expressed his own feelings, and provided the ingredients of secure attachment.

The mother felt increased confidence in her husband's parenting ability after observing the father-daughter interaction. Subsequent marital communication sessions focused on resolving anger and disappointment in the parents' relationship, and contracting to avoid triangulation in the future. The father apologized to his wife for being nonsupportive and for not understanding the serious nature of Annie's problems.

### Reenactment of Prior Patterns

Due to a history of maltreatment and lack of secure and loving attachment, these children compulsively reenact negative patterns of relating. For instance, they often unconsciously invite rejection and abuse. Parents with histories of attachment-related problems also reenact negative relationship patterns. A mother, for example, who was emotionally abandoned in her family-of-origin has a need for acceptance and love from her children, but her adopted (attachment disordered) child offers rejection and hate. She responds by rejecting the child, being angry and resentful, and distancing. This dynamic perpetuates old patterns, thereby creating a self-fulfilling prophecy for child and mother: It fulfills the child's expectation that mothers are untrustworthy and rejecting, and also fulfills mother's expectation that getting close only leads to emotional pain. Both are embroiled in an ongoing, mutually reinforcing pattern of negativity and disconnection. Changing this pattern involves three components:

- Therapeutic interventions address the mother's (or father's) attachment issues and patterns. The HNP is commonly employed to assist in identifying and modifying these patterns.

- Therapeutic interventions address the child's attachment issues and patterns.

- Parent-child interventions promote changes in relationship patterns. As the child and mother (or father) become more open and emotionally available, they are ready to interact with one another with improved communication, less anger and defensiveness, and increased closeness and trust.

## Case Example: Reenactment and Displacement

The first session with Annie was productive, and the following interventions were accomplished: rules of therapy, first-year-of-life cycle, and dialogue regarding her birth mother. Annie revealed her rage towards her birth mother for neglecting and abandoning her ("I want to kill her, cut her head off with a scissors, burn her house down"). The final part of the session focused on the relationship between Annie and adoptive mother; her mother held her in arms as they discussed Annie's progress in therapy.

**Therapist:** "You did a good job today, worked hard. Are you ready to tell your forever mom what we talked about?"

**Annie:** "Yeah!" (excited about seeing mother)

**Mother:** (Comes into treatment room and places Annie "in arms" on couch; Annie is receptive and cooperative.)

**Therapist:** "Look at your mom and tell her some of the things we talked about today."

**Annie:** "Mom, those things I told you I wanted to do to you—burn the house down, kick you, kill you—well, I really want to do those things to Angie (birth mother)."

**Mother:** "Wow. How do you feel now, after realizing all of that?"

**Annie:** "Better; half of my body got the anger out." (Annie and her mother are smiling at one another; Annie is relaxed in her mother's arms.)

Mother and daughter dialogue for the next 45 minutes about anger, the first-year-of-life cycle ("I didn't learn to trust"), and sexual abuse ("Angie's boyfriend touched me the wrong way"). The end of the session allowed "quiet attachment time" (eye contact, in arms, dimmed lights, relaxed closeness). The mother later reported this was the first time she experienced a close and positive connection with Annie since the adoption.

Between sessions Annie stayed in a "practice family" (therapeutic foster home), where she rehearsed anger management skills, cooperation with safe caregivers, responsibility, and reciprocity. The next session she expressed cognitive and emotional issues about compromised attachment with her birth mother: "I hate you/I love you; I needed you; you should have gone to parent school to learn to be a good mom." Again, mother-daughter attachment was facilitated during the final part of the session.

**Therapist:** (Speaks to therapeutic foster mother, who is participating in Annie's therapy.) "I think it would be good if Annie could now spend time with forever mom."

**Mother:** (Enters room; Annie gives her a hug, they hold one another for several minutes, rocking and talking.)

**Therapist:** "Annie, can you tell your forever mom what you worked on today?"

**Annie:** (looking in mom's eyes) "My birth mother didn't take care of me because she had to take drugs. I'm sad and mad about that. I take it out on you and dad."

**Mother:** "It's very sad that your birth mother made that choice, but you are making good choices to work on your life."

**Annie:** "I know. And I hate my birth mom, but I still love her too."

The therapist helped mother and Annie process the issues of her birth mother (love/hate, abandonment, anger, and loss) while in arms. The session ended with mother-daughter attachment time, followed by father-mother-daughter time together.

Annie revealed "four worries" in a subsequent session: "Mom will leave family; Mom and Dad will abuse me; Mom will leave me; I'll die." She shared these fears with both her mother and father. A plan was developed so that Annie can express her anxieties verbally, rather than act out with aggression and control.

**Annie:** "I'm afraid to love you, Mom." (sobbing, looking in mother's eyes, in arms)

**Therapist:** "Love is scary for you, Annie. Can you tell your Mom why?"

**Annie:** "I'm afraid you'll leave me, like Angie did. I'm afraid you or Dad will hurt me too."

**Mother:** (crying, holding daughter) "I'm sorry you were hurt. We will never hurt you or leave you. Maybe with time, you will learn to trust us. It's good you are using your words to tell me how you feel."

These mother-daughter sessions point out the importance of both content and process. Content includes the verbal sharing of important issues. Most important, however, is the process that is occurring; i.e., the context of the in arms attachment experience. The ingredients of secure attachment (eye contact, loving closeness and touch, empathy, gentle rocking, positive affect, protection) are experienced and rehearsed by mother and daughter.

## Case Example: Parent and Child Reenactment

Despite living in his adoptive family for three years, Adam did not develop an attachment to his parents. He was especially hostile, distant, punitive, and controlling with his adoptive mother. In addition to dealing with her son, the mother had her own difficult challenges: maltreatment and anxious attachment in her family of origin, unresolved grief regarding miscarriages and infertility, and ongoing and severe marital conflicts. Adam's hostile and rejecting demeanor triggered and exacerbated her pain, anger and depression.

Individual therapy sessions with Adam addressed early maltreatment and attachment issues, negative working model, and the development of prosocial coping skills. Sessions with the mother addressed prior losses, helped reduce the anger and fear in her reaction to Adam, and enhanced effective communication and problem solving with her husband. The groundwork was now established for initiating positive parent-child attachment. Following a successful "inner child" intervention with Adam, the mother was invited to participate in the session, while holding her son in arms.

**Therapist:** "OK, Adam, your forever Mom is now going to switch places with me."

(Adam eagerly places himself on mother's lap, gazes directly into her eyes, and smiles; he appears ready.)

**Adam:** "I want to give you a real hug." (hugs mother tightly)

**Mother:** "You do? OK." (seems amazed at his desire for closeness) "Jeepers, this feels good. I don't think you've ever given me a hug like this before."

**Therapist:** "Does it feel like Adam is giving you a real hug, and accepting yours?"

**Mother:** "Yes." (begins to cry) "Have you ever felt this before?"

**Adam:** "No." (Mother and son hold one another for several minutes.)

**Adam:** "Why are you crying?" (seems concerned about mother's tears)

**Mother:** "Part of me is sad, part of me is happy, and part just feels good."

**Adam:** "Do you think I'll be OK when we go home?"

**Mother:** "We are all working on it. I hope so."

It is important not to allow the content to get in the way of the process. Considerable time is spent in mother-child attachment "practice" (eye contact, gentle touch, rocking, holding, positive affect, smiles, attunement, and reciprocity)

**Therapist:** "Can you tell you mother what happened to baby Adam?"

**Adam:** "He had worms in his tummy, didn't get milk, good care, or a blanket." (good eye contact with mother).

**Therapist:** "You didn't get what you needed as a baby, but you can now. Let's pretend you are that little baby and your forever mom will take good care of you." (instructs mother to give Adam a bottle filled with fruit juice)

Adam and his mother spend half an hour in arms. He accepts the bottle, relaxes into mother's arms, and they remain quiet and close. The increase in mutual caring, empathy, and honest communication—as well as the decrease in anger, defensiveness, and control struggles—initiated the process of establishing secure attachment between mother and son. Subsequent sessions continued the Corrective Attachment Therapy.   ·

### Enhancing Intimacy and Affection

Once old destructive patterns are abated, positive patterns of relating can be experienced and rehearsed. Considerable therapy time is spent in practicing the behaviors and interactions of secure attachment. For example, to finish a session, a mother and child (or father and child) spend 20 to 30 minutes with the child lovingly held in arms.

### Case Example: Enhancing Closeness

Adoptive parents were considering relinquishing their daughter Kelly after several years of escalating problems and unsuccessful prior treatment. Mother was particularly angry and demoralized when they came to our program for help. She reported being "totally closed, I don't want to get hurt by Kelly anymore." The parents worked on their own issues (anger, hopelessness, lack of effective parenting skills), while Kelly was seen separately to address early maltreatment and attachment issues. On day four of the two-week treatment program, mother and daughter were ready to discuss their relationship and begin the process of attachment.

**Therapist:** (to mother) "Is there any part of you that gets worried about becoming close to Kelly now?"

**Mother:** "She's hurt me a lot, been there, done that. I don't want to get my heart broken again."

**Therapist:** "Can you tell your daughter what it's like to get your heart broken?"

**Mother:** (starts to cry) "When you hurt me or hurt yourself, it's like cutting a part of me off, because you are a part of me; you're my daughter!" (sobs)

**Therapist:** "Kelly, what feeling does your mom have now?"

**Kelly:** "She's sad, she's crying."

**Therapist:** "Do you know why she's sad? Can you tell her?"

**Kelly:** "Mom, you're sad about what I've done in the past, that I wouldn't let you love me, and I wouldn't love you."

**Therapist:** "You wouldn't take your mom's love, and wouldn't give your love to her?"

**Kelly:** "No."

**Therapist:** "So your mom is sad because she's not getting love, just like baby Kelly felt sad when she didn't get love?"

**Kelly:** "Yeah, I know that my mom is sad too."

**Therapist:** "What are you feeling now?"

**Kelly:** "I feel sad too; I feel sad about what I've done to you, not let you love me and try to help me." (Kelly starts to cry; mother and daughter seem relaxed and genuinely close.)

**Therapist:** "Should your mom worry, if she opens her heart to you now, when you go home you will hurt her again?"

**Kelly:** "No, because I'm learning how to let other people's love into me, and let my love go back to them." (smiles at mother, mutual eye contact)

**Therapist:** "Tell your mom."

**Kelly:** "I'll let your love go into my heart and my love go into your heart."

**Therapist:** "That would be nice. But are you all ready now, or do you have to work on it more? Tell your mom if you are ready, and if this will be easy or hard."

**Kelly:** "Mom, I want that, but I have more work to do. It will be hard, but I'm working on it."

This dialogue was followed with half an hour of "quiet attachment time." Next, therapist helped mother and daughter contract regarding new behaviors and coping skills: Kelly agreed to express feelings verbally, "eye-to-eye" with mother, rather than act out with aggression and distancing; her mother agreed to work on learning to trust and be emotionally available again. The father joined them towards the end of the session, and they held one another, talked, and laughed.

## Case Example: Father-Son Connecting

Parents can reenact and displace prior unresolved emotional and family issues onto their children, just as their children do to them. Honest and open parent-child communication in arms facilitates positive change.

Father (adoptive) had been furious at Adam and expressed guilt and shame about losing his temper ("I hit him; even thought about him dying"). Additionally, his prior unresolved losses (death of siblings; wife's miscarriages) exacerbated his negative reactions to his son. The following in arms dialogue initiated a process of sharing and connecting:

> **Father:** "I'm glad we can do this. I'm glad you're hugging mom and me. I used to get angry at you because you rejected me and mom and you wouldn't obey. That hurt!" (They hug one another.)
>
> **Therapist:** "Can you tell you son what you're afraid might happen if you open your heart and start loving him?"
>
> **Father:** "I built an imaginary wall between you and me. I didn't want to love you anymore because of all the hurt. Now I'm trying to get rid of that wall, just like you. I feel bad I got so mad at you in the past. I do love you."
>
> **Adam:** (Starts to cry, buries his head in father's chest.)
>
> **Therapist:** "Can you tell your father why you are so sad?"
>
> **Adam:** "When he told me he built a wall, I want him to love me." (sobs, father also cries; they hold one another close)

Father and son spent the next hour discussing plans for the future. They made agreements about better ways to express their anger ("talk about it together, not get hurtful or rejecting"). The session ended with 30 minutes of quiet, relaxed holding.

### Ecological Patterns

Changes occur in the relationship between the family system and other social systems (i.e., school, mental health and social service agencies, extended family, and other support networks). For example, parents are encouraged to join support groups in their local community. Also, identifying and facilitating effective follow-up therapy is important to maintain positive change. The treatment team is instrumental in helping the parents develop positive attitudes and working relationships with resources outside the family.

## Case Example: Social Systems

Madison's birth mother was an 18-year-old college student who was raped. Mother was angry during her entire pregnancy and rejected Madison at birth. Madison spent her first month of life in the hospital with medical complications, was placed in a foster home, and then adopted at 3 months of age. Parents reported that Madison would not attach throughout infancy and early childhood, and became destructive and violent by preschool. By age 8, she had attacked teachers and mother, killed small animals, and showed total lack of remorse.

At the time of treatment there were serious problems not only in the family, but also between the family and external systems. Madison fabricated a story about her mother abusing her, which the school counselor reported to social services. Social service initiated a child abuse investigation. The parents felt betrayed and wrongly accused by the school and social services. A major therapeutic goal, therefore, was to develop a collaborative treatment team; i.e., parents, school, social services, and therapists united in order to help Madison and empower her parents.

This goals was accomplished in several ways: 1) educating school and social services about attachment disorder, 2) ongoing communication with school and social services regarding therapeutic progress and helpful interventions for dealing with Madison, 3) including school personnel and social service case workers in follow-up treatment planning, and 4) clarifying roles, responsibilities, and intervention strategies for all parties involved.

These interventions facilitated the necessary structure and limits for Madison, and provided the parents with understanding and support. The school placed Madison in a special needs program. Social services terminated the child abuse investigation. Parents now had renewed motivation and energy to learn effective parenting attitudes and skills. Madison could no longer triangulate one system against the other, and she began genuine participation in therapy.

# 10
# Two-Week Treatment Program

## Structure and Format

The child, parents, and, when appropriate, other family members (e.g., siblings, grandparents) participate in 30 hours of therapy over a two-week period (three hours per day for 10 consecutive working days). This therapy format—the "two-week intensive"—was originally developed at Evergreen Consultants to provide treatment to children and families in need of services unavailable in their own geographic locale [Levy & Orlans 1995b]. Families traveled to Evergreen from every region of the United States, as well as abroad, to receive specialized treatment for attachment disorder. We realized this short-term format provided an array of clinical advantages for typically highly resistant, controlling, and nontrusting children. The consistency and intensity of daily therapeutic contact created a context in which defenses were reduced, motivation increased, and a trusting therapeutic relationship was established. Although significant and dramatic changes often occur during the two-week experience, this therapy was never intended to be a "magical cure." Intense confrontation of emotional issues, in conjunction with strong support and nurturance, "opens the door" for conventional therapy to be more effective. Follow-up therapy is essential. (See Appendix G for a historical perspective of attachment therapy.)

Another advantage of this therapy format is our ability to observe and modify family relationships and dynamics. Parent-child, marital, family-of-origin, and sibling issues become evident in daily therapy sessions. Also, we encourage referring therapists to participate in the treatment process whenever possible. This increases the likelihood of effective follow-up, and provides training and supervision to mental health professionals interested in learning about this modality.

The therapeutic setting incorporates a treatment room and observation area separated by a one-way mirror. This provides the therapist with the option of working with the family as a unit or having the parents observe the child's therapy from behind the one-way mirror. The reasons for using the one-way mirror are fourfold:

- It allows the parents to be a part of the treatment process while interrupting destructive and inhibiting relationship patterns,

- It provides the parents with effective role models regarding the management of behavioral and emotional problems of their child,

- It enables the therapist to assess the affective responses and emotional availability of the parents as they observe their child in therapy, and

- It provides parental feedback on child's honesty. These sessions are routinely videotaped in order to offer feedback to family members, serve as teaching tools in the training and supervision of therapists, and provide valuable clinical information to the follow-up therapist.

The multidisciplinary treatment team consists of co-therapists, therapeutic foster parents, and ancillary professionals (e.g., referring social service caseworkers, follow-up therapists, psychiatric consultant). A male-female co-therapy team promotes balance and flexibility and is helpful for both individual and family intervention. For example, as one therapist works with the child, the other can provide support and guidance to the parents as they observe the therapy. Therapeutic foster parents are specifically trained to understand and work with children with attachment disorder and their families. They provide a therapeutic milieu for the child during the two-week treatment. This "practice family" offers the child a valuable learning environment, provides the parents with much needed respite, and serves as role models of effective parenting skills and attitudes. Therapeutic foster parent involvement varies based on the clinical needs of each child and family. Some families benefit from child placement for the entire two weeks, while for other families limited or no placement is more appropriate.

### Session One

Therapeutic goals:

- Parent interview and assessment

- Further assessment of the child

- Developing a therapeutic context

- Contracting.

In the first session, the role and purpose of the therapeutic foster home ("practice family") is explained to the parents and the child. Each session begins with a dialogue between the parents and the treatment team. The therapeutic foster parents ("treatment parents") report on the child's behavior, mood, and attitude in their home, and the child's response to specific therapeutic tasks. Therapy issues and progress are discussed with the parents in addition to answering questions and responding to any concerns. At the conclusion of each session, the parents and treatment team meet again to process the specific issues covered in that day's session.

The parent interview provides detailed information regarding the child's early history, current symptoms and behavior, parenting styles, and family dynamics. Important issues to identify include strengths and deficits of marital relationship; support systems of the parents; similarities and differences in the parents' perception of the child's behavior; level of functioning of the siblings; parents' level of stress, frustration, and emotional availability to the child; effectiveness of specific parenting attitudes and techniques; and parents' prior attempted solutions. Parents are asked to bring such historical records as life books, family albums, court documents, diaries, social service reports, and letters and adoption records, which provide additional information and can be used therapeutically at a later time.

Parents often present as highly frustrated, desperate, wary, and exhausted. For example, adoptive parents are often told by professionals, "All this child needs is love and a stable home." However, the child with attachment disorder has little or no foundation to understand or accept love and, therefore, the parents typically experience rejection, feelings of inadequacy, despair, and hostility towards the child. They are often blamed for their child's inability to respond positively to the family environment. One of the primary goals of the initial session is to join with the parents and let them know we understand the nature of their frustration. The parents are educated about the causes and consequences of attachment disorder, and that knowledge enables them to be more objective and feel less responsible and guilty regarding their child's problems. The therapists provide considerable empathy, support, and validation in order to build a working alliance with the parents.

Another primary goal is the development of a specific treatment contract in which parents and therapists agree on certain desired outcomes (e.g., learn parenting skills or reduce resentment towards child). It is important that parents end the initial session with a sense of hope and enhanced expectation of success, thereby increasing their investment in the treatment process. Also during the initial session, the child is asked to fill out a sentence completion questionnaire (Appendix C) that provides information about content (attitudes, perceptions, and emotions) and process (how the child responds to the task).

Finally, the child is introduced to the therapeutic foster parents. The rules and expectations of that home are explained, including the reason why chores are emphasized. The manner in which the child accomplishes chores is diagnostic of responsibility, reciprocity, compliance, and family involvement. The child is told, "This is a practice family where you will learn new skills, behavior, and ways of relating to parents." The child's questions are answered and he or she leaves with the foster parents. Despite issues of rejection, abandonment, mistrust, and fear, the children typically leave with the treatment parents without much emotional fanfare. Children with attachment disorder lack the loving and intimate relationships that promote grief and anxiety upon separation.

## Case Example

The following case example demonstrates selected aspects of a two-week treatment process. The clinical interventions and dialogues are authentic, but were considerably more comprehensive during the actual therapy.

Ryan, age 10, was physically and sexually abused by his biological parents until age 5. Protective services removed him and his two siblings from the home. Ryan was placed in a foster home and, after five months of severe acting out (fire setting, cruelty to pets, destructive behavior), he was removed from the home and hospitalized. He was then placed in another foster home where he was adopted at age 6. For the next four years he was seen by seven different psychologists and psychiatrists and hospitalized four additional times. He was diagnosed with posttraumatic stress disorder and depression. The adoptive parents were told by therapists that Ryan had no conscience, and they recommended his removal from their home. Ryan's symptoms included frequent rage reactions involving physical aggression and destruction of property; oppositional, defiant, and controlling behavior; sexual abuse of younger children; emotional detachment and lack of affection; suicidal ideation and attempts. His older brother was placed in a series of foster homes and hospitals. His younger sister was hospitalized with a diagnosis of multiple personality disorder.

## Session One Illustration

The session began with the parent interview and the introduction of the treatment team. The mother said, "It seems he thinks he will die if he lets go of control," and, "We are desperate and at wit's end." The father shared, "We considered giving him up because he was destroying our family." They reported that Ryan kicks, screams, and throws things during his rages, experiences severe guilt in reference to the prior vicious sexual abuse of his sister, and attempted suicide recently by leaping in front of a car. The mother shared her goal for Ryan: "If he is not a serial killer, I'll be happy."

The father appeared somewhat distant, reticent and wary of the treatment process. The mother seemed more engaged and motivated, and was the spokesperson in the marriage. The therapists provided support, empathy, and a conceptual framework for understanding attachment disorder. Both parents expressed frustration about Ryan's behavior, but the father was more intolerant and the mother more accepting, even though Ryan acted out more consistently towards her. Although marital issues were not the focus of the first session, we observed a moderate level of stress and conflict regarding the handling of Ryan's problems. The parents were given a general overview of treatment and agreement was reached on a specific treatment plan (contract). Ryan was then introduced to the therapeutic foster parents, was told why he was spending time at their home, and was given the opportunity to ask questions.

### Session Two

Therapeutic goals:

- Educate and provide a cognitive frame for parents and child

- Contract with child

- Continue rapport building with parents and child

- Teach parenting skills

Initial contact with the child includes a review of the sentence completion task and an explanation of the first-year attachment cycle (Figure 1), while the child is in the holding-nurturing position. When presented in a nonchalant manner, most children do not question or protest being "in arms" with the therapist, which seems to reflect their innate need for safety, comfort, and structure. The explanation of the first-year-of-life attachment cycle is as follows (with variations in age- and stage-appropriate language):

> The first year of life involves four stages: *needs, arousal, gratification,* and *trust.* The baby is a bundle of needs, and expresses those needs and dis-

comfort through signals (cries, screams, kicks, moves). The sensitive and loving parent or caregiver gratifies the baby's needs (smiles, eye contact, love, affection, nourishment, rocking, holding, touch), which leads to the development of trust and secure attachment. When the baby's needs are not met and his discomfort is not reduced because of unreliable and insensitive care or because of lack of care, the baby learns to mistrust and anxious attachment occurs.

The child is informed about the consequences of anxious attachment: anger and rage; discomfort with touch, closeness, and intimacy; lack of eye contact for affection; unable to trust others and self; views self as defective and "bad"; views relationships as unsafe; inordinate need to control situations and people; lack of compassion and remorse; and oppositional and defiant behavior.

Educating the child about his or her early attachment experiences and the resultant psychosocial difficulties gives the message, "We understand how you got to be this way, and we can help you." Further, this positive reframing gives the message, "This is not your fault, but rather, an appropriate and predictable response to unfortunate circumstances." This sets the stage for cognitive-affective revision, the development of positive regard for self and others, and the working through of emotional trauma.

Contracting with the child is a crucial component of treatment with children of latency age or older. The contract is typically between the therapists and parents with younger children. (Contracts are agreements about specific behaviors between the therapists and child.) There is a direct correlation between the strength of the treatment contract and the desire, commitment, and motivation to change. The specific contract is based on the first-year-of-life attachment cycle "story," the sentence completion, and child's self-report (list of problems). To facilitate a contract with the child the following questions are posed:

- What happened to you in the past?

- How have past experiences affected you?

- How is your life going now?

- How will you be in the future if you remain the same?

- How will you be as an adult, parent, employee, husband?

- Are you willing to do what it takes to work on your life?

- Are you willing to accept our rules?

Once the child acknowledges the nature and severity of his or her problems, and agrees to work collaboratively with the therapist, the child is informed about the ground rules of therapy:

- Eye contact when communicating.

- Quick answers are expected.

- "I don't know" is not acceptable (guess or ask for help).

- We will work hard, but you must work hardest on your life.

- We believe actions, not just words.

After the child agrees to adhere to the ground rules, the therapist conveys his or her commitment ("We will go the distance with you") and instills hope ("We can help you change"). The information provided and contracts created in Session Two set the stage for the therapeutic interventions that follow.

### Session Two Illustration

We began with a discussion of Ryan's behavior in the therapeutic foster home. He was described as slow, passive-aggressive, and moderately noncompliant. He had to do his chores over several times before successful completion. Following the parent-treatment team discussion, we started our work with Ryan. A review of the sentence completion revealed that Ryan wrote: "I like to win"; "I lose control when I get mad"; "My parents did bad things to me when I was young." The first-year-of-life attachment story was now explained, with Ryan in the holding-nurturing position.

The following are excerpts from the dialogue during this portion of the session:

**Therapist M:** "How do you feel in this position?"

**Ryan:** "I don't like being here; I don't feel anything." (starts to cry)

**Therapist M:** "What did you learn in your first year of life?"

**Ryan:** "I had bad parents, learned to be bossy; to not trust anyone."

**Therapist M:** "Do you want your own family someday?"

**Ryan:** "I don't like to get close to people. I have a wall around my heart."

**Therapist T:** "How were you treated in your birth family?"

**Ryan:** "My parents did bad things to me, but it's hard to talk about."

**Therapist T:** "How did that little boy feel about himself?"

**Ryan:** "He thought he was a bad boy."

**Therapist M:** "Why is it hard for you to look into my eyes?"

**Ryan:** "I don't like to look in anyone's eyes. I had a bad life. I don't want people to see me."

**Therapist M:** "How do you feel about your birth parents?"

**Ryan:** "I still love them. I love and hate them.

Despite being apprehensive and somewhat guarded, Ryan disclosed valuable information regarding his feelings and perceptions. The therapists offered validation and support: "You have a good heart. You learned to be controlling for survival. We will teach you safe ways of expressing your feelings and about healthy touch. It wasn't your fault that your birth parents did bad things to you." The ground rules of therapy were discussed as part of the contract. For the final contract, Ryan was encouraged to maintain eye contact with each therapist, one at a time, and verbalize his request for help:

**Ryan:** "I want to work on my life. Will you help me?"

**Therapist M:** "I will help you improve your life."

**Therapist T:** "I will help you improve your life."

### Session Three

Therapeutic goals:

- Manage resistant and controlling behavior

- Provide validation and support

- Recontract

- Initiate cognitive and affective interventions

- Teach parenting skills

The Holding Nurturing Process (HNP), introduced in the preceding session, is used throughout the remainder of the treatment. The child's oppositional and controlling behaviors typically escalate as a result of deliberate therapeutic confrontation and structure. In contrast to other modalities, where the expression of the child's intense affect is discouraged, our goal is to encourage the release of these emotions and disturbing behavior as a first step towards constructive change. The therapists' messages to the child are: "We care about you and we will help you"; "We will take charge and you will be safe"; "You are not omnipotent"; "We can handle your controlling behaviors"; "You are safe in this situation to express your intense anger, hurt, and fear." The child begins to learn that the therapist is not intimidated by his or her anger, cannot be manipulated, and that the child will not be abandoned even at his or her worst.

The therapist is prepared for the child's resistance and responds in one of several ways:

- Acknowledge and accept: "I understand it is difficult for you to look at this issue now."

- Prescribe the behavior: "Try holding in your feelings even more."

- Give permission: "It's all right to resist, change is scary."

- Direct encouragement: "I know you can handle these feelings."

A specific therapeutic style and response is essential for treatment to be effective. The therapist must provide a balance of confrontation and support, be nurturing yet firm, avoid power struggles, maintain a positive focus, provide validation and encouragement, and instill hope.

The child's negative working model is now addressed. Specific perceptions and expectations are identified: "I am bad, defective, and deserve to be abandoned and abused"; "Adult caregivers can never be trusted"; "To survive I must be in control at all times"; "It was my fault that I was maltreated"; "If I get close to people I will be hurt and abandoned." We begin to challenge the child's belief system through a variety of strategies that will be explained in the next session.

## Session Three Illustration

During the treatment team discussion, the therapeutic foster father reported an interchange with Ryan from the previous evening.

**Foster Father:** "Why do you think you do chores so poorly?"

**Ryan:** "It's hard for me to do anything well." (starts to sob)

The parents discussed how Ryan is unable to handle confrontation at home as well, and described his pattern of "needing to fail." The therapists reframed Ryan's need to fail as a manifestation of self-contempt, and described parenting techniques designed to minimize power struggles. The mother described numerous power struggles at home and Ryan's typical violent responses. She referred to Ryan as a "potential rapist" due to his intense anger towards women. The therapeutic phase of the session with Ryan focused mostly on his angry, resistant, controlling, and defensive demeanor:

**Therapist M:** "What is your worst fear if you let your parents in your life?"

**Ryan:** (silence)

**Therapist M:** "What feelings did you have when you were young?"

**Ryan:** "I don't remember."

**Therapist T:** "Some feelings are sad, mad, glad, scared. Which ones did you have?"

**Ryan:** "I don't know."

**Therapist T:** "You learned to be in control to survive, but in here you have to give up some control to get better. You decide if you want to work on your life. We cannot force you. You have a choice."

**Ryan:** (four minutes of silence) "I guess I'll do it."

**Therapist M:** "Great! Now show us you really mean it by kicking your legs up and down in a swimming motion."

This interchange depicts an effective therapeutic response to deliberate attempts to control and manipulate. The therapists remained emotionally neutral, gave Ryan permission to be resistant, and empowered him by giving him the choice. The kicking technique provided a physical demonstration of his compliance, facilitated activation of emotions and attention, and released tension and anxiety (see pp. 132-134 for complete discussion of this technique).

### Session Four

Therapeutic goals:

• Amplify cognitive and affective interventions

• Manage resistant and controlling behavior

• Initiate positive (secure) attachment behavior between parent and child

• Teach parenting skills

- Explore family of origin (parents)

The session begins with a review of the child's thoughts, feelings, and behavior regarding therapy and specifically, the therapeutic foster home. Foster home issues include practicing compliance and reciprocity by accomplishing chores, learning to verbally communicate needs and feelings, and learning about choices and consequences. Contracting is once again emphasized; the therapist and child agree to work on certain issues resulting from their discussion. The child is often reluctant to comply at this point in the treatment process as a function of the changes in the dynamics and structure of his or her environment. Unlike the home environment, where the child maintains control by acting out or passive-controlling behavior, the new context (foster home and therapy) offers an entirely different experience—one in which the child is responsible for choices and the consequences of those choices. For example, the child who is unwilling to cooperate in treatment is informed of two choices and consequences: work hard in therapy, change, and have the possibility of a loving and satisfying family life, or do not cooperate, remain as you are, and face the consequences. One consequence may be that the parents set limits, informing the child that his or her disruptive behavior will no longer be tolerated in the family, and, "We will always love you but it might have to be from a distance." (The parents have been prepared for this limit-setting strategy in prior discussions with the therapists.) Choices are given in an empathic and nonpunitive fashion, and the child is free to select either option, thereby circumventing power struggles and control battles.

We now begin to focus on specific treatment issues regarding attachment and prior trauma. The therapist and child review reports and records that provide details about significant events in his or her early years. Some mental health professionals believe it is contraindicated to delve into the details of child maltreatment, because it may be too threatening to the child. It is our experience, as previously stated, that honest and open discussion of abuse and neglect is crucial to the healing process, and that most children are capable of effectively dealing with these issues with proper support and guidance. This review process sets the stage for a variety of therapeutic experiences. An array of thoughts and feelings emerge for the child as we review the records. We begin to provide the child with an effective framework to identify and express these thoughts and feelings. The child is helped to label specific emotions (sad, mad, scared, glad) and to verbalize feelings (face-to-face, eye-to-eye) in contrast to acting out or avoiding. This skill of direct verbal communication is emphasized and encouraged throughout treatment.

When age appropriate, the child is helped to understand the relationship between current behavior and prior traumatic experiences. This information is not provided with the premise that insight produces change, but rather, because it helps the child realize that he or she was a victim of others' maltreatment, reducing the burden of self-blame and shame. The therapists offer empathy and validation, giving the message: "It was not your fault. You were not responsible for the maltreatment, but you are responsible for your behavior and choices now and in the future."

The therapists begin to challenge the child's belief system, providing empathy for negativistic perceptions ("I understand that you don't trust adults because you were abused"), while simultaneously showing the child new possibilities and options ("Your adoptive mother didn't abuse you, and yet you are mistrustful towards her"). When clinically appropriate, the primary caregiver participates directly. For example, the adoptive mother, who has been observing the child's therapy from behind the one-way mirror, is invited into the treatment room to interact with the child, using the holding-nurturing position. The mother has typically been the primary target of the child's hostility and rejection, and consequently, often believes that these problems are her fault. As a result of observing the child's therapy, the mother develops increased understanding and empathy, is relieved of the burden of self-blame and guilt, and becomes more emotionally available to the child. This mother-child therapeutic experience serves two purposes. First, it actuates the process of positive attachment. Second, it provides diagnostic information regarding emotional availability and capacity for change in both mother and child.

## Session Four Illustration

The therapeutic foster father reported that Ryan was somewhat more compliant, but still had to repeat chores and tended to "act dumb." The therapist described to the parents effective ways of responding to the child's passive-resistant behavior. The mother shared additional information regarding details of Ryan's incestuous relationship with his birth family and reported that the birth mother told Ryan, "If you tell, we will never see you again, and it will be your fault." Consequently, Ryan refused to discuss these issues in four years of prior therapy. The birth father was characterized as a passive and submissive husband, and a participant in the incestuous relationships.

Ryan's therapy began with him demonstrating resistant and controlling behavior. The following interchange occurred with Ryan in the holding-nurturing position:

**Ryan:** "I don't know." (repeated response to therapists' inquiries)

**Therapist M:** "Show me you want to work hard by kicking your legs." (Ryan's resistance is exemplified by half-hearted kicking.)

**Therapist T:** "This is not good kicking; is this how you work hard? Maybe you want to quit?"

**Ryan:** "I'm tired."

**Therapist M:** "I understand you are tired, but do you want to talk about being tired or about getting better?"

**Therapist T:** (directs comment to co-therapist) "He wants to do it his way. He wants to be the boss." (Third-party dialogue is an effective way to avoid power struggles with the child while making a point.)

**Therapist M:** "It's OK if you decide you don't want to work hard on your life. And you need to understand the consequences of your choice." (The parents are now invited into the session to clarify the consequences of his choice, and to shift the focus to the parent-child relationship.)

**Mother:** "If you don't want to work hard in therapy, it's your choice. But you cannot continue to live at home if you don't get better."

**Father:** "You can't continue to be this way and live at home anymore."

**Ryan:** (following a brief silence) "I will work hard."

Ryan now discloses his fear of relinquishing control and, with the support and encouragement of the therapists, reveals details of sexual abuse (all of Ryan's disclosures of abuse had been previously documented by social services). He expresses a range of emotions (rage, shame, guilt, fear) regarding incestuous experiences, and talks about one inherent conflict of sexual abuse ("sex with mother was wrong, but it felt good"). The therapists challenge Ryan's negative working model in reference to self-blame ("it was not your fault"). The mother is now invited back into the treatment room. Ryan is asked to share the previously discussed information and feelings with her while she holds him "in arms." The mother provides reassurance and acceptance, and the therapists validate Ryan's courage and healthy choices.

**Therapist M:** "You faced your memories and feelings today. How did it work out?"

**Ryan:** "I feel better. I'm okay."

**Therapist T:** "How do you feel about yourself?"

**Ryan:** "I don't hate myself now. I guess it was not my fault."

The session concludes with 20 minutes of mother-child secure attachment behavior (eye contact, positive affect, reciprocal smile, affectionate and nurturing touch, in arms). This is the first time Ryan allows such closeness and affection with mother.

### Session Five

Therapeutic goals:

- Continue child's treatment
- Enhance parent-child attachment
- Teach parenting skills
- Life script with parents (Appendix H).

The initial focus is on the specific parenting skills required to effectively manage the child's behavior. The parents and treatment team review the child's experiences in both the therapy sessions and the therapeutic foster home in order to clarify the salient aspects of child management. The parents are informed that conventional parenting skills are often ineffective with children who have attachment disorder, due to their desperate need to control, lack of trust with and attachment to the parents, and perception that authority figures are abusive, neglectful, and unreliable. The parenting skills taught in this session (and reviewed and reinforced throughout therapy) stress the importance of the parents "not getting hooked" into the child's attempts to manipulate, control, and compulsively replay prior dysfunctional relationship patterns. Parents are taught to stay neutral and provide logical consequences in an empathic manner, in contrast to becoming angry, hostile, and punitive. The angry, punitive parent is unknowingly "playing the child's game," allowing the child to maintain control and repeating prior patterns of parental hostility and rejection. These and other parenting techniques provide concrete tools that enhance the parents' sense of competency, improves their self-esteem, prevents further marital discord, and offers an alternative context in which the child's chances of changing are improved. (See Chapter 11 for a discussion on parenting skills.)

Often, it is necessary to help the parents identify and explore psychosocial issues from their family of origin. The parents complete the Life Script in a discussion session with the therapist to obtain such information as the roles, messages, and discipline techniques of their own parents; their parents as role models regarding conflict-management, communication, and affect; family relationship patterns; and their self-perceptions as children. The therapists encourage the parents to examine the association between attachment history, family of origin, and current marital and parent-child relationships.

The second part of the session focuses on continued treatment of the child. The child is encouraged to verbalize thoughts and feelings regarding maltreatment and attachment issues that were raised in previous sessions. Feelings regarding rejection, abandonment, abuse (physical, sexual, emotional), neglect, helplessness, hopelessness, and fear now begin to emerge. It is common at this point for the child to volunteer specific memories never before revealed. The child is guided through a discussion of these difficult emotions and of concomitant defenses.

The therapist provides a balance of challenge and support. The supportive message is, "We understand that you needed your defenses for protection and survival in the past." The challenging message is, "Those defenses are now preventing you from learning to love and trust, and we know you can handle these issues and emotions." This work with the child is preparatory for the experiential interventions that begin in Session Six.

At this point, we invite the mother to participate. We facilitate a mother-child dialogue in which the child reiterates the information shared with the therapist. This sharing serves several purposes, as the mother listens with acceptance and empathy:

• It reduces the child's shame about his or her role in prior traumatic events,

• The child's repeated airing of the "taboo" subjects reduces the negative emotional impact (desensitization), and

• It enhances the closeness and trust between mother and child.

The session ends with a review of the therapeutic issues from the entire week. The treatment team and parents address relevant issues and make plans for the parents to visit the therapeutic foster home over the weekend. One purpose of the visit is for the parents to observe the way in which the therapeutic foster parents deal with rules, responsibilities, discipline, problem solving, and communication. A second purpose is for the parents to practice their new parenting skills, giving the child and parents the opportunity to interact in a new and more positive way. Third, the parents and therapeutic foster parents are encouraged to interact in a cooperative and congenial manner, thereby presenting a united front to the child.

## Session Five Illustration

The therapeutic foster parents reported that Ryan was more oppositional, angry, and distant after yesterday's therapy session. This is a common and predictable reaction to the initial confrontation of emotional trauma and increased intimacy. The mother reported that her experience with Ryan at the conclusion of yesterday's session was "the first time he ever allowed genuine closeness." The father stated that this was the first time in four years of therapy that Ryan talked about his honest feelings regarding abuse in his birth family.

The focus now shifted to a discussion of effective parenting concepts and skills, including providing logical, nonpunitive consequences; teaching the child to be responsible, respectful, and resourceful; setting limits and avoiding control battles; modeling healthy attitudes and behavior; managing anger and frustration. The treatment team provided the parents with concrete examples of child management techniques.

Next, the parents' family-of-origin issues were explored using the Life Script data.

- **Mother's history.** Oldest of nine children, strong mother and unavailable father, often in a parental-child role, learned to be assertive, domineering, and affectionate.

- **Father's history.** Youngest of six children, domineering and punitive father and submissive, emotionally unavailable mother, learned to be a good provider, punitive, and unaffectionate.

A connection was made between these prior issues and current parenting practices. The mother tended to rescue and overcontrol Ryan, while the father became angry, punitive, and withdrawn. Based on the trusting therapeutic relationship established over five days, the parents were now open and responsive to the information.

Therapy with Ryan began with validation and support, followed by continued work on trauma and attachment issues.

**Therapist T:** "You are brave and you stick to your word. You came back."

**Ryan:** "I want to work on my life."

**Therapist T:** "What feelings do you have in this holding position?"

**Ryan:** "I have bad memories. I wasn't touched in the right way. I'm scared."

**Therapist T:** (to Therapist M) "He is being honest about his scared feelings."

**Ryan:** "I'm scared, but I'll work hard anyway."

**Therapist T:** "Start kicking and let me know when you are ready to talk about what happened; then give me a loud 'Ready.' "

**Ryan:** "Ready!" (shares details of abuse)

**Therapist T:** "How do you feel about your birth mother for what she did to you?"

**Ryan:** "I hate her for that."

**Therapist M:** "Did she put love or hate in your heart?"

**Ryan:** "They put hate in my heart. I am full of hate." (He repeats this several times with increased intensity.)

**Therapist M:** (shows Ryan a photo of birth mother) "What do you want to say to her?"

**Ryan:** "I hate you for abusing me. I don't want you running my life anymore." (screams)

**Therapist T:** "You are doing a great job."

**Ryan:** "I'm learning to get my feelings out and to trust."

Ryan is beginning to direct his rage towards the perpetrators, rather than toward his adoptive parents or himself. He is breaking the "code of silence," communicating verbally rather than acting out behaviorally, and learning to allow others to help him. He begins to examine a loyalty conflict, both hating his parents for abandonment and abuse, and desiring a positive connection with his roots.

The final portion of the session included contracting for new behaviors and positive attachment to adoptive mother. Ryan and therapeutic foster parents discussed new ways of handling noncompliance. Ryan agreed to discuss his feelings directly regarding the need for control rather than demonstrating them through oppositional actions. The session ended with Ryan hugging both therapists, followed by 20 minutes of close contact with Mother.

### Sessions Six, Seven, Eight

Therapeutic goals:

- Introduce experiential interventions

- Continue emotional resolution and cognitive revision

- Enhance attachment to mother and father

This phase of treatment builds on the foundation constructed during the first five sessions, shifting into a deeper and more intensive focus on direct emotional experience. A primary therapeutic method used is *psychodramatic reenactment*. As previously described, the child and treatment team role play prior traumatic scenarios, giving the child the opportunity to direct anger towards those responsible for maltreatment; experience and release the fear, pain, and sadness associated with loss and helplessness; and to experience vulnerability in a safe and secure context. Over the course of Sessions Six, Seven, and Eight, the child progresses developmentally in the reenactment experiences from a posture of pain, resignation, hopelessness, and victimization to a more hopeful position of emotional and interpersonal mastery, leading to improved self-esteem. The specific therapeutic results include an increase in the sense of personal power, a reduction in the self-perception of "victim," removal of the negative emotional charge associated with traumatic events, revision of unrealistic perceptions and fantasies about self and others (e.g., birth family), and development of a positive alliance with primary caregivers.

Some health care providers fear that these experiential methods will retraumatize children, assuming they are emotionally fragile and will suffer further psychological damage. Our experience, however, is that despite their dreadful early life experiences, most children are capable of confronting these harsh realities and that they do benefit significantly from deep and emotionally genuine therapeutic experiences and demonstrate positive changes, which are reported in follow-up interviews. For example, children consistently report, that although the therapy is difficult and challenging, they are pleased that they participated, feel a sense of relief and increased well-being, and would recommend it to others with similar problems.

Another primary therapeutic method used is the *inner child metaphor*. The recent popularity of "the child within" concept in current psychology self-help manuals has caused some observers to view this method as faddish and trendy. We have found, however, that when utilized in a specific therapeutic manner, this metaphoric technique is a powerful tool for positive change. The child, while in the holding-nurturing position, is gently guided back to a time in his or her life that is associated with traumatic events, and is asked to visualize him- or herself as that little boy or girl.

The desired outcome of the inner child metaphor is twofold: the healing of prior trauma and the development of the social skills and emotional capacity necessary for healthy relationships. The therapeutic interventions described above provide the child with positive attachment experiences that did not occur at earlier developmental stages. During these new attachment experiences the child may become threatened, sensing a loss of identity and control. To reduce this anxiety, it is crucial to provide the child with a new sense of self. We use the metaphor "letting go of the rage and darkness in your heart, and replacing them with love and lightness."

Mother-child attachment experiences are repeated many times during treatment. The emphasis on the attachment to a mother figure is based on the primacy of the mother-infant bond. The regressive experience enables the child to simulate that original mother-infant attachment. We often use baby bottles and blankets during the attachment exercises to enhance authenticity. It is interesting to note that although older children may initially be embarrassed by the use of these items, they rarely object and most often enjoy the experience.

The role of the father figure during therapy is important, despite the initial emphasis on mother-child attachment. The father learns parenting skills that increase the likelihood of positive family involvement at home. He is encouraged to provide support to his wife throughout the treatment process in order to strengthen and unify the parental dyad. During the mother-child attachment exercise, the father often sits next to his wife, his arm around her shoulders, giving support to her and to the mother-child relationship. Subsequently, the focus shifts to father-child attachment. Father uses the holding-nurturing position and proceeds through the phases of the attachment exercise with the child.

### Session Six Illustration

Ryan was described as considerably more affectionate and emotionally genuine over the weekend. The parents found the home visit helpful, as they were able to observe parenting skills in action. Ryan is informed we will now use role playing to further resolve emotional issues. The dialogue begins with recontracting.

**Ryan:** "I don't like doing this."

**Therapist T:** "I know this is hard, but will you do it anyway?"

**Ryan:** "I promised not to quit, so I'll work hard."

**Therapist M:** "The harder it is, the more you can get out of it. What do you want to tell your birth mom (role played by female counselor)?"

**Ryan:** (to birth mother) "I don't want to be around you. I hate what you did to me. You taught me to have a sick mind."

**Therapist M:** "Use powerful words!" (Ryan becomes physically agitated.)

**Ryan:** "I want to kill you!" (screams)

**Therapist T:** "Was anyone there to help or protect you?"

**Ryan:** "No, my father didn't help me: he was on my mom's side." (sobs)

**Therapist M:** "Who do you have in your life now to protect you?"

**Ryan:** "My mom."

**Therapist M:** "Call her."

**Ryan:** "Mom, help me!" (repeats several times)

The mother enters the treatment room, holds and comforts Ryan, and they both tell the "birth mother" to leave. Ryan now shifts his allegiance to his adoptive mother, allowing her to be protective and nurturing. The session ends with extended dialogue and closeness between Ryan and his mother.

## Session Seven Illustration

The foster parents stated that Ryan was more controlling, bossy, and did his chores poorly last night. We reassured the parents that regression is common and explained that this is a manifestation of the fear of change. We then prepared them for the technique of "firing" the child from therapy. This technique is commonly used to avoid power struggles and places the responsibility for change on the child. Ryan was predictably resistant and controlling in treatment. The therapists dialogued with one another about his resistance, and informed him that he can only come back to therapy if he earns it by showing that he wants to work hard. Ryan left with the foster parents, obviously angry and conflicted.

## Session Eight Illustration

Foster parents reported that Ryan was antagonistic and belligerent after being "fired." However, as the day progressed Ryan became more cooperative and "did a great job" with his chores. Ryan began therapy by expressing his feelings, "I'm angry you fired me, and I want to work hard today." The paradoxical technique of firing the child the day before had the desired effects: it gave him the opportunity to make his own choice about participating in therapy; it prevented a therapist-child power struggle; and it solidified his commitment and increased his motivation.

The following are excerpts from the psychodramatic reenactment regarding birth mother.

**Birth Mother:** "You can't change, you will always be just like me."

**Ryan:** "I am changing."

**Therapist M:** "You are doing great. Now, stand up, look her in the eyes, and tell her how you are changing."

**Ryan:** "I'm not afraid of you anymore. I'm not helpless."

**Therapist T:** "How are you feeling now?"

**Ryan:** "I feel stronger now, but how do I get my sad feelings out?"

The preceding intervention gave Ryan the opportunity to feel, think, and behave in a genuinely powerful and self-confident manner in reference to his birth mother. The inner child metaphor that follows facilitated the expression of vulnerability, the process of grieving over losses, and the resolution of self-contempt.

**Therapist M:** "Close your eyes. Picture yourself as a little boy. How old is he? What is he thinking and feeling?"

**Ryan:** "I'm four years old. I'm feeling alone and scared."

**Therapist M:** "Here is a little bear. Pretend this is you when you were that little boy. Tell him what he needs."

**Ryan:** "You need protection and someone to trust. You are sad because of what your parents did to you."

**Therapist M:** "Tell him what happens in his life."

**Ryan:** "You get abused, you can't trust anyone, your mother never meets your needs, you go to an orphanage, and you are adopted by a family that loves you, but you can't love them back."

**Therapist T:** "This little boy was very hurt and disappointed. How did he learn to feel about himself?"

**Ryan:** "He learned to hate himself!"

**Therapist T:** "Have you taken very good care of him?"

**Ryan:** "No, I thought he was bad."

**Therapist T:** "Ask him if he can forgive you for not taking good care of him and if he wants to learn how to love."

**Ryan:** "Yes, he wants to forgive me, but he is afraid."

**Therapist T:** "Do you know anyone who can help you learn to love this little boy?"

**Ryan:** (Calls for his mother. She comes in and holds Ryan and the bear.) "Could you teach me how to love?"

**Mother:** "Of course I will help you."

**Therapist T:** "Tell your mom you are scared, but you don't have to push her away anymore."

**Ryan:** "I still am scared, but I won't push you away. I'm learning to love and trust."

Ryan is confronting and resolving the losses of attachment figures while simultaneously forming a positive attachment to his adoptive mother. The father is now invited to participate. He is told to sit next to his wife, place his arm around her, and provide support. Ryan agrees to drink juice from a baby bottle, while experiencing 20 minutes of family attachment. He maintains eye contact with his mother while allowing closeness and comfort from both parents.

### Session Nine

Therapeutic goals:

- Enhance father-child attachment

- Facilitate grieving and forgiveness

- Reinforce effective parenting skills

Birth father issues, such as abuse and abandonment, become the central focus. Psychodramatic reenactment is utilized to provoke and resolve traumatic issues between child and birth father. The child is in the holding-nurturing position and given the opportunity to further complete the grieving process regarding the loss of birth parents.

Grieving and mourning loss is an essential component of the healing process. Although sad and painful, it promotes a letting go of the past, creates the possibility of a new future, and can lead to the beginning of forgiveness. A *"magic wand"* technique is used, in which the child can speak directly to "birth parents," who are role played by others. The child is told, "For the next ten minutes your birth parents will be healthy. They will be open, honest, and available to address your comments, questions, and concerns." The child can move toward closure on birth parent issues by expressing feelings of loss and asking questions about the parents' lives. For example, the "parents" may explain what happened to them in their own childhoods that influenced them to be abusive or neglectful. The child's increased understanding of the parents serves several purposes. It helps the child understand that he or she now has the tools to break the cycle of abuse. Unlike the parents, the child is receiving help and is now free to make different and better choices. Second, it promotes a more empathic and forgiving attitude. The concept of forgiveness has several meanings. Therapeutically, forgiveness involves the release of pain and anger associated with a traumatic event. The goal is for the child to acknowledge the parents' responsibility for maltreatment, but also to release him or herself from the burden of emotional pain.

Parent-child reunification occurs no later than Session Nine. Instead of going back to the therapeutic foster home, the child leaves with his or her own parents. This gives the parents an opportunity to apply the parenting skills they have learned and is diagnostic of the child's progress. The child's confidence is increased as he or she experiences a concrete demonstration of parental effectiveness.

## Session Nine Illustration

The parents shared their experience regarding another visit to the foster home the prior evening. They reported that Ryan was cooperative, animated, and communicative. Therapy with Ryan began with birth father issues, using psychodramatic reenactment.

**Ryan:** (speaking to "birth father") "I needed you to help me. I hate you for not helping." (screams)

**Therapist T:** "Tell your birth father how you would have turned out if you did not get help."

**Ryan:** "I worried I'd be like you."

**Therapist M:** "You are breaking the cycle."

**Ryan:** "Yes, I'm breaking the cycle. I'm learning to care, love, and trust."

**Father:** (Adoptive father storms into the treatment room and forcibly evicts the "birth father.") "I am here to protect you now." (Father holds Ryan and comforts him.)

**Ryan:** "Thank you for protecting me. I love and trust you 100 percent."

**Father:** "We love you 100 percent."

**Ryan:** "I was afraid I'd be like my birth father, abuse kids, and go to jail."

**Father:** "You don't have to worry about that anymore. You're getting the help you need."

**Ryan:** (Discloses "secrets" to his father.) "My parents made me watch them have sex and taught me how to do it. I'm ashamed of what I did and am afraid I would become a homosexual."

Father and son spend considerable time relating positively and discussing the prior issues. The mother then joins them and they prepare for the "magic wand" forgiveness ritual. Ryan speaks directly to his "birth parents" (in the role-playing format).

**Therapist M:** "Pretend we have a magic wand. Your birth parents are healthy and can hear what you have to say. Ask them why they treated you poorly."

**Birth Parents:** "We didn't know any better. We were also abused."

**Therapist M:** "What do you want to say to them, Ryan?"

**Ryan:** "It was your fault and your parents' fault. You should have gotten help. Will you ever get help?"

**Birth Parents:** "No, but we are glad you are getting help."

**Therapist T:** "Ryan, ask your birth parents how they feel about you being in a loving family now."

**Birth Parents:** (responding to Ryan) "We are happy you are in a good family and getting the love you deserve. Can you ever forgive us for how we treated you?"

**Ryan:** "Maybe some day I will forgive you for what you guys did to me."

*Session Ten*

Therapeutic goals:

- Review and summarize treatment

- Develop follow-up plans and goals

- Closure and termination

The final session begins with a report by the parents regarding the child's overnight visit. The treatment team, parents, and child process the family interactions and issues. Positive changes in parenting style, child's coping skills, and family dynamics are validated and supported. A discussion now ensues regarding the entire 10 sessions. We review major treatment issues and the learning experiences of each family member. A specific follow-up plan is developed collaboratively. The treatment team, parents, and child provide input regarding: type and frequency of follow-up therapy; unresolved treatment issues that need further attention; strengths and resources of child and family; medication evaluation, if appropriate; and availability of current treatment team for future consultations with parents, therapists, school, and case-workers. (See Appendix I for sample follow-up treatment plan.)

The parents typically have many questions for the treatment team. We provide concrete answers as well as give information about what can be expected in the future. The parents are informed that children often test their parents upon returning home, which is their attempt to determine the reliability of the parents, and is only transitional in nature. Parents are also informed that children commonly have a major setback, referred to as "the last hurrah," after a long period of improvement. This brief period of escalating negativity represents a "last ditch effort" to hold onto old destructive patterns. We help the parents prepare for this setback by emphasizing the importance of using their newly acquired parenting skills consistently.

Final closure involves a group exercise in which the treatment team, parents, and child respond to the following question: "What has this two-week therapy experience been like for you?" The intensity and emotionality of the two-week experience creates a sense of intimacy and connectiveness between all participants. This closure exercise gives everyone the chance to share personal reactions and feelings of appreciation.

## Session Ten Illustration

The parents report that the overnight visit went well. Ryan's mood was positive, and he related in a close and comfortable way. The father stated, "He was more respectful, did what was asked, and seems to have made a 180-degree turnaround." The mother shared, "He seems more like a little boy—he's softer." Next, plans were made for the future. The therapists informed the parents and Ryan what they can expect (e.g., testing, regression), and discussed follow-up therapy. A family meeting was recommended after returning home so that Ryan could share his therapy experience with his siblings and apologize for prior negative behaviors.

Therapy ended with the closure ritual: Each person shared what their two-week experience had meant to them. Family members and treatment team expressed their feelings and thoughts. The mother stated, "This has given Ryan the solid foundation he never had before." The father shared, "At first I thought this was hocus-pocus, but now I realize this has done a world of good for Ryan and our family." Ryan said, "I'm doing great! Thanks for helping me. This was hard work but I'm glad I did it."

## Follow-Up and Outcomes

Follow-up interviews were conducted at three, six, nine, and 18 months.  The parents reported continued steady progress at six and nine months. They reported Ryan's newfound ability to deal with disappointments, a cessation of violent outbursts, and a consistent demonstration of loving and affectionate behaviors. He showed no signs of depression, was genuinely kind and protective of siblings, and earned straight A's in school. He appeared at peace with himself and had become a team player (soccer and basketball). The parents also felt overall improvement in the quality of family life, including a significant reduction in stress and increased harmony among all family members.

The 18-month follow-up revealed similar positive results. Although Ryan's grades dropped to B's, he still responded well to rules and authority and was easily correctable. He was initiating hugs on a daily basis and expressing anger appropriately. Ryan was maintaining friendships and a talent for art and music was beginning to emerge. The mother had stopped rescuing and the father no longer disciplined in a punitive fashion. The mother wrote the following letter 18 months after treatment:

> Hi, I thought I would write you a little note to update you on Ryan and all of our progress. Ryan is doing great! I never thought I would be able to say those words about Ryan, but I can. He is just so content with himself. It is a hard thing to describe the way he is now but he seems at peace with himself for lack of a better word. He is still very opinionated and very verbal about his wants and needs, but when disappointed with not getting his own way he is just that, disappointed, not out of control. He did great in soccer this year and is now playing basketball (Dad is his coach) and truly is a team player. He is affectionate and loving now, he is still giving lots of hugs and kisses and because of him we all are doing a lot more hugging and kissing and truly loving it. He is genuinely kind to his brothers and sisters (yes, sisters) most of the time and is really kind.
>
> We owe you a great debt of thanks, for Ryan's healing was also helpful in our own healing. The disruptiveness of Ryan's everyday habits left us exhausted with just dealing with him on a day-to-day basis and you helped us to get back on the right track after being on the side of the road for so long. We keep you in our prayers daily and hope all is wonderful in your life for you truly deserve happiness for all that you give to others. Thanks again."

A five-year follow-up, when Ryan was 15, revealed the following information. Academically, Ryan maintains mostly A's and B's in advanced classes. He was recently awarded an art scholarship to a well-respected parochial high school. He participates in sports, excels in lacrosse, and placed third in wrestling in the region. Ryan demonstrates appropriate social skills, has a number of long-term friends, and positive sibling relationships. Although opinionated and moody at times, there are no signs of depression. He is appropriately compliant to rules and authority, including teachers, coaches, and parents. His parents consider him a warm and loving child.

## Treatment Outcome Research

There has been a vast amount of research done on attachment patterns in families, and on the beneficial effects of early intervention, attachment, and child development. However, little research has been compiled on the effectiveness of treatment that focuses specifically on children with attachment disorder. Two recent studies on treatment outcome are described below.

Goodwin [1996] measured changes in psychosocial functioning among children who completed the two-week treatment program at the Attachment Center at Evergreen (ACE). Using the Attachment Disorder Symptom Checklist (ADSCL), Goodwin found significant reductions in 18 of 19 symptoms. Only eating problems showed no significant treatment effects. The positive results of treatment did not diminish over time; 24-month follow-up revealed that the improvements were maintained. The results of this study, however, are limited by methodological concerns. The ADSCL is a nonstandardized instrument, posttreatment data was collected at varying times, and there was no control group.

Myeroff [1997] also investigated the effectiveness of children who participated in the two-week treatment program at ACE. Randolph [1997] focused on children who completed the two-week treatment program and remained in long-term treatment while in a therapeutic foster home at ACE. Both studies compiled pre- and posttreatment data on children ages 4 to 14, using the Child Behavior Checklist (CBCL) [Achenbach & Edelbrock 1983]. The CBCL is widely used for measuring psychosocial symptoms in children, has good reliability and validity, and yields eight subscales that are divided into three categories: internalizing, externalizing, and general problems. Myeroff's study examined the impact of treatment on externalizing problems. She found significant reductions in aggressive and delinquent behavior for children one week and six months posttreatment, compared to controls. The control group was matched regarding gender, race, age, preadoption placements, and income of parents. The Randolph study examined all eight CBCL subscales with children who remained in the ACE program (ongoing therapy; therapeutic foster home) for six to 12 months. Significant improvements were found on Anxiety-Depression, Thought-Attention Problems, Withdrawn Behavior, and Aggressive-Delinquent behaviors after six months. Significant decreases into subclinical range were found on all subscales after one year. This study indicates that children receiving both the two-week treatment and long-term program showed considerable improvement in all areas of psychosocial symptoms measured by the CBCL. The greatest improvements after six months of treatment were with externalizing problems (delinquent and aggressive behavior), while internalizing problems (withdrawal and anxious-depressed) improved more after one year. This finding suggests that acting-out behavior is modified more readily, while internalizing problems show steady improvement over time.

# 11

# Parenting the Child with Attachment Disorder

Learning to be an effective parent, particularly with special needs children, is an ongoing process. Most people do not possess the information and skills to parent effectively, although some have a natural temperament that increases the likelihood of success. Although all parenting is a challenging (and rewarding) task, parenting the child with attachment disorder is especially arduous. These children are commonly mistrustful, angry, irresponsible, defensive, dishonest, destructive, and do not give or accept affection and love. Parenting requires the firmness to set limits, the maturity to remain calm and centered, and the flexibility to meet the child's unique needs.

Learning to effectively parent children with attachment disorder involves gathering information, developing understanding, and considerable time spent in "practicing" skills. Parents who are open to this learning process usually develop the essential attitudes and skills over time. The remainder of this chapter focuses on the concepts, goals, and methods inherent in effective parenting with traumatized and acting-out children who have histories of disrupted and compromised attachment.

## Basic Concepts

- **Parents' background.** Parents' or caregivers' attachment histories play a significant role in their current lives. They must be aware of how prior family-of-origin issues influence their parenting attitudes and practices, marital relationships, and current psychosocial functioning. Parents invariably raise their children the way they were raised. Either they copy the behaviors modeled by their own parents ("replicative script") or they exert considerable effort in order to change what was done to them ("corrective script"). These reactionary strategies are seldom effective when the parents have unresolved family issues.

- **Attachment begins with the parents.** Parents and caregivers are responsible for creating a framework of love, sensitivity, empathy, caring, security, and protection. They must model effective communication, coping skills, problem solving, and management of emotions for their children. Parents must stay calm "in the eye of the storm"; i.e., they stay in control emotionally when the child is out of control emotionally or behaviorally. In order to accomplish this challenging task, parents must always follow the number one rule of good parenting, "Take good care of yourself."

- **New ideas and skills.** Parenting concepts and techniques that are effective with many children fail miserably with children who have attachment disorder. Parents often receive well-meaning but inappropriate advise on how to deal with these children. They become frustrated and hopeless as their child's problems continue to escalate. Parents must be willing and able to learn totally new concepts and techniques of parenting that are effective with children with attachment disorder.

- **Parenting for attachment.** Effective parenting with children with attachment disorder must provide the same key ingredients as secure parent-infant attachment. Parents provide a balance of structure and nurturance that changes based on the developmental needs and capabilities of the child. The child initially requires considerable structure ("box with a velvet lining") in order to feel safe and secure with the caregiver. This is a competency-based philosophy of parenting. As the child demonstrates healthy skills, attitudes, and behaviors, the structure is diminished and the child is given more freedom to make independent choices.

- **The "Four Rs."** Parents are taught that children are expected to be *responsible, respectful, resourceful* and *reciprocal.* Children are held accountable for their choices and actions and for responsibilities as a family member (e.g., chores). Children must demonstrate respectful attitudes and behavior toward parents, caregivers, siblings, and others. By treating their parents with respect, they learn self-respect. Children must learn to develop and use inner strengths and resources in order to solve problems and cope with life. Self-serving, controlling, and manipulative behavior must be replaced by a healthy "give and take" reciprocity with caregivers and others.

- **Support.** Support is crucial. Parenting children with attachment disorder is a demanding, challenging, and stressful responsibility. Parents must have sufficient support from both inside and outside of the family. A united front is crucial in the parental team, as is support from extended family. Extrafamilial support systems (e.g., social services, support groups) assist and empower the parents in meaningful ways.

- **Hope.** After years of unresolved conflict and failed attempts to remedy the problem, most parents come to us hopeless, demoralized, and burned out. They are angry at their child for his or her continual disruptiveness, at their partner for lack of understanding and support, at social service and mental health professionals for failing to "cure" the problem, and at themselves for feeling inadequate and powerless in their efforts to promote positive change. They have lost trust and faith in "the system," and in the possibility of a positive outcome for themselves and their family. The parenting framework must instill and enhance a sense of hopefulness, enabling parents to experience success.

- **Basic objectives for effective parenting.** Parenting attitudes, concepts, and techniques are designed to help their children with the following;

  - Develop the capacity to form secure attachments and reciprocal relationships; the ability to give and receive love and affection.

  - Develop the internal resources necessary to make healthy choices, solve problems, and manage adversity effectively.

- Cultivate a positive and realistic sense of self, and self-in-relation to the world.

- Learn to identify, manage, and express emotions in a constructive manner.

- Learn prosocial values and morality, and the self-discipline and self-control necessary to function successfully in society.

- Develop the capacity for joy, playfulness, and a positive meaning in life.

## Parenting Goals and Methods

Parents of children with attachment disorder often do not have clear and realistic goals in dealing with day-to-day difficulties. Some have the correct goals in mind, but lack the means to achieve those goals. Through more than 25 years of experience in working with children who have attachment disorder and their families, the current authors and colleagues have developed practical and effective strategies and solutions. Listed below are specific parenting goals and methods:

### Creating a Healing Environment

Parents cannot "fix" children with attachment disorder, but can establish and maintain a family climate conducive to positive change, attachment, and healing. Sustaining the healing environment is difficult with children who rebuff love, nurturance, and human contact, and requires that parents have achieved a substantial degree of maturity, positive self-regard, and resolution of prior emotional and attachment issues.

### Methods

- Set a positive family tone, rather than allowing the child to set a negative emotional tone in the family.

- Provide frequent and genuine nurturance, attention, and love, both physically and emotionally.

- Encourage the child to be affectionate on "parental terms." Parents take the lead in providing affection to reduce control and manipulation by the child.

- Avoid angry, sarcastic, or demeaning responses.

**Rule #1.** Parents (adoptive and foster) did not create the original problem, but are responsible for creating an environment conducive to solutions.

### Creating Clear and Consistent Structure

Children with attachment disorder are emotionally and behaviorally disorganized and need a predictable sense of order. Children learn trust, respect, and self-control in the context of appropriate parental structure. The more severe the child's attachment difficulties, the more the child requires the secure containment of a firm structure.

## Methods

- Establish control by setting appropriate rules and realistic limits.

- Maintain an organized home; e.g., consistent bedtime and dinnertime provides predictable routines that enhance feelings of safety.

- Avoid triangulation by setting clear boundaries; e.g., child cannot "play" one parent against the other, or a teacher against a parent.

- Inform the child of expectations, standards and rules, and hold the child consistently accountable.

**Rule #2:** Providing structure engenders feelings of safety and security in the child.

### Caring for Self and Partner

A burned-out parent is of little value to a challenging child, himself or herself, or other family members. Parents must take good care of themselves emotionally, physically, socially and spiritually. Parents often confuse self-care with selfishness. The selfish parent is overly concerned with his or her own needs, having little concern for the children or others. Parents who practice self-care are more available to meet the needs of their children and other family members, because they are of sound mind and body. The parent who takes good care of him- or herself has the energy available to help the child, and also models self-respect and self-love. Maintaining a fulfilling and supportive marital relationship is required for a well functioning family.

## Methods

- Maintain social supports, interests, and activities so that life remains enjoyable.

- Utilize such stress management techniques as physical exercise, meditation, yoga, dance, music, and other relaxation techniques.

- Place a priority on the marital relationship through quality time together and good communication.

**Rule #3:** Take good care of yourself and your partner.

### Communicating Effectively

The parents' style of communication with children is crucial. Messages have both an overt and covert component. The overt component is the content of what is said ("Put your coat on, it's cold outside"). The covert component is the "message behind the message" ("You are not smart enough to make your own decisions, so I will make the decision for you"). Parents must be aware of the messages they send, and the impact those messages have on their children.

## Methods

- Send warm, loving, accepting messages.

- Use eye contact and touch (e.g., hands on shoulder) to facilitate effective listening.

- Use "thinking" rather than "fighting" words. Make positive statements ("Feel free to join us for lunch when your chores are done"), in contrast to negative statements ("You can't eat until you do your chores"). Thinking words promote positivity and cooperation. Fighting words promote animosity, defiance, and conflict.

- Messages of praise or approval must be specific to a behavior or accomplishment. Children with negative working models (poor self-image) cannot accept or integrate praise and approval, because it deviates from their negative beliefs about themselves. In fact, these children often escalate negative acting-out behaviors following positive feedback from others. Children typically respond in two ways to receiving unconditional positives: 1) "You must be stupid, you don't know me and you don't know what you are talking about; don't you see that I am a bad person"; or 2) "If you tell me I am good I need to act worse in order to defy your authority and maintain control." Messages must be presented in the form of specific conditional positives, such as, "I like the way you cleaned your room"; or "Thanks for using words to express your anger."

- Save the pizzazz for the positives! Emotionality reinforces behavior. Rather than becoming highly emotional in response to a child's negativity, it is more productive to remain emotionally neutral and become emotionally animated in response to positive behaviors.

- Use a resource model of questioning the child, i.e., a method of communicating that encourages the child to find his or her own solutions and avoids power struggles with the parent. ("Tell me what happened? What did you think and feel at the time? How did you handle it? How did it work out for you? How can you handle it differently in the future?")

**Rule #4:** It's not only what you say, but how you say it!

### Providing Consequences Rather than Punishment

Consequences and punishment are different. The goal of consequencing is to teach the child a lesson that leads to positive choices and behaviors. The goal of punishment is to inflict pain and seek revenge. Angry parenting is punitive and ineffectual. Children with attachment disorder feel a sense of power and control when they provoke angry responses from their caregivers. Additionally, a punitive and angry parental approach feeds into the child's negative sense of self, replicating early abuser-victim patterns. Consequencing lead to self-examination—the child examines the results of choices and actions. Punishment leads to resentment; i.e., the child and parent remain angry and attribute blame to one another. Consequencing is designed to meet the child's needs for learning, firm and caring structure, and accountability. Punishment is designed to meet the parent's needs for reprisal, tension reduction, and domination.

Parents often report that consequencing is ineffective as a tool in teaching personal responsibility or promoting behavioral change. This is in fact true; due to lack of cause-and-effect thinking and a chronic need to control at all costs, children with severe attachment disorder do not accept or learn from consequences. In such cases, appropriate therapeutic interventions are necessary prior to the application of consequential parenting techniques.

## Methods

- **Provide naturally occurring consequences when possible.** "The real world operates on consequences. If we do a consistently lousy job at work, our boss doesn't take away our VCR. He fires us!" [Cline & Fay 1990, p. 90]. Children who learn to accept the consequences of their choices and actions are simultaneously learning cause-and-effect thinking. Example: A child goes outside without a jacket and is cold, or misses dinner and is hungry; the parent does not rescue the child from his or her choices.

- **Impose consequences when naturally occurring consequences are not available.** Imposed consequences are most effective when they are enforceable, match the behavior, and are delivered in a warm and empathic manner. Example: The child with poor table manners is excused from the table by the parent and told, "feel free to eat with the family when you have good table manners, but for now you can eat in the other room."

- **Consequencing takes thought and does not have to be presented immediately.** Well-thought-out consequences are more effective than those presented impulsively. Example: Mom says to child, "I'm not sure what to do about this right now, but Dad and I will discuss it and we will get back to you. That will give you and us plenty of time to think it over." Taking time allows the parents to respond without anger and allows the child time to consider his or her actions.

**Rule #5:** Punitive parenting is ineffective and damaging.

### Identifying Units of Concern

Individuals can experience various degrees of concern regarding a particular problem or situation. Parents commonly take on too much of the concern for a child's problem, leaving the child with too little concern. When the parents are overresponsible, the child is not invested in creating a solution. Children are motivated when they "own" the problem. Without ownership there is little responsibility or motivation.

## Methods

- **The first step is to determine, "Who owns the problem?"** To determine ownership of a particular problem a parent must ask the following questions: "To what extent does this impact on my life, directly or indirectly? Whose choices and actions led to the problem? Who is responsible for the remedy?"

- **Assume there are 10 units of concern for any particular problem.** Parents are asked to determine the number of units of concern that they have and that their child has. For example, a child is demonstrating little effort academically. Mother is asked how many units of concern she is taking (mother replies, "6 units").

Father is asked the same question (father replies, "4 units"). This leaves the child with no units of concern for his or her problem. The child is left with no ownership of the problem, no motivation to find a solution, and no sense of responsibility or accountability.

- **Responsibility for solving a problem must be shifted from the parents to the child, so the child has the appropriate units of concern.** The parents might say to the child, "I will be glad to give you lots of support in your efforts to work things out with your teachers and counselor at school; let me know if you need my support."

**Rule #6:** Parents who take too much responsibility have children who take too little.

### Participating in the Family

An important way to enhance a child's involvement in a family is through chores. Chores help a child learn "life skills" by assuming responsibility and functioning independently. They also increase self-esteem and a sense of accomplishment. Further, important family values are learned by doing chores ("everyone in the family pulls their weight; take pride in what you do"). Due to the fact that children with attachment disorder are typically noncompliant and lack reciprocity, chores are particularly crucial. Chores provide assessment of, as well as practice with, reciprocity and compliance; both are important for secure attachment.

### Methods

- **Children are encouraged to do chores in the following way:** "Fast and snappy, right the first time, Mom and Dad's way."

- **Parents must avoid control battles when the child refuses to do a chore, or does it incorrectly or incompletely.** Parents provide a consequence and identify acceptable choices. For example, the child's chore is to set the dinner table, and he refuses. The parents sets the table minus the child's plate. The child asks where his plate is and the parent replies, "Feel free to eat with the family next time if you choose to do your chore. Tonight you can have your dinner apart from the family."

**Rule #7:** Chores help a child feel good about himself and about being part of a family.

### Giving Choices

Commands and directives from parents lead to control battles and power struggles with oppositional and controlling children. Providing the child with choices is more constructive and effective. Choices invite the child to think, problem solve, and learn from mistakes. Choices set up a win-win scenario: The parents win because they are providing the choices; the child wins because he or she is empowered by having the opportunity to select one of the choices. Additionally, a positive message is conveyed to the child ("I will respect your choice"). It is imperative that all choices given are ones that are acceptable to the parents. This is a version of an Ericksonian technique called the illusion of alternatives; the alternative of not responding at all is not offered.

## Methods

- **Only give choices that you can live with.** The parent must be willing to allow the child to experience the consequences of his or her choices. For example: "You can wear the same clothes again and I will drop you off with the sitter, or you can put clean clothes on and go with us to the movie."

- **Remain emotionally neutral** when the child attempts to introduce other choices, and calmly reiterate the original choices.

**Rule #8:** Give choices you can live with.

### Parenting Creatively

Parenting a child who has attachment disorder is challenging and it helps to have a "framework for freedom": strategies and methods that prevent the child from "ruffling your feathers." Parenting strategies must be creative, safe, and appropriate to the characteristics of the child, family, and situation. The methods listed below have been found to enhance learning opportunities for children and increase confidence and competence of parents.

## Methods

- **Hassle time.** Increases reciprocity by repayment: "You owe me a half hour of work as repayment for annoying me in the store." This allows the parent to feel better about the child instead of remaining angry and resentful. It also enables the child to demonstrate accountability and "clean the slate."

- **Parent on strike.** When a child refuses to be compliant and responsible, the parent can discontinue services. Only the basics for survival and protection are provided: "Sorry, honey, I won't be giving you a ride to your friend's house. Please ask again when you decide to be a responsible family member." It is more constructive for the parent to discontinue services than to provide services while feeling angry and resentful. It also teaches the child about appreciation and reciprocity.

- **One-minute reprimand.** At times a parent must confront a child directly regarding poor choices and negative behaviors. This is done eye-to-eye, face-to-face, with firm and caring touch (e.g., hands on child's arms or shoulders). The parent is honest and explicit about his or her anger or frustration, without attacking or threatening. This procedure allows the parent to "vent" honestly and openly, to model appropriate verbal expression of anger, and enables the child to be confronted on the realities and consequences of his or her behavior. After this time-limited confrontation, the parent offers warmth, support, and love, and reaches out to hug the child.

- **Double binding.** Oppositional children sometimes need to be told to do more of a negative behavior ("prescribe the symptom"). This creates a double bind: If the child displays the negative behavior, it is expressed at the request of and under the control of the parent; if the child refuses to display the negative behavior, the parent is pleased with the child's decision not to act out. For example: A parent might say, "Great temper tantrum, can you scream louder?" Prior to giving the child a chore, a parent might say "I really want you to do a very bad job with this chore, do it slowly and don't finish it." Ironically, contrary children typically do not follow the parental directive, i.e., they do it right!

- **Think-it-over spot.** This is a three-step problem resolution process. First, the child who is acting out is told to sit for a brief period of time (depending on the chronological and emotional age of the child). This de-escalates stress and anger for both parent and child. Second, both the parent and child "think it over." The child is asked to think about choices, behaviors, and consequences. The parent thinks about the best way to handle his or her own emotions and how to attain a positive outcome for the child. Third, when the time-out is over, the parent and child communicate about the nature of the problem and possible constructive solutions.

- **One-liners.** Parents often need a phrase or expression that prevents negative engagement with an acting-out child. One-liners are short phrases, expressed with empathy rather than anger or sarcasm, that focus the problem back to the child. Examples: "Sorry you feel that way honey. That's an interesting thought. That was a bad choice—how sad for you. What do you think I think? A smart kid like you can figure it out. Is that taking good care of yourself? Well, who lies a lot? Do you think I just fell off the 'dumb mom' truck?"

- **Fake it until you make it.** New choices, behaviors, and ways of relating initially feel unnatural to children and parents. They are instructed to rehearse new behavior; over time, these new ways of relating begin to feel more comfortable and lead to positive changes. Example: An angry parent is instructed to provide communication and consequences "as if they weren't angry." This results in more effective anger management and anger reduction.

**Rule #9:** Be creative, have fun, stay light.

### Parenting Is Competency Based

Secure attachment is an ongoing process of structure and freedom, closeness and separateness, dependence and independence. The secure base during the early stages of attachment serves as a springboard for later autonomy, competence, and mastery. The infant is helpless and vulnerable and totally dependent on primary caregivers. These caregivers are responsible for fulfilling the infant's basic needs and for providing protection and security. As the infant develops, the sensitively attuned caregiver allows more opportunities for autonomous exploration and independent activity. The ongoing balance between connection and autonomy changes developmentally in accordance with the needs and capabilities of the child.

As development unfolds, the child who is securely attached is able to demonstrate competency in four areas: *knowledge, skills, judgment,* and *self-control* (Figure

6). Security of attachment provides a foundation for optimal information processing, the attainment of personal and social skills, the judgment to make appropriate choices, and the ability to regulate emotions and impulses. Children with attachment disorder, in contrast, have not developed competency in these four areas. They do not demonstrate (or, in many cases, possess) the knowledge, skills, judgment, and self-control necessary to be caring and responsible. There is a huge difference between their chronological and psychosocial ages. They have physical characteristics of their age, but think, act, and relate on a much younger level. For example, a 10-year-old child with a history of disorganized attachment may act as if he is independent (i.e., not needing anyone, making own decisions, discarding guidance and adult direction). In truth, the child is incapable of such independence and autonomy, and typically demonstrates ineptitude through irresponsible, defiant, and immature choices and actions.

The key to effective parenting (and treatment) with children with attachment disorder is to *contain them within the boundaries of their capabilities*. The structure provided must correspond to their emotional, behavioral, and developmental level of functioning.

## Methods

In Figure 6, each circle represents family rules and structure, starting with the totally dependent infant and moving outward until adulthood. Contained within each circle is 1) responsibility/obligation and 2) power/freedom. It is important that these two features are balanced. If you have a child who is handling responsibility/obligation, yet is denied appropriate power/freedom, then it is likely that he or she will become rebellious. Conversely, if you have a child who has considerable power/freedom, yet demonstrates insufficient responsibility/obligation, then you invariably will have a "spoiled" child. The attainment of increased responsibility and privileges should be competency based. As a child shows increased mastery, he or she moves further toward autonomy. On this path, the child should be in charge of everything within his or her circle. However, each newly attained parameter should be earned through demonstration of responsible behavior [Buenning 1995].

**Rule #10:** Contain children within the boundaries of their capabilities.

In conclusion, parenting a child with attachment disorder is a challenging task. Parents often say, "I really blew it with my kid. I'll never understand how to do it right. I will never get over my hurt and anger." Providing information, skills, and ongoing support to parents reduces their frustration, helplessness and pessimism, and increases their sense of confidence and empowerment. Finally, a sense of humor in parenting difficult children is crucial. Sometimes laughter is the best medicine. Not only does humor provide relief for the parent, but it also avoids negative interactions with the child.

## Figure 6. The Autonomy Circle

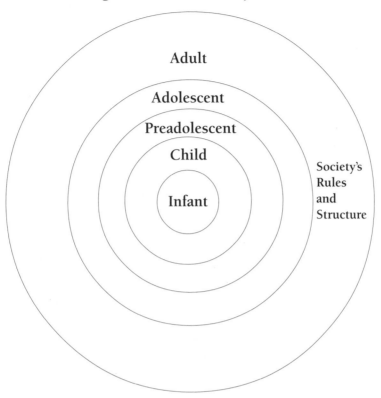

Family's Rules and Structure
Must balance
Responsibility/obligation
Power/freedom

Four competency areas:
Knowledge
Skills
Judgment
Self-control

# 12

# The Child Welfare System & Public Policy

Attachment disorder permeates the social service, mental health, and child welfare system in the United States. This chapter will examine the problems and challenges inherent in foster care, adoption, and substitute child care, and provide possible solutions. Early intervention, education, and prevention programs, which have successfully enhanced healthy family attachment and child development, will be described.

## Foster Care: A System in Turmoil

An increasing number of disturbed children have entered the foster care system recently; since 1985 the foster care population has more than doubled. These children often stay in foster homes for years as overwhelmed caseworkers try to help biological parents with the problems that made them abusive or neglectful. Ninety-four percent of infants entering foster care were found to have a history of maternal drug abuse [Halfon et al. 1995], and 75% of children entering care had a family history of mental illness or drug and alcohol abuse [Chernoff et al. 1994]. The federal government spends $3.5 billion annually (matched by states) to finance these out-of-home placements.

Children entering foster care have an abundance of risk factors and an absence of protective factors: abuse and neglect; poverty; lack of prenatal care; prenatal drug and alcohol exposure; teenage pregnancy and birth; family history of mental illness, substance abuse, and criminality; violent homes and neighborhoods; anxious and disorganized attachments with caregivers. These traumatic experiences are confounded by multiple losses—separations from biological parents, siblings, communities, and cultural ties.

The crisis in foster care can be attributed to a number of factors [Klee et al. 1997]:

- Ballooning foster care population;

- Inadequate public funding, severely limiting resources to meet the needs of children and foster parents;

- Increased emotional, behavioral, and medical needs of children in out-of-home care, and more serious problems of their biological parents;

- Increased stress on the staff of child welfare agencies, including difficulties in recruiting and retaining caseworkers due to high case loads, inadequate salaries, and burnout;

- Diminishing numbers of foster parents, due to the poor image of foster care, inferior pay, and inadequate support and training; and

- Community services that are uncoordinated, inaccessible, or nonexistent.

## Historical Overview

Prior to 1800, children rarely were involved in public care. In the 19th century, the development of public concern and policy for dependent, abused, and neglected children came almost exclusively from private, secular agencies like Societies for the Prevention of Cruelty to Children. These organizations were the leaders in protecting children, advocating for better legislation and public sector support for safeguarding children's interests. Only one state, Indiana, had a governmental body to overlook child welfare. The community's responsibility for abandoned and unwanted babies led to the creation of foundling hospitals in the early 19th century, and the practice of institutionalizing children [Schene 1996].

In 1920, the Child Welfare League of America was founded. The CWLA helped to standardize national child welfare programs that stressed temporary rather than permanent institutional care for dependent children, and attempted to preserve the natural family whenever possible. By the 1930s, the private humane societies functions of child protection were being taken over by public organizations. The Social Security Act of 1935 marked the first federal government attempt to fund child welfare services. Title IV-A, later Aid to Families with Dependent Children (AFDC), addressed the financial needs of children deprived of parental support. Title IV-B (Child Welfare Services) encouraged the expansion of services to vulnerable children by providing states with formula grants. Funds were available through IV-B to pay for foster care, but not to provide supportive services to biological families

In the 1930s and 1940s, the development of social casework methodologies led to a change in child protection from a law enforcement, punitive model, to an emphasis on an aggressive social service rehabilitative model. In the 1960s and early 1970s there was a significant increase in federal funding for state social service programs. Child abuse emerged as an issue of major importance. Reporting laws were passed in all states mandating professionals to identify children who needed protection.

The Child Abuse Prevention and Treatment Act, passed in 1974, provided funds to assist in developing programs and services for abused and neglected children and families. The Adoption Assistance and Child Welfare Act of 1980 was the federal government's first attempt to develop and implement a national policy regarding child welfare. A major goal of this policy was to maintain and reunite children with their families (family preservation) and to reduce the large number of children who were drifting permanently in the foster care system [Schene 1996]. This legislation initiated federal adoption assistance, which spurred the effort to find homes for children with "special needs" by offering monthly subsidies to families who would adopt. The term "special needs" was introduced as social service agencies began to increase their efforts to find homes for hard-to-adopt children. This group included children who had varying racial backgrounds, were older, in multisibling situations, and were physically and/or mentally disabled. Prior to the 1970s most adoptions were with healthy same-race infants. Today, approximately 90% of children adopted from agencies are "special needs."

Most social service and mental health programs did not realistically anticipate special needs problems and were not adequately prepared to respond. Adoption agencies and social services had little experience or training to deal with the problems confronting this new wave of adoptees and their families. The system became severely taxed in its ability to meet the needs of children in placement. In 1989, the Select Committee on Children, Youth and Families of the U.S. House of Representatives issued a report entitled "No Place to Call Home: Discarded Children in America." The report exposed the nation's failure to provide for children and families in crisis, and documented a dramatic deterioration in the foster care, juvenile justice, and mental health systems during the 1980s. The report concluded that there was a massive failure at all levels of government to enforce the laws that provide children with services and protection: "As a result, children bounce from one system to another, and fail to receive the counseling and safeguards necessary to enable them to find permanent families and essential services" [U.S. Select Committee on C.Y.F. 1989, p. 3]. The report also found the child welfare service system to be totally overwhelmed; an estimated 70 to 80% of emotionally disturbed children received inappropriate mental health services or no services at all. Excessive caseloads contributed to overburdening the system's ability to provide minimal care and appropriate services.

A 1989 study, funded by the Casey Foundation, found that the quality of foster care deteriorated as a result of several factors: a national preoccupation with child abuse and neglect, cutbacks in federal funds, federal legislation that denigrates foster care, and the belief that the needs of troubled families are best met with a minimum of government intervention [Kamerman & Kahn 1989]. The goal of the Federal Adoption Assistance and Child Welfare Act of 1980 was to preserve families. However, political agendas and subsequent funding cutbacks left the social service system unable to provide services to address serious family problems, such as increased drug abuse, homelessness, poverty, violence, teenage pregnancy, and AIDS. The goals of child protective services were to remove children from dangerous and maltreating homes and place them in alternative environments, such as foster homes. Again, foster parents lacked adequate emotional support, economic support, and specialized training to handle these damaged children. To date, our society has done little to remedy this situation. Consider the following:

- The number of children in foster care increased over 75% from 1985 (280,000) to 1995 (490,000). There may be 1 million children in foster care by the year 2000 [CWLA 1996].

- During the last 10 years, the number of licensed foster homes dropped due to lack of agency support, low reimbursements coupled with increased cost of living, and increased needs of foster children [CWLA 1996].

- Rates of psychopathology among children in foster care have been found to be between 40-80%, including numerous emotional, social, developmental, and medical problems [Schneiderman et al 1998].

- Forty percent of foster children stay in care longer than two years, and 15% remain over four years [CWLA 1996].

- Former foster children make up 17% of America's state prison population [Craig 1995].

- Seventy-five percent of placements are a result of severe abuse and/or neglect [Risley-Curtiss 1996].

In November 1997, President Clinton signed into law the most significant overhaul of the nation's foster care system in 17 years—the Adoption and Safe Families Act. This legislation is designed to improve the safety of children, to promote adoption and other permanent homes, and to support families. It includes an adoption incentive plan where states are paid bonuses for each foster child adopted and for each special needs adoption. The law also requires states to document reasonable efforts to place a child for adoption (including kinship care), and provides health care coverage to all special needs children who receive adoption assistance. States continue to be required to make reasonable efforts to reunify families; however, the child's health and safety is the paramount concern. It is a well-meaning and worthy goal to place children in permanent adoptive homes. This goal, however, will only lead to more frustration and failure without appropriate preplacement assessment of children and families and effective treatment for children with attachment disorder. Adoptive families must be prepared to effectively respond to the special needs of these angry and mistrustful children. Additionally, postplacement treatment and support reduces the likelihood of disruption.

### Siblings in Foster Care

There are approximately 500,000 children who are currently in foster care in this country. Sixty-five to 85% of these children have at least one sibling and 30% have four or more siblings. Seventy-five percent of sibling groups are separated after they enter the foster care system [Phillips 1998]. In theory, siblings are supposed to be placed together; however, this is the exception rather than the rule. The reasons for separating siblings groups in foster care are numerous, but the most common reasons are logistical. Foster homes tend to fill their placement quotas with children from several different homes and lack sufficient space when a sibling group needs placement [Lawrence & Lankford 1997]. Siblings are also separated because it is difficult to find families willing to accept a sibling group.

Relationships with siblings over a lifetime are usually our most enduring. The intensity of the sibling bond is enhanced by several factors: accessibility of siblings to one another, lack of parental protection and need fulfillment, and the ongoing search for personal identity. Children who enter the foster care system rely heavily on sibling attachments due to inadequate parental attachments. The presence of a sibling relationship minimizes the trauma of parental separation and loss. When siblings are separated through foster care and adoption, they experience further trauma [Schooler 1997].

There are situations, however, when the separation of siblings groups is warranted. Quite often members of a sibling group are suffering from severe attachment disorder. If one sibling has attachment disorder, it is likely that other siblings have varying degrees of this problem. Taking on the special needs of such a sibling group can be overwhelming for one foster family. This can place the family at risk for disruption and jeopardize the well-being of other children in the home. Another legitimate reason for separating siblings occurs when one has victimized another (physical or sexual abuse). Even the most diligent foster parent cannot watch the siblings 24 hours a day. The abused sibling(s) are at risk for further victimization. Making the decision to separate siblings is never easy for courts and social service agencies. A comprehensive attachment disorder assessment is often helpful in determining placement appropriateness for sibling groups.

*Recommendations*

### Family Preservation

The goal of keeping families together failed because the child welfare and mental health systems could not keep pace with the vast increases in drug abuse, poverty, violence, and resulting child maltreatment. The "myth of family preservation" [Pelton 1997] suggests that there have actually been two child welfare systems operating— one oriented toward preserving families, and the other toward removing children from maltreating homes. The reality is, it is impossible to keep families together when children are at risk for abuse and neglect. Removing a child from a dangerous environment, placing him or her in temporary foster care, then returning that child to abusive parents is not family preservation—it is insanity!

Early intervention and prevention programs that focus on training and supporting high-risk parents and encouraging secure parent-child attachment in the first three years of life, offer the best hope for family preservation. Programs that identify high-risk families and provide education, support, and appropriate treatment before and during pregnancy, and during the crucial early developmental stages of infancy and toddlerhood, have been successful in preventing family disruption, establishing secure attachments, and improving psychosocial functioning of children as they develop.

### Place Early—Don't Move

Children in the foster care system who are subjected to multiple placements are deprived of stability, continuity of caregivers, and the opportunity for developing secure attachments. Children who are placed at any early age, and remain in that family for at least 10 years, have the lowest rates of behavioral problems, delinquency, adult violence, and criminality [Widom 1991]. Children not adopted out of the system benefit from establishing long-term secure attachments with foster parents.

### Early Assessment and Intervention

There are increasing numbers of children who enter the foster care system with severe behavioral and emotional problems. These antisocial children lack conscience and morality, lie and steal, defy and mistrust authority, and are hostile, aggressive, and controlling. In short, they have severe attachment disorder. Research shows that these are the children who experience frequent placement moves, because they are dangerous and disruptive in foster homes [Widom 1991]. It is imperative to accurately diagnose attachment disorder prior to placement in order to 1) provide the appropriate therapeutic foster care placement, and 2) provide proper corrective attachment therapy and parenting.

### Training and Support of Foster Parents

Children with severe attachment disorder must be placed with therapeutic foster parents who receive ongoing training and support. Specialized foster parents must be skilled in Corrective Attachment Parenting and serve as a member of a unified treatment team. Support must be ongoing, including emotional support from placing agencies, appropriate financial reimbursement, and available and appropriate respite. It is a well-known fact that foster parents do not receive adequate recognition or reimbursement. In many states, foster parents do not receive sufficient compensation to cover the cost of caring for a child [Vick 1997]. Foster parents—the true heroes of child welfare—are commonly angry and frustrated due to lack of agency and community support, understanding, and recognition. They are charged with the responsibility of maintaining disturbed children in their homes 24 hours a day, seven days a week, yet the child welfare system has not been responsible in assisting them in this task.

### Kinship Care

Fifty percent of foster care placements in larger states are now through kinship care—placing children with grandparents, aunts and uncles, cousins, or other extended family. Siblings are more likely to be placed together through kinship care than within traditional foster homes. Relatives are more likely to make a commitment to a sibling group, and the children are better able to maintain a sense of identity, connection, and continuity. Since attachment disorder and its causes (maltreatment, poverty, violence, drug abuse) are intergenerationally transmitted, it is crucial that extended kin are evaluated regarding their ability to care for the children being placed.

## Adoption: A Crisis in America

Although many children with attachment disorder are adopted, not all adopted children have severe attachment problems. Many infants, if adopted early, will develop secure attachments to their adopted parents and live healthy, productive lives [Schaffer & Lindstrom 1989]. The key factors in regard to severity of attachment disorder are the child's age at adoption, the number of prior moves, and abuse and neglect in the first two years of life. These factors seriously affect children's ability to form close relationships throughout their lives. Unfortunately, a high number of adoptive children fall into the attachment disorder category, and are coming to the attention of the mental health, social service, and criminal justice systems.

Developmental research pertaining to the adjustment of adopted children indicates they are at greater risk for developing emotional, social, behavioral, and/or academic problems than nonadopted children [Bohman & Sigvardsson 1980, 1985; Borgatta & Fanshel 1965; Brodzinsky et al. 1984; Kenny et al. 1967; Lindholm &

Touliatos 1980; cited in Brodzinsky & Schechter 1990]. Adopted children, who comprise only 2% of children under 18 in this country, represent approximately one-third of children who are placed in residential treatment and adolescent psychiatric centers. Adopted children are referred for psychological treatment two to five times more frequently than their nonadopted peers; they are twice as likely to display psychosocial problems in childhood or later life, and are two to three times more likely to display psychopathic conduct disorder behaviors [Jones 1997]. Attention deficit disorder is 10 times higher among adoptees. An inordinate number of adoptees are sexually promiscuous and become pregnant or impregnate someone in adolescence. They have a higher incidence of running away and have more difficulties in school, both academically and socially, than nonadopted children. Adopted children are involved in disproportionate numbers in the criminal justice system [Verrier 1994].

Adoption may trigger issues of abandonment. There are two quite opposite responses to being abandoned as a child. One way adoptees deal with their abandonment fears is to provoke rejection by others ("I'll reject you before you reject me"). They accomplish this by provocation, aggression, and other antisocial behaviors. The other coping strategy is to be acquiescent, compliant, and withdrawn ("If I please you and stay out of your way, you won't leave me"). Regardless of which approach is used, most children who have been abandoned have issues in one or more of the followings areas: separation and loss, trust, rejection, guilt, shame, intimacy, identity, loyalty, power, and control.

Although, as previously stated, many infants adopted early do establish secure attachments, it is not uncommon for children adopted at birth or soon after to display attachment difficulties. Recent advances in prenatal psychology have provided insight into why this is so. The fetus and mother shared a nine-month experience where they were biologically and emotionally bonded. For example, the womb is a sound chamber where the fetus is never beyond the range of mother's voice or heartbeat. A newborn will recognize and respond to mother's voice, face, and biorhythms [Stern 1985]. Neonates can also recognize mother's smell: sweat, urine, breath, saliva, and breast milk all contain scent-communicating chemicals [Furlow 1996]. At birth, the newborn "knows" who his or her mother is and is not.

A child's primary connection is the lifeline to his or her biological family, no matter how insufficient or limiting it is. Even children with strong, enduring attachments with adoptive parents have this lifeline to biological parents. The best adoptive parents cannot replace what the child yearns for. This longing is always there, either on the surface or unconsciously. Until they are able to come to terms with deep unresolved feelings toward their birth family, children may continue to experience both profound grief over their loss and rage directed toward a world that hurt them [Jernberg 1990].

### An Adoption Saga

Genuinely warm and caring parents adopt children and bring them into their homes with the intent of offering a stable, loving environment and a commitment to make them a part of the family. They have a vision of bestowing on the child all the love required, and believe they will be loved and appreciated in return. However, it does not take long before some children are showing their skills and imagination in maintaining chaos in the family. No parenting methods seem to work, and punishment only seems to make the child worse. After vacillating between techniques, and experiencing confusion, anger and despair, some parents finally give up [Orlans 1993].

An adoptive parent writes:

> We've tried point systems, rewards for good behavior, and taking privileges away. I have never been successful making time-out work. Our family has been torn apart by him. We have a hard time finding baby-sitters who can handle him, so we don't go anywhere anymore. We feel totally helpless and hopeless. We are tired of all this craziness and manipulation. We just feel terribly frustrated, angry, and want to give up. We want to believe that somewhere out there is a way to break the stronghold on him and offer our whole family the bright future that could be.

The desperate family begins to seek help, but counselors unfamiliar with attachment issues offer few solutions. They are told by therapists and social workers that "all the child needs is love and a stable home." Little do these professionals realize that these children have no foundation upon which to understand or accept love. The parents have exhausted every resource only to receive frustration, placation, and even condemnation for their efforts. Uneducated friends and extended family also add to the adoptive parents frustration. Another adoptive parent writes:

> As far as others are concerned, Sarah is a perfectly normal ... even "sweet" little girl. When we attempt to correct her in front of my family, they make excuses for her: "Oh, that's just little girls," or "It's the age," or "I don't mind, she's so cute," or "Don't be so hard on her."

A vicious cycle soon develops where, due to extreme exasperation, the parents (particularly the mother) appear increasingly angry and frustrated. The child is an expert at appearing charming and engaging to others, and the problem is assumed to be due to rejection and hostility from the adoptive parents. Unwitting professionals see this anger and frustration as reaffirming of their assumptions that the parents need to "lighten up" and be more loving. This total lack of understanding serves to further alienate the family and to increase their isolation, resentment, and hostility. Many mental health professionals are still under the false presumption that a loving adoptive home is a cure for children who have been abused and neglected and who have attachment disorder. We have learned, however, that abuse most often has lingering effects that love alone is incapable of curing. The child with severe attachment disorder who comes into an adoptive home is unable to respond positively to stability or love. He or she is bent on maintaining chaos, perpetuating hostility, and avoid closeness.

## International Adoption

After the Korean War, the adoption of foreign-born children became increasingly more common in the United States. The nationalities most adopted were Korean, South American, and East Indian. Two million Americans want to adopt babies each year, but only 50,000 manage to do so, and then only often after years of bureaucratic delays. This has made international adoptions more and more appealing as an alternative for those who want to adopt. In 1997, 13,620 children were adopted from outside the United States, compared to 5,315 children in 1978. Children were adopted most often from the following countries [Adoptive Families 1997b]:

| | |
|---|---|
| Russia | 3,816 |
| China | 3,597 |
| South Korea | 1,654 |
| Guatemala | 788 |
| Romania | 621 |

Adoption of children from former Eastern Bloc countries (Russia, Romania, other ex-USSR) quadrupled from 1992 through 1996. For example, Americans could travel to Romania and adopt a child in as little as two weeks. Adoption was not only much quicker, but also became easier for people in single and alternative lifestyles. These Romanian children, although malnourished, appeared cute and charming to their hopeful prospective parents. After adoption, serious emotional problems began to appear. What the adoptive parents did not realize was the extreme degree of deprivation the children had experienced, and the impact this would have on their behavior. Romania's dictator, Nicolae Ceausescu, required each woman of child-bearing age to have five children for the state. His plan was to raise workers and soldiers to do his bidding. He did not plan for adequate nutrition and prenatal care, which led to a skyrocketing infant mortality rate. Low birth weight babies were classified as miscarriage and denied treatment. Those who managed to survive ended up in one of 78 state orphanages. There were often as few as one or two caregivers for hundreds of children, and an estimated 25 cents per day was spent on feeding each child. They were barely given the attention necessary to survive, let alone to form healthy attachments. Many would lag years behind in emotional, physical, and cognitive development [McKelvey & Stevens 1994].

In our experience treating children with attachment disorder, adopted from all over the world, we have found that the former "Eastern bloc" children to be some of the most severely disturbed. Their experiences have taught us a great deal about the effects of extreme deprivation on the body and the mind, but at an enormous cost. The problems that these children bring to their adoptive families can become insurmountable. These adoptions have already begun to disrupt. This invariably places a greater strain on our already taxed and inadequate child welfare resources for severely disturbed children.

### Transracial Adoption

Approximately 50,000 children per year are legally free for adoption, and more than one-half are children of ethnic and/or cultural minorities, primarily African American [Child Welfare League of America 1993]. Nationally, these children constitute more than 60% of the 500,000 children in foster care, which is twice their representation in the total U.S. child population (47% African American compared to 15% of the U.S. child population). The number of European American children entering foster care each year is greater than the number of African American children. Yet, African Americans make up a disproportionate and increasing number of children who remain in the system [Adoptive Families 1997a]. African American and interracial families adopt at a higher rate than any other group in our population. Generally, agencies try to place African American children with African American families. However, due to the high numbers of African American children in need of homes, the minority community has been stretched to its limits. If they are not to grow up in institutions or the foster care system, many of these children will have to be adopted by European American families [Schaffer & Lindstrom 1989].

An institutional belief persists that the emotional and developmental needs of minority children can only be met by adoption into families of the same race and culture. To date, there is no scientific evidence suggesting that African American children raised in European American or interracial homes are poorly adjusted and/or isolated from the African American community [Vroegh 1997]. More than 20 years of transracial adoption (TRA) research has confirmed that it is better for African American children to be placed with European American families than to remain without permanent homes [Silverman 1993]. In one long-term study of 300 midwestern families in which European American parents had adopted African American children, it was found that these children developed into teenagers and adults who fared well personally and in their families. They had little problem with racial identification and did not develop more psychosocial problems than other adoptees [Simon & Alstein 1992]. Another longitudinal study, begun in 1969, compared African American children adopted transracially and within race. No differences were found among adoptees regarding general adjustment, self-esteem, racial self-identity, and family relationships [Shireman & Johnson 1986]. Opponents of transracial adoption suggest that it undermines a child's sense of racial identity and leads to a form of racial and cultural genocide [National Association of Black Social Workers 1994].

Although secure attachment patterns develop and are maintained in transracially adopted families, raising a child from another culture or race requires knowledge and sensitivity. Parents must be aware that the child has a right and a need to know who he or she is, culturally and racially, as well as confirming the child's identity as a family member. Parents also need to be conscious about the prejudicial reactions of others toward the child and family [Schaffer & Lindstrom 1989]. Vroegh [1997, p. 568] writes, "The ideology of transracial adoption opponents appears to lie in an adult political agenda of separatism rather than in a humanist agenda of fulfilling children's best interests." Secure attachment in the family, including trust, intimacy, and morality, appears to be more important for the healthy psychosocial development of children than racial and cultural differences.

Courtney [1997, p. 765] writes; "A consideration of available evidence suggests that TRA does not have the potential at anytime in the near future to move a significant proportion of African American children from out-of-home care." He cites considerable evidence to suggest that the major reasons for out-of-home placements (poverty, substance abuse, child maltreatment) are prevalent among African American families, which results in these children being placed in the category of "special needs." A child's race, even more than physical or emotional disability, influences the preferences of potential adopters. Consequently, Courtney suggests, minority children have an extremely low chance of adoption, transracially or otherwise. "Nothing short of a massive effort to improve the condition of impoverished families is likely to significantly stem the tide of children being placed in out-of-home care" [Courtney 1997, p. 768].

## Adoption and Attachment

It is estimated that adoption affects the lives of 40 million Americans. In many cases, particularly with infant adoptions, the child and family fare well. There are, however, many other adoptive children and families who struggle with severe emotional and relationship problems, sometimes leading to relinquishment, and the child being placed back into "the system." Many of these adoptive children are classified as "special needs" due to age (over 5 in foster care system); ethnic and cultural background; members of a sibling group who must stay together; infants born drug-exposed, HIV positive, or with Fetal Alcohol Syndrome; or otherwise physically and/or psychologically challenged. Currently, there are more than half a million such children waiting to be placed in homes. More than half the children in the adoption/foster care system are considered high-risk because of prenatal vulnerabilities, problems resulting from early maltreatment, multiple out-of-home placements, and compromised attachment.

Children who have experienced insufficient, disrupted, or pathological attachment relationships in their early years are high-risk for disruption. These are the children and parents that are in need of specialized services in order to prevent disruption. Adoptive families who receive ongoing support and effective therapeutic services are more stable and better able to manage stress and adversity, than those who do not. The following factors increase the probability of successful adoption [McKelvey & Stevens 1994]:

• Place early: infants do best adjusting to adoptive homes.

• Minimize moves: frequent moves and foster placements are traumatizing.

• Plan for permanency: developed at the time child enters the child welfare system.

• Preplacement services: to assess, educate, and support parents and child, and ease the transition.

• Fit: attempt to match temperaments between child and parents.

• Full disclosure: child's history, including realistic appraisal of risks.

• Postplacement services: support and intervention prior to crises.

• Ongoing help: education, support, and therapeutic services for family, lasting through adolescence.

There are a variety of issues that are salient to adoptive children and parents. These issues, listed below, are even more dramatic when applied to children with serious attachment disorders prior to adoption. This information is informed, in part, by Fahlberg [1991].

## Separation and Loss

The adoptive family is a system built upon "necessary losses." Experiences of separation and loss are fundamental to all members of the adoption triad. The child has lost his or her original bond with birth mother and early attachment to birth parents or other caregivers (e.g., grandparents, foster parents). Despite neglectful or abusive care, there is still a sense of loss when the child is separated from birth parents. There is often a loss of self-worth and self-identity for the child, who wonders, "Why did they give me up?" Separations from siblings, extended kin, friends, and teachers are also common. Birth parents have lost a biological child, and experience feelings of inadequacy, failure, damaged self-esteem, and a sense of loss of control over their lives. Many birth parents suffer unresolved losses stemming from their early years, which has both contributed to and exacerbated current losses. Adoptive parents struggle with a variety of losses. Many have dealt with the pain of infertility for years: feelings of inadequacy, strain on the marriage, lack of understanding and support from extended family, lost fantasy of a biological child. Despite popular belief, adoption does not "fix" the pain of infertility, and feelings of loss often continue for years. Adoptive parents also have feelings of loss associated with miscarriage, death, sense of inadequacy, lack of control over their own bodies and events, and the difference between the fantasy of the child they planned to adopt and the reality of the child who entered their home.

A child's reaction to separation and loss is determined by two major factors: the nature and quality of the attachment being disrupted, and the abruptness of the separation. The stronger the relationship, the more traumatic the loss. The more abrupt the transition, the more difficult it is to work through the loss. Fahlberg [1991] describes additional factors that influence a child's reaction to loss of an attachment figure:

- Age and developmental stage,

- Attachment to birth parents/caregivers,

- Prior separation experiences,

- Child's perception and interpretation,

- Preparation for move,

- Parting and welcoming messages received,

- Child's temperament, and

- Environment child is leaving and moving to.

Infants can feel the effects of separation and loss associated with a disruption of the maternal bond, inadequate early care, and multiple moves. It is between the ages of 6 months to 4 years, however, that the loss of attachment figures can cause the most emotional damage. Loss at this stage of development often results in a lack of trust in caregivers, and problems with autonomy, identity formation, and social adjustment. Children commonly react to loss with regression of recently acquired skills. The toddler, for example, may display regressive eating, sleeping, or elimination behaviors. Important developmental tasks may not be accomplished when the child is preoccupied with feelings of loss. The child with multiple moves, for instance, may show little reaction to another separation, as a defense against emotional pain. This child will lag behind developmentally, be less likely to form subsequent attachments, and is more likely to act out in ways that lead to additional moves. Studies show that children with attachment disorder have numerous moves in the foster care system [Widom 1991].

## The Grief Process

Grief is a natural and necessary reaction to the loss of an attachment figure. Children who have experienced early attachment failures and disruptions are struggling with, or stuck at some point in, the grieving process. As previously described, children typically go through three stages when they are separated from attachment figures: protest, despair, and detachment. The child who feels despair is preoccupied and depressed, but can still grieve for her or his unavailable caregiver. The detached child, however, has "shut down" emotionally and has not completed the grieving process. Children in this latter category are routinely placed in adoptive homes, but will not trust, relate positively, or attach.

The grieving process as a reaction to separation and loss has been described as a series of stages culminating in resolution [Jewett 1982; Kubler-Ross 1969]:

• Shock and numbing;

• Alarm reaction ("fight, flight, or freeze");

• Denial;

• Intense emotions (anger, sadness, guilt, shame, fear);

• Yearning and bargaining;

• Despair and disorganization; and

• Reorganization and resolution.

Children with attachment disorder are grieving losses, or defending against those losses and the accompanying emotional pain. It is important that child welfare and mental health professionals, as well as adoptive parents, understand the nature and depth of their grief. Children who are withdrawn, emotionally detached, and unwilling to connect with caregivers, may be demonstrating a reaction to loss and grief, rather than symptoms of severe disturbance. Adoptive parents must be taught to be proactive, not reactive; i.e., not withdraw from the reticent child, but rather, provide support, patience, empathy, and appropriate structure. Adoptive parents or other family members who are unresolved in their own grief process will be limited in their ability to help the child through his or her own losses and grief.

Honest and open communication is often helpful, creating an "empathic bridge" between parent and child. (see pp. 134-135 for examples of sharing the pain of loss).

## Bonding and Attachment

*Bonding* is the physical and psychological connection between mother and infant that begins at conception, grows during pregnancy, intensifies at birth, and exists forever. All children are bonded to their biological mothers, regardless of what transpires after birth. *Attachment* is the enduring emotional connection between caregivers and child, characterized by the development of trust, security, and the desire for closeness, particularly when the child is under stress. In most cases, parents who adopt infants must provide a context in which attachment is learned. Parents who adopt toddlers or older children, especially with a history of separations and loss, must help them overcome attachment fears and disorders.

A child's adaptation to an adoptive home depends on the nature, quality, and patterns of prior attachments, as well as his or her reactions to separation and loss. The grief process affects subsequent attachments; *unresolved grief inhibits the development of future attachment*. Attachment disorder also results from prior family dynamics and traumatic experiences (abuse, neglect, domestic violence); vulnerabilities of the child (biological depression, fetal alcohol syndrome, fetal alcohol effects, temperament); and multiple out-of-home placements. These children are commonly placed with an adoptive family, but do not form positive or meaningful attachments to their new caregivers. They are fearful of trusting and loving, certain that it will only lead to pain once again, and hide these fears under angry, aggressive, and controlling behaviors. Confusion about loyalties also prevents attachment, as children struggle with relationships with birth, foster, and adoptive parents. Unresolved attachment issues of the adoptive parents can prevent the establishment of a family atmosphere conducive to healing and promoting attachment. These parents function in a reactive mode, rather than being proactive and utilizing effective parenting approaches with the angry, frightened, and mistrustful child. Parents must work through their own losses to help a child with loss.

In general, facilitating secure attachment with adoptive children involves the same three processes as with biological children: *attachment cycle, positive interaction cycle,* and *claiming*. In the attachment cycle, the caregiver gratifies the child's needs in a sensitive, appropriate, and consistent manner, resulting in a reduction of anxiety and discomfort, and feelings of security, safety, and trust. Parents initiate the positive interaction cycle, creating an ongoing positive reciprocal relationship in which the child learns to respond favorably to feelings, messages, limits, and behaviors. Claiming helps the child feel "a part of" the family, a sense of belonging.

## Intense Emotions

Children commonly are dealing with a variety of powerful and confusing feelings associated with loss, grief, and compromised attachment: anger (often rage), sadness, fear, helplessness, hopelessness, shame, guilt. It is crucial that adoptive parents are given training and support so they can respond in helpful ways to this emotionality. Effective therapy can aid the child in managing and resolving emotional difficulties, as well as provide education and support to the parents. The child's pain cannot be avoided. Again, parents with unresolved emotional issues may be "triggered" by the negative emotionality of the child, which can result in destructive responses and negative ongoing relationship dynamics.

## Belief Systems

Negative perceptions and interpretations (i.e., cognitive appraisals) of separation and loss have long-term harmful influences on the development and stability of children. The child may believe, "I was given away (not wanted); taken away (angry at 'the system'); or it was my fault (feels responsible)." Young children employ magical thinking, a natural component of the egocentric stage of development and blame themselves for the losses. This leads to self-contempt, damages further self-worth and identity, and prevents the formation of future attachment ("I am not worth loving"). Preparing children for transitions can prevent damaging perceptions.

## Loyalty Conflicts

As previously stated, every child has a bond with birth mother. Children in foster or adoptive families must deal with several sets of parents (birth, legal, parenting). Caregivers must accept the place of birth parents in the child's emotional life. Children who have experienced abuse, neglect, and abandonment from birth parents need a way to "come to terms" with those important biological attachment figures. Children must be protected from adult conflicts and rivalries, whether these are legal battles (e.g., visitation, custody, termination of parental rights), or emotional battles. Adoptive parents often feel threatened by a child's desire to maintain ties with biological or prior foster parents. These ties, however, when appropriate and supervised, can enhance the child's sense of self, reduce internal emotional conflict, and allow more energy available for current family relationships.

## Belonging

Feeling alienated, isolated, and disconnected, are common feelings for children in adoptive families. They lack a secure attachment to both prior and current caregivers, and often act out to get attention. It is important that the child and family learn to feel they belong to one another ("claiming") and develop a family identity that includes the adoptive child. Parents are sometimes impatient and need to realize that trust and attachment take time, particularly when the child has a history of painful loss.

## Moves

Losses are psychologically traumatizing and interrupt the necessary tasks of child development. Abrupt, unplanned moves are most traumatic for children and adults alike. It is common, however, to move children through the foster care system; one study reported an average of between three and five moves for children in foster care in a five-year period [Widom 1991]. It is easy to blame "the system" for these placement moves, but research shows that, in fact, it is usually the acting-out children with attachment disorder who are moved most. Approximately 75% of children in out-of-home placements are victims of abuse, neglect, or abandonment. The emotional and behavioral problems of these children result in more frequent placements, as foster parents are not able to tolerate the difficulties and disruptions on family life [Widom 1991]. Again, the best outcomes for children in the foster care system are associated with two factors: 1) place early (those placed under 1 year old did best), and 2) do not move (those who remained in one home did best).

When a child must be moved, the transition can be eased by appropriate preplacement planning and preparation. The child (and adults involved) need understanding, support, and help learning to cope with the emotions associated with separation and loss. Additionally, children do better when they have a sense of control during stressful times; explaining to the child what is happening and what they can expect is often helpful. (See Table 13.)

## Trust, Autonomy, and Identity

Trust develops during the first-year-of-life attachment cycle: need, arousal, gratification and trust. The baby learns to trust *caregivers* (reliable and sensitive; will meet my needs); *self* (my needs are acceptable; I am worthwhile); and the *external world* (I feel safe and protected, my world is OK). The development of basic trust is a primary development task of the first year of life and serves as a foundation for future emotional and social growth. Maltreatment, abandonment, and out-of-home placements contribute to the lack of trust in children who are adopted. The child's lack of trust in prior caregivers is projected onto the current (adoptive) caregiver. Adoptive parents must be emotionally prepared to deal with this mistrust, and the associated anger, acting out, and low self-esteem.

The emergence of a sense of autonomy is an important developmental task of the second and third years of life. Dependence on a caregiver and independence from that caregiver are continuously balanced within the context of the attachment relationship. The child with a "secure base" can explore autonomously, knowing he or she is safe and protected. Children with attachment disorder do not have this safety net; they either become afraid to explore (clingy, overdependent), or develop an ingenuine type of independence ("I do not need anyone"). The adopted child with attachment disorder is needy, fearful, and emotionally immature, but compensates by working hard at demonstrating "pseudoindependence."

Identity is who the child believes him- or herself to be. Identity formation is based on the child's experiences, interpretation of those experiences, other's reactions to the child, and the significant role models the child identifies with [Van Gulden & Bartels-Rabb 1994]. Self-worth is at the core of identity. Children with attachment disorder develop a shame-based identity, due to abandonment, real or perceived, and their sense of self as flawed, unlovable, and "bad." They carry this negative working model into the adoptive family, pushing away the nurturance and love they believe is not deserved. Lacking a positive and clear sense of identity, these children are at risk for antisocial behavior, susceptibility to negative peer influence, and a chronic feeling of alienation in the adolescent years.

### Table 13. Minimizing the Trauma of Moves: Developmental Considerations

**Infants**: Emphasis on transferring attachment and caregiving routines during preplacement contacts. Maintain as many routines as possible in new setting. After move, provide consistency and *meet needs on demand.*

**Toddlers:** Preplacement preparation is crucial to reduce long-term anxiety and fear regarding separation, loss, and lack of safety with caregivers. Primary goal during moving process is to transfer attachment; best facilitated by cooperative contact between the parents the child is leaving and new parents/caregivers. Provide support and understanding if regression occurs after move; undue pressure may have negative long-term effects. Note events surrounding the move on the child's permanent record, as this information may help caregivers and helping professionals understand the child's future actions and issues. Postplacement contacts with previous caregivers are important so that children understand the reasons for the move as they grow older.

**Preschool Years:** Explaining in "child-friendly" language what is occurring and why reduces magical thinking and helps the child attain a sense of control over events. Preplacement services aid in transferring attachment to new caregivers and initiating the process of grieving. Identifying and modifying the child's negative perceptions (e.g., "It is my fault I lost my mom") prevents future emotional problems. As child develops increased cognitive skills, around 8 or 9 years old, caregivers and/or helpers need to review the past, so that the child is not misinterpreting those events.

**Grade School Age:** Despite increased cognitive and verbal skills, it remains necessary to identify and correct magical thinking and misperceptions. It is important to help the child understand what is happening, and to provide aid in identifying and constructively expressing emotions. Adults are responsible for decision making, but the child needs to be included as an active participant in the moving process. The child is encouraged to share feelings, worries, and desires regarding the transition. After the move, discussions about grief-related (or other) feelings helps the child free up energy for social, academic, and additional activities and accomplishments.

**Adolescence:** Moves during early adolescence (12 to 14) are more difficult than in later adolescence, because individuation is a major developmental task of this stage. It is difficult to encourage attachment to new caregivers when the child is in the process of emotionally separating from family. Parents need to be sensitive to these development issues; children do best with a clear and concrete commitment ("contract") to the new caregivers. Adolescents need to have input into decision making about their lives and future, consistent with their need to have increasing control over life events in general. They should be a part of the process of deciding where to live, except in special situations (e.g., displaying poor judgment). Commitments and contracts are helpful in clarifying and attaining goals. Parents, caregivers, and helping professionals can assist the adolescent "come to terms" with prior losses and trauma, and encourage a healthy balance of dependence and independence [adapted from Fahlberg 1991].

## Fit

Adoptive parents go through a "psychological pregnancy," as they prepare for and fantasize about the new child entering their family. The closer the child is to his or her fantasy prior to adoption, the stronger the attachment. Children with attachment disorder deviate from these parents' fantasies; they distance themselves emotionally, are angry and aggressive, and do not accept limits and authority. A poor fit also occurs when the child and adoptive parents are different in temperament (e.g., active and energetic child, subdued and restrained parents). Although it is not possible to match a child and prospective parents on all dimensions, efforts should be made to consider these factors. Preplacement services aid the parents in developing a realistic appraisal of the child, which may differ considerably from their desires and fantasies.

## Shifts in the Family System

The addition of a new member is a critical transition that always requires an adjustment in the family system. An adoptive family is extremely vulnerable to these changes, because of the tentative nature of the tie between the adopted child and the family [Reitz & Watson 1992]. The place and role of the child in the new family must be determined. An adopted infant has special status, and is typically able to form attachments with appropriate and sensitive parenting. The older adopted child, however, brings roles, patterns of relating, and expectations learned in prior families (birth, foster). The family and child may have difficulty in adjusting to one another. "To return to its prior equilibrium, any system tends to cast off what it perceives as foreign" [Reitz & Watson 1992, p. 131]. The adopted child who continues prior behaviors and roles in the new family is vulnerable to rejection and scapegoating, a major reason for relinquishment.

## Preplacement Preparation

Planned transitions help to minimize the trauma of separation and loss and facilitate the development of new attachments. The process of moving children out of biological homes, through the child welfare system, and into adoptive families, must incorporate the following factors:

- Address the fears, anxieties, and emotions of the child, the parents/caregivers the child is separating from, and the new caregivers.

- Recognize and support the grieving process for child and adults.

- Educate, support, and empower the new parents.

- Encourage realistic expectations for child and new parents. Providing full disclosure of the child's history and psychosocial difficulties helps parents develop realistic expectations. Discussions and training sessions enhance preparation. Parents can role play not only parenting strategies but also "being the child," to increase understanding, empathy, and skills. Talking to experienced foster and adoptive parents ("old timers") provides insight and support.

- Help child develop accurate perceptions and reduce harmful effects of self-blame.

- Consider the messages that child is given. What are the "parting messages" as a child leaves a family (supportive, blaming, vague)? What are the "welcoming messages" received as the child enters the new family (apprehensive, surprised, confident, mistrustful)?

- Preplacement contacts and visits with the new family are useful in diminishing anxiety about the unknown, dealing with loss and grief, and beginning the process of transferring attachment. Visits are usually supervised and evaluated.

- Commitments to work together in the future from everyone involved in the child's life (prior and new caregivers, child, caseworker) ease the transition and help to achieve long-term goals.

## Postplacement Services

A major component of effectively dealing with separation, loss, and disruption of attachment is the quality of the new family environment that the child moves to. The new adoptive parents must be prepared to provide a healthy balance of structure and caring, help the child cope with grief and other emotions, and make decisions regarding the role played by prior attachment figures in the child's current and future life. Postplacement services involve the following:

- Ongoing support, education, and treatment services available for the child and new parents. This encourages effective coping and significantly reduces disruption rates.

- Allow contacts with prior attachment figures when appropriate. This decreases the child's magical thinking, loyalty conflicts, denial of feelings, and enhances self-worth, resolution of separation issues, and the transfer of attachment. Contacts are preferably in person, but can also occur through phone calls, letters, or audio/video tapes. *Interrupt contact when prior caregivers sabotage the goals and send damaging messages to the child.* Contact is not recommended when prior caregivers had been severely abusive.

- Assessment process is necessary in order to measure success in achieving specific goals with the child, prior caregivers and new caregivers. Positive changes in family dynamics, parenting practices, coping skills, and the development of new attachments, should be evaluated on a regular basis, as a part of an ongoing follow-up plan.

## Helping Services

There are many studies that indicate adopted children are at greater risk for emotional, social, behavioral, and academic problems than their nonadopted peers [Brodzinsky et al. 1984, 1990]. Adopted children are more likely to come to the attention of the mental health system. This occurs for two possible reasons: 1) due to early insecure attachment and loss and 2) as they reach school age, these children develop the cognitive skills to understand the implications of adoption (e.g., abandonment and identity issues). It is not possible, however, to place all adopted children into one category. Each child is unique, with differences in biological/genetic background, early life experiences, cultural influences, and placement procedures. Long-term prognosis is good for many adopted children with attachment disorder when they receive effective services during childhood and their adoptive parents are well-prepared for the challenging task. The confidence and competence of the parents, combined with support from social services, mental health professionals and extended family, are important components of successful outcome.

## Substitute Child Care:
## Who Is Watching the Babies?

The use of out-of-home, substitute child care has become a necessity for the majority of families with children in our society. Economic and social conditions often force both parents to work, penalize those who put their careers on hold for several years, and provide little support to parents. More than 50% of preschoolers in the United States are in some form of substitute child care (30% in a child care facility, 17% in provider's home, and 5% at home with baby-sitters) [Kantrowitz 1997]. Traditionally, families benefited from an abundance of secondary attachment figures. Families tended to remain in one place, and were surrounded by relatives and life-long neighbors who helped with child care. Currently, one out of five families moves every year.

### Research and Discussion

The issue of substitute infant and child care has prompted a significant amount of debate and research within the public policy and scientific arenas. The relationship between early substitute child care and children's psychosocial development (as reflected in attachment style), has received considerable attention. Some studies found that nonmaternal infant care is strongly correlated with insecure attachment patterns, while others found that attachment is influenced by a combination of factors, including the quality of child care, time spent in child care, and maternal sensitivity during the first 15 months [Belsky & Rovine 1988; NICHD 1996].

The National Institute on Child Health and Human Development (NICHD) began a large-scale longitudinal study in 1989 to examine the effects of day care on child development. The researchers found that more than one-half of the babies at age 15 months displayed insecure attachment patterns when their mothers were insensitive and unresponsive, or showed signs of depression and anxiety. The risk of insecure attachment was compounded by poor quality day care, being in day care for 10 hours or more a week, and switching child care arrangements [NICHD 1996]. Thus, the combination of poor quality day care and unresponsive maternal care was most damaging for healthy attachment and subsequent child development.

While the effects of day care remain a topic of debate, there is a general consensus that the better the quality of care, the better the outcomes for children [Young et al. 1997]. Overall quality of care includes training and education of caregivers, staff/child ratios and group size, and appropriateness of care provided (i.e., meeting infants' and toddlers' social, cognitive, physical, and emotional needs). However, even infants and toddlers who attended a high-quality day care program were found to be more aggressive in kindergarten than children who stayed home [Haskins 1985; cited in Moore 1996, p. 305]. In addition to the quality of substitute child care, two other factors have been found to determine attachment and psychosocial development: the number of hours per week in substitute care, and the age and developmental stage of the children in care. Moore [1996] found that the effects of substitute care vary with the child's age and developmental level, as well as amount of time spent. Boys developed more behavior problems than girls as the total amount of time in substitute care increased (aggressive and oppositional behavior in preschool). Moore concluded, "While the first year of life has been viewed as a critical period, the present findings suggest that this critical period should be extended to 2 1/2 years" [Moore 1996, p. 308]. Other studies found that 24 to 36 months of age is an important transition time for behavioral and emotional reorganization. Bowlby [1982] suggested that after 3 years of age, most children are able to feel secure with a subordinate attachment figure. Bowlby writes, "after children have reached their third birthday, they are usually much better able to accept mother's temporary absence . . . this change seems to take place almost abruptly, suggesting that at this age some maturational threshold is passed" [Bowlby 1982, p. 205].

A decade ago, Young and Zigler [1986] reviewed the status of day care regulations, and analyzed the extent to which day care requirements were followed. They found that not one state met the recommended standards for quality day care. Ten years later, they found similar deficiencies: 67% of the states received overall ratings of poor or very poor; not one state received an overall rating of good [Young et al. 1997]. Their findings indicate that current state regulations for infant and toddler day care do not establish minimally acceptable thresholds of quality. These researchers conclude, "as a society, it is time we recognize that the sound development of an increasing proportion of children is compromised by inappropriate care during their most formative years" [Young et al. 1997, p. 543].

## Recommendations

- **Continuity of caregivers.** Infants and toddlers need one consistent, responsible, and loving caregiver. Day care programs should assign a specific caregiver for each child, and this provider should move up the age range, caring for the same children from infancy through preschool.

- **Stability of child care.** For children under the age of 3, the staff child ratio must be 1:4, with a maximum group size of eight.

- **Qualifications for day care providers.** Infant and toddler caregivers must have the training, experience, and personal emotional maturity necessary to develop consistent, stable, and supportive relationships with young children. These care providers should receive wages and benefits compatible with their level of training and experience. Providers should be knowledgeable in the fields of infant and child development, emphasizing trust and emotional security, safe exploration, and effective communication with parents.

- **Parents as partners.** Infant and toddler care providers should be trained in facilitating a partnership with parents. Establishing a relationship with parents which includes discussions of the child's development, and the parents' role in it, is extremely important.

- **Businesses as partners.** Employers should be required to provide job-protected parental leave for at least one year following child birth and adoption. Additionally, companies should be encouraged to provide high-quality in-house day care to their employees. Infants and young children can be cared for on premises, and the employees should have flexible access to their children.

## Early Intervention and Prevention

The goal of early intervention and prevention programs is to make books that focus on the treatment of children with attachment disorder, such as the book you are reading right now, less necessary and relevant. Primary prevention focuses on intervening early in the life of families, infants, and children, to create healthy patterns; meet the physical, psychosocial, and cognitive needs of children; and strengthen families. Secondary prevention identifies at-risk children (e.g., crime committed, referred to mental health agency), or parents (e.g., child abuse and neglect, substance abuse, poverty, teenage pregnancy), with the goal of preventing additional problems in the future. The following discussion focuses on early intervention and primary prevention that provide education and support to families during the initial phases of the parent-child relationship. This is the time when families face both their highest risk for severe maltreatment, and at the same time, their greatest opportunities for creating positive and enduring parent-child interaction and attachment patterns [Guterman 1997].

### Concepts and Goals

Early intervention and primary prevention concepts are not new. In 1920, Christian Carstens, the founder of the Child Welfare League of America, stated that child protective agencies should work toward the prevention of cruelty and neglect, not merely to the prevention of its reoccurrence. In 1991, the U.S. National Advisory Board on Child Abuse and Neglect recommended a system of neonatal home visiting support programs to prevent maltreatment. In 1992, the National Committee to Prevent Child Abuse initiated the development of early child abuse and neglect prevention programs, which resulted in the establishment of more than 150 programs in 28 states [Healthy Families American 1996; Guterman 1997]. In 1995, the Administration for Children, Youth and Families awarded funds to 63 community-based programs to serve low-income families with infants, toddlers, and pregnant women. This marked the beginning of Early Head Start, which is based on the following guiding principles: "All children from birth to age three need early child development experiences that honor their unique characteristics and provide love, warmth, and positive learning experiences; and all families need encouragement and support from their community so they can achieve their own goals and provide a safe and nurturing environment for their very young children" [Advisory Committee on Services for Families with Infants and Toddlers 1994; cited in Lally & Keith 1997, p. 3].

The American Psychological Association launched a large-scare search for effective prevention programs. Once identified, these model programs could serve as examples to be repeated in other settings [Price et al. 1989]. This APA Task Force found that effective prevention programs share a number of features:

- **Programs are targeted.** Their focus is shaped by an understanding of the risks and problems encountered by the target group.

- **Long-term change.** Programs are designed to alter the life trajectory of participants; to set individuals on a new developmental course, opening opportunities, providing social support, changing life circumstances, and teaching new skills.

- **Strengthen natural support.** These programs strengthen the existing support found in family, community, or school settings.

- **Research.** Programs collect vigorous research evidence to document success and effectiveness.

### Sample Programs

Although there are many successful early intervention and prevention programs operating currently, the list below includes programs that have been found to effectively enhance healthy parent-child attachment and prevent an array of child and family problems

## Home Visitation 2000

- **Intervention.** Low-income women during pregnancies and the first two years of children's lives: paraprofessional and nurse teams made home visits in order to improve prenatal health, provide support, teach emotionally sensitive caregiving, improve children's health and development, and enhance women's personal development.

- **Outcome.** Mothers made better use of community resources and improved their health pre- and postnatally; significantly less abuse and neglect of children during first two years; fewer parent-child coping problems and maltreatment at 50-month follow-up [Robinson & Glaves 1996].

## Perry Preschool Project

- **Intervention.** Preschoolers at-risk for school failure from low socioeconomic families: children participated in two years of special education to enhance cognitive skills; parent involvement via groups, and weekly home visits by teachers and staff.

- **Outcome.** Children received higher grades, stayed in school longer, more likely to graduate high school, with significant decrease in crime and delinquency (50% less likely to be arrested by age 19) [Berrueta-Clement et al. 1984].

### Seattle School Development Program

- **Intervention.** Families at-risk for maltreatment and preschoolers at-risk for antisocial behavior: provided parent training and support and special programs for children, focusing on family, school, peers, and community at different stages of child development.

- **Outcome.** Behavioral problems (antisocial behaviors) significantly reduced in children by fifth grade [Zigler 1994].

### Healthy Start Program

- **Intervention.** Serving low-income, high-stress (substance abuse, depression) families: paraprofessionals made home visits to provide parent education and support, coordination with community services, support groups for parents.

- **Outcome.** Mothers showed greater positive involvement and sensitivity to infants at 6 months of age; reduction of abuse and neglect at 12 months [Center on Child Abuse Prevention Research 1996].

### Houston Parent-Child Program

- **Intervention.** Serving low-income Mexican American families with 1-year-old child: home visits by paraprofessionals to teach baby care and improve home environment; children participate in special nursery school during second year, while mothers attend child management classes.

- **Outcome.** Children showed less aggression, less hostility, and more empathy, five to eight years after program [Johnson & Walker 1990].

### Teen Mother Program

- **Intervention.** Single, teenage mothers (16.5 years old average), delivered first child within past two years: 12 one-hour group sessions to teach stress management, problem solving, child care, and provide social support.

- **Outcome.** Significant increase in caregiving competency and baby care, and decrease in violence and abuse toward infants [Schinke et al. 1986].

### Yale Child Welfare Program

- **Intervention.** Home visits by professionals and paraprofessionals to low-income mothers: provided parent education, pediatric services, support, and linkage to community services during the first 17 months of first-born children.

- **Outcome.** Ten years later, mothers were more likely to be self-supporting and had better parent-child relationships; children had better school adjustment, less aggression and anger, and were more compliant with parents [Zigler 1994].

These early intervention and prevention programs identify and build on the strengths of families and communities. They provide health care, parent support and education, child care and development information, and help in linking parents and children to community resources. By helping parents to understand and fulfill their children's emotional, social, cognitive, and physical needs, they encourage secure attachment and produce lasting improvements in children's psychosocial competence. Further, benefits from prevention programs increase over time. Benefits accrue over time as children engage in less crime, depend on welfare-type services less, and reap the benefits of higher levels of education [Price et al. 1989]. For example, a benefit-cost analysis of the Perry Preschool Program showed a total net benefit to each preschool child of $5,000. At 19 years of age, however, the total net benefit was estimated at $23,000, due to less need for services and less crime [Gramlich 1984; cited in Price et al. 1989, p. 56].

# Sample Intake Packet

## Appendix A

### Forms

Child Registration Form
Symptom Checklist
Child's Biography
Parents' Autobiographies
Hometown "Follow-up" Therapist Form

### Information

What Is Attachment Disorder?
Attachment Therapy Program
Recommended Readings

# Child Registration Form

Date
_____

Child's Name _____    Date of Birth _____

Parent's Name    Father _____    Mother _____

Address:  Street _____    City _____    State _____ ZIP _____

Telephone
_____

Date of Parent's Marriage(s), Separation(s), and Divorce(s)
_____

_____

Level of Education:    Father _____    Mother _____

Others Living at Home: _____    Sex _____    Birth Date _____    School & Grade _____

Others Living at Home: _____    Sex _____    Birth Date _____    School & Grade _____

Others Living at Home: _____    Sex _____    Birth Date _____    School & Grade _____

Others Living at Home: _____    Sex _____    Birth Date _____    School & Grade _____

Father's Employer _____    Occupation _____

Mother's Employer _____    Occupation _____

Family Physician
_____

Referred By _____    Telephone Number _____

Primary Complaint and Problem
_____

_____

_____

_____

# Developmental History

❐ Yes ❐ No    Was pregnancy planned?

❐ Yes ❐ No    Were there complications?

What? _____

Complications of birth and delivery _____

❐ Yes ❐ No    Is child adopted?

Age if/when adopted _____

❐ Yes ❐ No    Problems with feeding, eating, sleeping?

When did they start? _____

Duration? _____

❐ Yes ❐ No    Have there been any physical or emotional separations (i.e., death, hospitalizations, depression) between child and caretaking adult during the first 26 months of life?

❐ Yes ❐ No    Is there, as far as you know, any possible history that could be considered abusive?

Please describe: _____

_____

_____

If it is hard to remember ages please simply check the problem areas or areas you feel were/are advanced or slow in development:

| *Age he/she:* | | *Does he/she:* | | *Is he/she:* | |
|---|---|---|---|---|---|
| Held head up | _____ | Have blank spells | _____ | Shy or timid | _____ |
| Crawled | _____ | Rock | _____ | Affectionate | _____ |
| Walked with help | _____ | Shun attention | _____ | Well-coordinated | _____ |
| Used sentences | _____ | Have temper tantrums | _____ | Impulsive | _____ |
| Fed self | _____ | Have falling spells | _____ | Right- or left-handed | _____ |
| Dressed alone | _____ | Have unusual fears | _____ | Clumsy | _____ |
| Turned over | _____ | Bump head | _____ | | |
| Sat | _____ | Hold his/her breath | _____ | | |
| Walked alone | _____ | Show daredevil behavior | _____ | | |
| Was weaned | _____ | Have sleep problems | _____ | | |
| Said "No" to everything | _____ | Have eating problems | _____ | | |
| Smiled at parents | _____ | | | | |
| Pull up at crib | _____ | | | | |
| Said 4-10 words | _____ | | | | |
| Helped with dressing | _____ | | | | |
| Dry during day | _____ | | | | |
| Dry during night | _____ | | | | |

Previous testing or therapy _____

Dates _____    Place _____

Findings

# School Information

School of Patient

Grade                                    Teacher

Year Enrolled                            School Telephone Number

School Social Worker or Psychologist

Previous Schools

Please fill in where appropriate:

*My child has been:*                                    *I have been told by the school that my child:*

Tutored in                  _____        Gets along well with adults        _____

Date                        _____        Gets along poorly with adults      _____

Enrolled in special class   _____        Gets along poorly with students    _____

Which class                 _____        Procrastinates                     _____

Expelled                    _____        Has few friends                    _____

Date                        _____        Is bored                           _____

Suspended                   _____        Is above/below average IQ          _____

Date                        _____        Is "hyperactive"                   _____

Commendations & awards      _____        Has trouble on bus/playground      _____

_____

Repeated grade              _____

Cuts class                  _____

Frequently                  _____

Cutting class since         _____

## Family Information (Optional)

Who wanted help?

Five adjectives describing mother

Five adjectives describing father

Five adjectives describing parental relationship

Mother's main concern

Child's main concern

# Symptom Checklist

_____

Child's Name                                          Date

_____

Completed by

Please place a mark in the appropriate column for each symptom as it pertains to your child. On a separate sheet of paper, please give a brief description of your child's behavior regarding each of the symptoms checked as moderate or severe.

|  | NONE | MILD | MODERATE | SEVERE |
|---|---|---|---|---|
| 1. Lack of impulse control | _____ | _____ | _____ | _____ |
| 2. Self-destruction | _____ | _____ | _____ | _____ |
| 3. Destruction of property | _____ | _____ | _____ | _____ |
| 4. Aggression toward others | _____ | _____ | _____ | _____ |
| 5. Consistently irresponsible | _____ | _____ | _____ | _____ |
| 6. Inappropriately demanding and clingy | _____ | _____ | _____ | _____ |
| 7. Stealing | _____ | _____ | _____ | _____ |
| 8. Deceitful (lying, conning) | _____ | _____ | _____ | _____ |
| 9. Hoarding | _____ | _____ | _____ | _____ |
| 10. Inappropriate sexual conduct and attitudes | _____ | _____ | _____ | _____ |
| 11. Cruelty to animals | _____ | _____ | _____ | _____ |
| 12. Sleep disturbance | _____ | _____ | _____ | _____ |
| 13. Enuresis and encopresis | _____ | _____ | _____ | _____ |
| 14. Frequently defies rules (oppositional) | _____ | _____ | _____ | _____ |
| 15. Hyperactivity | _____ | _____ | _____ | _____ |
| 16. Abnormal eating habits | _____ | _____ | _____ | _____ |
| 17. Preoccupation with fire, gore, or evil | _____ | _____ | _____ | _____ |
| 18. Persistent nonsense questions and incessant chatter | _____ | _____ | _____ | _____ |
| 19. Poor hygiene | _____ | _____ | _____ | _____ |
| 20. Difficulty with novelty and change | _____ | _____ | _____ | _____ |
| 21. Lack of cause-and-effect thinking | _____ | _____ | _____ | _____ |
| 22. Learning disorders | _____ | _____ | _____ | _____ |
| 23. Language disorders | _____ | _____ | _____ | _____ |
| 24. Perceives self as victim (helpless) | _____ | _____ | _____ | _____ |
| 25. Grandiose sense of self-importance | _____ | _____ | _____ | _____ |

# **Symptom Checklist** (continued)

Please place a mark in the appropriate column for each symptom as it pertains to your child. On a separate sheet of paper, please give a brief description of your child's behavior regarding each of the symptoms checked as moderate or severe.

|  | NONE | MILD | MODERATE | SEVERE |
|---|---|---|---|---|
| 26. Not affectionate on parent's terms | _____ | _____ | _____ | _____ |
| 27. Intense displays of anger (rage) | _____ | _____ | _____ | _____ |
| 28. Frequently sad, depressed, or hopeless | _____ | _____ | _____ | _____ |
| 29. Inappropriate emotional responses | _____ | _____ | _____ | _____ |
| 30. Marked mood changes | _____ | _____ | _____ | _____ |
| 31. Superficially engaging and charming | _____ | _____ | _____ | _____ |
| 32. Lack of eye contact for closeness | _____ | _____ | _____ | _____ |
| 33. Indiscriminately affectionate with strangers | _____ | _____ | _____ | _____ |
| 34. Lack or or unstable peer relationships | _____ | _____ | _____ | _____ |
| 35. Cannot tolerate limits and external control | _____ | _____ | _____ | _____ |
| 36. Blames others for own mistakes or problems | _____ | _____ | _____ | _____ |
| 37. Victimizes others (perpetrator, bully) | _____ | _____ | _____ | _____ |
| 38. Victimized by others | _____ | _____ | _____ | _____ |
| 39. Lacks trust in others | _____ | _____ | _____ | _____ |
| 40. Exploitative, manipulative, controlling, and bossy | _____ | _____ | _____ | _____ |
| 41. Chronic body tension | _____ | _____ | _____ | _____ |
| 42. Accident prone | _____ | _____ | _____ | _____ |
| 43. High pain tolerance | _____ | _____ | _____ | _____ |
| 44. Tactily defensive | _____ | _____ | _____ | _____ |
| 45. Genetic predispositions | _____ | _____ | _____ | _____ |
| 46. Lack of meaning and purpose | _____ | _____ | _____ | _____ |
| 47. Lack of faith, compassion, and other spiritual values | _____ | _____ | _____ | _____ |
| 48. Identification with evil and the dark side of life | _____ | _____ | _____ | _____ |
| 49. Lack of remorse and conscience | _____ | _____ | _____ | _____ |

# Child's Biography

Please write an autobiography on your child and include as much of the following information as possible.

- Describe what you know about your child's birth family (if adopted). Age of parents, number of siblings, family dynamics, amount of abuse and/or neglect.

- List the number of disruptions (moves away from a family) your child has experienced, the reason for each, the length of time and age of your child in each placement and what degree of abuse, neglect, or nurturing she/he received in each placement.

- Discuss any medical problems your child has experienced: inner ear problems, colic, hospitalizations, premature birth, lack of prenatal care, etc.

- If this is your birth child, please detail family dynamics during your child's first three years of life:

  - How was the prenatal care, birth, and postnatal care?

  - Did the mother suffer postpartum depression?

  - How did the child respond to holding, eye contact, being alone, etc.?

  - What kind of emotional support was there for the mother during the child's early years?

  - How did you react to the baby's fussiness?

- Please describe the progression of your child's disruptive behavior, how you've dealt with it, and the behavior that bothers you the most.

- Discuss your child's positive attributes.

- Discuss what previous therapy your child has had, its duration, and the results.

- Discuss your hopes for bringing your child and family to this program.

# Parents' Autobiographies

Please write an autobiography on each parent and include as much of the following information as possible.

Family of Origin:

- Describe your mother and father (positive and negative comments).

- How did your parents show affection to each other and their children?

- How did your parents handle disagreements and conflicts and what were their main methods of discipline?

- How many siblings do you have and what role did each sibling play in the family dynamics?

- Discuss any history of alcohol or drug abuse, any occurrences of physical or sexual abuse, and any history of mental or emotional illnesses in the family, and how they were dealt with.

*Medical History:*

- List any current/past illnesses/injuries that has impacted you or your family.

*Marital History:*

- Describe your current marriage (positive and negative comments).

- Write a brief description of any previous marriage(s).

*Current Family:*

- List your children and give a brief description of each child.

- What are your main methods of discipline and how effective have they been?

- What concerns do you have with any other member of the family?

- How large of a role (if any) does religion play in your family?

# Hometown (Follow-Up) Therapist

_____

Date

_____

Name                    ·

_____

Address

_____

_____

Telephone

CLINICAL BACKGROUND:

_____

_____

_____

_____

_____

EXPERIENCE WITH ATTACHMENT DISORDER, CHILDHOOD TRAUMA, FAMILY INTERVENTION:

_____

_____

_____

_____

_____

ADDITIONAL INFORMATION:

_____

_____

_____

_____

# What Is Attachment Disorder?

Attachment Disorder is developed when children, for a myriad of reasons, do not form a trusting bond in infancy and early childhood. A lack of trust generates feelings of aloneness, being different, pervasive anger, and an inordinate need for control. A trusting bond is essential in continued personality and conscience development, and serves as the foundation for future intimate relationships.

There are a variety of conditions that place a child at-risk for attachment disorder. They include, but are not limited to, the following:

- Neglect;
- Physical, sexual, or emotional abuse;
- Painful or undiagnosed illness or injury;
- Sudden separation from primary caregiver;
- Prenatal abuse including alcohol and/or drug abuse, and poor nutrition;
- Frequent foster placements and failed adoptions;
- Pathological or inadequate childcare;
- Physical or psychological abandonment by mother; and
- Premature birth.

Children who have attachment disorder display symptoms that are very controlling and confounding. These may include the following:

- Superficially engaging and "charming";
- Lack of eye contact on parental terms;
- Indiscriminately affectionate with stranger;
- Not affectionate on parent's terms (not cuddly);
- Destructive to self, others, and material things (accident prone);
- Cruel to animals;
- Stealing;
- Lying about the obvious (crazy lying);
- No impulse control (frequently acts hyperactive);
- Learning lags;
- Lack of cause-and-effect thinking;
- Lack of conscience;
- Abnormal eating patterns;
- Poor peer relationships;
- Preoccupation with fire;
- Persistent nonsense questions and incessant chatter;
- Inappropriately demanding and clingy;
- Abnormal speech patterns; and
- Sexual acting out.

Because these symptoms are not only controlling, but also extremely effective at keeping parents at arms' length, increasing attempts at closeness by the parents are met with greater resistance by the child. Over time the child's behavior becomes more disruptive while the parents become more frustrated.

# Attachment Therapy Program

The following is a description of the brief intensive outpatient attachment therapy as practiced at Evergreen Consultants. The therapy is designed to work with children who have a diagnosis of reactive attachment disorder of infancy. Some children have been given a diagnosis of oppositional defiant disorder, posttraumatic stress disorder, or conduct disorder and many are also diagnosed as having attention deficit/hyperactivity disorder and mood disorder. All suffer from a prolonged or delayed grief reaction in response to one or more significant losses early in childhood.

A number of therapists are involved in attachment therapy at our center. Each therapist is unique and has evolved a way of working that has been successful with difficult children and adolescents. Each client is also unique. The therapists, although they may use different approaches or techniques, all subscribe to attachment theory as the organizing construct that underlies their work. Therapy techniques vary to take advantage of the strengths of the therapist and to meet the specific needs of the client.

Most children we treat are severe in their pathology. Many have lived in one or more foster homes and have suffered neglect and physical and/or sexual abuse. A high percentage of children treated here are adopted. Some experienced medical/pain trauma as infants or prolonged or frequent separations from primary attachment figures during the first two years of life. Almost all have had several years of therapy with one or more therapists. Some have been hospitalized one or more times. Whatever the help, there is little evidence of positive change as measured by improvement in the child's behavior and in his or her ability to trust. The following elements describe the attachment work done at Evergreen Consultants.

## Structure and Duration

We work for ten consecutive days (two weeks), three to four hours per day. This is an outpatient facility. Families stay at local hostelries or with friends or family nearby. Two therapists are generally used. If indicated, the child may stay in a therapeutic foster family for all or part of the two weeks. The time in therapy is divided between working with the parents, with the child/adolescent, and sometimes with other members of the family. Referring therapists are encouraged to come with the family and be a part of the therapeutic team, if they are available to follow-up with the family after the two-week intensive.

## Family Focus

Treatment always involves a child and the parents. Sometimes we involve siblings as the child has often abused them and corrective work is needed for these relationships. The parents are involved in all 30 hours of treatment. They are either in the therapy room directly or are watching therapists work with the child from an observation room.

Many of the parents are feeling "burned out" by their child's pathology. They have often been emotionally abused, particularly the mother. Since one of the goals of therapy is to help the parents get "in charge" in a good way, the parenting coalition must be solid. To that end, sometimes the therapy process will focus on the parents' release of old anger, on relationship issues, and sometimes on unaddressed emotional issues of one or both parents, which inhibit the formation of strong attachment bonds.

## Attachment Therapy

Therapy has three components. The first is educational, designed to help parents understand children with attachment disorder: how they feel, how they think, and their internal psychological dynamics. The teaching of consequential parenting skills comprises the second part. These skills are designed to help the parents protect themselves from the child's pathology and to provide necessary corrective parenting experiences for the child. Consequential parenting also serves to heighten the child's motivation for treatment by allowing them to experience the pain of their condition rather than displacing it on the parents. The third component involves intensive emotional work with the child. This part constitutes a significant portion of the treatment.

The basic purpose of treatment is to help the child resolve a dysfunctional attachment. The goal is to help the child bond to the parents and to come to grips with the disappointment and anger at his/her first attachment figure(s) and their failure to parent (well). Said another way, the goal is to resolve the fear of loving and being loved. All of the children who come for treatment have authority or control issues. Control, trust, and intimacy issues are prominent features of their pathology and the resolution of these issues is a major treatment objective.

## Experiential

In addition to using standard verbal psychotherapy techniques, we use techniques designed to engage the child in corrective emotional experiences. Our child clients made decisions about trust early in their lives. These survival decisions were made as infants or very young children, made before they had language to encode the meaning of what was happening, even to themselves. Their trauma is locked into the experience of having felt pain at a time when they were powerless to get the help they needed. A variety of therapeutic techniques (psychodrama, imagery, social skill-building, and holdings) are used to elicit and correct the child's pathology.

## Regressive Work

A major dynamic in treatment is helping the child regress to the period that produced the pathology. This allows the child to access deep, genuine, and intense emotions associated with the events and people who created those feelings. The corrective experience is orchestrated to allow the child to express these feelings, recognize and recall them, and identify the events and the people involved. This experience then provides an opportunity for resolution of significant old pathological emotions while simultaneously creating powerful new bonds with trustworthy and reliable parents.

## Affective Emphasis

The therapy has a major emotional or affective emphasis. We operate with the philosophy that emotions have a major causative effect on behavior. We believe that when the emotions that cause the behavior change, the behaviors will change, often with little or no discussion. In our experience, the trauma the children have experienced, which often includes the loss of their birth mothers, neglect, and abuse, produces three major emotions: fear, sadness, and anger. These emotions provide the causal energy for most of the child's pathological behavior. These emotions underlie their avoidance of attachment. Consequently, the regressive work that helps them access their fear, sadness, and anger is a process that helps them heal from their emotional trauma(s).

Historically, the therapy focused extensively on the child's anger because most of the children exhibited angry, aggressive symptoms. Hence, the therapy was called "Rage Reduction Therapy" by many. Currently, we work with whatever disturbing emotion is most prominent. When the major underlying emotion is sadness, then grief work becomes the main focus. If it is fear, that becomes the therapeutic focus. In most children, however, we see all three emotions playing a significant contributing role in the child's pathology.

## Confrontive

In contrast to play therapy or client-centered therapy, in which the child chooses the subject matter, the therapists and parents are in charge and direct the course of therapy. In our experience, children with attachment disorder will not voluntarily face their painful emotions. Denial, avoidance, and dissociation are the defenses that allowed them to survive their trauma and they are not disposed to give them up easily.

"Confrontive" does not mean hostile or punishing. It means dealing directly with the heart of the client's experience. A contract made with the child includes an agreement that the therapists direct the therapy. The child is given the difficult choice of facing the consequences of not resolving problems or going through the painful work of solving them. This choice is given to the child genuinely and repeatedly but in a compassionate, understanding, and supportive manner. Consequently, therapy is quite confrontive and the child, as part of the contract, must agree to acknowledge the problems that brought the family to treatment and ask us for help. In our experience, when addressed in a forthright, open, and realistic manner, children almost always respond in the affirmative.

## Contractual

In essence, all therapy conducted at Evergreen Consultants is done under three clear contracts. The most essential is the one between the parent and the child. The parent must be able to get the child to acknowledge and accept the reality of the problems and get the child to know that, while not responsible for the cause, he/she must accept responsible participation in its cure. The other two contracts are between the parents and the therapists and between the therapists and the child.

## Summary

The course of therapy takes into account the unique needs of each family and child. Perhaps the most critical factor in positive treatment outcomes are parents who are strong, committed, compassionate, and open to their own emotional growth and to learning and applying parenting skills specific to their child's needs. The skill of the clinicians in selecting and implementing treatment strategies most appropriate to each child and family is also a considerable factor in outcomes of this therapy.

Attachment therapy at Evergreen Consultants is often the treatment of choice in cases where able parents have a child who had a traumatic first two years of life and defends against accepting parental control and good judgment.

# Recommended Readings

Ainsworth, M. (1967). *Infancy in Uganda: Infant care and the growth of love.* Baltimore, MD: The Johns Hopkins University Press.

Ainsworth, M. D. S., Blehar, M., Waters, E., & Wall, S. (1978). *Patterns of attachment.* Hillsdale, NJ: Erlbaum.

Barth, R. P., & Berry, M. (1988). *Adoption and disruption.* Hawthorne, NY: DeGruyter.

Belsky, J., & Nezworsky, T. (Eds.) (1988). *Clinical implications of attachment.* Hillsdale NJ: Lawrence Erlbaum Associates.

Bolton, F.G., Jr. (1983). *When bonding fails.* Beverly Hills, CA: Sage.

Bowlby, J. (1973). *Attachment and loss. Vol. 2: Separation.* New York: Basic Books.

Bowlby, J. (1980). *Attachment and loss. Vol. 3: Loss, sadness and depression.* New York: Basic Books.

Bowlby, J. (1982). *Attachment and loss. Vol. I* (rev. ed.). New York: Basic Books.

Bowlby, J. (1988a). *A secure base: Parent-child attachment and healthy human development.* New York: Basic Books.

Bowlby, J. (1988b). *A secure base: Clinical applications of attachment theory.* London: Routledge.

Brazelton, T. B., & Cramer, B. G. (1990). *The earliest relationship.* New York: Addison-Wesley.

Briere, J. (1989). *Therapy for adults molested as children: Beyond survival.* New York: Springer.

Briere, J., Berliner, L., Buckley, J. A., Jenny, C., & Reid, T. (Eds.) (1996). *APSAC handbook on child maltreatment.* Thousand Oaks, CA: Sage.

Brodzinsky, D. M. & Schechter, M. D. (1990). *The psychology of adoption.* New York: Oxford University Press.

Byng-Hall, J. (1995). *Rewriting family scripts.* New York: Guilford Press.

Child Welfare League of America (1996). *Family foster care survey.* Washington, DC: Author.

Children's Defense Fund (1997). *The state of America's children: Yearbook 1997.* Washington, DC: Author.

Cline, F. W. (1982). *Parent education text.* Evergreen, CO: EC Publications.

Cline, F. W. (1992). *Understanding and treating the severely disturbed child.* Evergreen, CO: EC Publications.

Cline, F. W. (1995). *Consciousless acts, societal mayhem.* Golden, CO: Love and Logic Press.

Cline, F., & Fay, J. (1990). *Parenting with love and logic.* Colorado Springs, CO: Pinon Press.

Colin, M., Stevenson-Hinde, J., & Marris, P. (Eds.) (1991). *Attachment across the life cycle.* New York: Routledge.

Colin, V.L. (1996). *Human attachment.* New York: McGraw-Hill.

Courtney, M. E., (1997). The politics and realities of transracial adoption. *Child Welfare 76*(6), 749-779.

Crittenden, P. (1988). Relationships at risk. In J. Belsky & T. Nezworski (Eds.), *Clinical implications of attachment* (pp. 136-176). Hillsdale, NJ: Erlbaum.

Delaney, R. J. (1991). *Fostering changes.* Ft. Collins, CO: Corbett

Delaney, R. J., & Kunstal, R. (1993). *Troubled transplants: Unconventional strategies of helping disturbed foster and adoptive children.* Portland, ME: National Child Welfare Center, University of Southern Maine.

Dunn, J., & Plomin, R. (1990). *Separate lives: Why siblings are so different.* New York: Basic Books.

Egeland, B., & Farber, E. A. (1984). Infant-mother attachment: Factors related to its development and changes over time. *Child Development, 55,* 753-771.

Fahlberg, V. (1991). *A child's journey through placement.* Indianapolis, IN: Perspective Press.

Feeney, J., & Noller, P. (1996). *Adult attachment.* Thousand Oaks, CA: Sage.

Friedrich, W. N. (1990). *Psychotherapy of sexually abused children and their families.* New York: Norton.

Fromm, E. (1973). *The anatomy of human destructiveness.* New York: Holt, Rinehart and Winston.

Gil, E. (1991). *The healing power of play.* New York: Guilford.

Gil, E. (1996). *Treating abused adolescents.* New York: Guilford.

Goleman, D. (1995). *Emotional intelligence.* New York: Bantam.

Grabe, P. V. (1990). *Adoption resources for mental health professionals.* New Brunswick, NJ: Transaction Publishers.

Greenberg, M. T., Cicchetti, D., & Cummings, E. M. (1990). *Attachment in the preschool years: theory, research and intervention.* Chicago, IL: University of Chicago Press.

Guralnick, M. J. (1997). *The effectiveness of early intervention.* Baltimore: Brookes.

Herman, J. (1992). *Trauma and recovery.* New York: Basic Books.

Hughes, D. (1997). *Facilitating developmental attachment.* Northvale, NJ: Jason Aronson.

James B. (1989). *Treating traumatized children.* Lexington, MA: Lexington Books.

James, B. (1994) *Handbook for treatment of attachment-trauma problems in children.* New York: Lexington.

Keck, G., & Kupecky, R. (1995). *Adopting the hurt child.* Colorado Springs, CO: Pinon Press.

Jewett, C.L. (1982). *Helping children cope with separation and loss.* Cambridge, MA: Harvard Common Press.

Kagan, J. (1994). *Galen's prophecy: Temperament in human nature.* New York: Basic Books.

Karen, R. (1994). *Becoming attached: Unfolding the mystery of the infant-mother bond and its impact on later life.* New York: Warner Books.

Kubler-Ross, E. (1969). *On death and dying.* New York: Macmillan.

Lamb, M.E. (1997). *The role of the father in child development* (3rd ed.). New York: Wiley.

Levy, T., & Orlans, M. (1995a). Intensive short-term therapy with attachment disordered children. In. L. VandeCreek, S. Knapp, & T.L. Jackson (Eds.), *Innovations in clinical practice: A source book,* Vol. 14 (pp. 227-251). Sarasota, FL: Professional Resource Press.

Levy, T., & Orlans, M. (1995b). Attachment theory and assessment. In C. A. McKelvey (Ed.), *Give them roots, then let them fly: Understanding attachment therapy* (pp. 36-53). Evergreen, CO: Attachment Center Press.

Levy, T., & Orlans, M. (1995c). Two week intensive. In C.A. McKelvey (Ed.), *Give them roots, then let them fly: Understanding attachment therapy* (pp. 135-164). Evergreen, CO: Attachment Center Press.

Levy, T., & Orlans, M. (1998). *Attachment, trauma, and healing: Understanding and treating attachment disorder in children and families.* Washington, DC: CWLA Press.

Levy, T. (In press). *Handbook of attachment interventions.* San Diego, CA: Academic Press.

Liedloff, J. (1975). *The continuum concept.* New York: Addison-Wesley.

Lieberman, A. (1993). *The emotional life of the toddler.* New York: The Free Press.

Lifton, B. J. (1979). *Lost and found: The adoption experience.* Harper & Row.

Magid, K., McKelvey, C. A. (1988). *High risk: Children without a conscience.* New York: Bantam Books.

McCreight, B. (1997). *Recognizing and managing children with fetal alcohol syndrome/fetal alcohol effects.* Washington, DC: Child Welfare League of America.

McKelvey, C. A. (Ed.) (1995). *Give them roots, then let them fly: Understanding attachment therapy.* Evergreen, CO: Attachment Center Press.

McKelvey, C. A., & Stevens, J. (1994). *Adoption crisis. The truth behind adoption and foster care.* Golden, CO: Fulcrum.

Melina, L.R. (1986). *Raising adopted children: A manual for adoptive parents.* New York: Harper and Row

Montagu, A., (1986). *Touching: The human significance of skin.* New York: Harper and Row.

Parkes, C. M., & Stevenson-Hinde, J. (Ed.) (1982). *The place of attachment in human behavior.* New York: Basic Books.

Parkes, C. M., Stevenson-Hinde, J., & Marris, P. (Ed.). (1991). *Attachment across the life cycle.* New York: Routledge.

Pearce, J. W., & Pezzot-Pearce, T. D. (1997). *Psychotherapy of abused and neglected children.* New York: Guilford.

Peterson, C., Maler, S., & Seligman, M. (1993). *Learned helplessness.* New York: Oxford.

Raine, A. (1993). *The psychopathology of crime.* New York: Academic Press.

Reitz, M., & Watson, K. W. (1992). *Adoption and the family system.* New York: Guilford.

Samenow, S. E. (1991). *Before it's too late.* New York: Times Books.

Schooler, J. E. (1993). *The whole life adoption book: Realistic advice for building a healthy adoptive family.* Colorado Springs, CO: Pinon Press.

Schore, A. N. (1994). *Affect regulation and the origin of the self: The neurobiology of emotional development.* Hillsdale NJ: Lawrence Erlbaum Associates.

Sears, W. & Sears, M. (1993). *The baby book.* Little Brown & Co.

Stern, D. N. (1985). *The interpersonal world of the infant: A view from psychoanalysis and developmental psychology.* New York: Basic Books.

Streissguth, A. (1997). *Fetal alcohol syndrome.* Baltimore, MA: Brookes.

Terr, L. (1990). *Too scared to cry.* New York: Harper & Row.

van der Kolk, B. A., McFarlane, A. C., & Weisaeth, L. (1996). *Traumatic stress.* New York: Guilford Press.

Verny, T., & Kelly J. (1981). *The secret life of the unborn child.* New York: Delta Publishing.

Verny, T., & Weintraub, P. (1991). *Nurturing the unborn child.* New York: Dell Publishing.

Verrier, N. N. (1994). *The primal wound: Understanding the adopted child.* Baltimore, MD: Gateway Press.

Waldmann, C. H., & Mansfield, L. G. (1994). *Don't touch my heart.* Colorado Springs, CO: Pinon Press.

Welch, M. (1988). *Holding time.* New York: Simon and Schuster.

Werner, E., & Smith, R. (1992). *Overcoming the odds: High-risk children from birth to adulthood.* Ithaca, NY: Cornell University Press.

West, M. L., & Sheldon-Keller, A. (1994). *Patterns of relating: An adult attachment perspective.* New York: Guilford Press.

Yochelson, S., & Samenow, S. E. (1993). *The criminal personality: A profile for change.* New Jersey: Jason Aronson.

Zeanah, C. (Ed.) (1993). *Handbook of infant mental health.* New York: Guilford Press.

ZERO TO THREE (1994). *Diagnostic classification of mental health and developmental disorders in early childhood.* Arlington, VA: ZERO TO THREE/National Center for Clinical Infant Programs.

ZERO TO THREE (1997). *How I grow in your care from zero to three.* Arlington, VA: National Center for Infants, Toddlers and Families.

# A Day in the Life ...
## Appendix B

### A Day in the Life of Michael (age 10)

A typical day in the life of Michael starts out with a long list of refusals. He typically refuses to get up on time, refuses to get ready for school, and refuses to take care of his wet bed clothes (i.e., taking the wet bed clothes to the laundry room). The morning normally continues with him arguing about what he should wear to school. He usually wants to wear something that is dirty and in the laundry or something that is inappropriate. From here he moves on to breakfast, where he whines and complains that there is nothing to eat. He refuses to take his medication, Ritalin. He usually makes it out the door just in time to catch the school bus. In response to this behavior, we press him to comply just short of him going into a tantrum and leave him alone. Once he goes into a tantrum we cannot get him to comply with anything. Consequently, we clean up his wet bed clothes and he goes to school without his medication, wearing dirty or inappropriate clothes.

Once at the school bus stop or on the school bus, Michael often teases his sister, making fun of her and calling her obscene names. We believe that this behavior makes him feel big or important in the eyes of the older boys, so our punishments (denying him dessert or some other treat) have had no long-term effectiveness.

At school Michael is somewhat uncooperative, trying to do what he wants to do when he feels like it. Further, he teases and bothers the classmates around him. He marginally obeys the teacher, giving her defiant stares while he slowly and marginally carries out her instructions. He has displayed his defiance a couple of times to the school principal. His interaction with his classmates and neighborhood friends is fairly good in that he has won their approval/acceptance because he is a good athlete. Of course, he gets along with them best when he is in control and they are complying with his wishes. His interaction with his peers nearly always centers around a competition (sports or a competitive video game) and is accompanied with constant boasting and bragging on his part. Not surprisingly, Michael is a sore-loser and behaves best after he has beaten someone at some game.

Upon returning from school, Michael continues his defiant behavior by refusing to do his homework and sneaking out to play when he is supposed to be doing his homework. Sometimes we can coerce him into doing his homework by refusing to take him to sports practice, but on occasion he has outwitted us by claiming he has no homework. If it is an evening that he has a therapy session he frequently runs away long enough to miss session. To counter his running away, we intentionally do not tell him what time the session is. However, while he doesn't get a chance to run away, getting him into the car evolves into a major wrestling match with one of us holding him and the other driving. After a holding session at the therapist's office, Michael is usually rather compliant the remainder of the evening (what little is left of it) and he is generally calm. If it is an evening where Michael doesn't have a therapy session, he often targets his teasing at the family as a whole, or an individual member by screaming or doing some other inappropriate action while we/they are watching a favorite TV program, reading, or while his brother/sister are doing their homework.

Michael seldom goes to bed at his assigned time. We generally give him about 15 minutes leeway, before we really press him. Again, if he throws a tantrum someone gets hurt or he destroys the house or somebody's property. At times we have to physically drag him to his room and place him in bed. Sometimes he stays in his room and sometimes he doesn't. If he stays in his room he normally screams and jumps on his bed for a while before settling down and going to sleep.

The neighbor's reaction to Michael is mixed. Generally he gets along with them, but we have had a couple of incidences where the neighbors came to us and complained about him. In one case we paid for the damage (a broken window), which seemed to pacify the situation. In the other case, he got into a fight with a girl with asthma who was teasing him. The fight brought on an asthma attack, which scared and upset our neighbor. Luckily, this neighbor was a school teacher, who seemed more willing to understand his situation. She stated that, "Although she was extremely upset, she knew we were trying to take care of the situation and doing the best we could."

## A Day in the Life of April (age 8)

April's typical good behaviors are pleasant, intelligent conversation, and creative play. Her other behaviors at any given moment may include hitting, kicking, biting, cursing, screaming, punching holes in the wall, throwing objects, slamming doors, stealing, etc… I used to respond in anger and embarrassment. I now respond with removal from the situation, time out, loss of toys.

April doesn't have really much to do with the boys. She doesn't play well with other children. She has one girl that she plays well with (5 years old), but other than that she doesn't do that well with peers.

It bothers me that she has to be in control so much, that she will jeopardize anything to get her way. April's strong will is both positive and negative. Her winning smile and cunning intelligence are positive. She is a good reader and speller. Her school behavior has been awful. She is in an ALC (Alternative Learning Center) most of the day and does much better. She is never great at responding to authority, because it challenges her own. She does, however, have an understanding that Mrs. Smith has more control than any other teacher at school.

Most of the school and church community have been supportive. They are appalled at April's behavior. Most have had no concept, until this last hospitalization that it was anything other than strong-willed behavior on her part and lenient discipline on my part. Now that we have documentation that April has an actual physical/mental problem, it has helped people at least understand my reactions. It is quite unnerving to have your child brought to you screaming and crying, while you are in a rehearsal with 40 fourth, fifth, and sixth graders. It took three teachers to carry April kicking, biting, and cursing, and the teachers were shocked because I didn't immediately "spank the fire" out of her. Instead, I isolated her to an empty room, got my sister-in-law, who is great with April, to be with her. Then I spent the next ten minutes bandaging the bitten hand of one teacher while explaining her explosive behavior to the others. Of course, we left church early and she was remanded to her room.

April is constantly challenging me. Every day, every way. In the store, at home, at church, at play. I must constantly be on my guard. I have to watch what I say and do, and keep my wits about me at all times. On a bad day, she really zeros in and works overtime to get me upset, as though she has won.

She is now challenging Jim with statements like, "I don't have to mind you!" She is less likely to disobey him, but it does happen.

This child has been a definite challenge. She has strengthened our marriage in many respects. We know we can't handle too much alone. We need each other. If I call the print shop, exasperated, Jim will come home. If he senses a rough day, he'll take her to the shop or soccer fields. If I sense he's had it, I make plans to divert her attention so he gets a break. It has been quite a financial strain. On our lifestyle— we don't take April to important places or functions. We sit at the back and leave early if we have a problem. The boys don't have a lot of friends to the house because April embarrasses them so often. They never want her at school events. Our house is messed up all the time with her "stuff." They call her "the bag lady." She has made approximately 25 holes in the wall. We have locks on all the boy's bedroom doors, linen closet, sewing room, and pantry to keep her out. She steals their money, breaks their radios, ruins games. Strangely enough, they each profess to love her and are kind to her the majority of the time. Since we now know that April's left brain is deficient, we have talked to the boys about her being mentally handicapped instead of just "mean spirited." This has really helped them deal with her situation better.

Personally, I am worn out. Some days I just don't want to come home. I often have nightmares of April dying, and wake up feeling incredible remorse. I am working so hard to see April's strengths and hope that in the long term she will be able to contribute to society in a positive way. I need a rest, but it would take a week just to unwind and no one can handle April for that long outside our immediate family.

The only parenting techniques that work with April are time-outs, removal from the areas of dispute, therapeutic holds, and taking away of personal property. A soft voice is a must. Punishment must be swift and strong. No wishy-washy what to do. Action must be immediate with a determination to outlast her best effort. The least effective is spanking. This really revs her up. We have tried EVERYTHING. Nothing that ever worked with any of the boys works for her. Grounding is ridiculous, charts don't work. She cannot be reasoned with. Washing out her mouth was a real challenge. She would curse right through the bubbles. She'd curse till she threw up.

When the idea of permanent residential care was first mentioned, I cried for two days. I couldn't eat. I still felt there must be more we could do because "good" parents would never entertain that thought. Now, even with high dosages of medicine, I do not see major results. I do see an increased attention span. But I see more and more weird behaviors. More and more acting out and violence at school. I am terrified that the school will say, "She's too dangerous, take her home." I am coming more and more to the reality that I am not equipped to deal with this type of behavior. I'm certainly better than I was eight years ago, and my friends marvel at my newfound patience. But I fear it is not enough.

Tim is the most physically threatened. April picks on him the most. He is most kind to her and hates to hit her back or even protect himself from her. She has hit him with a baseball bat, plastic but very hard, bit him innumerous times, hit, kicked, etc. He probably loves April more than any of the boys.

My worst fear is that April will commit some awful crime or injure some child or teacher at school or church. My best hope is that you will be able to help April and she will develop a conscience and stop the violence.

# Sentence Completion Form
## Appendix C

I would like to get to know you better, and one way I thought might be easiest, would be for you to tell me what you think and how you feel about these things:

I'm afraid _____

I know I can _____

Other kids _____

People often _____

I secretly _____

My greatest worry _____

I just can't _____

My mind _____

At home _____

There is nothing _____

My mother won't _____

My family _____

I wish I could stop _____

Mother and I _____

When I get mad _____

Most girls _____

When I was very young _____

I'm different because _____

I hurt when _____

I'm sad when _____

When I grow up _____

I need _____

Father and I _____

I wish _____

I hate _____

It would be funny _____

Most boys/girls _____

I want to know _____

My school _____

Three wishes I have are _____

259

# Patterns of Adult Attachment
## Appendix D

The Berkeley Adult Attachment Interview was used to assess parents' patterns of attachments [Main et al. 1985]. This interview procedure elicits details of early family life, relationships with parents, and unresolved emotional issues. It assesses the adults' early attachment experiences and their current "state of mind" about attachment. Based on their responses, adults are assigned to one of four categories, each equivalent to and predictive of infant/childhood attachment patterns (secure, dismissing, preoccupied, and unresolved):

### 1. Secure-autonomous

- Coherent view of attachment.

- Secure base provided by at least one of their parents.

- Do not portray their childhoods as trouble free; objective regarding the positive and negative qualities of their parents.

- Able to reflect on selves and relationships (little self-deception); comfortable talking about attachment issues; communicate in a clear, direct, and honest manner.

- Worked through painful issues from childhood and can discuss these issues without much anxiety or stress; insight into the effects of early negative emotional and family experiences; understanding and some level of forgiveness towards their parents.

- Able to depend on others; accept the importance of relationships in their lives.

- Most of their own children were rated as *securely attached*.

### 2. Dismissing

- Unable or unwilling to address attachment issues in coherent and serious way; dismiss the value and importance of attachment relationships.

- Guarded and defensive answers; often not able to accurately remember their childhoods; do not want to reflect on their past.

- Idealized their parents; deny true facts and feelings associated with negative parental behavior (e.g., abuse and neglect).

- Avoided the pain of early rejection and their need for love and affection through various defensive strategies.

- Three-fourths of their own children were *avoidantly attached*.

### 3. Preoccupied

- Confused and incoherent regarding memories; unresolved about early hurt and anger in family relationships.

- Childhoods characterized by disappointment, frustrating efforts to please their parents, and role reversals ("parentification").

- Remain emotionally enmeshed with parents and family-of-origin issues; unaware of own responsibility in current relationship problems.

- Most of their own children have *ambivalent attachments*.

### 4. Unresolved

- Experienced severe trauma and early losses; have not mourned lost attachment figures and not integrated those losses into their lives.

- Frightened by memories and emotions associated by early trauma; may dissociate to avoid pain; confused and incoherent regarding past events.

- Extremely negative and dysfunctional relationships with their own children, including abuse and neglect; script their children into past unresolved emotional patterns and dramas.

- Produce *disorganized-disoriented attachments* in their children.

# Symptom Comparison:
## ADHD, Bipolar Disorder, Reactive Attachment Disorder
### Appendix E

| Symptom | ADHD | Bipolar I Disorder | Reactive Attachment Disorder |
|---|---|---|---|
| Age of onset | Birth, 6, 13 | 2-3, 7, 13-35 | Birth to 3 |
| Family history | ADHD, academic difficulties, alcohol & substance abuse | Mood disorders, academic difficulties, alcohol & substance abuse, adoption, ADHD | Abuse and neglect, severe emotional & behavioral disorders, alcohol & substance abuse, abuse & neglect in parent's own early life |
| Incidence | Approximately 6% of general population | 2-3% of general population | 3-6% of general population |
| Cause | Genetic, exacerbated by stress | Genetic, exacerbated by stress & hormones | Psychological secondary to neglect, abuse, abandonment |
| Duration | Chronic & unremittingly continuous, tends toward improvement | May or may not show clear behavioral episodes & cyclicity; worsens over years with increased severe and dramatic symptoms | Dependent on life circumstances, including treatment & innate temperament; worsens over years without treatment, resulting in antisocial character disorders |
| Attention span | Short, leading to lack of productivity | Dependent on interest & motivation, distractible | Usually prolonged secondary to hypervigilance, under stress can shorten |
| Impulsivity | Secondary to inattention or oblivious, regret | Driven, "irresistible," grandiosity, thrill-seeking, counterphobia, little regret | Usually deliberate actions; poor cause-and-effect thinking; no remorse |
| Hyperactivity | 50% are hyperactive, disorganized | Wide ranges, with hyperactivity common in children | Common |
| Self-esteem | Low, rooted in ongoing performance difficulties | Low because of inherent unpredictability of mood | Low, rooted in abandonment, feel worthless & unlovable, masked by anger |
| Attitude | Friendly in a genuine manner | Highly unpredictable, dysphoric, moody, negativistic | Superficially charming, phoney, distrusting, emotionally distant, nonintimate |

| Symptom | ADHD | Bipolar I Disorder | Reactive Attachment Disorder |
|---|---|---|---|
| Control issues | Tend to desire to seek approval; get into trouble by inability to complete tasks | Intermittent desire to please (based on mood), tend to push limits and relish power struggles | Controlled and controlling, only for self-gain, under-handed, covert & punitive |
| Oppositional/ defiant | Argumentative, but will relent with some show of authority, redirectable | Usually overtly & prominently defiant, often not relenting to authority | Covertly or overtly defiant, passive aggressive |
| Blaming | Self-protective mechanism to avoid adverse consequences | Disbelief/denial they caused something to go wrong | Rejecting of responsibility, lack of empathy |
| Lying | Avoid adverse consequences | Enjoys "getting away with it" | "Crazy lying," self-centered "primary process" distortions, remain in control |
| Fire setting | Play with matches out of curiousity, nonmalicious | Play with matches/fire setting | Revenge motivated, malicious; danger seeking secondary to despair |
| Anger, irritability, temper, rage | Situational, in response to over stimulation, low frustration tolerance & need for immediate gratification; rage reaction is usually short lived | Secondary to limit setting or attempts by authority figures to control their excessive behavior, can last for extended periods of time; overt, assaultive | Chronic, revenge oriented; eternal "victim" position, with rationalizations for destructive retaliation; hurtful to innocent others and pets |
| Entitlement | Overwhelming need for immediate gratification | Feel entitled to get what they want, grandiose | Compensation for abandonment & deprivation |
| Conscience development | Capable of demonstrating remorse when calmed down | Limited conscience development, less cruel than RAD | Very "street smart," good survival skills, con artists, calculating, lack of remorse |
| Sensitivity | Oblivious to their circumstances, inappropriateness shows as result | Acutely aware of circumstances and are "hot reactors" | Hypervigilant, compensating for past helplessness; limited emotional repertoire, insensitive |
| Perception | Flooded by sensory overestimation, hyperactive, distractible, shuts down | Self-absorbed, preoccupied with internal need fulfillment, narcissistic. | Self-centered, primary process, primitive distortions |

| Symptom | ADHD | Bipolar I Disorder | Reactive Attachment Disorder |
|---|---|---|---|
| Peer relationships | Makes friends easily, but not able to keep them | Can be charismatic or depressed, depending on mood; conflicts are the rule | Very poor, controlling & manipulative; not able to maintain relationships |
| Sleep disturbances | Overstimulated, once asleep "sleeps like a rock" | Inability to relax because of racing mind; nightmares common | Hypervigilance creates light sleepers; tends to need little sleep, arise early in a.m. |
| Motivation | Less resourceful, more adult dependent; OK starters, poor finishers | Grandiose: believe they are resourceful, gifted, creative; self-directed, variable energy & enthusiasm | Consistently poor initiative, limited industriousness, intentional inefficiency |
| Learning difficulties | Commonly have auditory perceptual difficulties, lack fine motor coordination | Nonsequential, nonlinear learners, verbally articulate | Brain maturational delays secondary to maternal drug/alcohol effects, early life abuse/neglect can create diverse learning problems |
| Anxiety | Uncommon, unless performance related | Emotionally wired & have high potentials for anxiety, fears & phobias. Somatic symptoms common, needle phobic | Appear invulnerable; poor recognition, awareness or admission of fears |
| Sexuality | Emotionally immature & sexually naive | Sexual hyperawareness, pseudomaturity, and high activity level | Uses sex as means of power, control, or of infliction of pain, sadistic |
| Substance abuse | Strong tendencies, more out of coping mechanisms for low self-esteem | Strong tendencies in attempt to medically treat either hypomanic/depressive moods | Sporadic/uncommon, need to maintain control |
| Optimal environment | Low stimulation & stress, support & structure | Clear & assertive, limits, encouragement | Balance of security & stability, limits and clear expectations, nurturance and encouragement |
| Psychopharmacology | Medications very helpful: Ritalin, Dexedrine, Cylert, Wellbutrin; Clonidine, Imipramine & Nortriptyline useful as adjunctive treatments | Medications helpful to stabilize mood: Lithium, Carbamazepine, Valproic Acid, Verapamil, Risperdal | Antidepressants, Clonidine, may help decrease hypervigilance, does not help characterological traits |

# The Effective Corrective Attachment Therapist

## Appendix F

- Tolerance, empathy, patience, and compassion.

- Emotionally nonreactive; ability to remain "centered."

- Accepting, nonjudgmental, and supportive.

- Comfortable with anger and other strong emotions.

- Free of personal abuse issues.

- Confident and able to instill confidence.

- Genuine sense of humor, devoid of sarcasm and ridicule.

- Able to give and receive love.

- Resolved with grief, loss, and "wounded child" issues.

- Continue to grow and evolve as therapist and person.

- Sensitive to cultural backgrounds and differences.

- Adept at dealing with resistance in creative and flexible manner.

- Able to work effectively with a treatment team.

- Realistic and able to maintain hope and optimism.

- Knowledge and skills regarding attachment formation and disorder and both child and family systems therapy.

- Emotionally able and professionally willing to utilize nontraditional interventions (e.g., Holding Nurturing Process).

# Historical
# Perspective
## Appendix G

Sigmund Freud can be credited with revolutionizing our knowledge of the human psyche. At 29, the young neurologist traveled to Paris to study with the great master Jean Charot. Charot was head of Salpetriere Hospital and was considered to be the leading neurologist of his time. Freud was extremely impressed with Charot's use of hypnosis in the treatment of hysteria [Woodworth & Sheehan 1964].

Upon his return to Vienna, Freud collaborated with his good friend and eminent physiologist, Joseph Breuer. Breuer observed that while a hypnotized woman was freely discussing her problems, she displayed unexpectedly powerful emotions. Upon awakening from the hypnotic state, she reported significant feelings of relief. Breuer used the term "abreaction" to describe this release of blocked emotional charge. He believed it could be released through conscious awareness and physical movement [Coleman 1964].

Freud and Breuer published the results of their clinical case studies. In these studies, Freud referred to this discharge of emotions as "catharsis." He believed that a cathartic experience could be employed to eliminate the source of psychological problems by relating them to past emotional experiences. He further concluded that childhood traumas produce emotional energy that can become repressed in the unconscious mind. Freud believed that these blocks manifest themselves as neurosis, and that he could assist patients to recall and discharge this energy through the use of hypnosis [Badcock 1988].

Freud soon realized that there were certain drawbacks to this approach. He noticed that results tended to be temporary and that some neurotics were difficult to hypnotize. This led to the incorporation of new techniques and the elimination of the hypnotic state totally. Freud and Breuer discovered that they could encourage patients to relax and freely discuss their thoughts, no matter how illogical or absurd. This new method was call "free association." The principles used to analyze this information and the methods used to facilitate insight came to be called "psychoanalysis." While free associating, patients would occasionally describe vivid dreams. Freud was fascinated by these dreams, and he soon began analyzing his own dreams and those of others. *The Interpretation of Dreams* [1900] was his first major psychoanalytic work [Hunt 1993].

Psychoanalysis has received criticism over the years for being too verbal, cumbersome, sexually focused, lengthy, costly, and pessimistic of man's inherent nature. However, Freud's contributions are found in the theoretical foundation of most modern psychotherapies, both traditional and alternative. Freud normalized psychopathology by his belief that patients' symptoms represent attempts to manage their problems as best they can. He also was the first true holistic practitioner, recognizing the role of psychology, biology, and social factors in the development of the personality. He emphasized the dynamic role of the unconscious and the importance of early childhood experiences in later emotional development. He encouraged the revisiting of past traumas that lie repressed and unexpressed in the unconscious. His desire was to assist his patients in exploring the painful past and to release the pain and subsequently blocked emotional energies. Where the various schools of therapeutic thought differ is mostly in the techniques they employ to accomplish this task.

During his lifetime, many of Freud's theories were actively challenged and discounted. Particularly in England and the United States, his ideas received widespread professional condemnation. In the United States, his theories did not gain full recognition and acceptance until he was in his eighties and close to death. His influence was so profound that history will remember him as one of the great minds of humanity.

Some of Freud's disciples began to differ with him regarding his emphasis on sexuality as the central factor in the development of psychological disturbance. C. G. Jung developed his own approach, called Analytic Psychology. His concepts included the collective unconscious, psychological types, and the distinction between the introvert and the extrovert. Alfred Adler moved on to found the School of Individual Psychology, focusing on social motivations, and developed the concept of an inferiority complex [Roazen 1975].

Another intimate student of Freud's was Austrian psychoanalyst Wilhelm Reich. As many of Freud's colleagues were moving away from an emphasis on sexuality, Reich emphasized it further. Reich also advocated an integrated body-mind approach to healing in psychotherapy and is considered the patriarch of body work. He concluded that in childhood, we learn to tense certain muscles as a body defense against intolerable feelings. Our bodies tend to hold the effect of suppressed feelings that become manifest in adulthood in certain facial expression, body postures, and personality traits. He called this muscular defense "body armor." He also believed that talk therapy was insufficient to penetrate these deeply ingrained blocks. Reich was convinced that these resistances of blocked energy could be released by hitting out, screaming, and crying. He worked primarily with body armor and resistances without necessarily connecting them to the accompanying psychological issues. Reich believed that sexual fulfillment was crucial for mental health and that sexual orgasmic energy could be measured. He developed the "orgone box" to harness this energy that he believed could cure a wide range of psychological disorders [Robinson 1969].

The McCarthyism of the early 1950s was not a receptive time for Reich's controversial sexual views. At that time it was forbidden to even say the work "pregnant" on television. In 1951, the federal government brought charges of fraud against him. After losing an appeal, he eventually was imprisoned. The U.S. Food and Drug Administration destroyed his orgone boxes and burned his publications. After one year in prison, he died of a heart attack. After Reich's death, many of his ideas were discredited and abandoned. However, the climate of the 1960s, with the emergence of the human potential movement, led to a renaissance in body-mind work. Techniques that began to gain popularity included Gestalt Therapy, Eriksonian

Hypnosis, and other techniques that promoted therapeutic change through the release of long-withheld emotions (Bioenergetics, Feldenkreis, Alexander technique, Hakomi, Rolfing, and Rage Reduction Therapy).

Reich's belief in the body-mind connection had a direct influence on psychoanalyst Frederick Pearls, who founded Gestalt therapy. Gestalt therapy places an emphasis on awareness of restrictions in articulation and body posture. Gestalt techniques assist patients in projecting parts of themselves onto inanimate objects. Chairs are typically used to facilitate a dialogue between the objects in order to reveal inner conflicts. The release of explosive or aggressive emotions concerning the past is encouraged. This is followed by an examination of behaviors that were adopted to deal with these past traumas, which are then reevaluated as to their current relevancy.

Reichian student Alexander Lowen developed Bioenergetic Analysis based on the belief that past emotional trauma creates specific tensions in the body. These muscular tensions are the physical counterpart of emotional conflict. By employing various techniques to charge and discharge the body, muscular tensions are released, enabling the memory of trauma to return. The revealed feelings are then explored in therapy [Lowen 1988]. Psychodrama, developed by Vienese psychiatrist Jacob Moreno, is another technique that advocated acting out and reexperiencing a painful past to facilitate an emotional catharsis. This release may be quite dramatic and explosive. Moreno believed that we all have parts of our inner selves crying out for expression, which creates conflicts and emotional problems. Primal Scream, originated by Arthur Janov, is a dramatic form of self-exploration where patients reexperience repressed primal pain in a highly emotional and expressive manner.

The idea of using "holding" to facilitate therapeutic change is not new. Ann Sullivan used holding as a fundamental method to reach her breakthroughs with Helen Keller. In 1955, Paul Roland, a physical therapist at the Veterans Administration Hospital began using "touch" in his work with catatonic schizophrenics. He began by sitting with a tactilely defensive patient. After a time he touched the patient's arm. Eventually he was able to increase contact. From that point on, rehabilitation of the patient proceeded quite rapidly. Gertrude Schwing also was able to achieve remarkable breakthroughs with schizophrenic children through therapeutic holdings [Montague 1986].

In 1966, Robert Zaslow, a professor at San Jose State University, began integrating theories of attachment and holding therapy into his clinical work in infantile autism. His work emphasized the correlation between aggression, rage, and resistance behavior. He called his holding technique "Rage Reduction Therapy," which was later changed to the Z-process [Zaslow & Breger 1969]. He eventually expanded his technique to be used with a wide variety of childhood disorders including psychosis, identity disorder, hyperactivity, and learning problems [Zaslow & Menta 1975].

Interestingly, others around the world were simultaneously achieving significant results by employing holding techniques with autistic children. In England, Dr. Gerald O'Gorman used institutionalized girls to cuddle autistic children. The autistic children showed immediate and dramatic improvement, including the development of coordinated behavior and speech [Montague 1986].

Martha Welch, M.D., began holding autistic children at the Albert Einstein College of Medicine and later continued at the Mothering Center in Greenwich, Connecticut. She achieved success by assisting mothers in holding their autistic children, promoting a predictable sequence of fighting and resisting, followed by calming and relating. Dr. Welch found that her technique of "Holding Time" is effective in addressing a wide variety of child and family problems [Welch 1988]. Additionally, Dr. Michele Zapella, of the Ospedale Regionale of Siena, began using an approach to autistic children where touching and holding play a crucial role [Montague 1986].

In his holding work with schizophrenics, Dr. Zaslow consistently found that by eliciting high levels of contained anger, patients did not feel more "crazy" or hostile, but instead, felt more peaceful, integrated, loving, responsive, and connected to other people. Zaslow's impressive results were beginning to gain considerable attention. His method was presented at the Tavistoc Clinic in London, the same clinic where Robertson and Bowlby began their ground-breaking attachment research in the early 1950s.

Although Dr. Zaslow's techniques were effectively producing dramatic results in a wide variety of disorders, there were several aspects of his work that were controversial. One contested part of his methodology had to do with the extensive use of tactile stimulation (rubbing the rib cage) in order to activate rage and breakthrough resistances. The other major area of contention was the "Who's the Boss" issue. Zaslow believed that individuals who lacked appropriate parental boundaries and limits have difficulty in controlling themselves. Therefore, in order to make significant therapeutic progress, they first need to be controlled appropriately by a therapist. This necessitates high confrontation that lead to the goal of deep expression of anger and capitulation to the therapist, followed by experience of relief and closeness [Zaslow & Menta 1976].

In 1972, Dr. Zaslow was brought to Forest Heights Lodge, a noted psychiatric residential facility in Evergreen, Colorado, to do extensive training. Russ Colburn, Director of the Lodge, invited child psychiatrist, Foster W. Cline, to participate in this process. Zaslow's marathon sessions were characterized by their depth of intensity and duration. They could continue for as long as it took to achieve expression and resolution; 8 to 10 hours was not uncommon. Dr. Cline significantly reduced the time it took to achieve results, partly due to his mastery in dealing with resistance. In 1973, Dr. Cline founded Evergreen Consultants in Human Behavior, a group of clinicians in private practice who specialize in the innovative treatment of severely disturbed children and their families.

Evergreen Consultants eventually abandoned the use of tactile stimulation and rigid adherence to the use of heavy confrontation required to gain therapeutic control. Even though we found it to be therapeutically effective, we did not believe that tactile stimulation would ever be widely understood or accepted by the professional community. We also feared that this technique could be easily abused by an untrained or emotionally unstable therapist.

We continued to believe that establishing therapeutic control was important. However, we began to see that a child only required a level of control equal to his level of resistance. We found that resistance could be successfully addressed through the use of many different therapeutic modalities and began to use psychodramatic reenactment, visualization, inner-child work, and a strong therapeutic contract, as a replacement for the heavy emphasis on control and capitulation. Orlans found that when a good working contract with the older disturbed child is established, significant therapeutic change is possible. He also placed a heavy emphasis on family systems work in the treatment process. These techniques gave the holding work a softer and more nurturing quality.

Orlans co-developed the "two-week intensive" (30 hours of intensive therapy over 10 days), as a viable and practical means of treating disturbed children and their families. He eventually introduced the two-week intensive to the Attachment Center at Evergreen, and it is now an integral part of treatment in many other attachment centers throughout the United States.

Many forms of holding therapy have evolved over the years. All holding therapies tend to be grouped together as one technique. In fact, there are many variations of holding work. Some are more intrusive, some are less. Variations in treatment philosophies and individual therapist style contribute to a wide spectrum of techniques.

# Life Script
## Appendix H

This questionnaire is completed with the therapist. It is useful as a tool to facilitate discussion about family-of-origin issues.

1. Write 4 to 6 adjectives that describe each parent, from your perspective as a child.

2. Write 4 to 6 adjectives that describe yourself as a child.

3. Why did your father marry your mother?

   Why did your mother marry your father?

4. What were the major messages your father gave you about yourself and how to deal with life? What was your response to him?

   What were the major messages your mother gave you about yourself and how to deal with life? What was your response to her?

5. What did you learn from your father about men and women?

   What did you learn from your mother about men and women?

6. How did your parents handle conflict, emotion, and discipline of children?

7. Who was your favorite childhood hero or heroine?

8. What was your favorite childhood story or fairy tale?

9. What would you write on the tombstone or epitaph for your father, your mother, yourself?

# Follow-Up Treatment Plan
## Appendix I

Date

Child's Name                  Date of Birth        Age

Therapist                  Treatment Family

Hometown Therapist/Agency

Clinical Director             Treatment Dates

## Diagnosis

| Axis | Code | Diagnosis |
|------|------|-----------|
| I | 313.89 | Reactive Attachment Disorder |
| | 313.81 | Oppositional Disorder |
| | 309.89 | Posttraumatic Stress Disorder |

## Strengths

Parents' commitment, understanding, and willingness to learn.

Support of hometown agency and therapist.

Extended family support.

Child's intelligence and desire for family.

Spiritual faith and support of family.

Parents working to strengthen marriage.

## Treatment Issues

Child's oppositional, defiant, and aggressive behaviors.

Child's lack of trust, reciprocity, and negative working model.

Parenting skills; high frustration and stress.

Mother's depression and demoralization.

Father's resolution of family-of-origin issues.

# Treatment Goals and Plans

## Emotional/Relationships

Goal 1  Family will create a safe and secure environment to facilitate trust and attachment.

Goal 2  Child will increase ability to be reciprocal, trusting, affectionate, and appropriately compliant with parents.

Goal 3  Parents will enhance marital communication and unity, address individual family of-origin issues, and improve parenting skills.

Goal 4  Family will establish necessary external supports to reduce stress level and achieve goals.

## Description of Services

| Services: | Intensity / Frequency: |
|---|---|
| Individual, marital, and family therapy. | Regular schedule with hometown therapist. |
| Telephone contact with therapeutic foster parent. | Weekly/ongoing |
| Follow-up medication monitoring and management. | As per hometown psychiatrist. |
| Parents establish respite system with help of hometown agency. | ASAP; with hometown agency. |
| Conference calls with treatment team. | As per schedule and/or as needed. |

By signing this treatment plan, I agree to follow through with my role in carrying out the plan or will contact the Clinical Director with any changes or concerns.

| | |
|---|---|
| Parent | Parent |
| Child | Treatment Parents |
| Clinical Director | Hometown Therapist |
| Primary Therapist | Date |

# References

Abrams, S. M., Field, T., Scafidi, F., & Prodromidis, M. (1995). Newborns of depressed mothers. *Infant Mental Health Journal, 16,* 231-237.

Achenbach, T. M., & Edelbrock, C. (1983). *Manual for the child behavior checklist and revised child behavior profile.* Burlington, VT: University of Vermont.

Adoptive Families. (1997a). Families for kids of color. *Adoptive Families Magazine, 30*(6), 9–10.

Adoptive Families. (1997b). *International adoption statistics released, 30*(6), 6.

Advisory Committee on Services for Families with Infants and Toddlers. (September 1994). *Statement of the advisory committee on services for infants and toddlers.* Washington, DC: U.S. Department of Health and Human Services.

Ainsworth, M. (1967). *Infancy in Uganda: Infant care and the growth of love.* Baltimore, MD: The Johns Hopkins University Press.

Ainsworth, M. D. S. (1973). The development of infant-mother attachment. In B. M. Caldwell & H. N. Ricciuti (Eds.), *Review of child development research,* Vol. 3 (pp. 1-94). Chicago, IL: University of Chicago Press.

Ainsworth, M. D. S., Blehar, M., Waters, E., & Wall, S. (1978). *Patterns of attachment.* Hillsdale, NJ: Erlbaum.

Ainsworth, M. D. S., & Wittig, B. A. (1969). Attachment and the exploratory behavior of one year olds in a strange situation. In B. M. Foss (Ed.), *Determinants of infant behavior,* Vol. 4 (pp. 113-136). London: Methuen.

Alexander, P. D. (1992). Application of attachment theory to the study of sexual abuse. *Journal of Consulting and Clinical Psychology, 60,* 185-195.

Alexander, R., & Moskal, M. (1997). Drugs in children: Exposure before and after birth. *APSAC Advisor, 10*(1), 10-14.

Allen, B., & Borgen, K. (1994). Multimodel therapy for survivors of sexual abuse with developmental disabilities. *Sexuality and Disability, 12*(3), 201-206.

Alston, J. F. (1995). *New findings in diagnosis correlation between bipolar disorder and reactive attachment disorder.* Personal communication.

Amato, P. R. (1986). Marital conflict, the parent-child relationship and child self-esteem. *Family Relations, 35,* 403-410.

American Psychiatric Association. (1994). *Diagnostic and statistical manual of mental disorders* (4th ed.). Washington, DC: Author.

Anisfeld, E., Casper, V., Nozyce, M., & Cunningham, N. (1990). Does infant carrying promote attachment? *Child Development, 61,* 1617-1627.

Arnstein, H. A. (1975). *The roots of love.* New York: Bobbs-Merrill.

Badcock, C. (1988). *Essential Freud.* New York: Basil Blackwell.

Bakwin, H. (1942). Loneliness in infants. *American Journal of Diseases of Children, 63,* 30-40.

Bain, L. J. (1991). *A parent's guide to attention deficit disorder.* New York: Dell.

Banks, R. (1980). Health and spiritual dimensions. *Journal of School Health, 50,* 195-202.

Barnett, D. (1997). The effects of early intervention on maltreating parents and their children. In M. Guralnick (Ed.), *The effectiveness of early intervention* (pp. 147-170). Baltimore, MD: Brookes.

Barrera, M., Rosenbaum R., & Cunningham, C. (1986). Early home intervention with low birth weight infants and their parents. *Child Development, 57*(1), 20-33.

Bath, H. (1994). The physical restraint of children: Is it therapeutic? *American Journal of Orthopsychiatry, 64,* 40-49.

Beach, S. R. H., & Nelson, G. M. (1990). Pursuing research on major psychopathology from a contextual perspective: The example of depression and marital discord. In G. Brody and I. Sigel (Eds.), *Methods of family research: Biographies of research projects: Vol 2. Clinical populations.* Hillsdale, NJ: Erlbaum.

Beeghly, M., & Cicchetti, D. (1994). Child maltreatment, attachment and the self system: Emergence of an internal state lexicon in toddlers at high social risk. *Development and Psychopathology, 6,* 5-30.

Behavioral Health Treatment. (1997). *Mother's depression passes to baby* (Vol. 2). Providence, RI: Manisses Communication Group.

Beitchman, J. H., Zucker, K. J., Hood, J. E., daCosta, G. A., & Ackman, D. (1991). A review of the short-term effects of child sexual abuse. *Child Abuse & Neglect, 15,* 537-556.

Bell, C. C., & Jenkins, E. J. (1993). Community violence and children on Chicago's southside. *Psychiatry, 56,* 46-54.

Belsky, J. (1979). The interrelation of parental and spousal behavior during infancy in traditional nuclear families: An exploratory analysis. *Journal of Marriage and the Family, 41,* 749-755.

Belsky, J. (1995). *Mother's representations and family interactions.* Paper presented at Research Symposium, Institute for Behavioral Research, Jan. 12, 1995. Athens, GA: University of Georgia.

Belsky, J., Gilstrap, B., & Rovine, M. (1984). The Pennsylvania Infant and Family Development Project, I: Stability and change in mother-infant and father-infant interaction in a family setting at one, three and nine months. *Child Development, 55,* 692-705.

Belsky, J., & Isabella, R.A. (1988). Maternal, infant, and social-contextual determinants of attachment security. In J. Belsky & T. Nezworski (Eds.), *Clinical implications of attachment* (pp. 41-94). Hillsdale, NJ: Erlbaum.

Belsky, J., & Nezworsky, T. (Eds.). (1988). *Clinical implications of attachment.* Hillsdale NJ: Lawrence Erlbaum Associates

Belsky, J., & Rovine, M. (1988). Nonmaternal care in the first year of life and the security of attachment. *Child Development, 59,* 157-167.

Belsky, J., Rovine, M., & Fish, M. (1989). The developing family system. In M. R. Gunnar & E. Thelen (Eds.), *Systems and development: The Minnesota Symposia of Child Psychology, Vol. 22* (pp. 119-166). Hillsdale NJ: Lawrence Erlbaum Associates.

Belsky, J., Rovine, M., & Taylor, D. (1984). The Pennsylvania Infant and Family Development Project III: The origins of individual differences in infant-mother attachment: Maternal and infant contributions. *Child Development, 55,* 718-728.

Belsky, J., & Vondra J. (1989). Lessons from child abuse: The determinants of parenting. In D. Cicchetti & V. Carlson (Eds.), *Child maltreatment: Theory and research on the causes and consequences of child abuse and neglect* (pp. 153-202). New York: Cambridge University Press.

Belsky, J., Youngblade, L., Rovine M., & Volling, B. (1991). Patterns of marital change and parent-child interaction. *Journal of Marriage and the Family, 53,* 487-498.

Bender, L., & Yarnell, H. (1941). An observation nursery: A study of 250 children on the psychiatric division of Bellevue Hospital. *American Journal of Psychiatry, 97,* 1158-1174.

Berliner, L. (1991, June). Effects of sexual abuse on children. *Violence Update,* 1-11.

Berliner, L., & Elliott, D. M. (1996). Sexual abuse of children. In J. Briere, L. Berliner, J. A. Buckley, C. Jenny, & T. Reid (Eds.), *APSAC handbook on child maltreatment* (pp. 51-71). Thousand Oaks, CA: Sage.

Berman, S. L., Kurtines, W. M., Silverman, W. K., & Serafini, L. T. (1996). The impact of exposure to crime and violence on urban youth. *American Journal of Orthopsychiatry, 66* (3), 329-336.

Bernard, J., & Sontag, L. (1947). Fetal reactions to sound. *Journal of Genetic Psychology, 70,* 209-210.

Berrueta-Clement, J. R., Schweinhart, L. J., Barnett, W. S., Epstein, A. S., & Weikart, D. P. (1984). *Changed lives: The effects of the Perry Preschool Program on youths through age 19* (Monographs on the High/Scope Educational Research Foundation, No. 8). Ypsilanti, MI: High/Scope.

Besharov, D. J. (1994). *When drug addicts have children.* Washington, DC: Child Welfare League of America.

Biller, H., & Meredith, D. (1974). *Father power.* New York: David MacKay.

Binstock, W. A. (1973). Purgation through pity and terror. *International Journal of Psycho-analysis, 54,* 499-504.

Bohman, M., & Sigvardsson, S. (1980). A prospective, longitudinal study of children registered for adoption: A 15-year follow-up. *Acta Psychiatrica Scandinavica, 61,* 339-355.

Bohman, M., & Sigvardsson, S. (1985). A prospective longitudinal study of adoption. In A.R. Nicol (Ed.), *Longitudinal studies in child psychology and psychiatry.* New York: Wiley.

Borgatta, E. F., & Fanshel, D. (1965). *Behavioral characteristics of children known to psychiatric outpatient clinics.* New York: Child Welfare League of America.

Borysenko, J., & Borysenko, M. (1994). *The power of the mind to heal.* Carson, CA: The Hay House, Inc.

Bouchard, T. J., Lykken, D. T., McGue, M., Segal, N. L., & Tellegen, A. (1990). Sources of human psychological differences: The Minnesota study of twins reared apart. *Science, 250,* 223-228.

Bowlby, J. (1944). Forty-four juvenile thieves: Their characters and home-life. *International Journal of Psycho-Analysis, 25,* 19-52, 107-127. Reprinted (1946) as monograph. London: Bailiere, Tindall & Cox.

Bowlby, J. (1951). Maternal care and mental health. Geneva, Switzerland: *World Health Organization Monograph Series* (2).

Bowlby, J. (1969). *Attachment and loss. Vol. I: Attachment.* New York: Basic Books.

Bowlby, J. (1970). *Child care and the growth of love.* Harmondsworth: Pelican.

Bowlby, J. (1973). *Attachment and loss. Vol. 2: Separation.* New York: Basic Books.

Bowlby, J. (1980). *Attachment and loss. Vol. 3: Loss, sadness and depression.* New York: Basic Books.

Bowlby, J. (1982). *Attachment and loss, Vol. I* (Rev. ed.). New York: Basic Books.

Bowlby, J. (1988a). *A secure base: Parent-child attachment and healthy human development.* New York: Basic Books.

Bowlby, J. (1988b). *A secure base: Clinical applications of attachment theory.* London: Routledge.

Boyer, D., & Fine, D. (1991). Sexual abuse as a factor in adolescent pregnancy and child maltreatment. *Family Planning Perspectives, 24,* 4-19.

Brazelton, T. B. (1981). *On becoming a family: The growth of attachment.* New York: Delacorte Press.

Brazelton, T. B., & Als, H. (1979). Four early stages in the development of mother-infant interaction. In A. Schluit (Ed.), *The psychoanalytic study of the child,* Vol. 34 (pp. 33-55). New York: Wiley.

Brazelton, T. B., & Cramer, B.G. (1990). *The earliest relationship.* New York: Addison-Wesley.

Brazelton, T. B., Koslowski, B., & Main, M. (1974). The origins of reciprocity: The early mother-infant interaction. In M. Lewis & L. Rosenblum (Eds.), *The effect of the infant on its caregiver* (pp. 68-93). New York: Wiley.

Bretherton, I. (1985). Attachment theory: Retrospect and prospect. In I. Bretherton & E. Waters (Eds.), Growing points of attachment theory and research. *Monographs of the Society for Research in Child Development, 50,* (1-2, Serial No. 209), 66-104.

Briere, J. (1988). The long-term clinical correlates of childhood sexual victimization. *Annals of New York Academy of Sciences, 528,* 327-334.

Briere, J. (1989). *Therapy for adults molested as children: Beyond survival.* New York: Springer.

Briere, J., & Runtz, M. (1987). Post-sexual abuse trauma: Data and implications for clinical practice. *Journal of Interpersonal Violence, 2,* 367-379.

Briggs, D. (1997). Forgiveness, first step in healing process. *Denver Post,* Dec. 20, 1997.

Brodzinsky, D. M., Ramsay, D., Singer, L. M., Stein, M., & Waters, E. (1990). Mother-infant attachment in adoptive families. In P.V . Grabe (Ed.), *Adoption resourcesfor mental health professionals* (pp. 121-135). New Brunswick, NJ: Transaction Publishers.

Brodzinsky, D. M., & Schechter, M. D. (1990). *The psychology of adoption.* New York: Oxford University Press.

Brodzinsky, D. M., Schechter, D. E., Braff, A. M., & Singer, L. M. (1984). Psychological and academic adjustment in adopted children. *Journal of Consulting and Clinical Psychology 52,* 582-590.

Brody, G. H., Pillegrini, A. D., & Sigel, I. E. (1986). Marital quality and mother-child and father-child interactions with school aged children. *Developmental Psychology, 22,* 291-296.

Brohl, K. (1996). *Working with traumatized children: A handbook for healing.* Washington DC: CWLA Press.

Brown, D., & Fromm, E. (1986). *Hypnotherapy and hypnoanalysis.* Hillsdale, NJ: Erlbaum.

Browne, A., & Finkelhor, D. (1986). Impact of child sexual abuse: A review of the research. *Psychological Bulletin, 99,* 66-77.

Bruner, J. (1995). *Acts of meaning.* Cambridge, MA: Harvard University Press.

Buenning, W. (1995). *The autonomy circle.* Personal communication.

Burgess, A. W., & Holmstrom, L. L. (1984). Rape trauma syndrome. *American Journal of Psychiatry, 131*(9), 981-986.

Buss, D. M. (1995). Psychological sex differences. *American Psychologist, 50,* 164-168.

Butterfield, F. (1997, July 21). Juvenile courts on way out? *Denver Post,* 18.

Byng-Hall, J. (1995a). Creating a secure family base: Some implications of attachment theory for family therapy. *Family Process, 34*(1), 45-58.

Byng-Hall, J. (1995b). *Rewriting family scripts.* New York: Guilford Press.

Calhoun, B. C., & Watson, P.T . (1991). The cost of maternal cocaine use. *Obstetrics and Gynecology, 78,* 731-734.

Campbell, S. B. (1991). Longitudinal studies of active and aggressive preschoolers: Individual differences in early behavior and in outcome. In D. Cicchetti & S. L. Toth (Eds.), *Internalizing and externalizing expression of dysfunction: Rochester Symposium on Developmental Psychopathology,* Vol 2 (pp. 57-89). Hillsdale, NJ: Erlbaum.

Cannon, A. (1997). Animal/human cruelty linked. *Denver Post,* August 10, 1997.

Carlson, V., Cicchetti, D., Barnett, D., & Braunwald, K. (1989). Disorganized-disoriented attachment relationships in maltreated infants. *Developmental Psychology, 25,* 525-531.

Center on Child Abuse Prevention Research. (1996, June 15). *Intensive home visitation: A randomized trial, follow-up and risk assessment study of Hawaii's Healthy Start Program* (Final report, prepared for the National Center on Child Abuse and Neglect). Chicago, IL: National Committee to Prevent Child Abuse.

Chapin, H. D. (1915). A plea for accurate statistics in children's institutions. *Transactions of the American Pediatric Society, 27,* 180-185.

Chandler, G. M. (1993). A hypnotic intervention for anger reduction and shifting perceptual predispositions. *Journal of Mental Health Counseling, 15*(2), 200-205.

Chernoff, R., Combs-Orne, T., Risley-Curtiss, C., & Heisler, A. (1994). Assessing the health status of children entering foster care. *Pediatrics, 93,* 594-601.

Chess, S., & Thomas, A. (1987). *Origins and evolution of behavior disorders.* Cambridge, MA: Harvard University Press.

Chess, S., Thomas, A., & Birch, H. (1959). Characteristics of the individual child's behavioral responses to the environment. *American Journal of Orthopsychiatry, 29,* 791-802.

Child Welfare League of America. (1993). *Charting the new course: Children's legislative agenda.* Washington, DC: Author.

Child Welfare League of America. (1996). *Family foster care survey.* Washington, DC: Author.

Children's Defense Fund. (1996). *The state of America's children.* Washington, DC: Author.

Children's Defense Fund. (1997). *The state of America's children: Yearbook 1997.* Washington, DC: Author.

Chu, J. A., & Dill, D. L. (1990). Dissociative symptoms in relation to childhood physical and sexual abuse. *American Journal of Psychiatry, 147,* 887-892.

Clarke-Stewart, K. A. (1978). And daddy makes three: The father's impact on mother and young child. *Child Development, 49,* 466 - 482.

Cline, F. W. (1982). *Parent education text.* Evergreen, CO: Evergreen Consultants in Human Behavior, EC Publications.

Cline, F. W. (1992). *Understanding and treating the severely disturbed child.* Evergreen CO: Evergreen Consultants in Human Behavior, EC Publications.

Cline, F. W. (1995). *Consciousless acts, societal mayhem.* Golden, CO: Love and Logic Press.

Cline, F., & Fay, J. (1990). *Parenting with love and logic.* Colorado Springs, CO: Pinon Press.

Cohen, J., & Mannarino, A.P. (1988). Psychological symptoms in sexually abused girls. *Child Abuse & Neglect, 12,* 571-577.

Colapinto, J. A. (1995). Dilution of family process in social services: Implications for treatment of neglectful families. *Family Process, 34*(1), 59-74.

Colapinto, J., Minuchin, S., & Minuchin, P. (1989). *Home-based family service manual.* New York: Family Studies, Inc.

Cole, P., & Putnam, F. W. (1992). Effect of incest on self and social functioning: A developmental psychopathology perspective. *Journal of Consulting and Clinical Psychology, 60,* 174-184.

Coleman, J. C. (1964). *Abnormal psychology and modern life.* Los Angeles, CA: Scott Foresman.

Colin, V. L. (1996). *Human attachment.* New York: McGraw-Hill.

Conte, J. R., & Schuerman, J. R. (1987). Factors associated with an increased impact of child sexual abuse. *Child Abuse & Neglect, 11,* 201-211.

Cook, E. T., Greenberg, M. T., & Kusche, C. A. (1994). The relations between emotional understanding, intellectual functioning, and disruptive behavior problems in elementary school-aged children. *Journal of Abnormal Child Psychology, 22,* 205-219.

Courtney, M. E. (1997). The politics and realities of transracial adoption. *Child Welfare* 76(6), 749-779.

Craig, C. (1995). What I need is a mom. *Policy Review.* Washington, DC: Heritage Foundation.

Crittenden, P. M. (1985). Maltreated infants: Vulnerability and resilience. *Journal of Child Psychology and Psychiatry, 26*(1), 85-96.

Crittenden, P. M. (1988). Relationships at risk. In J. Blesky & T. Nezworski (Eds.), *Clinical implications of attachment* (pp. 136-176). Hillsdale, NJ: Erlbaum.

Crittenden, P. M. (1992a). Children's strategies for coping with adverse home environments: An interpretation using attachment theory. *Child Abuse and Neglect, 16*(3), 329-343.

Crittenden, P. M. (1992b). Treatment of anxious attachment in infancy and early childhood. *Development and Psychopathology, 4,* 575-602.

Crittenden, P. M. (1994). Peering into the black box: An exploratory treatise on the development of self on young children. In D. Cicchetti & S. L. Toth (Eds.), *Rochester Symposium on Developmental Psychopathology,* Vol. 5 (pp. 79-148). Rochester, NY: University of Rochester Press.

Crittenden, P. M., & Ainsworth, M. D. S. (1989). Child maltreatment and attachment theory. In D. Cicchetti and V. Carlson (Eds.), *Child maltreatment: Theory and research on the causes and consequences of child abuse and neglect* (pp. 432-463). New York: Cambridge University Press.

Crittenden, P. M., & DiLalla, D. (1988). Compulsive compliance: The development of an inhibitory coping strategy in infancy. *Journal of Abnormal Child Psychology, 16,* 585-599.

Crockenberg, S. B. (1981). Infant irritability, mother responsiveness, and social support influences on the security of infant-mother attachment. *Child Development, 52,* 857-865.

Crowell, N., & Leepers, E. (1994). America's fathers and public policy. Board on Children and Families, Institute of Medicine. Washington, DC: National Academy Press.

Cummings, E. M. (1994). Marital conflict and children's functioning. *Social Development, 3,* 16-36.

Cummings, E. M., & Davis, P. T. (1994a). *Children and marital conflict: The impact of family dispute and resolution.* New York: Guilford.

Cummings, E. M., & O'Reilly, A.W. (1997). Fathers in family context: Effects of marital quality on child adjustment. In M.E. Lamb (Ed.), *The role of the father in child development,* (3rd ed.), (pp. 49-65). New York: Wiley.

DeAngelis, T. (1995). New threat associated with child abuse. *APA Monitor, 24*(4), 1-38.

DeCasper, A., & Fifer W. (1980). Of human bonding: Infants prefer their mother's voices. *Science, 208,* 1174-1176.

DeFrancis, V. (1969). *Protecting the child victim of sex crimes committed by adults: Final report.* Denver, CO: The American Humane Association.

DeMulder, E. K., & Radke-Yarrow, M. (1991). Attachment with affectively ill and well mothers: Concurrent behavioral correlates. *Development and Psychopathology, 3,* 227-242.

Dickenson, S., & Parke, R. D. (1988). Social referencing in infancy: A glance at fathers and marriage. *Child Development, 59,* 506-511.

Dodge, K. A., Bates, J. E., & Pettit, G. S. (1990). Mechanisms in the cycle of violence. *Science, 250,* 1678-1683.

Donahue, P. (1985). *The human animal.* New York: Simon and Schuster.

Donley, M.G. (1993). Attachment and the emotional unit. *Family Process, 32*(1), 3-20.

Dubowitz, H., Black, M., Starr, R. M., & Zuvarin, S. (1993). A conceptual definition of child neglect. *Criminal Justice and Behavior, 20,* 8-26.

Dunn, J., & Brown, J. (1991). Relationships, talk about feelings, and the development of affect regulation in early childhood. In J. Garber & K. A. Dodge (Eds.), *The development of emotion regulation and dysregulation* (pp. 89-108). New York: Cambridge University Press.

Dunn, J., & Plomin, R. (1990). *Separate lives: Why siblings are so different.* New York: Basic Books.

Easterbrooks, M. A., & Goldberg, W. A. (1991). Security of toddler-parent attachment. In M. Greenberg, D. Cicchetti, & E. M. Cummings (Eds.), *Attachment in the preschool years* (pp. 221-244). Chicago: University of Chicago Press.

Egeland, R. (1988). Breaking the cycle of abuse: Implications for prediction and intervention. In K. D. Browne, C. Davies, & P. Stratton (Eds.), *Early prediction and prevention of child abuse* (pp. 87-99). New York: Wiley.

Egeland, B., & Farber, E. A. (1984). Infant-mother attachment: Factors related to its development and changes over time. *Child Development, 55,* 753-771.

Egeland, B., Jacobvitz, D., & Sroufe, L. A. (1988). Breaking the cycle of abuse: Relationship predictions. *Child Development, 59,* 1080-1088

Egeland, B., Pianta, R., & O'Brien, M. A. (1993). Maternal intrusiveness in infancy and child maladaptation in early school years. *Development and Psychopathology, 5,* 359-370.

Einbender, A. J., & Friedrich, W. N. (1989). Psychological functioning and behavior of sexually abused girls. *Journal of Consulting and Clinical Psychology, 57,* 155-157.

Eisenberg, N., & Mussen, P. (1989). *The roots of prosocial behavior in children.* Cambridge, England: Cambridge University Press.

Elicker, J., Englund, M., & Sroufe, L. A. (1992). Predicting peer competence and peer relationships in childhood from early parent-child relationships. In R. Parke & G. Ladd (Eds.), *Family-peer relationships: Modes of linkage* (pp. 138-161). Hillsdale, NJ: Erlbaum.

Elliott, D. M., & Briere, J. (1994). Forensic sexual abuse evaluations: Disclosures and symptomatology. *Behavioral Sciences and the Law, 12,* 261-277.

Erickson, E. (1950). *Childhood and society.* New York: Norton.

Erickson, M. F., & Egeland, B. (1996). Child neglect. In J. Briere, L. Berliner, J. A. Buckley, C. Jenny, & T. Reid (Eds.), *APSAC handbook on child maltreatment* (pp. 4-20). Thousand Oaks, CA: Sage.

Erickson, M., Egeland, B., & Pianta, R. (1989). The effects of maltreatment on the development of young children. In D. Cicchetti & V. Carlson (Eds.), *Child maltreatment: Theory and research on the causes and consequences of child abuse and neglect* (pp. 647-684). New York: Cambridge University Press.

Erickson, M., Sroufe, L. A., & Egeland, B. (1985). The relationship between quality of attachment and behavior problems in preschool and a high risk-sample. In I. Bretherton & E. Waters (Eds.), Growing points of attachment theory and research. *Monographs of the Society for Research in Child Development, 50* (1-2, Serial No. 209), 147-166.

Estrin, R. (1996, January 20). Juvenile firesetting. *Denver Post,* 22.

Everstine, D. E., & Everstine, L. (1989). *Sexual trauma in children and adolescents.* New York: Brunner/Mazel.

Fahlberg, V. (1991). *A child's journey through placement.* Indianapolis, IN: Perspective Press.

Faller, K.C. (1989). The myths of the "collusive mother": Variability in the functioning of mother of victims of intrafamilial sexual abuse. *Journal of Interpersonal Violence, 3,* 190-196.

Field, T. (1987). Interaction and attachment in normal and atypical infants. *Journal of Consulting and Clinical Psychology, 55,* 853-859.

Field, T. (1995). Infants of depressed mothers. *Infant Behavior and Development, 18,* 1-13.

Field, T. (1997). The treatment of depressed mothers and their infants. In L. Murray and P. J. Cooper (Eds.), *Postpartum depression and child development* (pp. 221-236). New York: Guilford.

Field, T., Grizzle, N., Scafidi, F., & Abrams, S. (1996). Massage therapy for infants of depressed mothers. *Infant Behavior and Development, 19,* 107-112.

Finkelhor, D. (1979). What's wrong with sex between adults and children? Ethics and the problem of sexual abuse. *American Journal of Orthopsychiatry, 49,* 692-697.

Finkelhor, D. (1987). The trauma of child sexual abuse: Two models. *Journal of Interpersonal Violence, 2,* 348-366.

Finkelhor, D. (1990). Early and long-term effects of child sexual abuse: An update. *Professional Psychology, 21,* 325-330.

Finkelhor, D. (1994). Current information on the scope and nature of child sexual abuse. *The Future of Children, 4,* 31-53.

Finkelhor, D., & Baron, L. (1986). Risk factors for child sexual abuse. *Journal of Interpersonal Violence, 1,* 43-71.

Finkelhor, D., & Browne, A. (1985). The traumatic impact of child sexual abuse: A conceptualization. *American Journal of Orthopsychiatry, 55*(4), 530-541.

Finkelhor, D., Hotaling, G., Lewis, I. A., & Smith, C. (1990). Sexual abuse in a national survey of adult men and women: Prevalence, characteristics, and risk factors. *Child Abuse & Neglect, 14,* 19-28.

Finkelhor, D., Williams, L., & Burns, N. (1988). *Nursery crimes: Sexual abuse in day care.* Newbury Park, CA: Sage.

Flaherty, J. A., & Richman, J. A. (1986). Effects of childhood relationships on the adult's capacity to form social supports. *American Journal of Psychiatry, 143,* 851-855.

Fonagy, P., Target, M., & Steele, M. (1997). Morality, disruptive behavior, borderline personality disorder, crime, and their relationships to security of attachment. In C. Atkinson & K. J. Zucker (Eds.), *Attachment and Psychopathology* (pp. 223-274). New York: Guilford.

Franz, D. C., McClelland, C. D., Weinberger, J., & Peterson, C. (1994). Parenting antecedents of adult adjustment: A longitudinal study. In C. Perris, W. A. Arrindell, & M. Eisemann (Eds.), *Parenting and psychopathology* (pp. 127-144). Chicester, England: Wiley.

Friedrich, W. N. (1990). *Psychotherapy of sexually abused children and their families.* New York: Norton.

Friedrich, W. N., Beilke, R. L., & Urquiza, A. (1987). Children from sexually abusive families: A behavioral comparison. *Journal of Interpersonal Violence, 2,* 391-402.

Frodi, A., & Thompson, R. (1985). Infant's affective responses in the strange situation: Effects of prematurity and quality of attachment. *Child Development, 56,* 1280-1290.

Fromm, E. (1973). *The anatomy of human destructiveness.* New York: Holt, Rinehart and Winston.

Furlow, F. B. (1996). The smell of love. *Psychology Today, 4,* 38-45.

Gale, J., Thompson, R. J., Moran, T., & Sack, W. H. (1988). Sexual abuse in young children: Its clinical presentation and characteristic patterns. *Child Abuse & Neglect, 12,* 163-171.

Gallup, G. H., Moore, D. W., & Schussel, R. (1995). *Disciplining children in America: A Gallup Poll Report.* Princeton, NJ: The Gallup Organization.

George, C., Kaplan, N., & Main, M. (1984). *Attachment interview for adults.* Unpublished manuscript, University of California at Berkeley.

Gil, E. (1991). *The healing power of play.* New York: Guilford.

Gil, E. (1996). *Treating abused adolescents.* New York: Guilford.

Gold, E. R. (1986). Long-term effects of sexual victimization in childhood: An attributional approach. *Journal of Consulting and Clinical Psychology, 54,* 471-475.

Goldberg, W. A., & Easterbrooks, M. A. (1984). The role of marital quality in toddler development. *Developmental Psychology, 20,* 504-514.

Goleman, D. (1995). *Emotional intelligence.* New York: Bantam.

Gomes-Schwartz, B., Horowitz, J., & Cardarelli, A. (1990). *Child sexual abuse: The initial effects.* Newbury Park, CA: Sage.

Goodman, G. S., Bottoms, B. L., & Shaver, P. R. (1994). *Characteristics and sources of allegations of ritualistic child abuse.* Executive summary of the final report to the National Center on Child Abuse and Neglect. Washington, DC: National Center on Child Abuse and Neglect.

Goodwin, L. (1996). *Attachment therapy: Treatment for the attachment disordered child.* Unpublished doctoral dissertation.

Grabe, P. V. (1990). *Adoption resources for mental health professionals.* New Brunswick, NJ: Transaction Publishers.

Gramlich, E. M. (1984). Commentary on *Changed lives.* In J. R. Berrueta-Clement, L. J. Schweinhart, W. S. Barnett, A. S. Epstein, & D. P. Weikart (Eds.), *Changed lives: The effects of the Perry Preschool Program on youths through age 19* (Monographs of the High/Scope Educational Research Foundation, No. 8, pp. 200-203). Ypsilanti, MI: High/Scope.

Greenberg, M. T., DeKlyen, M., Speltz, M. L., & Endriga, M. C. (1997). The role of attachment processes in externalizing psychopathology in young children. In L. Atkinson & K.J. Zucker (Eds.), *Attachment and psychopathology* (pp. 196-222). New York: Guilford Press.

Greenberg, M. T., Speltz, M. L., DeKlyen, M., & Endriga, M. C. (1991). Attachment security in preschoolers with and without externalizing problems: A replication. *Development and Psychopathology, 3,* 413-430.

Greenberg, M., & Morris, N. (1974). Engrossment: The newborn's impact on the father. *American Journal of Orthopsychiatry, 44,* 526-536.

Grimsley, K. D. (1998, February 16). U.S. less generous with new mothers. International Labor Organization, *Denver Post,* 16.

Grossman, F., Eichler, L., & Winnickoff, S. (1980). *Pregnancy, birth, and parenthood.* San Francisco, CA: Jossey-Bass.

Grossman, K., & Grossman, K. (1991). Attachment quality as an organizer of emotional and behavioral responses in a longitudinal perspective. In C. M. Parkes, J. Stevenson-Hinde, & P. Marris (Eds.). *Attachment across the life cycle* (pp. 93-114). New York: Routledge.

Grych, J. M., & Fincham, F. (1990). Marital conflict and children's adjustment: A cognitive-contextual framework. *Psychological Bulletin, 108,* 267-298.

Guralnick, M. J. (1997). *The effectiveness of early intervention.* Baltimore, MD: Brookes.

Guterman, N. B. (1997). Early prevention of physical child abuse and neglect: Existing evidence and future directions. *Child Maltreatment 2*(1), 12-34.

Hafen, B. Q., Karren, K. J., Frandsen, K. J., & Smith, N. L. (1996). *Mind/body health.* Needham Heights, MA: Allyn and Bacon.

Halfon, N., Medononca, H., & Berkowitz, G. (1995). Health status of children in foster care: The experience of the Center for the Vulnerable Child. *Archives of Pediatrics and Adolescent Medicine, 149,* 386-392.

Hamburg, D. (1992). *Today's children: Creating a future for a generation in crisis.* New York: Times Books.

Hann, D. M., Castino, R. J., Jarosinski, J., & Britton H. (1991). Relating mother-toddler negotiation patterns to infant attachment and maternal depression with an adolescent mother sample. In J. Osofsky & L. Hubbs-Tait (Chairs), *Consequences of adolescent parenting: Predicting behavior problems in toddlers and preschoolers.* Symposium conducted at the biennial meeting of the Society for Research in Child Development. Seattle, WA.

Hare, R. D. (1993). *Without conscience: The disturbing world of psychopaths among us.* New York: Pocket Books.

Harlow, H. (1958). The nature of love. *The American Psychologist, 3,* 673-685.

Harnish, J., Dodge, K., & Valente, E. (1995). Mother-child interaction quality as a partial mediator of the roles of maternal depression symptomatology and socioeconomic status in the development of child behavior problems. *Child Development, 66* (3), 739-753.

Haskins, R. (1985). Public school aggression among children with varying day-care experience. *Child Development, 56,* 689-703.

Healthy Families America. (1996). *Fourth year progress report.* Unpublished manuscript. Chicago: National Committee to Prevent Child Abuse.

Heinssen, R., Levendusky, P., & Hunter, R. (1995). Client as colleague. *American Psychologist, 50* (7), 522-532.

Hellman, D., & Blackman, N. (1966). Enuresis, firesetting and cruelty to animals: A triad predictive of adult crime. *American Journal of Psychiatry, 122,* 1431-1435.

Herbert, M. (1987). *Conduct disorders of childhood & adolescence.* New York: Wiley.

Herman, J. L. (1992). *Trauma and recovery.* New York: Basic Books.

Herrenkohl, E. C., Herrenkohl, R. C., & Egoff, B. (1994). Resilient early school-age children from maltreating homes: Outcomes in late adolescence. *American Journal of Orthopsychiatry, 64*(2), 301-309.

Hibbard, R. A., Ingersoll, G. M., & Orr, D. P. (1990). Behavior risk, emotional risk, and child abuse among adolescents in a nonclinical setting. *Pediatrics, 86,* 896-901.

Hoffman, M. (1983). Empathy, guilt, and social cognition. In W. F. Overton (Ed.), *The relationship between social and cognitive development* (pp. 12-23). Hillsdale, NJ: Lawrence Erlbaum.

Hoffman-Plotkin, D., & Twentyman, C.T. (1984). A multimodel assessment of behavioral and cognitive deficits in abused and neglected preschoolers. *Child Development, 55,* 794-802.

Horney, K. (1959). The holistic approach. In H. Kelman (Ed.), *American Handbook of Psychiatry.* New York: Basic Books.

Howard, J. (1994). Barriers to successful intervention. In D. Besharov (Ed.), *When drug addicts have children* (pp. 91-100). Washington, DC: Child Welfare of America.

Howard, P. J. (1994) *The owner's manual for the brain: Everyday applications from mind-brain research.* Austin, Texas: Leornian Press.

Huesman, L. R., Eron, L. D., Lefkowits, M. M., & Walder, L. O. (1984). Stability of aggression over time and generations. *Developmental Psychology, 20,* 1120-1134.

Hughes D. (1997). *Facilitating developmental attachment.* Northvale, NJ: Jason Aronson.

Hunt, M. (1993). *The story of psychology.* New York: Doubleday.

Hutchins, J. (1995). Disconnected dads. *Family Therapy News, American Association of Marriage and Family Therapy, 26(5),* 27-28.

Jacobson, J. L., & Wille, D.E. (1986). The influence of attachment pattern on developmental changes in peer interaction from the toddler to the preschool period. *Child Development, 57,* 338-347.

Jaffe, J. P., Wilson, S., & Wolfe, D. (1988). Specific assessment and intervention strategies for children exposed to wife battering: Preliminary empirical investigations. *Canadian Journal of Community Mental Health, 7,* 157-163.

James, B. (1994) *Handbook for treatment of attachment-trauma problems in children.* NY: Lexington.

Jaudes, P. K., & Ekwo, E. E. (1997). Outcomes for infants exposed in utero to illicit drugs. *Child Welfare, 77(4),* 521-534.

Jernberg, A. M. (1990). Enhancing attachment for adopted children. In P. Grabe (Ed.), *Adoption resources for mental health professionals* (pp. 271-279). New Brunswick, NJ: Transaction Publishers.

Jewett, C. L. (1982). *Helping children cope with separation and loss.* Cambridge, MA: Harvard Common Press.

Johnson, D. L., & Walker, T. (1990). The primary prevention of behavior problems in Mexican-American children. *American Journal of Community Psychology.*

Jones, A. (1997). Issues relevant to therapy with adoptees. *Psychotherapy, 34(1),* 64-68.

Jones, S. (1983). *Crying babies, sleepless nights.* New York: Warner.

Judith, A. (1996). *Eastern body, western mind.* Berkeley, CA : Celestial Arts.

Jung, C.G. (1969). *Essays on a science of mythology: The myth of the divine child.* Princeton, NJ: Bollingen Series.

Kachur, S. P., Stennies, G. M., Powell, K. E., & Lowery, R. (1994). School-associated violent deaths in the United States, 1992-1994. *Journal of American Medical Association, 275,* 1729-1734.

Kagan, J. (1981). *The second year: The emergence of self-awareness.* Cambridge, MA: Harvard University Press.

Kagan, J. (1984). *The nature of the child.* New York: Basic Books.

Kagan, J. (1989, August). *The return of temperament in psychological theory.* Paper presented at the 97th annual convention of the American Psychological Association. New Orleans, LA.

Kagan, J. (1994). *Galen's prophecy: Temperament in human nature*. New York: Basic Books.

Kagan, J., & Moss H. A. (1962). *Birth to maturity*. New York: Wiley.

Kamerman, S., & Kahn, A. (1989). *Social services for children, youth and families in the United States*. New York: Annie E. Casey Foundation.

Kamerman, S., & Kahn, A. (1990). Social services for children, youth, and families in the United States. *Children and Youth Services Review* (Special issue), 12 (1/2).

Kantrowitz, B. (1997, November 10). Keeping your kids safe. *Newsweek, 80*(19), 63.

Karen, R. (1994). *Becoming attached*. New York: Warner Books.

Keefer, C. H., Tronic, E. Z., Dixon, S., & Brazelton, T. (1982). Specific differences in motor performance between Gusii and American newborns and a modification of the Neonatal Behavioral Assessment Scale. *Child Development, 53*, 754-759.

Kellert, S., & Felthous, A. (1983). Childhood cruelty toward animals among criminals and non-criminals. Manuscript submitted for publication.

Kelley, H. H. (1973). The process of causal attribution. *American Psychologist, 28*, 107-128.

Kelley, S. J. (1989). Stress responses of children to sexual abuse and ritualistic abuse in day care centers. *Journal of Interpersonal Violence, 4*(4), 502-513.

Kelley, S. J. (1996). Ritualistic abuse of children. In J. Briere, L. Berliner, J. A. Buckley, C. Jenny, & T. Reid (Eds.), *APSAC handbook on child maltreatment* (pp. 90-99). Thousand Oaks, CA: Sage.

Kendall-Tackett, K. A., Williams, L. M., & Finkelhor, D. (1993). Impact of sexual abuse on children: A review and synthesis of recent empirical studies. *Psychological Bulletin, 113*, 164-180.

Kenny, T., Baldwin, R., & Mackie, J. B. (1967). Incidence of minimal brain injury in adopted children. *Child Welfare, 46*, 24-29.

Kerr, M. E., & Bowen, M. (1988). *Family evaluation*. New York: W.W. Norton.

Kitzinger, J. (1989). *The crying baby*. New York: Viking.

Klass, C. S. (1996). *Home visiting*. Baltimore, MD: Brookes.

Klause, M., & Kennel, J. (1982). *Parent-infant bonding*. St. Louis, MO: C.V. Mosby.

Klee, L., Kronstadt, D., & Zlotnick, C. (1997). Foster care's youngest: A preliminary report. *American Journal of Orthopsychiatry, 67*(2), 290-299.

Kolko, D. J. (1996). Child physical abuse. In J. Briere, L. Berliner, J. A. Buckely, C. Jenny, & T. Reid (Eds.), *APSAC handbook on child maltreatment* (pp. 21-50). Thousand Oaks, CA: Sage.

Kosmicki, F. X., & Glickauf, C. (1997). Catharsis in psychotherapy. *Psychotherapy, 34*(2), 154-159.

Kotelchuck, M. (1976). The infant's relationship to the father: Experimental evidence. In M. E. Lamb (Ed.), *The role of the father in child development*. New York: Wiley.

Kubler-Ross, E. (1969). *On death and dying*. New York: Macmillan.

Lally, R. J., & Keith, H. (1997). Early head start: The first two years. *ZERO TO THREE, 18*(2), 3-8.

Lamb, M. E. (1997). *The role of the father in child development* (3rd ed.). New York: Wiley.

Lawrence, C., & Lankford, V. (1997). Sibling loss: The hidden tragedy of the child welfare system. *Adoptive Families, 30*(6), 16-17.

LeDoux, J. (1992). Emotion and the limbic system. *Concepts in Neuroscience, 2*, 2-16.

Letourneau, N. (1997). Fostering resilience in infancy and young children through parent-infant interaction. *Infants and Young Children, 9*(3), 36-45.

Levine, I. S. (1996). Preventing violence among youth. *American Journal of Orthopsychiatry, 66* (3), 320-322.

Levy, D. (1937). Primary affect hunger. *American Journal of Psychiatry, 94,* 643-652.

Levy, T., & Orlans, M. (1995a). Intensive short-term therapy with attachment disordered children. In. L. VandeCreek, S. Knapp, & T. L. Jackson (Eds.), *Innovations in clinical practice: A source book,* Vol. 14, (pp. 227-251). Sarasota, FL: Professional Resource Press.

Levy, T., & Orlans, M. (1995b). Attachment theory and assessment. In C. A. McKelvey (Ed.), *Give them roots, then let them fly: Understanding attachment therapy* (pp. 36-53). Evergreen, CO: Attachment Center Press.

Levy, T., & Orlans, M. (1995c). Two week intensive. In C.A. McKelvey (Ed.), *Give them roots then let them fly: Understanding attachment therapy* (pp. 135-164). Evergreen, CO: Attachment Center Press.

Lewis, W. A., & Bucher, A. M. (1992). Anger, catharsis, the reformulated frustration-aggression hypothesis, and health consequences. *Psychotherapy, 29*(3), 385-392.

Lieberman, A. F., & Pawl, J. H. (1988). Clinical implications of attachment theory. In J. Belsky & T. Nezworski (Eds.), *Clinical implications of attachment* (pp. 327-351). Hillsdale, NJ: Lawrence Erlbaum.

Lieberman, A. F., Wiedes, S., & Fenichel, E. (1997). *The DC: 0-3 casebook.* Washington, DC: ZERO TO THREE/National Center for Infants, Toddlers and Families.

Liedloff, J. (1975). *The continuum concept.* New York: Addison-Wesley.

Lindholm, B. W., & Touliatos, J. (1980). Psychological adjustment of adopted and non-adopted children. *Psychological Reports, 46,* 307-310.

Lloyd, D. (1991). Ritual child abuse: Understanding the controversies. *Cultic Studies Journal,8*(2), 122-133.

Lobato, D. (1990). *Brothers, sisters and special needs.* Baltimore, MD: Paul Brookes.

Londerville, S., & Main, M. (1981). Security of attachment, compliance, and maternal training methods in the second year of life. *Developmental Psychology, 17,* 289-301.

Lorenz, K. C. (1971). Gestalt perception as a source of scientific knowledge. In K. C. Lorenz (Ed.), *Studies in animal and human behavior* (Vol. 2). Cambridge, MA: Harvard University Press.

Lowen, A. (1988). *Love, sex, and your heart.* New York: Penguin Books.

Lung, C. T., & Daro, D. (1996). *Current trends in child abuse reporting and fatalities.* Chicago, IL: National Committee to Prevent Child Abuse.

Lyons-Ruth, K. (1991). Rapproachment or approachment: Mahlers theory reconsidered from the vantage point of recent research in early attachment relationships. *Psychoanalytic Psychology, 8,* 1-23.

Lyons-Ruth, K. (1996). Attachment relationships among children with aggressive behavior problems: The role of disorganized early attachment patterns. *Journal of Consulting and Clinical Psychology, 64, 1,* 64-73.

Lyons-Ruth, K., Alpern, L., & Repacholi, B. (1993). Disorganized infant attachment classification and maternal psychosocial problems as predictors of hostile-aggressive behavior in the preschool classroom. *Child Development, 64,* 572-585.

Lyons-Ruth, K., Bronfman, E., & Parson, E. (1994). *Atypical maternal behavior and disorganized infant attachment strategies.* Manuscript submitted for publication.

Lyons-Ruth, K., Repacholi B., McLeod, S., & Silva, E. (1991). Disorganized attachment behavior in infancy: Short-term stability, maternal and infant correlates, and risk-related subtypes. *Development and Psychopathology, 3,* 377-396.

MacFarlane, J. (1975). Olfaction in the development of social preference in the human newborn. In M. Hofer (Ed.), *Ciba Foundation Symposium: Parent-infant interaction.* Amsterdam: Elsevier.

MacLean, P. D. (1982, Winter). The co-evolution of the brain and the family. *The L.S.B. Leakey Foundation News, 1,* 14-15.

MacLean, P. D. (1978). A mind of three minds: Educating the triune brain. In *Education and the brain.* The National Society for the Study of Education. Chicago, IL: University of Chicago Press.

Main, M., & Cassidy, J. (1988). Categories of response with the parent at age six: Predicted from infant attachment classifications and stable over a one month period. *Developmental Psychology, 24,* 415-426.

Main, M., & Goldwyn, R. (in press). Adult attachment rating and classification systems. In M. Main (Ed.), *A typology of human attachment organization assessed in discourse, drawings and interviews.* New York: Cambridge University Press.

Main, M., & Goldwyn, R. (1984). Predicting rejection of her infant from mother's representation of her own experience. *Child Abuse and Neglect, 8,* 203-217.

Main, M., & Goldwyn, R. (1985-1993). *Adult attachment scoring and classification system.* Unpublished manuscript, Department of Psychology, University of California, Berkeley.

Main, M., & Hesse, E. (1990) Parent's unresolved traumatic experiences are related to infant disorganization attachment status: Is frightened and/or frightening parental behavior the linking mechanism? In M. T. Greenberg, D. Chicchetti, & E. M. Cummings (Eds.), *Attachment in the preschool years: Theory, research and intervention* (pp. 161-184). Chicago, IL: University of Chicago Press.

Main, M., Hesse, E., & van IJzendoorn, M. H. (1994). *Unresolved status in the adult attachment interview: Related to dissociation, absorption, and unusual beliefs.* Manuscript submitted for publication.

Main, M., Kaplan, N., & Cassidy, J. (1985). Security in infancy, childhood and adulthood: A move to the level of representation, In I. Bretherton & E. Waters (Eds.), Growing points of attachment theory and research. *Monographs of the Society for Research in Child Development, 50,* (1-2, Serial No. 209), 66-104.

Main, M., & Solomon, J. (1986). Discovery of an insecure, disorganized/disoriented attachment pattern: Procedures, findings, and implications for the classification of behavior. In M. Yogman & T. B. Brazelton (Eds.), *Affective development in infancy* (pp. 66-104). Norwood, NJ: Ablex.

Main, M., & Solomon, J. (1990). Procedures for identifying infants as disorganized/disoriented during the Ainsworth Strange Situation. In M. Greenberg, D. Chicchetti, & E. M. Cummings (Eds.), *Attachment in the preschool years: Theory, research, and intervention* (pp. 121-160). Chicago, IL: University of Chicago Press.

Main, M., & Weston, D. (1981). The quality of the toddler's relationships to mother and to father as related to conflict behavior and readiness to establish new relationships. *Child Development, 52,* 932-940.

Main, M., & Weston, D. (1982). Avoidance of the attachment figure in infancy: Descriptions and interpretations. In C. M. Parkes & J. Stevenson-Hinde (Eds.), *The place of attachment in human behavior* (pp. 31-59). New York: Basic.

Malphurs, J., Larrain, C., Field, T., Pickens, J., Pelaez-Nogueras, M., Yando, R., & Bendell, D. (1996). Altering withdrawn and intrusive interaction behaviors of depressed mothers. *Infant Mental Health Journal, 17,* 152-160.

Mannarino, A. P., Cohen, J. A., & Berman, S. R. (1994). The Children's Attributions and Perceptions Scale: A new measure of sexual abuse-related factors. *Journal of Clinical Child Psychology, 23,* 204-211.

Mannarino, A. P., & Cohen, J. A. (1996). A follow-up study of factors which mediate the development of psychological symptoms in sexually abused girls. *Child Maltreatment, 1*(3), 246-260.

Marvin, R. S. (1977). An ethological-cognitive model for the attenuation of mother-child attachment behavior. In T. Alloway, L. Krames, & P. Pliner (Eds.), *Advances in the study of communication and affect: Vol 3. Attachment behavior* (pp. 25-60). New York: Plenum.

Marvin, R. S., & Stewart, R. B. (1990). A family systems framework for the study of attachment. In M. T. Greenberg, D. Cicchetti, and E. M. Cummings (Eds.), *Attachment in the preschool years* (pp. 61-86). Chicago, IL: University of Chicago Press.

Mason, W. A., & Berkson, G. (1975). Effects of maternal mobility on the development of rocking and other behaviors in rhesus monkeys. *Developmental Psychobiology, 8,* 197-221.

Masterson, J. F. (1985). *The real self: A developmental, self and objective relations approach.* New York: Brunner/Mazel.

May, R. (1972). *Power and innocence.* New York: W.W. Norton.

McCreight, B. (1997). *Recognizing and managing children with fetal alcohol syndrome/fetal alcohol effects.* Washington, DC: CWLA Press.

McFarlane, A. C. (1988). Recent life events and psychiatric disorder in children: The interaction with preceding extreme diversity. *Journal of Clinical Psychiatry, 29*(5), 677-690.

McGuire, K. N. (1991). Affect in focusing and experiential psychotherapy, In J. D. Safran & L. S. Greenberg (Eds.), *Emotion, psychotherapy, and change* (pp. 227-251). New York: Guilford.

McKelvey, C. A., & Stevens, J. (1994). *Adoption crisis.* Golden, CO: Fulcrum.

McLeer, S. V., Deblinger, E., Atkins, M. S., Ralphe, D. L., & Foa, E. (1988). Posttraumatic stress disorder in sexually abused children. *Journal of the American Academy of Child and Adolescent Psychiatry, 27,* 650-654.

Mead, M. (1964). Cultural factors in the cause of pathological homicide. In *Bulletin of Menniger Clinic, 28,* 11-22.

Meyer, D., & Vadasy, P. (1994). *Sib shops.* Baltimore, MD: Paul Brookes.

Miller, A. (1983). *For your own good: Hidden cruelty in childrearing and the roots of violence.* New York: Farrar, Strauss, Giroux.

Miller, P. A., Eisenberg, N., & Gular, S. (1989). Mother's emotional arousal as a moderator in the socialization of children's empathy. *New Directions for Child Development, 44,* 65-83.

Moffitt, T. E. (1993). The neuropsychology of conduct disorder. *Development and Psychopathology, 5,* 135-151.

Montagu, A., (1986). *Touching. The human significance of skin.* New York: Harper and Row.

Moore, D. (1996). Substitute child care at different ages: Relationship to social-emotional functioning in preschool. *American Journal of Orthopsychiatry, 66*(2), 305-308.

Moreno, J. L. (1977). *Psychodrama.* New York: Beacon House.

Morris, D. (1967). *The naked ape.* New York: McGraw Hill.

Morris, D. (1994). *The human animal.* New York: Crown Publishers.

Murray, B. (1996). Getting by with a little help from some friends. *American Psychological Association Monitor, 27*(1), 41.

Myeroff, R. (1997). *Attachment therapy: An outcome study.* Unpublished doctoral dissertation.

National Association of Black Social Workers (1994). *Position statement: "Preserving African American families."* Detroit, MI: Author.

National Center on Child Abuse and Neglect. (1993). *A report on the maltreatment of children and disabilities.* Washington, DC: U.S. Department of Health and Human Services.

National Center on Child Abuse and Neglect. (1995). *National child abuse and neglect data systems. Third national incidence study of child maltreatment.* Washington, DC: U.S. Government Printing Office.

National Institute of Child and Human Development Early Child Care Research Network (1996, April). *Infant child care and attachment security: Results of the NICHD study of early care.* Symposium presented at the International Conference on Infant Studies, Providence, RI.

Neal, M. (1968). Vestibular stimulation and developmental behavior of the small premature infant. *Nursing Research Report, 3,* (1).

Neubauer, P. B., & Neubauer, A. (1990). *Nature's thumbprint: The new genetics of personality.* Reading, MA: Addison-Wesley.

Nichols, M. (1986). Catharsis: History and theory. In M. Nichols & T. Paolino (Eds.), *Basic techniques of psychodynamic psychotherapy: Foundations of clinical practice.* New York: Gardner.

Offord, D. R., Boyle, M. C., & Racine, Y. A. (1991). The epidemiology of antisocial behavior in childhood and adolescence. In D. J. Pepler & K. H. Rubin (Eds.), *The development and treatment of childhood aggression* (pp. 31-54). Hillsdale, NJ: Erlbaum.

Orlans, M. (1993). Adoption: An American crisis. In B. Harting, *Uncharted waters: Parenting an attachment disordered child.* Self-published.

Ornstein, R. (1995). *The roots of self.* San Francisco: Harper.

Osofsky, J. D. (1995a). Children who witness domestic violence. The invisible victims. *Social Policy Report, Society for Research in Child Development, 9,* No. 3.

Osofsky, J. D. (1995b). The effects of exposure to violence on young children. *American Psychologist, 50,* 782-788.

Osofsky, J. (1994). Introduction: Caring for infants and toddlers in violent environments. Arlington, VA: *ZERO TO THREE.*

Parke, R. D. (1990). In search of fathers: A narrative of an empirical journey. In I. Sigel & G. Brody (Eds.), *Methods of family research,* Vol. 1. Hillsdale, NJ: Erlbaum.

Pastor, D. L. (1981). The quality of mother-infant attachment and its relationship to toddler's initial sociability with peers. *Developmental Psychology, 17,* 323-335.

Pearce, J. C. (1992). *Evolutions end.* New York: Harper Collins.

Pearce, J. W., & Pezzot-Pearce, T. D. (1994). Attachment theory and its implications for psychotherapy with maltreated children. *Child Abuse and Neglect, 18,* 425-438.

Pearce, J. W. & Pezzot-Pearce, T. D. (1997). *Psychotherapy of abused and neglected children.* New York: Guilford.

Pedersen, F. (1980). Parent-infant and husband-wife interactions observed at five months. In F. A. Pedersen (Ed.), *The father infant relationship.* New York: Praeger.

Pedersen, F., Yarrow, L., Anderson, B., & Cain, R. (1978). Conceptualization of father influences in the infancy period. In M. Lewis & L. A. Rosenblum (Eds.), *The social network of the developing infant.* New York: Plenum.

Pelton, L. H. (1997). Child welfare policy and practice: The myth of family preservation. *American Journal of Orthopsychiatry, 67*(4), 545-553.

Perry, B. D. (1994). Neurobiological sequelae of childhood trauma. In M. Murberg (Ed.), *Catecholamine function in posttraumatic stress disorder* (pp. 233-255). Washington, DC: American Psychiatric Press.

Perry, B. D. (1995). Incubated in terror: Neurodevelopmental factors in the 'cycle of violence.' In J. D. Osofsky (Ed.), *Children, Youth and Violence* (pp. 45-63). New York: Guilford.

Peters, S. D. (1988). Child sexual abuse and later psychological problems. In G.E. Wyatt & G. J. Powell (Eds.), *The lasting effects of child sexual abuse* (pp. 101-107). NewburyPark, CA: Sage.

Peterson, C., Maler, S., & Seligman, M. (1993). *Learned helplessness.* NY: Oxford.

Peterson, J., & Thoennes, N. (1990). Custody after divorce: Demographic and attitudinal patterns. *American Journal of Orthopsychiatry, 60,* 233-249.

Phillips, C. (1998). Foster care system struggles to keep siblings living together. *American Psychological Association Monitor, 29*(1), 26-27.

Piaget, J. (1952). *The origins of intelligence in children.* New York: International Universities Press.

Piaget, J. (1965). *The moral judgment of the child.* New York: Free Press.

Pianta R., Egeland, B., & Erickson, M. F. (1989). The antecendents of maltreatment: Results of the mother-child interaction research project. In D. Cicchetti & V. Carlson (Eds.), *Child maltreatment* (pp. 203-253). New York: Cambridge University Press.

Prescott, J. W. (1971). Early sematosensory deprivation as an ontogenetic process in the abnormal development of the brain and behavior. In I. E. Goldsmith & J. Moor-Jankowski (Eds.), *Medical primatology.* New York: S. Karger.

Price, R. H., Cowen, E. C., Lorion, R. P., & Ramos-Mckay, J. (1989). The search for prevention programs. *American Journal of Orthopsychiatry, 59*(1), 49-58.

Pruett, K. D. (1997), How men and children affect each other's development. *Bulletin of ZERO TO THREE, 18*(1), 3-11.

Putnam, F. (1991). Behavioral and psychophysiological correlates of sexual abuse. Paper presented at the American Academy of Child and Adolescent Psychiatry, San Francisco.

Putnam, F. (1995). Development of dissociative disorders. In D. Cicchetti & D.J. Cohen (Eds.), *Development psychopathology,* Vol. 2 (pp. 581-608). New York: Wiley.

Raine, A. (1993). *The psychopathology of crime.* New York: Academic Press.

Ramey, C. T., & Ramey, S. L. (1998). Early intervention and early experience. *American Psychologist, 53*(2), 109-120.

Randolph, E. (1997). *Does attachment therapy work: Results of two preliminary studies.* Evergreen, CO: The Attachment Center Press.

Reitz, M., & Watson, K. W. (1992). *Adoption and the family system.* New York: Guilford.

Renken, B., Egeland, B., Marvinney, D., Mangelsdoft, S., & Sroufe, L. A. (1989). Early childhood antecedents of aggression and passive-withdrawal in early elementary school. *Journal of Personality, 57,* 257-281.

Richters, J. E., & Martinez, P. (1993). The NIMH community violence project: Children as victims of and witnesses to violence. *Psychiatry, 56,* No. 1, 7-21.

Risley-Curtiss, C. (1966). Child protective services: The health status and care of children in out-of-home care. *APSAC Advisor, 9*(4), 1-7.

Roazen, P. (1975). *Freud and his followers.* New York: Alfred A. Knopf.

Robertson, J., & Robertson, J. (1989). *Separation and the very young*. London: Free Association Books.

Robinson, J. L., & Glaves, L. (1996). Supporting emotion regulation and emotional availability through home visitation. *Bulletin of ZERO TO THREE, 17*(1), 31-35.

Robinson, P. A. (1969). *Reich: The Freudian left*. New York: Harper & Row.

Russell, D. E. H. (1986). *The secret trauma: Incest in the lives of girls and women*. New York: Basic Books.

Sagi, A. (1990). Attachment theory and research from a cross cultural perspective. *Human Development, 33*, 10-22.

Salk, L. (1960). *The effects of normal heart beat sound on the behaviors of the newborn infant*. Paper delivered at the World Federation of Mental Health, Edinburgh, Scotland.

Samuel, M., & Samuel, N. (1986). *The well pregnancy book*. New York: Simon and Schuster.

Scarr, S. (1998). American child care today. *American Psychologist, 53*(2), 95-108.

Schaffer, J. S., & Lindstrom C. (1989). *How to raise an adopted child*. New York: Crown Publishers.

Scharff, D. E., & Scharff, J. S. (1987). *Object relations family therapy*. Northvale, NJ: Jason Aronson.

Scheff, T. J. (1979). *Catharsis in healing, ritual, and drama*. Berkeley: University of California Press.

Schene, P. (1996). Child abuse and neglect policy: History, models, and future directions. In J. Briere, L. Berliner, J. A. Buckley, C. Jenny, & T. Reid (Eds.), *The APSAC handbook on child maltreatment* (pp. 385-397). Thousand Oaks, CA: Sage.

Schinke, S. P., Schilling, R. F., Barth, R. P., Gilchrist, L. D., & Maxwell, J. S. (1986). Stress-management intervention to prevent family violence. *Journal of Family Violence, 1*(1), 13-26.

Schneider-Rosen, K., Braunwald, K. G., Carlson, V., & Cicchetti, D. (1985). Current perspectives in attachment theory: Illustration from the study of maltreated infants. In I. Bretherton & E. Waters (Eds.), *Monographs of the Society for Research in Child Development, 50*(1-2), 194-210.

Schneiderman, M., Connors, M. M., Fribourg, A., Gries, L., & Gonzales, M. (1998). Mental health services for children in out-of-home care. *Child Welfare, 77*, 29-40.

Schooler, J. (1997). When siblings are separated. *Adoptive Families, 30*(6), 14-19.

Showalter, J. E. (1983). The use and abuse of pets. *Journal of the American Academy Child Psychiatry, 22*, 68-72.

Schulman, M., & Mekler, E. (1994). *Bringing up a moral child*. New York: Doubleday.

Seligman, M. (1993). *Helplessness: On depression, development, and death*. San Francisco, CA: Freeman.

Seligman, M., Peterson, C., Kaslow, N. J., & Abramson, L. (1984). Attributional style and depressive symptoms in children. *Journal of Abnormal Psychology, 83*, 235-238.

Shireman, J. F., & Johnson, P. (1986). A longitudinal study of black adoptions: Single parent, transracial, and traditional. *Social Work, 31*, 172-176.

Silverman, A. R. (1993). Outcomes of transracial adoption. *The Future of Children, 3*(1), 104-118.

Simon, R. J., & Alstein, H. (1992). *Adoption, race, and identity: From infancy through adolescence*. New York: Praeger.

Simon, S. (1976). *Caring, feeling, touching*. New York: Argus Communications.

Smith, L. H. (1976). *Improving your child's behavior chemistry.* New York: Pocket Books.

Solter, A. (1995). Why do babies cry? *Pre and Perinatal Psychology Journal,* Vol. 10 (1), 21-43.

Sontag, L. W. (1970). Parental determinants of postnatal behavior. In H. Weisman & G. Kerr (Eds.), *Fetal growth and development* (pp. 265-281). New York: McCraw-Hill.

Spaccarelli, S. (1994). Stress appraisal and coping in child sexual abuse. *Psychological Bulletin, 116,* 340-362.

Spieker, S. J., & Booth, C. (1988). Maternal antecedents of attachment quality. In J. Belsky & T. Nezworski (Eds.), *Clinical implications of attachment* (pp. 300-323). Hillsdale, NJ: Erlbaum.

Spitz, R. (1947). *Grief: A peril in infancy* (Film). University Park, PA: Penn State Audio Visual Services.

Spitz, R. (1965). *The first year of life.* New York: International Universities Press.

Sroufe, L. A. (1983). Infant-caregiver attachment patterns of adaptation in preschool: The roots of maladaptation and competence. In M. Perlmutter (Ed.), *Minnesota symposium in child psychology,* Vol. 16 (pp. 41-81). Hillsdale, NJ: Erlbaum.

Sroufe, L. A. (1988). The role of infant-caregiver attachment in development. In J. Belsky & T. Nezworski (Eds.), *Clinical implications of attachment* (pp. 18-38). Hillsdale, NJ: Erlbaum.

Sroufe, L. A., Carlson, E., & Shulman, S. (1993). *The development of individuals in relationships: From infancy through adolescence.* Unpublished manuscript.

Sroufe, L. A., Egeland, B., & Kreutzer, T. (1990). The fate of early experience following developmental change. *Child Development, 61,* 1363-1373.

Sroufe, L. A., & Waters, E. (1977). Attachment as an organizational construct. *Child Development, 48,* 1184-1199.

Starn, J. (1992). Community health nursing visits for at-risk women and infants. *Journal of Community Health Nursing, 9*(2), 103-110.

Stayton, D., Hogan, R., & Salter-Ainsworth, M. (1971). Infant obedience and maternal behavior: The origins of socialization reconsidered. *Child Development, 42,* 1057-1069.

Stein, J.A., Golding, J. M., Siegel, J. M., Burnam, M. A., & Sorensen, S. B. (1988). Long-term psychological sequelae of child sexual abuse: The Los Angeles Epidemiological Catchment Area Study. In G.E. Wyatt & G.J. Powell (Eds.), *The lasting effects of child sexual abuse* (pp. 135-154). Newbury Park, CA: Sage.

Stern, D. N. (1985). *The interpersonal world of the infant: A view from psychoanalysis and developmental psychology.* New York: Basic Books.

Strauss, M. A. (1993). Ordinary violence, child abuse and wife-beating: What do they have in common? In D. Finkelhor, R. J. Gelles, G. T. Hotelling & H. Strauss (Eds.), *The dark side of families.* New York: Sage Publications.

Suomi, S. J., & Harlow, H. F. (1978). Early experience and social development in rhesus monkeys. In M. Lamb (Ed.), *Social and personality development.* New York: Holt, Rinehart, & Winston.

Takahashi, K. (1990). Are the key assumptions of the "Strange Situation" procedure universal? A view from Japanese research. *Human Development, 33,* 23-30.

Tapia, F. (1971). Children who are cruel to animals. In *Child Psychiatry and Human Development, 2,* 70-77.

Terr, L. (1990). *Too scared to cry.* New York: Harper & Row.

Thomas, A., Chess, S., & Birch, H. G. (1969). *Temperament and behavior disorders in children.* New York: New York University Press.

Tinbergen, N. (1951). *The study of instinct*. London: Oxford University Press.

Tolman, L. (1995). Attachment holding therapy: An evolution. *Family Attachment Institute Newsletter, 3*, 2.

Trepper, T. S., & Barrett, M. J. (1989). *Systemic treatment of incest: A therapeutic handbook*. New York: Brunner/Mazel.

Trepper, T. S., Nieder, D., Mika, L., & Barett, M. J. (1996). Family characteristics of intact sexually abusing families: An exploratory study. *Journal of Child Sexual Abuse, 5*(4), 1-18.

Tronick, E. Z., & Weinberg, M. K. (1997). Depressed mothers and infants: Failure to form dyadic states of consciousness. In L. Murray & P. Cooper (Eds.), *Postpartum depression and child development* (pp. 54-84). New York: Guilford Press.

Troy, M., & Sroufe, L. A. (1987). Victimization among preschoolers: The role of attachment relationship history. *Journal of the American Academy of Child and Adolescent Psychiatry, 26*, 166-172.

Truman, K. K. (1991). *Feelings buried alive never die*. Las Vegas, NV: Olympus Distributing.

Turiel, E. (1983). Domains and categories in social-cognitive development. In W. F. Overton (Ed.), *The relationship between social and cognitive development* (pp. 53-89). Hillsdale, NJ: L. Erlbaum.

U. S. Department of Justice (1995). *Juvenile offenders and victims: A national report*. Washington, DC: Office of Juvenile Justice and Delinquency Prevention.

U.S. Select Committee on Children, Youth and Families. (1989). *No place to call home: Discarded children in America*. Washington, DC: U.S. House of Representatives.

van den Boom, D.C. (1988). *Neonatal irritability and the development of attachment*. Unpublished doctoral dissertation, University of Leiden, The Netherlands.

van der Kolk, B. (1996). The complexity of adaptation to trauma. In van der Kolk, B., McFarlane, A. C., & Weisaeth, L. (Eds.), *Traumatic stress* (pp. 182-213). New York: Guilford Press.

van der Kolk, B., & Fisler, R. (1994). Childhood abuse and neglect and loss of self-regulation. *Bulletin of the Menninger Clinic, 58*(2), 145-168.

van der Kolk, B. A., McFarlane, A. C., & Weisaeth, L. (1996). *Traumatic stress*. NY: Guilford Press.

van Gulden, H., & Bartels-Rabb, L. M. (1994). *Real parents, real children: Parenting the adopted child*. New York: Crossroad.

van IJzendoorn, M. H. (1995). Adult attachment representations, parental responsiveness, and infant attachment: A meta-analysis on the predictive validity of the Adult Attachment Interview. *Psychological Bulletin, 117*, 387-403.

van IJzendoorn, M. H., & Bakermans-Kranenburg, S. (1997). Intergenerational transmission of attachment: A move to a contextual level. In L. Atkinson & K.J. Zucker (Eds.), *Attachment and psychopathology* (pp. 135-170). New York: Guilford Press.

Verny T., & Kelly J. (1981). *The secret life of the unborn child*. New York: Delta Publishing.

Verrier, N. N. (1994). *The primal wound: Understanding the adopted child*. Baltimore, MD: Gateway Press.

Vick, C. (1997). Foster parents: The heroes of child welfare. *Adoptive Families, 30*(6), 8-13.

Vroegh, K. S. (1997). Transracial adoptees: Developmental status after 17 years. *American Journal of Orthopsychiatry, 67*(4), 568-575.

Waterman, J., Kelly, R. J., McCord, J., & Oliveri, M. K. (Eds.). (1993). *Behind playground walls: Sexual abuse in day care*. New York: Guilford Press.

Waters, E. (1978). The stability of individual differences in infant-mother attachment. *Child Development, 49,* 483-494.

Waters, E., Wippman, J., & Sroufe, L. A. (1979). Attachment, positive affect, and competence in the peer group: Two studies in construct validation. *Child Development, 50,* 821-829.

Watson, J. B. (1928). *Psychological care of infant and child.* New York: Norton.

Weaver, T. L., & Clum, G. A. (1995). Psychological distress associated with interpersonal violence: A meta-analysis. *Clinical Psychology Review, 15,* 115-140.

Welch, M. (1988). *Holding time.* New York: Simon and Schuster.

Werner, E. (1989). High-risk children in young adulthood: A longitudinal study from birth to 32 years. *American Journal of Orthopsychiatry, 59*(1), 72-81.

Werner, E., & Smith, R. (1992). *Overcoming the odds: High-risk children from birth to adulthood.* Ithaca, NY: Cornell.

West, M., & Konner, M. J. (1976). The role of the father: An anthropological perspective. In M. Lamb (Ed.), *The role of the father in child development* (pp. 185-216). New York: Wiley.

Weston, J. (1968). The pathology of child abuse. In R. Helfer and C. Kempe (Eds.). *The battered child* (pp. 118-136). Chicago, IL: University of Chicago Press.

Whitfield, C. (1987). *Healing the child within.* Deerfield Beach, FL: Health Communications.

Widom, C.S. (1991). The role of placement experiences in mediating the criminal consequences of early childhood victimization. *American Journal of Orthopsychiatry, 61*(2), 195-209.

Winnicott, D. (1965). *The family and individual development.* London: Tavistock.

Winnicott, D. W. (1985). *Collected papers.* New York: Basic Books.

Wolff, P. M. (1969). The natural history of crying and other vocalizations in infancy. In B. M. Foss (Ed.), *Determinants of infant behavior,* Vol. 4 (pp. 81-109). London: Methuen.

Wolinsky, S. (1993). *Quantum consciousness. The guide to experiencing quantum psychology.* Norfolk, CT: Bramble Books.

Woodworth, R. S., & Sheehan, M. R. (1964). *Contemporary schools of psychology.* New York: The Ronald Press Co.

Wyatt, G. E. (1985). The sexual abuse of Afro-American and white-American women in childhood. *Child Abuse & Neglect, 9,* 507-519.

Yochelson, S., & Samenow, S. (1976). *The criminal personality: A profile for change.* Northvale, NJ: Jason Aronson.

Yochelson, S., & Samenow, S. E. (1993). *The criminal personality: A profile for change.* Northvale, NJ: Jason Aronson.

Yogman, M. (1989). Father-infant play with pre-term and full-term infants. In F. A. Pedersen & P. Berman (Eds.), *Men's transitions to parenthood: Longitudinal studies of early family experience* (pp. 175-196). Hillsdale, NJ: Erlbaum.

Young, K.T., Marsland, K. W., and Zigler, E. (1997). The regulatory status of center-based infant and toddler child care. *American Journal of Orthopsychiatry, 67*(4), 535-544.

Young, K. T., & Zigler, E. (1986). Infant and toddler day care: Regulation and policy implications. *American Journal of Orthopsychiatry, 56,* 43-55.

Zahn-Waxler, C., Cummings, E. M., Iannotti, R. M., & Radke-Yarrow, M. (1984). Young offspring of depressed parents: A population at-risk for affective problems. In D. Cicchetti & K. Schneider-Rosen (Eds.), *New directions for child development: No. 26. Childhood depression* (pp. 81-105). San Francisco, CA: Jossey-Bass.

Zahn-Waxler, C., Radke-Yarrow, M., Wagner, E., & Chapman, M. (1992). Development of concern for others. *Developmental Psychology, 28,* 126-136.

Zaslow, R. W., & Breger, L. (1969). A theory and treatment of autism. In L. Breger (Ed.), *Clinical-cognitive psychology: Models and integration.* Englewood Cliffs, NJ: Prentice-Hall.

Zaslow, R. W., & Menta, M. (1975). *The psychology of the z-process: Attachment and activation.* San Jose, CA: San Jose State University.

Zaslow, R. W., & Menta, M. (1976). *Face-to-face with schizophrenia.* San Jose, CA: San Jose State University.

Zeanah, C. H., Mammen, O. K., & Liebermen, A.F . (1993). Disorders of attachment. In C.H. Zeanah (Ed.), *Handbook of Infant Mental Health* (pp. 332-349). New York: Guilford Press.

Zeanah, C. H., & Scheeringa, M. (1996). Evaluation of posttraumatic symptomology in infants and young children exposed to violence. In J. Osofsky & E. Fenichel (Eds.), *Islands of safety* (pp. 9-14). Arlington, VA: ZERO TO THREE.

Zeanah, C. H., & Zeanah, P. D. (1989). Intergenerational transmission of maltreatment: Insights from attachment theory and research. *Psychiatry, 52,* 177-196.

ZERO TO THREE. (1994). *Diagnostic classification of mental health and developmental disorders in early childhood.* Arlington, VA: ZERO TO THREE/National Center for Clinical Infant Programs.

ZERO TO THREE. (1997). *How I grow in your care from zero to three.* Arlington, VA: National Center for Infants, Toddlers and Families.

Zigler, E. (1994). Early intervention to prevent juvenile delinquency. *Harvard Mental Health Letter, 11*(3), 5-7.

Zuckerman, B. (1994). Effects on parents and children. In D. Besharov (Ed.), *When drug addicts have children* (pp. 49-63). Washington, DC: Child Welfare League of America.

Zuravin, S. J. (1991). Research definitions of child physical abuse and neglect. In R. H. Starr & D. W. Wolfe (Eds.), *The effects of child abuse and neglect.* New York: Guilford Press.

# Index

# About the Authors

**Terry M. Levy, Ph.D., B.C.F.E.,** is a Licensed Clinical Psychologist in Colorado and Florida, and a Board Certified Forensic Examiner in Clinical and Family Psychology. He is a clinical member of the American, Colorado, and Florida Psychological Associations; American and Colorado Associations of Marriage and Family Therapy; American Family Therapy Academy; and the National Register of Health Service Providers in Psychology. He was founder and Director of the Family Life Center (Florida) and the Miami Psychotherapy Institute, both treatment and training centers, and co-founder and President of the Board of Directors of the Association for Treatment and Training in the Attachment of Children (ATTACh).

Dr. Levy has been providing psychotherapy treatment and training for more than 25 years. He has taught seminars on therapeutic issues for the American Psychological Association, the American Professional Society on the Abuse of Children, and numerous mental health, social service, and school systems nationwide. Currently, Dr. Levy has a private practice in Evergreen, Colorado, at Evergreen Consultants in Human Behavior.

**Michael Orlans, M.A., B.C.F.E., D.A.P.A.,** is in private practice and Director of Training with Evergreen Consultants in Human Behavior. He is a Marriage and Family Therapist with more than 25 years of clinical experience. In addition to his work in private practice and in the public sector, Michael has taught on the faculty of several universities. He is a nationally known lecturer and trainer, with expertise in working with severely emotionally disturbed children and their families. He has served as a consultant to therapeutic foster care programs, child welfare agencies, and is on the Advisory Council of the National Alliance for Rational Children's Policy. He is co-founder of the Association for Treatment and Training in the Attachment of Children. He is also a Diplomate, Board Certified Forensic Examiner, and founding executive board member and Diplomate of the American Psychotherapy Association.